Revision and Printing History

January 1990·   First Printing

Small Print

The X Window System Series

The books in the X Window System series from O'Reilly and Associates
are based in part on the original MIT X Window System documentation,
but are far more comprehensive and easy to use. Over 20 computer
vendors recommend or license volumes in the series. In short, these are the
definitive guides to the X Window System.

Volume 0, X Protocol Reference Manual. A complete programmer's
reference to the X Network Protocol, the language in which computers
communicate all the information between the X server and X clients. 414
pages, $30.00

**Volumes 1 and 2, Xlib Programming Manual and Xlib
Reference Manual.** Complete guides to programming with the X library
(Xlib), the lowest level of programming interface to X. 664 and 725 pages,
$34.95 each, or $60.00 as a set.

Volume 3, X Window System User's Guide. Describes window
system concepts and the most common client applications available for X,
Release 3. For experienced users, later chapters explain customizing the X
environment and include an alternate *.uwmrc* file. 576 pages, $26.95

**Volumes 4 and 5, X Toolkit Intrinsics Programming Manual and
X Toolkit Intrinsics Reference Manual.** Complete guides to
programming with the Xt Intrinsics, the library of C language routines
created to facilitate the design of user interfaces, with reusable components called widgets. 582 and 545 pages, $30.00 each, or $55.00 as a set.

Volume 7, XView Programming Manual. XView is an easy-to-use
toolkit, not just for Sun developers. This volume provides complete
information on the XView toolkit, from concepts to creating XView
applications to reference pages. 566 pages. $30.00.

For orders or a free catalog of all our books, please contact us. For
international orders (outside U.S. or Canada) see our list of distributors in
the back of this book.

O'Reilly & Associates, Inc.

Creators and publishers of Nutshell Handbooks
632 Petaluma Avenue • Sebastopol CA 95472
email: uunet!ora!nuts • 1-800-338-6887 • in CA 1-800-533-6887 • +1 707-829-0515

Table of Contents

Preface

About the X Toolkit

The X Toolkit is the collective name for two C language subroutine libraries (Xt and Xaw) designed to simplify the development of X Window System applications using reusable components called *widgets*. Typical widgets include scrollbars, menus, dialog boxes, text-editing areas, drawing areas, etc. Each widget is made up of its own X window, but most of the work that goes on in that window has already been taken care of—all the application programmer has to do is assemble the widgets and write application-specific code that will be called in response to events in the widgets.

The Xt library (the Intrinsics) consists of routines for using and building widgets. Widgets are defined using an object-oriented classing mechanism. The Xaw widget library is based on Xt and provides a small number of widgets that can be used to write simple application programs

The Xt Intrinsics are written using Xlib, the lowest level C language interface to the X Window System. Both the Xt Intrinsics and Xlib are required by the X standard (established by the X Consortium) on any system that allows programming of X applications

Xaw was developed by MIT's Project Athena, and the acronym Xaw stands for *Athena Widgets*. Primarily, Xaw was designed as a simple demonstration and test of the Intrinsics—not as a complete set of widgets for writing demanding applications There are numerous other widget sets provided by system vendors to implement particular user-interface styles. Most notably, HP has supplied a fairly extensive widget set (referred to as the *HP Widgets*) that is also provided on the MIT X release tape In the future, though, the dominant widget set is likely to be one provided by OSF, as part of a product called OSF/*Motif*. Motif includes a widget set based on the HP Widgets and an extended version of the Intrinsics developed by Digital Equipment Corporation. There will also be widget sets that implement an AT&T user interface standard called *OPEN LOOK*.

The X Toolkit Intrinsics will work the same way with any of these Xt-compatible widget sets In fact, it is possible, though not always aesthetically or economically desirable, to combine widgets from different widget sets in the same application.*

---

*Note that there are other X toolkits (note the lower-case "t" in "toolkits") that have nothing whatever to do with the X Toolkit (Xt), except that they have similar goals—namely, to make it easier to write standard X applications These toolkits include Andrew (from Carnegie-Mellon University), InterViews (from Stanford), and Xview (from Sun) These are not merely different widget sets but are entirely different toolkits They are not compatible with Xt.

About This Book

This book is the fifth volume in the O'Reilly & Associates X Window System Series. It includes reference pages for each of the Xt Intrinsics functions, for useful macros and function prototypes, for the base widget classes defined by the Intrinsics, and for the Athena Widgets. Reference pages are organized alphabetically for ease of access; a permuted index and numerous appendices and quick reference aids are also provided

Volumes Four and Five are designed to be used together Volume 4 provides an explanation of the X Toolkit, including tutorial material and numerous programming examples Arranged by task or topic, each chapter brings together a group of X Toolkit functions, describes the conceptual foundation they are based on, and illustrates how they are most often used in writing applications This volume is structured so as to be useful as a tutorial and also as a task-oriented reference

To get the most out of the examples in Volume Four, you will need the exact calling sequences of each function from Volume Five. To understand fully how to use each of the functions described in Volume Five, all but the most experienced Toolkit "hacker" will need the explanation and examples in Volume Four

Even though the Toolkit is intended to hide the low-level X interface provided by Xlib, there are times in writing widgets when Xlib functions will be necessary because no Xt feature exists to do the same thing. Volume Four describes the most common occasions for using Xlib but does not provide a reference to the particular functions involved For that, see Volume One, *Xlib Programming Manual*, and Volume Two, *Xlib Reference Manual*.

How This Book is Organized

Volume Five consists of reference pages for Toolkit functions. It also contains numerous helpful appendices

The book is organized as follows

Preface   describes the organization of the book, and the conventions it follows

Chapter 1,   *Introduction*, provides an overview of the functional areas the reference pages fall into.

Permuted Index provides a standard UNIX ptx for all reference pages, regardless of section.

Section 1,   *X Toolkit Intrinsics Functions and Macros*, contains reference pages for the Intrinsics functions and macros. The header on each reference page states whether the function applies to using or building widgets, but all are organized alphabetically.

Section 2,   *Prototype Procedures*, lists the prototypes used for declaring application callback routines, actions, widget methods, and other user-supplied functions

Section 3,   *Intrinsics-mandated Widget Classes*, contains reference pages for the required widget classes—Core, Composite, Constraint, and Shell

Section 4, *Athena Widgets*, contains reference pages for the Athena widgets

Appendix A, *Alphabetical and Group Summaries*, provides quick reference tables that list each Intrinsics function alphabetically and by logical groups.

Appendix B, *X Toolkit Data Types*, lists and explains, in alphabetical order, the structures, enums and other typedefs used for arguments to Xt functions and macros

Appendix C, *Event Reference*, describes each event type in a reference page format Each page includes information on how to select the events, when they are generated, the contents of the event structures, and notes on how to use them.

Appendix D, *Standard Errors and Warnings*, lists the possible errors or warnings returned by the X Toolkit, along with their possible cause.

Appendix E, *Resource File Format*, explains the EBNF syntax used the resource file.

Appendix F, *Translation Table Syntax*, explains the EBNF syntax used the translation table It discusses modifiers and event types

Appendix G, *StringsDefs h Header File*, groups the identifiers found in *StringDefs h*

Appendix H, *Release Notes*, summarizes the changes between these two releases.

Master Index provides a thorough, combined index to Volumes Four and Five, making it easy to look up all the appropriate references to a topic, in either volume.

Assumptions

This book makes no assumptions about the reader's knowledge of object-oriented programming or the X Window System However, for many advanced topics, the reader will need to consult the earlier volumes in this series—Volume One, *Xlib Programming Manual*, and Volume Two, *Xlib Reference Manual*.

Readers should be proficient in the C programming language, although examples are provided for infrequently used features of the language that are necessary or useful when programming with the X Toolkit. In addition, general familiarity with the principles of raster graphics will be helpful.

Conventions Used in This Book

Italics are used for:

*   UNIX pathnames, filenames, program names, user command names, and options for user commands.

*   New terms where they are defined.

`Typewriter Font` is used for:

*   Anything that would be typed verbatim into code, such as examples of source code and text on the screen

*   The contents of include files, such as structure types, structure members, symbols (defined constants and bit flags), and macros.

*   Xt functions.

*   Names of subroutines of the example programs.

Italic Typewriter Font is used for:

*   Arguments to Xt functions, since they could be typed in code as shown but are arbitrary names that could be changed.

Helvetica Italics are used for:

*   Titles of examples, figures, and tables.

Boldface is used for:

*   Chapter and section headings.

Requests for Comments

Please write to tell us about any flaws you find in this manual or how you think it could be improved in order to help us provide you with the best documentation possible.

Our U.S. mail address, e-mail address, and telephone numbers are as follows:

O'Reilly and Associates, Inc.
632 Petaluma Avenue
Sebastopol, CA 95472
800-338-6887, in CA 800-533-6887
international +1 707-829-0515

UUCP: uunet!ora!tim   ARPA: tim@ora.com

Bulk Sales Information

This manual is being resold as the official X Window System documentation by many workstation manufacturers. For information on volume discounts for bulk purchase, call O'Reilly and Associates, Inc., at 800-338-6887 (in California, 800-533-6887), or send e-mail to linda@ora.com.

For companies requiring extensive customization of the book, source licensing terms are also available.

Obtaining the X Window System Software

The X Window system is copyrighted but freely distributed. The only restriction this places on its use is that the copyright notice identifying the author and the terms of use must accompany all copies of the software or documentation. Thanks to this policy, the software is available for nominal cost from a variety of sources. See Appendix G, *Sources of Additional Information*, in Volume Four, *X Toolkit Intrinsics Programming Manual*, for a listing of these sources.

Acknowledgements

As mentioned above, this manual is based in part on the *Xt Toolkit Intrinsics—C Language Interface*, by Joel McCormack, Paul Asente, and Ralph Swick, and on the *X Toolkit Athena Widgets—C Language Interface*, by Ralph Swick and Terry Weissman. We have done our best to incorporate all the useful information from these documents, while reorganizing them into alphabetical reference manual pages. We have clarified and expanded the descriptions of Intrinsics functions, added examples and cross references, and in general tried to make it useful for reference purposes.

We would like to thank the authors of this document, and the X Consortium, for the copyright policy that allows others to build upon their work. Their generosity of spirit not only has made this book possible, but is the basis for the unparalleled speed with which the X Window System has been adopted as a *de facto* standard.

We would also like to thank the reviewers of the companion volume, *X Toolkit Programming Manual*. Even though they didn't directly review this book, their comments are often reflected in its pages. They were David Lewis and Peter Winston of Integrated Computer Solutions (ICS), Wendy Eisner of Sunquest Information Systems, Dan Heller of Island Graphics, Inc. (now working with O'Reilly and Associates), Miles O'Neal of Systems and Software Solutions, Inc., Chris Peterson of MIT Project Athena, and Ian Darwin of SoftQuad. Extra thanks are due to Ralph Swick and Chris Peterson, who answered many questions during the development of these books.

We are grateful to Sony Microsystems for the loan of a Sony NEWS workstation running their implementation of the X Window System. The speed and power of the Sony workstation, and the support of their staff, was a great help in developing these books. Additional development was done on a Sun-3 workstation running MIT's sample server, a Visual 640 X Display Station, and an NCD16 Network Display Station.

Mark Langley edited an early version of this book. He also authored the introduction to the current version and provided some of the examples on the reference pages. His help is greatly appreciated.

Many staff members of O'Reilly and Associates assisted in producing this manual, particularly Donna Woonteiler, who coordinated the final production. The cover design is by Edie Freedman. Kathryn Ellis produced the master index. Other assistance came in many different forms from Daniel Gilly, Lenny Muellner, Linda Mui, Sue Willing, and Ruth Terry.

Of course, we alone take responsibility for any errors or omissions that remain.

—Tim O'Reilly

1
Introduction

The classic problem in constructing software manuals is how to resolve the conflicting needs of tutorial and reference Over time, we have found that the alphabetical "man page"* approach of the *UNIX Reference Manual* has consistently made it the most accessible reference manual we have ever used However, as has often been pointed out by detractors of UNIX, this approach can make the manual impenetrable to a novice.

We believe that the ideal solution is a programming manual/reference manual pair, in which the tutorial programming manual gives an understanding of the whole and the alphabetical reference manual supplies all of the additional details However, in order to make this reference manual more useful as a stand-alone document, we have also added a level of structure beyond alphabetization

First, the manual is divided into four major sections (plus appendices): the Xt Intrinsics (and macros), function typedefs for widget methods and other internal routines, Intrinsics-mandated widget classes, and the Athena widgets Pages themselves are unnumbered, however, cross-references to pages in other sections use the familiar UNIX parenthetical section notation—e g., Core(3). Within the first section, which includes Intrinsics function calls and macros, the page header indicates a general subject area for related routines

In this introduction, we have also provided a high-level discussion of various general topics, ranging from the Widget Lifecycle to Event Handling. Table 1-1 below associates various reference pages in Section 1 with the corresponding section in this introduction In addition, the See Also section of each reference page refers back to the appropriate discussion in this introduction, as well as to relevant chapters in Volume Four, *X Toolkit Intrinsics Programming Manual*.

---
*That is, manual page—or reference page, as we'll call it.

Table 1-1. Overview of the Intrinsics

Introduction Topic	Using Widgets	Building Widgets	Function typedefs

Widget
 	
Lifecycle
	XtCreateApplication-
	   Shell
	XtCreateManaged-
	   Widget
	XtCreateWidget
	XtDestroyWidget
	XtInitialize
	XtIsManaged
	XtIsRealized
	XtMainLoop
	XtManageChild
	XtManageChildren
	XtRealizeWidget
	XtUnmanageChild
	XtUnmanageChildren
			XtExposeProc
			
			XtInitProc
			XtProc
			XtRealizeProc
			XtWidgetProc

Classes and Subclasses Core, etc.	XtApplicationClass XtApplicationName XtClass XtCreateWidget XtIsSubclass XtSuperclass	XtIsSubclass	
Application Interface	XtAddActions XtAddCallback XtAddCallbacks XtMergeArgLists XtOverrideCallback XtSetArg See also Resource Management below	XtCallCallbacks XtHasCallbacks XtRemoveAllCallbacks XtRemoveCallback XtRemoveCallbacks	XtCallbackRec

Events	Translations
	XtMainLoop
		RemoveTimeOut
		XtAddEventHandler
		XtAddInput
		XtAddRawEvent-
		   Handler
		XtAddTimeOut
		XtAppProcessEvent
		XtDispatchEvent
		XtHasInput
		XtNextEvent
		XtPeekEvent
		XtRemoveEvent-
		   Handler
		XtRemoveInput
		XtRemoveRawEvent-
		   Handler
			Event masks
			XEvent

Table 1-1. Overview of the Intrinsics (continued)

Introduction Topic	Using Widgets	Building Widgets	Function typedefs

Translations and Actions	MenuPopup
	MenuPopdown
	XtAddActions
	XtAugment-
	   Translations
	XtOverride-
	   Translations
	XtParseTranslation-
	   Table
			XtActionProc

Graphics		XtDestroyGC XtGetGC XtReleaseGC	
Popups	MenuPopdown MenuPopup XtCallbackExclusive XtCallbackNone XtCallback- Nonexclusive XtCallbackPopdown XtCreatePopupShell XtPopdown XtPopup	XtMoveWidget XtNameToWidget	

Resource Management	XtGetValues
	XtSetValues
		XtAddConverter
		XtConvert
		XtDirectConvert
		XtGetApplication-
		   Resources
		XtGetResources
		XtGetSubResources
		XtGetSubvalues
		XtStringConversion-
		   Warning
			XtSetValuesFunc

Geometry Management	XtConfigureWidget XtMakeGeometryRequest XtMakeResizeRequest XtMoveWidget XtQueryGeometry XtResizeWidget XtResizeWindow XtUnmanageChild XtUnmanageChildren	XtAddExposureToRegion	Composite XtArgsProc
Xlib Interface		XtDisplay XtScreen XtWindow	

Table 1-1. Overview of the Intrinsics (continued)

Introduction Topic	Using Widgets	Building Widgets	Function typedefs
Misc.	XtIsSensitive XtNameToWidget XtWindowToWidget	XtAddGrab XtCalloc XtError XtErrorMsg XtFree XtMalloc XtParent XtRealloc XtRemoveGrab XtSetWarningHandler XtWarning XtWarningMsg	

1.1 Widget Lifecycle

A widget goes through several distinct stages in its lifetime. It is consecutively created, managed, realized, mapped (this is usually performed automatically), and destroyed.

For any program to use the X Toolkit, it must first create and initialize the Toolkit itself, create an application context, and open the display. These operations can be combined using XtInitialize. XtInitialize returns a top-level shell widget that can be the parent of the rest of the application. If an application wishes to open windows on multiple screens simultaneously, these operations can be done individually. (See XtInitialize-Toolkit, XtAppCreateContext, and XtDisplayInitialize).

Next, the application is ready to create widgets. It does this with XtCreateWidget or XtCreateManagedWidget. Widget creation causes the Intrinsics to invoke the widget's private initialize method. The methods, or procedures, associated with a widget are summarized in Core(3).

In the initialize method, the widget performs customized initialization and processes the arguments that are passed to it as resource arguments in the call that created it. (See Section 1.7, "Resources.")

XtCreateManagedWidget combines creation with the obligatory step of bringing the widget's placement under the dominion of its parent's geometry manager. (See Section 1.8, "Geometry Management.") A widget created with XtCreateWidget must be separately managed with a call to XtManageWidget.

Finally, widgets must be realized; this step causes them to be displayed. (Realization is separate from creation in order to allow all geometry negotiation between widgets to occur before anything is drawn.) To cause all widgets in an application to be realized, it is sufficient to realize the top-level widget with XtRealizeWidget. The Intrinsics recursively realize children before their parents. (See XtRealize, XtRealizeProc, and Core(3) for more on realization.)

Most widgets are mapped automatically by virtue of having a mapped_when_managed Boolean set in the Core instance record Otherwise, mapping can be controlled by XtMap-Widget and XtUnmapWidget.

Before a widget can actually draw anything on the display, it must receive events telling it to do so. When an application calls XtMainLoop, the Intrinsics begin to process the events sent by the server and dispatch the appropriate handlers. This is how the widget's other methods get invoked: namely, they are called in response to some server event.

Most widgets are not explicitly destroyed When a program exits and the connection is closed, the widget's data structures on the server vanish.

1.1.1 Example Program

The following program fragment is sufficient to create, manage, and display a single Label widget.

```
#include <stdio.h>
#include <X11/Xlib.h>
#include <X11/Intrinsic.h>
#include <X11/StringDefs.h>
#include "Label.h"

Arg args[] = {
   XtNlabel, (XtArgVal) "Stuff",
};

main(argc, argv)
int argc;
char **argv;
{
   Widget toplevel, label;
   WidgetClass wc;
   int i;

   toplevel = XtInitialize(argv[0], "my-widget", NULL, 0, &argc, argv);
   wc = labelWidgetClass;      /* ... from widget include file */
   label = XtCreateManagedWidget(label,/* widget name   */
                     wc,       /* widget class */
                     toplevel,/* parent widget*/
                     args,     /* argument list*/
                     XtNumber(args)/* arglist size */
                     );
   fprintf(stderr, "status of creating label widget %d\n", label);
   XtRealizeWidget(toplevel);
   XtMainLoop();
}
```

1.2 Classes and Subclasses

The class mechanism allows X Toolkit programs to exploit object-oriented programming techniques. The *widget* is the basic object in the Toolkit, it is a template containing code and providing fields for data. In particular, a widget is defined by a *class* and *instance* structure

For more details on particular classes supplied with the X Toolkit, see Core, Composite, Constraint, and Shell in Section 3 of this manual.

For a detailed description of how widget class and instance structures are implemented, see Chapters 5 and 6 in Volume Four, *X Toolkit Intrinsics Programming Manual.*

1.3 Application Interface

An application program can communicate with widgets in several ways. A widget makes certain state information available through resources, which an application can both read and write. A widget can also pass control back to an application to handle some designated event.

When an application creates a widget, it passes an argument list of *resources* that specify how a widget is to do its job These argument lists can be created statically or can be controlled at run time with XtSetArg. (To see a complete example of this, see Chapter 3, *Other Widget Programming Techniques*, in Volume Four, *X Toolkit Intrinsics Programming Manual.*)

The application program can write selected values inside a widget instance by using Xt-SetValues and can read values using XtGetValues. Using XtSetValues causes the widget to be notified of changes asynchronously through the Core set_values method, so the widget can be assured of working with current data These same resource mechanisms can be used analogously with nonwidget data, as well. (See XtSet-Subvalues and XtGetSubvalues.)

1.3.1 Callbacks

A widget can return control to the application using *Callbacks.* Namely, by specifying a resource of type XtRCallback, an application can pass a list of procedures for the widget to invoke when certain things happen (The types of events that result in a callback must be agreed upon between the widget and the application in advance.)

The Intrinsics maintain callback lists in an internal format, so once a resource of type Xt-RCallback is passed to a widget, it cannot be accessed directly. To access callback lists, use one of the functions XtAddCallback, XtAddCallbacks, XtRemove-Callbacks, or XtRemoveAllCallbacks

The name of the resource for which the application can supply a callback list is often exported from the widget's public include file If a widget has only one resource of type callback, it will probably be called XtNcallback.

Callbacks are described in detail with example code in Chapter 2, *Introduction to the X Toolkit*, in Volume Four, *X Toolkit Intrinsics Programming Manual*

1.4 Events

In Xlib, all the synchronization between server and client is done with events. Events can range from input typed at the keyboard to notifications from the server that a window is now available to receive input. The Toolkit default event processor loop is invoked after widgets are created and realized (see Section 1.1, "Widget Lifecycle") by calling XtMainLoop.

Using the X Toolkit, widgets can process events in one of two ways. The first way resembles the low-level X event mechanism. They can set up event handlers to capture events as they come in. To do this, a widget declares a handler with XtAddEventHandler and specifies the event mask that should cause the handler to be invoked. (This approach is discussed in depth in Chapter 8, *More Input Techniques*, in Volume Four, *X Toolkit Intrinsics Programming Manual*.

The second way involves setting up event translations for events. See Section 1.5, "Translations and Actions."

1.5 Translations and Actions

The translation manager allows an application or a widget to indicate interest in higher level user behavior. That is, instead of having to parse individual events in the widget, the widget can ask to be notified when the user performs a certain type of mouse click or types something in particular from the keyboard.

Translations can also be overridden by an application program or a widget's subclass.

MenuPopup and MenuPopdown are examples of translation actions that can be invoked directly. XtOverrideTranslations and XtAugmentTranslations allow a widget's translations to be appropriately manipulated.

Actions (the entities on the right-hand side of a translation) can also be added and augmented, either for a particular widget or for the application at large.

For more details, see Chapter 7, *Events, Translations and Accelerators*, in Volume Four, *X Toolkit Intrinsics Programming Manual*

1.6 Pop Ups

A pop-up widget is a widget that bypasses geometry management and appears to pop up and pop down again when it is no longer needed

Pop ups are treated in detail in Chapter 12, *Menus, Gadgets and Cascaded Pop Ups*, in Volume Four

Pop ups can be popped up or down as a result of a translation action (MenuPopup and MenuPopdown). They can also be popped up or down by specifying particular Intrinsics procedures in a callback list (namely, XtCallbackExclusive, XtCallback-Exclusive, XtCallbackNone, XtCallbackPopdown)

To use a pop up, first a shell must be created with XtCreatePopupShell Then it can be popped up specifically using XtPopup or one of the aforementioned techniques.

Any widget can have pop-up children it does not need to be a subclass of Composite(3) Subsequently, the pop-up shell created with XtCreatePopupShell can be given its single normal child with XtCreateManagedWidget, specifying the pop-up shell as parent It bypasses a widget's insert_child method, even if it has one

A pop up can be *spring*-loaded so that it pops up as a result of a translation A spring-loaded pop up invoked from a translation table already must exist at the time that the translation is invoked, so the translation manager can find the shell by name Creating the pop-up shell and child in advance makes the user's act of popping up faster.

Pop ups invoked explicitly with XtPopup or XtCallbackExclusive can be created as they are needed Delaying the creation of the pop up is particularly useful when you pop up an unspecified number of them The program does not have to create the shell until it is needed the first time, then after popping it down, it can preserve it until it is needed again

1.7 Resources

Resources are a list of name-value pairs The X server has a set of the name-value pairs that can be used as defaults The Intrinsics maintain name-value pairs in the same form in the widget structure Using resources, an application can communicate with a widget and vice versa Arguments to widgets are also passed as resources.

The X Window System maintains a database of resources and their values on the server Individual program execution may override the values obtained from the server's database for the context of the program's execution

XtInitialize sets up the original context for program execution.

The routines XtSetValues and XtGetValues use a resource list to set and get widget state. The updating of resource values from the widget class and the resource database occurs transparently to the widget The Intrinsics update the widget class structure before calling the widget's Initialize method.

The use of resources is not limited to widgets. Nonwidget structures can maintain lists of resources and make calls to the Intrinsics functions XtGetResourceList and XtGet-ApplicationResources explicitly to get the resource list updated from the resource database and the current execution context.

The Intrinsics also allow extensive conversion of resources and their types While most conversions are performed transparently, it is possible to use explicit conversion of resources profitably in data structures that are not widgets.

1.7.1 Data Structures

The resource data structure can be thought of as a template It lists a set of names, default values, and offsets. Subsequently, values for a whole resource list can be determined with reference to a single base address.

XtResource is defined in *<X11/Intrinsic h>*.

```
typedef struct _XtResource {
  String    resource_name;    /* Resource name */
  String    resource_class    /* Resource class */
  String    resource_type;    /* Representation type desired */
  Cardinal resource_size;     /* Size in bytes of representation */
  Cardinal resource_offset,/* Offset from base to put resource value */
  String    default_type;     /* Representation type of specified *
                               *      default */
  caddr_t  default_addr;      /* Address of resource default value */
} XtResource, XtResourceList;
```

The ArgList data structure is also defined there ArgLists are used for taking values to and from a base offset resource list In some Intrinsics routines, ArgLists also provide a set of values that can override whatever values the resource mechanism nominates XtGet-Values and XtGetSubvalues *returns* its values in an ArgList.

```
typedef struct {
    String    name;
    XtArgVal value;
} Arg, *ArgList;
```

ArgVal is a typedef for a longword/pointer quantity.

There are several routines that get and set resource values in widgets, resource data structures, and ArgLists Since the names of the routines are not particularly mnemonic, Table 1-2 below contrasts and summarizes the different functions.

In the table, Rlist+Base indicates that a resource list is used to offset a base address to obtain the actual location for a value. This is how resources are stored in widgets, using the XtOffset macro.

Table 1-2. Overview of Resource Management Functions

Procedure	From	To	Used for/Lookup by
XtSetValues XtGetValues	ArgList Widget	Widget ArgList	Widget instance variables
XtSetSubvalues XtGetSubvalues	ArgList RList+Base	RList+Base ArgList	Nonwidget resources
XtGetResourceList	Resource Manager	RList (defaults)	Default values
XtGetAppResources XtGetSubresources	Widget,ArgList Widget,ArgList	RList+Base RList+Base	By widget By name/class

Each function can be looked up separately to understand the exact details of the routine.

Routines to fetch values of resources, like XtGetApplicationResources, accept a list of resources and a base pointer. The portable and recommended way to access resources in a resource list is to declare a structure that contains fields for values and to pass a pointer to this structure as the base address. Then XtOffset can be used to determine the relative address of the field in the structure.

Here is a short program that sets up a resource argument list and accesses it.

```
/* res.c - access application resources */
#include <stdio.h>

#include <X11/Xlib.h>
#include <X11/StringDefs.h>
#include <X11/IntrinsicP.h>
#include <X11/Intrinsic.h>
/*
 * fields to be filled in from resources
 * Note that instance_variables must be defined as a pointer...
 */
typedef struct _instance_variables {
    String label;
    XFontStruct *font_struct;
    long foreground;
} instance_variable_rec, *instance_variables;
instance_variables InstanceVariables;

static XtResource resources[] = {
    {
    XtNforeground,
    XtCForeground,
    XtRPixel, sizeof(Pixel),
    XtOffset(instance_variables, foreground),
    XtRString, "XtDefaultForeground"
    },
    {
    XtNfont,
    XtCFont,
    XtRFontStruct, sizeof(XFontStruct *),
    XtOffset(instance_variables, font_struct),
    XtRString, "XtDefaultFont"
    },
```

```
{
XtNlabel,
XtCLabel,
XtRString, sizeof(String),
XtOffset(instance_variables, label),
XtRString, "Default Label"
},
},

Arg args[] = {
    XtNlabel, (XtArgVal) "Stuff",
},

main(ac, av)
int ac,
char **av;
{
    Widget toplevel,
    instance_variable_rec iv;

    toplevel = XtInitialize(av[0], "my-widget", NULL, 0, &ac, av);
    XtGetApplicationResources(toplevel,    /* widget */
                              &iv,          /* base address */
                              resources,    /* resource */
                              XtNumber(resources),/* how many */
                              NULL, 0);     /* ArgList to merge */

    printf("label=%s\n", iv.label);
}
```

1.7.2 Resource Names

The complete resource name for a field of a widget instance is the concatenation of the application name (from `argv[0]`) or the *-name* command-line option (see XtDisplay-Initialize), the instance names of all the widget's parents, the instance name of the widget itself, and the resource name of the specified field of the widget. Likewise, the full resource class of a field of a widget instance is the concatenation of the application class (from XtAppCreateShell), the widget class names of all the widget's parents (not the superclasses), the widget class name of the widget itself, and the resource name of the specified field of the widget.

1.7.3 Resource Types

Resource data types are represented as strings. The actual string definitions are in *<X11/StringDefs h>* The data types represented by the string identifiers are described in Table 1-3 below

The type of a resource is specified by a string. Existing types include XtRString, Xt-RInt, and XtRPointer

If an application needs to invent new data types, it merely must define a string to represent the data type. (See Volume Four, *X Toolkit Intrinsics Programming Manual.*) Just use a string of the form XtR*MyType*.

For more information, see XtGetApplicationResources, XtGetResources, XtSetResources, XtSetValues, XtGetValues, XtSetSubvalues, and Xt-GetSubvalues. XtDisplayInitialize describes more details of command line parsing.

Table 1-3. Resource Types

Resource Type Name	Data Type	Defined in <*XII/* ... >
XtRAcceleratorTable	XtAccelerators	*Intrinsic.h*
XtRBoolean	Boolean	*Intrinsic.h*
XtRBool	Bool	*Xlib.h*
XtRCallback	XtCallbackList	*Intrinsic.h*
XtRCallproc	. . .	. . .
XtRColor	XColor	*Xlib.h*
XtRCursor	Cursor	*X.h*
XtRDimension	Dimension	*Intrinsic.h*
XtRDisplay	Display	*Xlib.h*
XtRFile	FILE*	*Xos.h*
XtRFloat	float	. . .
XtRFont	Font	*X.h*
XtRFontStruct	XFontStruct *	*Xlib.h*
XtRFunction	(*)()	. . .
XtRImmediate	. . .	. . .
XtRInt	int	. . .
XtRPixel	Pixel	*Intrinsic.h*
XtRPixmap	Pixmap	*X.h*
XtRPointer	caddr_t	. . .
XtRPosition	Position	*Intrinsic.h*
XtRShort	short	. . .
XtRString	char *	. . .
XtRTranslationTable	XtTranslations	*Intrinsic.h*
XtRUnsignedChar	unsigned char	. . .
XtRWidget	Widget	*Intrinsic.h*
XtRWindow	Window	*X.h*

XtRCallProc and XtRImmediate are special cases; they can only be used as default values. Both of these resource types, by their very nature, defeat resource type checking and conversion.

The XtRCallProc type allows a widget to specify a procedure to actually determine the default value of the resource at run time. The XtRCallProc procedure is invoked as an XtResourceDefaultProc.

The `XtRImmediate` type indicates that the value in the default address field is the resource value itself, not a resource.

For the Intrinsics to find and correctly handle callback lists, they should be declared with a resource type of `XtRCallback`. Whenever a widget contains a callback list for use by clients, it also exports in its public *.h* file the resource name of the callback list. Applications and client widgets never access callback list fields directly. Instead, they always identify the desired callback list by using the exported resource name. The callback manipulation functions described here check that the requested callback list is implemented by the widget.

1.7.4 Command Line Arguments

Command line arguments given to a program can be used to set resource values. Any resource in a program can be accessed from the command line using the *–xrm* argument. For example, in the above program to change label, the following would work:

```
ride% cc res.c -lXt -lX11
ride% a.out -xrm '*label: New Label String'
```

The standard command line arguments are shown in Table 1-4.

Table 1-4. Command Line Arguments

Option	Resource	Value	Sets
-bg	`*background`	next argument	background color
-background	`*background`	next argument	background color
-bd	`*borderColor`	next argument	border color
-bw	`.borderWidth`	next argument	width of border in pixels
-borderwidth	`.borderWidth`	next argument	width of border in pixels
-bordercolor	`*borderColor`	next argument	color of border
-display	`.display`	next argument	server to use
-fg	`*foreground`	next argument	foreground color
-fn	`*font`	next argument	font name
-font	`*font`	next argument	font name
-foreground	`*foreground`	next argument	foreground color
-geometry	`.geometry`	next argument	size and position
-iconic	`.iconic`	"on"	start as an icon
-name	`.name`	next argument	name of application
-reverse	`*reverseVideo`	"on"	reverse video
-rv	`*reverseVideo`	"on"	reverse video
+rv	`*reverseVideo`	"off"	No Reverse Video
-selectionTimeout	`.selectionTimeout`	Null	selection timeout
-synchronous	`.synchronous`	"on"	synchronous debug mode
+synchronous	`.synchronous`	"off"	synchronous debug mode
-title	`.title`	next argument	title of application
-xrm	value of argument	next argument	depends on argument

New entries can be added to the Intrinsics' parsing table This is discussed in Volume Four, *X Toolkit Intrinsics Programming Manual* More extensive examples are also given there

1.8 Geometry Management

Geometry management allows a widget to control the size and layout of other widgets The controlling widget is called the parent, and the controlled widgets are called children

A parent becomes capable of siring children by being a subclass of Composite(3) The Composite class provides several methods that are invoked when children are created, managed, and destroyed

A widget is *managed* when it is placed on its parent's list of widgets whose layout is controlled explicitly by the parent. An application can manage a widget by calling `Xt-ManageWidget` or by creating it with `XtCreateManagedWidget`. A widget cannot be *realized* (i e., given an actual window) or *mapped* (positioned on the display) until it is managed.

Most widgets are *mapped_when_managed*. That means, when they are put under parental management, they will subsequently be mapped without any further intervention, the core `set_mapped_when_managed` Boolean can be set explicitly with `XtSetMapped-WhenManaged` Widgets that are not mapped when managed must call `XtMapWidget` explicitly. In any case, a widget cannot safely perform output until the X Server sends an Expose event, which will in turn cause the Intrinsics to invoke the child widget's Redraw method.

Geometry management is asymmetrical and can be considered from either the perspective of the child or the perspective of the parent. The following sections describe geometry management from both perspectives, with reference to the Composite(3) class methods used in each case In the following discussion, a reference to a "composite widget" (note the lower-case *c*) means "a widget that is a subclass of Composite, whereas a reference to the class "Composite" means the actual Composite class

1.8.1 Parent's Perspective

The Intrinsics invoke a parent's `insert_child` method when the application creates a child widget. When the application manages the child, the Intrinsics invoke the `change_managed` method. The Intrinsics invoke the `geometry_manager` method to lay out the widget's children

The `geometry_manager` can then determine the layout of its children as it sees fit. It sets the actual values of its core values using `XtConfigureWidget`, `XtResize-Widget`, or `XtMoveWidget`.

The insert and delete routines are of type `XtWidgetProc(2)`

To remove the child from the parent's children array, the XtDestroyWidget function eventually causes a call to the composite parent's class delete_child method. A delete_child method is of type XtWidgetProc(2)

Most widgets inherit the delete_child method from their superclass Composite widgets that create companion widgets define their own delete_child method to remove these companion widgets

To add a child to the parent's list of children, the XtCreateWidget function calls the parent's class routine insert_child The insert_child method for a composite widget is of type XtWidgetProc(2)

Most composite widgets inherit their superclass's operation The Composite class's insert_child method calls the insert_position method and inserts the child at the specified position.

Some composite widgets define their own insert_child method so that they can order their children in some convenient way, create companion controller widgets for a new widget, or limit the number or type of their children widgets

If there is not enough room to insert a new child in the children array (that is, num_children = num_slots), the insert_child method must first reallocate the array and update num_slots The insert_child method then places the child wherever it wants and increments the num_children field

Instances of composite widgets may need to specify the order in which their children are kept For example, an application may want a set of command buttons in some logical order grouped by function, and it may want buttons that represent file names to be kept in alphabetical order

Composite widgets that allow clients to order their children (usually homogeneous boxes) can call their widget instance's insert_position method from the class's insert_child method to determine where a new child should go in its children array Thus, a client of a composite class can apply different sorting criteria to widget instances of the class, passing in a different insert_position method when it creates each composite widget instance

The return value of the insert_position method indicates how many children should go before the widget Returning zero means before all other children, and returning num_children means after all other children The default insert_position function returns num_children and can be overridden by a specific composite widget's resource list or by the argument list provided when the composite widget is created

1.8.2 Child's Perspective

The child widget uses XtMakeGeometryRequest to petition its parent to change its geometry For simplified cases, the child can use XtMakeResizeRequest.

Some parents may be more democratic than others More open-minded parents can find out a child's ambitions by using XtQueryGeometry Calling XtQueryGeometry triggers a call to the Core query_geometry method. The parent is not bound by any of its child's suggestions.

A child's query_geometry method is expected to examine the bits set in.

    intended->request_mode,

evaluate the preferred geometry of the widget, and store the result in preferred_return (setting the bits in

    preferred_return->request_mode

corresponding to those geometry fields that it cares about). If the proposed geometry change is acceptable without modification, the query_geometry method should return XtGeometryYes. If at least one field in preferred_return is different from the corresponding field in intended or if a bit was set in preferred_return that was not set in intended, the query_geometry method should return XtGeometryAlmost. If the preferred geometry is identical to the current geometry, the query_geometry method should return XtGeometryNo After calling the query_geometry method or if the query_geometry field is NULL, XtQueryGeometry examines all the unset bits in·

    preferred_return->request_mode

and sets the corresponding fields in preferred_return to the current values from the widget instance. If StackMode is not set, the stack_mode field is set to XtSMDont-Change XtQueryGeometry returns the value returned by the query_geometry method or XtGeometryYes if the query_geometry field is NULL

Therefore, the caller can interpret a return of XtGeometryYes as not needing to evaluate the contents of the reply and, more importantly, not needing to modify its layout plans. A return of XtGeometryAlmost means either that both the parent and the child expressed interest in at least one common field and the child's preference does not match the parent's intentions or that the child expressed interest in a field that the parent might need to consider A return value of XtGeometryNo means that both the parent and the child expressed interest in a field and that the child suggests that the field's current value is its preferred value. In addition, whether or not the caller ignores the return value or the reply mask, it is guaranteed that the reply structure contains complete geometry information for the child.

Parents are expected to call XtQueryGeometry in their layout routine and wherever other information is significant after change_managed has been called. The change_managed method may assume that the child's current geometry is its preferred geometry. Thus, the child is still responsible for storing values into its own geometry during its initialize procedure

1.8.3 Constraint Widgets

A constraint widget (a subclass of Constraint(3)) is a widget class that allows the parent to provide per-child data in the child widget structure. The parent can use this as an aid in laying out the children or for some application-dependent function The per-child data is maintained as resources and is transparent to the child itself.

The constraint structure itself adds several new fields. The constraint class itself adds a resource set which gets propagated to its children. There are also `constraint_init`, `constraint_destroy`, and `constraint_set_values` methods which are invoked. They are passed the *child* widget.

The values passed to the parent constraint initialization procedure are the same as those passed to the child's class widget initialization procedure.

The constraint initialization procedure should compute any constraint fields derived from constraint resources. It can make further changes to the widget to make the widget conform to the specified constraints, for example, changing the widget's size or position.

If a constraint class does not need a constraint initialization procedure, it can specify NULL for the initialize field of the `ConstraintClassPart` in the class record.

The constraint destroy procedure is retrieved from the destroy field of the structure, is called for a widget whose parent is a subclass of `constraintWidgetClass`, and is of type `XtWidgetProc`. The constraint destroy procedures are called in subclass-to-superclass order, starting at the widget's parent and ending at `constraintWidgetClass`. Therefore, a parent's constraint destroy procedure only should deallocate storage that is specific to the constraint subclass and not the storage allocated by any of its superclasses.

If a parent does not need to deallocate any constraint storage, the constraint destroy procedure entry in its class record can be NULL.

1.8.4 Related Discussion

Detailed examples of widgets that do geometry management, and use constraints, are presented in Chapter 11, *Geometry Management*, in Volume Four, *X Toolkit Intrinsics Programming Manual*. See also Composite(3) and Constraint(3).

1.9 Xlib Interface

The X Toolkit relies on underlying Xlib structures of Windows, Displays, and Screens to perform input and output.

A widget performs output by using Xlib calls to draw graphics and text. A widget maintains Xlib structures in Core instance variables. To simplify access whenever an Xlib structure is used, *<X11/Intrinsic.h>* provides macros (for widget implementors) and functions (for widget users).

In particular, see `XtDisplay`, `XtWindow`, and `XtScreen`. The dimensions of the widget's window can be obtained from Core instance variables. Other data structures that a widget might need to perform its particular function more efficiently can be put in the widget data structures.

The Intrinsics also provide a scheme to improve the efficiency of Graphics Contexts. See also `XtGetGC` and `XtDestroyGC` Examples using these functions are presented in Volume Four

—Mark Langley

Permuted Index

How to Use the Permuted Index

The permuted index takes the brief descriptive string from the title of each command page and rotates (permutes) the string so that each keyword will at one point start the *second*, or center, column of the line. The beginning and end of the original string are indicated by a slash when they are in other than their original position; if the string is too long, it is truncated.

To find the command you want, simply scan down the middle of the page, looking for a keyword of interest on the right side of the blank gutter. Once you find the keyword you want, you can read (with contortions) the brief description of the command that makes up the entry. If things still look promising, you can look all the way over to the right for the name of the relevant command page.

The Permuted Index

instance of a data type XtNew   allocate storage for one   .   .   . XtNew(1)
XtMalloc   allocate storage   .   .   .. XtMalloc(1)
XtFree   free an   allocated block of storage   .   .   . XtFree(1)
XtRealloc   change the size of an   allocated block of storage   . ... XtRealloc(1)
XtRemoveInput   cancel source of   alternate input events   .   .   . XtRemoveInput(1)
/called by the Intrinsics when   another client claims his/   .   .   XtLoseSelectionProc(2)
scrolling of viewing area in   another widget /to control .... Scrollbar(4)
a widget's accelerators on   another widget /install .   ... .   XtInstallAccelerators(1)
its displays /destroy an   application context and close ....   XtDestroyApplicationContext(1)
widget /get the   application context for a given   .   .   XtWidgetToApplicationContext(1)
a display and remove it from an   application context /close .   .   .   XtCloseDisplay(1)
/create an   application context   .   .   .   XtCreateApplicationContext(1)
a display and add it to an   application context /initialize .   ..   .   XtDisplayInitialize(1)
and add a display to an   application context /initialize, ...   XtOpenDisplay(1)
window/ Shell Widget Class   application resources linking   .   ... .   Shell(3)
file as an input source for an   application /register a new .   ..   .   XtAddInput(1)
register a work procedure for an   application XtAddWorkProc   XtAddWorkProc(1)
a new resource converter for an   application /register   .. .. XtAppAddConverter(1)
as an input source for a given   application /register a new file   ..   XtAppAddInput(1)
a work procedure for a given   application /register .... XtAppAddWorkProc(1)
process input from a given   application XtAppMainLoop   .   .   XtAppMainLoop(1)
base-offset resource list (by   application) /update   .   .   ... .   XtGetApplicationResources(1)
/return next event from an   application's input queue . .   . XtAppNextEvent(1)
/examine the head of an   application's input queue . .   .. XtAppPeekEvent(1)
/if there are any events in an   application's input queue .   .   . .. XtAppPending(1)
/examine the head of an   application's input queue . ...   XtPeekEvent(1)
/if there are any events in an   application's input queue   .   . . . XtPending(1)
to control scrolling of viewing   area in another widget /widget   .   . . Scrollbar(4)
XtMergeArgLists   merge two   ArgList structures .   .   . . XtMergeArgLists(1)
list XtSetSubvalues   copy from   ArgList to base-offset resource . ..   XtSetSubvalues(1)
XtSetValues   copy resources from   ArgList to widget .. . .   XtSetValues(1)
XtSetArg   construct or modify an   argument list dynamically .   . .   XtSetArg(1)
base-offset resource list to the   argument list /copy from   ..   .   XtGetSubvalues(1)
resources from a widget to the   argument list XtGetValues   copy . .   XtGetValues(1)
zero XtCalloc   allocate an   array and initialize elements to   .. .. .   XtCalloc(1)
of elements in a fixed-size   array /determine the number   . . .   XtNumber(1)
when requested selection data   arrives /procedure called .... XtSelectionCallbackProc(2)
descendants /destroy the windows   associated with a widget and its   .   .   XtUnrealizeWidget(1)
other widgets gripWidgetClass   attachment point for dragging   .   . Grip(4)
/user input from modal widget   back to normal destination .   ..   .   XtRemoveGrab(1)
XtWorkProc   perform   background processing   .   . .   XtWorkProc(2)
application) /update   base-offset resource list (by   .. .. XtGetApplicationResources(1)
name/ XtGetSubresources   update   base-offset resource list (by   . . . . .   XtGetSubresources(1)
XtGetSubvalues   copy from   base-offset resource list to the/   .. .   XtGetSubvalues(1)
/copy from ArgList to   base-offset resource list . . .   .   XtSetSubvalues(1)
XtFree   free an allocated   block of storage . .. .   XtFree(1)
change the size of an allocated   block of storage XtRealloc .... XtRealloc(1)
XtStringConversionWarning   emit   boilerplate string conversion/   ..   XtStringConversionWarning(1)
geometry-managing   box widget boxWidgetClass   ..   .   Box(4)
dialogWidgetClass   dialog   Box widget .. ..   Dialog(4)
geometry-managing box widget   boxWidgetClass ..   .   . Box(4)
a widget MenuPopdown   built-in action for popping down .   .. MenuPopdown(1)
widget MenuPopup   built-in action for popping up a   . ..   MenuPopup(1)
commandWidgetClass   command   button activated by pointer/ .   . . . Command(4)
XtOffset   determine the   byte offset of a field within a/   ... .. XtOffset(1)
perform resource conversion and   cache result XtDirectConvert   . . . XtDirectConvert(1)
procedure XtCallAcceptFocus   call a widget's accept_focus   .   XtCallAcceptFocus(1)
handler XtAppErrorMsg   call the high-level fatal error   .. . . XtAppErrorMsg(1)

X Toolkit Intrinsics
Functions and Macros

This section contains alphabetically-organized reference pages for each Intrinsics function and macro.

Each page contains a synopsis of the routine's calling sequence, its arguments, a description of its function, and a reference to related routines.

MenuPopdown

Name
MenuPopdown — built-in action for popping down a widget.

Synopsis
```
void MenuPopdown(shell_name)
    String shell_name;
```

Arguments
`shell_name` Specifies the name of the widget shell to pop down.

Description
Pop-ups can be popped down through several mechanisms:

* A call to `XtPopdown`

* The supplied callback procedure `XtCallbackPopdown`

* The standard translation action `MenuPopdown`

To pop down a spring-loaded menu when a pointer button is released or when the pointer is moved into some window, use `MenuPopdown`.

`MenuPopdown` is known to the Translation Manager, which must perform special actions for spring-loaded pop ups. All that is necessary is to map it to some event or event sequence using a translation specification in a resource file. Calls to `MenuPopdown` in a translation specification are mapped into calls to a nonexported action procedure.

If a shell name is not given as an argument, `MenuPopdown` calls `XtPopdown` with the widget for which the translation is specified. If a `shell_name` is specified in the translation table, `MenuPopdown` tries to find the shell by looking up the widget tree starting at the parent of the widget in which it is invoked. If it finds a shell with the specified name in the pop-up children of that parent, it pops down the shell; otherwise, it moves up the parent chain as needed. If `MenuPopdown` gets to the application top-level shell widget and cannot find a matching shell, it generates an error.

See Also
`MenuPopup, XtCallbackPopdown, XtPopDown, XtPopup`.

MenuPopup

Name

MenuPopup — built-in action for popping up a widget.

Synopsis

```
void MenuPopup(shell_name)
    String shell_name;
```

Arguments

shell_name   Specifies the name of the widget shell to pop up.

Description

MenuPopup is a built-in action that pops up a widget. It must be specified in a translation for ButtonPress or an EnterNotify event.

MenuPopup is known to the Translation Manager, which must perform special actions for spring-loaded pop ups. All that is necessary is to map it to some event or event sequence using a translation specification in a resource file. Calls to MenuPopup in a translation specification are mapped into calls to a nonexported action procedure, and the translation manager fills in parameters based on the event specified on the left-hand side of a translation.

If MenuPopup is invoked on ButtonPress (possibly with modifiers), the translation manager pops up the shell with *grab_kind* set to XtGrabExclusive and *spring_loaded* set to TRUE. If MenuPopup is invoked on EnterWindow (possibly with modifiers), the translation manager pops up the shell with *grab_kind* set to XtGrabNonexclusive and *spring_loaded* set to FALSE. Otherwise, the translation manager generates an error.

When the widget is popped up, the following actions occur:

- Calls XtCheckSubclass to ensure *popup_shell* is a subclass of Shell.

- Generates an error if the shell's *popped_up* field is already TRUE.

- Calls the callback procedures on the shell's *popup_callback* list.

- Sets the shell *popped_up* field to TRUE and the shell *grab_kind* and *spring_loaded* fields appropriately.

- If the shell's *create_popup_child* field is non-NULL, it is called with *popup_shell* as the parameter.

- Calls:

```
XtAddGrab(popup_shell, (grab_kind == XtGrabExclusive),
          spring_loaded)
```

- Calls XtRealizeWidget with *popup_shell* specified.

- Calls XMapWindow with *popup_shell* specified.

(Note that these actions are the same as those for XtPopup.) MenuPopup tries to find the shell by searching the widget tree starting at the parent of the widget in which it is invoked. If it finds a shell with the specified name in the pop-up children of that parent, it pops up the shell with the appropriate parameters. Otherwise, it moves up the parent chain as needed. If

MenuPopup gets to the application widget and cannot find a matching shell, it generates an error.

See Also
MenuPopdown, XtPopDown, XtPopup.

XtAddActions

Name

XtAddActions — register an action table with the Translation Manager.

Synopsis

```
void XtAddActions(actions, num_actions)
    XtActionList actions;
    Cardinal num_actions;
```

Arguments

actions   Specifies the action table to register.

num_actions Specifies the number of entries in this action table

Description

All widget class records contain an action table In addition, using XtAddActions, an application can register its own action tables with the Translation Manager. An action table consists of a list of string names (which can be used in translation tables to associate an action with one or more events) and corresponding function pointers. The function pointer is of type Xt-ActionProc

By convention, the string and the function name are identical except that the function name begins with an upper-case letter, as in the example.

```
static XtActionsRec two_quits[] = {
    {"confirm", Confirm},
    {"quit", Quit},
},
```

This mapping from strings to function pointers is necessary to allow translation tables to be specified in resource files, which are made up entirely of strings.

For example, the Command widget has procedures to take the following actions:

- Set the appearance of the Command widget to indicate it is activated when a pointer button has been pressed in it.

- Unset the button back to its normal mode.

- Highlight the button borders when the pointer enters the Command widget.

- Unhighlight the button borders when the pointer leaves.

- Notify any callbacks that the button has been activated.

The action table for the Command widget class makes these functions available to translation tables written for Command or any subclass:

```
XtActionsRec actionTable[] = {
    {"Set", Set},
    {"Unset",      Unset},
    {"Highlight",  Highlight},
```



```
("Unhighlight",  Unhighlight)
("Notify",       Notify),
};
```

The actions specified in a translation can be registered before or after the translation table is parsed.

The items in an action list registered with `XtAddActions` are registered globally for the entire application. By contrast, the action list specified in a widget class structure is local—only translations specified by the widget itself can access local actions. However, a widget's local translation can access global actions, if there is no local action of the same name.

If an application registers more than one global action with the same name, the most recently registered action is used. The Intrinsics register an action table for `MenuPopup` and `Menu-Popdown` as part of X Toolkit initialization.

The Core class structure holds a list of translations and actions. Compare `XtParse-TranslationTable`. Chapter 7, *Events, Translations, and Accelerators*, in Volume Four, *X Toolkit Intrinsics Programming Manual*, contains general discussion and examples.

Structures

The `XtActionList` is a pointer to an `XtActionsRec`, defined as follows in *<X11/Xt-Intrinsic.h>*:

```
typedef _XtActionsRec    *XtActionList;

typedef struct _XtActionsRec {
    char *string;
    XtActionProc proc;
} XtActionsRec;
```

The string field is the name that you use in translation tables to access the procedure. The `proc` field is a pointer to a procedure that implements the functionality.

The form of an `XtActionProc` is described in `XtActionProc(2)`.

The `string` field is the name that you use in translation tables to access the procedure. The `proc` field is a pointer to a procedure that implements the functionality.

See Also

Section 1.5, "Translations and Actions,"
`XtAppAddActions, XtParseTranslationTable, MenuPopdown, MenuPopup,`
`XtActionProc(2),`
`Core(3).`

XtAddCallback

Name

XtAddCallback — add a callback procedure to a widget's callback resource

Synopsis

```
void XtAddCallback(w, callback_name, callback, client_data)
    Widget w,
    String callback_name;
    XtCallbackProc callback;
    caddr_t client_data;
```

Arguments

w   Specifies the widget.

callback_name
                 Specifies the resource name of the callback list to which the procedure is to
                 be appended See XtCallbackProc(2)

callback   Specifies the callback procedure to be added

client_data Specifies the argument to be passed to the specified callback procedure when
                 it is invoked by XtCallCallbacks, or specifies NULL

Description

Generally speaking, a widget expecting to interact with an application will declare one or more *callback lists* as resources, the application adds functions to these callback lists, which will be invoked whenever the predefined callback conditions are met. Callback lists are resources, so that the application can set or change the function that will be invoked

Callbacks are not necessarily invoked in response to any event, a widget can call the specified routines at any arbitrary point in its code, whenever it wants to provide a "hook" for application interaction. For example, all widgets provide an XtNdestroyCallback resource to allow applications to interpose a routine to be executed when the widget is destroyed.

Widgets can define additional callback lists as they see fit. For example, the Athena Command widget defines the XtNcallback callback list to notify clients when the widget has been activated (by the user clicking on it with the pointer) (This is actually a poor choice of names. It should have been given a more specific name, such as XtNnotifyCallback)

Callback functions are registered with a widget using a call to XtAddCallback or XtAdd-Callbacks. Even though callback lists are resources, callback functions cannot be added from resource files, since callback lists are maintained in a private internal form by the Intrinsics. They cannot be modified directly except through one of the calls (such as XtAdd-Callback) provided to access them.

XtAddCallback adds a new callback to the end of the callback list. A callback will be invoked as many times as it occurs in the callback list. See XtCallbackProc(2) for a description of the format of a callback function

Use XtAddCallbacks to add a list of callbacks to a widget's callback list

Callbacks differ from actions in the way that the registered function is invoked. For callbacks, the trigger is an abstract occurrence defined by the widget, which may or may not be event-related. The routines on a widget's callback lists are invoked by the widget code, using a call to XtCallCallbacks. Actions, on the other hand, are invoked directly by Xt, as the result of an event combination specified by the translations mechanism.

Another major difference between an action function and a callback function is that action functions are called with an event as an argument, while actions do not have the *client_data* or *call_data* arguments present for callback functions. This means the only way to pass application data into an action function is through global variables. On the other hand, the presence of the event argument means that you can use the contents of the event structure in the action function.

See Also
Section 1.3, "Application Interface,"
XtAddCallbacks, XtCallCallbacks, XtRemoveAllCallbacks, XtRemove-
Callback, XtRemoveCallbacks,
XtCallbackProc(2).

XtAddCallbacks

Name

XtAddCallbacks — add a list of callback procedures to a given widget's callback list.

Synopsis

```
void XtAddCallbacks(w, callback_name, callbacks)
    Widget w;
    String callback_name;
    XtCallbackList callbacks,
```

Arguments

w
: Specifies the widget

callback_name
: Specifies the resource name of the callback list to which the procedure is to be appended

callbacks
: Specifies the NULL-terminated list of callback procedures and corresponding client data

Description

Generally speaking, a widget expecting to interact with an application will declare one or more *callback lists* as resources, the application adds functions to these callback lists, which will be invoked whenever the predefined callback conditions are met. Callback lists are resources, so that the application can set or change the function that will be invoked

Callbacks are not necessarily invoked in response to any event, a widget can call the specified routines at any arbitrary point in its code, whenever it wants to provide a "hook" for application interaction. For example, all widgets provide an XtNdestroyCallback resource to allow applications to interpose a routine to be executed when the widget is destroyed

Widgets can define additional callback lists as they see fit. For example, the Athena Command widget defines the XtNcallback callback list to notify clients when the widget has been activated (by the user clicking on it with the pointer). (This is actually a poor choice of names It should have been given a more specific name, such as XtNnotifyCallback.)

Callback functions are registered with a widget using a call to XtAddCallbacks or XtAdd-Callback. Even though callback lists are resources, callback functions cannot be added from resource files, since callback lists are maintained in a private internal form by the Intrinsics They cannot be modified directly except through one of the calls (such as XtAddCallback) provided to access them.

XtAddCallbacks adds new callbacks to the end of the callback list. A callback will be invoked as many times as it occurs in the callback list. See XtCallbackProc(2) for a description of the format of a callback function.

Use XtAddCallback to add a single callback to a widget's callback list

Callbacks differ from actions in the way that the registered function is invoked. For callbacks, the trigger is an abstract occurrence defined by the widget, which may or may not be event-related. The routines on a widget's callback lists are invoked by the widget code, using a call to XtCallCallbacks. Actions, on the other hand, are invoked directly by Xt, as the result of an event combination specified by the translations mechanism.

Another major difference between an action function and a callback function is that action functions are called with an event as an argument, while actions do not have the client_data or call_data arguments present for callback functions. This means the only way to pass application data into an action function is through global variables. On the other hand, the presence of the event argument means that you can use the contents of the event structure in the action function.

There are many cases where you might want to add more than one callback function to the same callback list. The use of XtCallbackExclusive *et al.* provides a good case in point. There are Intrinsics-defined callback functions that can be used to pop up a widget. However, they do not place the pop up.

To pop up a dialog box upon the press of a command button, you would typically add two callback functions to the Command widget's XtNcallback list: one of the Intrinsics-supplied XtCallback* functions, and one of your own to place the pop up.

One way to add more then one callback function is to call XtAddCallback more than once. Another way is to call XtAddCallbacks, which takes an XtCallbackRect array as an argument. This array is usually initialized at compile time, as shown in the example below. The final NULL, NULL entry terminates the list. (This particular list registers the functions place_popup and XtCallbackExclusive and passes them both 0 as *client_data*.)

```
XtCallbackRec quit_callback_list[] = {
    {place_popup, 0}
    {XtCallbackExclusive, 0},
    {(XtCallbackProc) NULL, (caddr_t) NULL},
}
```

This form of XtCallbackRec list can also be used to replace a callback list with XtSet-Values (but not to *get* a callback list, because Xt compiles the list into an internal form).

Structures

```
typedef struct _XtCallbackRec*    XtCallbackList;

typedef struct _XtCallbackRec {
    XtCallbackProc callback;
    caddr_t client_data;
} XtCallbackRec, *XtCallbackList;
```

See Also

Section 1.3, "Application Interface,"
XtAddCallback, XtCallCallbacks, XtRemoveAllCallbacks, XtRemove-
Callback, XtRemoveCallbacks,
XtCallbackProc(2).

XtAddConverter

Name

XtAddConverter — register a new resource converter.

Synopsis

```
void XtAddConverter(from_type, to_type, converter, convert_args,
        num_args)
    String from_type;
    String to_type,
    XtConverter converter,
    XtConvertArgList convert_args;
    Cardinal num_args;
```

Arguments

from_type   Specifies the source type of the resource to be converted.

to_type   Specifies the destination type to which the resource is to be converted

converter   Specifies the converter procedure See XtConverter(2).

convert_args
     Specifies how to obtain additional arguments needed for the conversion; if no arguments are provided, this should be NULL See the Structures section below for a detailed description of the format of convert_args

num_args   Specifies the number of additional arguments to the converter or zero

Description

XtAddConverter obtains the default application context and invokes XtAppAdd-Converter. XtAddConverter is a simplified interface to XtAppAddConverter, and the calling sequences are identical, except that you do not need to specify an application context. Since most applications have only one application context, XtAddConverter does not require the application to pass app_context explicitly See XtAppAddConverter for additional details. See XtConverter(2) for a description of the contents of a resource converter.

Structures

```
typedef struct {
    XtAddressMode    address_mode;
    caddr_t          address_id,
    Cardinal         size,
} XtConvertArgRec, *XtConvertArgList,
```

See Also

XtAppAddConverter,
XtConverter(2)

XtAddEventHandler

Name

XtAddEventHandler — register a procedure to handle events.

Synopsis

```
void XtAddEventHandler(w, event_mask, nonmaskable, proc,
        client_data)
    Widget w;
    EventMask event_mask;
    Boolean nonmaskable;
    XtEventHandler proc;
    caddr_t client_data;
```

Arguments

w   Specifies the widget for which this event handler is being registered.

event_mask   Specifies the event mask for which to call this procedure.

nonmaskable   Specifies a Boolean value that indicates whether this procedure should be
               called on the nonmaskable events. (This argument should almost always be
               FALSE.)

proc   Specifies the procedure that is to be called. See XtEventHandler(2).

client_data   Specifies additional data to be passed to the client's event handler.

Description

XtAddEventHandler registers a procedure to be called when an event matching the
event_mask occurs in the specified widget. XtAddEventHandler can be called at any
time during the widget's lifetime; it ensures that Xlib will deliver the requested event by calling XSelectInput directly if the widget is realized, and it ORs the mask bits into the
widget's event mask otherwise. (Compare XtAddRawEventHandler.)

See XtEventHandler(2) for a description of an event handler procedure.

A procedure may be registered with the same client_data to handle multiple events. Further, more than one event handler can be registered for a given event. If multiple handlers are
registered, the handlers will be called, but in an indeterminate order. Translations and event
handlers can also be registered for the same event.

If a widget should wish to be informed when a nonmaskable event occurs, nonmaskable
should be set to TRUE. The nonmaskable events are GraphicsExpose, NoExpose,
SelectionClear, SelectionRequest, SelectionNotify, ClientMessage, and
MappingNotify. Ordinarily, nonmaskable events are of interest only to the Intrinsics.

Chapter 8, *More Input Techniques*, in Volume Four, *X Toolkit Intrinsics Programming Manual*,
provides example code for tracking pointer motion, pointer motion hints, and keyboard events.

Structures

The event_mask is formed by combining the event mask symbols listed in the first column of the table below using the bitwise OR operator (|). Each mask symbol sets a bit in the event_mask.

The table also briefly describes the circumstances under which you would want to specify each symbol.

Event Mask Symbol	Circumstances
NoEventMask	No events
KeyPressMask	Keyboard down events
KeyReleaseMask	Keyboard up events
ButtonPressMask	Pointer button down events
ButtonReleaseMask	Pointer button up events
EnterWindowMask	Pointer window entry events
LeaveWindowMask	Pointer window leave events
PointerMotionMask	All pointer motion events
PointerMotionHintMask	Fewer pointer motion events
Button1MotionMask	Pointer motion while button 1 down
Button2MotionMask	Pointer motion while button 2 down
Button3MotionMask	Pointer motion while button 3 down
Button4MotionMask	Pointer motion while button 4 down
Button5MotionMask	Pointer motion while button 5 down
ButtonMotionMask	Pointer motion while any button down
KeymapStateMask	Any keyboard state change on EnterNotify, LeaveNotify, FocusIn or FocusOut
ExposureMask	Any exposure (except GraphicsExpose and NoExpose)
VisibilityChangeMask	Any change in visibility
StructureNotifyMask	Any change in window configuration.
ResizeRedirectMask	Redirect resize of this window
SubstructureNotifyMask	Notify about reconfiguration of children
SubstructureRedirectMask	Redirect reconfiguration of children
FocusChangeMask	Any change in keyboard focus
PropertyChangeMask	Any change in property
ColormapChangeMask	Any change in colormap
OwnerGrabButtonMask	Modifies handling of pointer events

See Also

Section 1.4, "Events," Section 1.5, "Translations and Actions,"
XtAddRawEventHandler, XtRemoveEventHandler,
XtEventHandler(2).

XtAddExposureToRegion

Name

XtAddExposureToRegion — merge Expose and GraphicsExpose events into a region.

Synopsis

```
void XtAddExposureToRegion(event, region)
    XEvent *event;
    Region region;
```

Arguments

event   Specifies a pointer to the Expose or GraphicsExpose event.

region   Specifies the region object (as defined in <X11/Xutil.h>).

Description

The XtAddExposureToRegion utility function merges Expose and GraphicsExpose events into a region that clients can process at once rather than processing individual rectangles.

XtAddExposureToRegion computes the union of the rectangle defined by the exposure event and the specified region. Then it stores the results back in region. The Intrinsics pass an XRegion to a widget in the XtExposure method.

If the event argument is not an Expose or GraphicsExpose event, XtAddExposure-ToRegion returns without an error and without modifying region.

This function is used by the Intrinsics exposure compression mechanism. It is not ordinarily used explicitly by widgets.

Structures

A region is defined as an XRegion in <X11/region.h> among the private files for Xlib. A region is made up of these definitions:

```
typedef struct {
    short x1, x2, y1, y2;
} Box;

typedef struct _XRegion {
    short size;
    short numRects;
    Box *rects;
    Box extents;
} ;
```

See Also

Core(3)

XtAddGrab

Name

XtAddGrab — redirect user input to a modal widget.

Synopsis

```
void XtAddGrab(w, exclusive, spring_loaded)
    Widget w;
    Boolean exclusive;
    Boolean spring_loaded,
```

Arguments

w   Specifies the widget to add to the modal cascade.

exclusive   Specifies whether user events should be dispatched exclusively to this widget or also to previous widgets in the cascade.

spring_loaded

    Specifies whether this widget was popped up because the user pressed a pointer button

Description

XtAddGrab appends a widget to a *modal cascade*. Modal widgets are widgets that, except for the input directly to them, lock out user input to the application XtAddGrab affects only Xt's event dispatching —it does not request a key or button grab on the server.

When a modal menu or modal dialog box is popped up, user events (keyboard and pointer events) that occur outside the modal widget should be delivered to the modal widget or ignored In no case should user events be delivered to a widget outside the modal widget.

Menus can pop up submenus, and dialog boxes can pop up further dialog boxes to create a pop-up cascade In this case, user events may be delivered to one of several modal widgets in the cascade.

Display-related events should be delivered outside the modal cascade so that Expose events and the like keep the application's display up to date Any event that occurs within the cascade is delivered as usual The user events that are delivered to the most recent spring-loaded shell in the cascade when they occur outside the cascade are called remap events These events are KeyPress, KeyRelease, ButtonPress, and ButtonRelease The user events that are ignored when they occur outside the cascade are MotionNotify, EnterNotify, and LeaveNotify. All other events are delivered normally.

XtPopup uses the XtAddGrab and XtRemoveGrab functions to constrain user events to a modal cascade and subsequently to remove a grab when the modal widget goes away. Usually you should have no need to call them explicitly. XtAddGrab is called implicitly by Xt-CallbackExclusive and other calls

The XtAddGrab function appends the widget (and associated parameters) to the modal cascade and checks that *exclusive* is TRUE if *spring_loaded* is TRUE. If these are not both TRUE, XtAddGrab generates a warning and asserts an *exclusive* grab anyway

When the modal cascade holds at least one widget, XtDispatchEvent determines if the event should be delivered or held. It starts with the last cascade entry and follows the cascade till it finds the youngest cascade entry added with *exclusive* TRUE. If it finds a widget in the cascade interested in the event, it delivers the event to it.

This modal cascade, along with all descendants of the widgets it contains, comprise the *active subset*. User events that occur outside the widgets in this subset are ignored or remapped. Modal menus generally add pop-up submenus to the cascade with *exclusive* set to FALSE, so that the submenu can receive input event after it pops up. Modal dialog boxes that restrict user input to the most deeply nested dialog box add a subdialog widget to the cascade with *exclusive* set to TRUE. User events that occur within the active subset are delivered to the appropriate widget, which is usually a descendant of the modal widget.

Regardless of where they occur on the display, redirected events are always delivered to the most recent widget in the active subset of the cascade that has *spring_loaded* TRUE, if any such widget exists.

See Also

XtCallbackExclusive, XtCreatePopupShell, XtDispatchEvent, XtPopup, XtRemoveGrab.

XtAddInput

Name

XtAddInput — register a new file as an input source for an application

Synopsis

```
XtInputId XtAddInput(source, condition, proc, client_data)
    int source;
    caddr_t condition;
    XtInputCallbackProc proc;
    caddr_t client_data,
```

Arguments

source	Specifies the source file descriptor (on a UNIX-based system) or other operating-system-dependent device specification
condition	Specifies a mask that indicates a read, write, or exception condition or some operating-system-dependent condition.
proc	Specifies the procedure that is to be called when input is available. See Xt-InputCallbackProc(2).
client_data	Specifies the argument to be passed to the specified procedure when input is available.

Description

XtAddInput obtains the default application context and invokes XtAppAddInput Xt-AddInput is a simplified interface to XtAppAddInput, and except that you do not need to specify an application context, the calling sequences are identical. Since most applications have only one application context, XtAddInput does not require the application to pass app_context explicitly

While most applications are driven only by X events, some applications need to incorporate other sources of input XtAppAddInput allows an application to integrate notification of pending file data into the event mechanism. The application uses XtAppAddInput to register a file with the Intrinsics read routine. When I/O is pending on the file *source*, the registered callback procedure *proc* is invoked *source* is usually file input but can also be file output. (Note that "file" means any sink or source of data.)

XtAppAddInput also specifies the *condition* under which *source* can generate events The legal values for *condition* are operating-system-dependent On a UNIX-based system, the possible values are XtInputReadMask, XtInputWriteMask, or XtInputExcept-Mask. The masks cannot be ORed together These limit the invocation of *proc* to either a pending read, write, or exception condition on the *source* file See the UNIX system select call for discussion of these conditions.

Callback procedures that are used when there are file events are of type XtInputCallback-Proc.

Note that when reading from a socket, you should be careful not to close the end of the socket that is waiting before exiting the XtMainLoop. If you do this, you will get an infinite loop, in which the *proc* is called repeatedly, while the Intrinsics wait for an EOF to be read.

See Chapter 8, *More Input Techniques*, in Volume Four, *X Toolkit Intrinsics Programming Manual*, for a complete example using this function.

See Also

XtAppAddInput, XtRemoveInput,
XtInputCallbackProc(2).

XtAddRawEventHandler

Name

XtAddRawEventHandler — register an event handler without selecting for the event.

Synopsis

```
void XtAddRawEventHandler(w, event_mask, nonmaskable, proc,
        client_data)
    Widget w;
    EventMask event_mask;
    Boolean nonmaskable;
    XtEventHandler proc;
    caddr_t client_data;
```

Arguments

w   Specifies the widget for which this event handler is being registered.

event_mask Specifies the event mask for which to call this procedure. See XtAdd-
            EventHandler.

nonmaskable Specifies a Boolean value that indicates whether this procedure should be
            called on the nonmaskable events (GraphicsExpose, NoExpose,
            SelectionClear,   SelectionRequest,   SelectionNotify,
            ClientMessage, and MappingNotify).

proc   Specifies the procedure that is to be registered. See XtEventHandler(2).

client_data Specifies additional data to be passed to the client's event handler.

Description

XtAddRawEventHandler is similar to XtAddEventHandler except that it does not
affect the widget's mask and never causes an XSelectInput call to be made for its events.
The event mask in XtAddRawEventHandler indicates which events the handler will be
called in response to, but only when these events are selected elsewhere.

A raw event handler might be used to "shadow" another event handler (both added with the
same event mask), such that until a primary event handler is added, the shadow handler will
never be called. The primary handler will be added with XtAddEventHandler and will
alter the event mask, and then both handlers will be called when the appropriate events occur.

However, the "shadowing" technique is not necessary to assure that multiple calls to XtAdd-
EventHandler would not result in wasted XSelectInput calls in which the event mask
has not changed. Xt keeps a cache of the event masks of each widget and calls XSelect-
Input only when it is necessary to change the window's event mask attribute.

Raw event handlers are removed with a call to XtRemoveRawEventHandler.

A widget needs to register a raw handler only in extraordinary circumstances; most widgets use
XtAddEventHandler.

Xt Functions and Macros

See Also

Section 1.4, "Events,"
XtAddEventHandler, XtRemoveRawEventHandler,
XtEventHandler(2).

XtAddTimeOut

Name
XtAddTimeOut — create a timeout value.

Synopsis
```
XtIntervalId XtAddTimeOut(interval, proc, client_data)
    unsigned long interval,
    XtTimerCallbackProc proc;
    caddr_t client_data;
```

Arguments
interval   Specifies the time interval in milliseconds

proc   Specifies the procedure to be called when the time expires See XtTimer-
            CallbackProc(2)

client_data Specifies the argument to be passed to the specified procedure when it is
            called

Description
XtAddTimeOut obtains the default application context and invokes XtAppAddTimeOut. It
is retained as a simplified interface to XtAppAddTimeout. Since most applications have
only one *app_context*, XtAddTimeOut does not require the application to pass an
app_context explicitly

The Intrinsics invoke the specified *proc* when *interval* elapses and the timeout is removed
from the event queue

The return value XtIntervalID uniquely identifies the pending timer pseudo-event The
pending event can be deleted from the queue before the interval expires by calling Xt-
RemoveTimeOut.

The callback procedure pointer that is invoked when timeouts expire is of type XtTimer-
CallbackProc.

XtAppNextEvent and XtAppPeekEvent dispatch timer queue entries.

See Also
Section 1 4, "Events,"
XtAppAddTimeOut, XtAppNextEvent, XtAppPeekEvent, XtAppPending, Xt-
DispatchEvent, XtRemoveTimeOut,
XtTimerCallbackProc(2)

XtAddWorkProc

Name

XtAddWorkProc — register a work procedure for an application.

Synopsis

```
XtWorkProcId XtAddWorkProc(proc, client_data)
    XtWorkProc proc;
    caddr_t client_data;
```

Arguments

proc   Specifies the procedure to be called when the application is idle.

client_data Specifies the argument to be passed to the specified procedure when it is called.

Description

XtAddWorkProc obtains the default application context and invokes XtAppAddWork-Proc. It is a simplified interface to XtAppAddWorkProc. Since most applications have only one app_context, XtAddWorkProc does not require the application to pass an app_context explicitly.

XtWorkProc(2) discusses the responsibilities of the application's background processing routine.

See Also

XtAppAddWorkProc, XtRemoveWorkProc, XtWorkProc(2).

Name

XtAppAddActions — declare an action table and register it with the Resource Manager.

Synopsis

```
void XtAppAddActions(app_context, actions, num_actions)
    XtAppContext app_context,
    XtActionList actions;
    Cardinal num_actions;
```

Arguments

app_context   Specifies the application context.

actions   Specifies the action table to register.

num_args   Specifies the number of entries in this action table.

Description

All widget class records contain an action table In addition, using XtAddActions, an application can register its own action tables with the Resource Manager An action table consists of a list of string names (which can be used in translation tables to associate an action with one or more events) and corresponding function pointers. The function pointer is of type XtActionProc.

By convention, the string and the function name are identical except that the function name begins with an upper-case letter, as in the example

```
static XtActionsRec two_quits[] = {
    {"confirm", Confirm},
    {"quit", Quit},
},
```

This mapping from strings to function pointers is necessary to allow translation tables to be specified in resource files, which are made up entirely of strings.

For example, the Command widget has procedures to take the following actions

- Set the appearance of the Command widget to indicate it is activated when a pointer button has been pressed in it.

- Unset the button back to its normal mode

- Highlight the button borders when the pointer enters the Command widget.

- Unhighlight the button borders when the pointer leaves

- Notify any callbacks that the button has been activated.

The action table for the Command widget class makes these functions available to translation tables written for Command or any subclass.

```
XtActionsRec actionTable[] = {
    {"Set", Set},
    {"Unset",       Unset},
    {"Highlight",   Highlight},
```

```
    {"Unhighlight",  Unhighlight}
    {"Notify",       Notify},
};
```

The actions specified in a translation can be registered before or after the translation table is parsed.

The items in an action list registered with XtAddActions are registered globally for the entire application. By contrast, the action list specified in a widget class structure is local—only translations specified by the widget itself can access local actions. However, a widget's local translation can access global actions, if there is no local action of the same name.

If an application registers more than one global action with the same name, the most recently registered action is used. The Intrinsics register an action table for MenuPopup and Menu-Popdown as part of X Toolkit initialization.

The Core class structure holds a list of translations and actions. Compare XtParse-TranslationTable. Chapter 7, *Events, Translations, and Accelerators*, in Volume Four, *X Toolkit Intrinsics Programming Manual*, contains general discussion and examples.

If more than one action is registered with the same name, the most recently registered action is used. If duplicate actions exist in an action table, the first is used. The Intrinsics register an action table for actions called MenuPopup and MenuPopdown as part of X Toolkit initialization.

See Also
XtAddActions

XtAppAddConverter

Name

XtAppAddConverter — register a new resource converter for an application

Synopsis

```
void XtAppAddConverter(app_context, from_type, to_type,
        converter, convert_args, num_args)
    XtAppContext app_context;
    String from_type;
    String to_type,
    XtConverter converter;
    XtConvertArgList convert_args;
    Cardinal num_args;
```

Arguments

app_context	Specifies the application context
from_type	Specifies the source type of the resource to be converted.
to_type	Specifies the destination type to which the resource is to be converted.
converter	Specifies the converter procedure See XtConverter(2).
convert_args	Specifies how to obtain additional arguments needed for the conversion, if no arguments are provided, this should be NULL See the Structures section below for a detailed description of the format of convert_args
num_args	Specifies the number of additional arguments to the converter or zero

Description

Resource converters provide a general way to pass specific data structures, and to hide the details of the data structures themselves. Using XtAppAddConverter or XtAdd-Converter, an application can register a converter to transform data of a given type to another specified type. The types themselves are arbitrary, and are specified by a string. For example, the converter mechanism can convert data of type String to an application data type of Menu if the application has registered the appropriate converter; to the application, the data type Menu is opaque

Some converters need additional arguments, which can be obtained from fields within the widget or as constants The enumerated type XtAddressMode and the structure Xt-ConvertArgRec specify how each argument is derived. These are defined in <X11/Convert h>, as follows.

```
typedef enum {
    /* address mode parameter representation */
    XtAddress,              /* address */
    XtBaseOffset,           /* offset */
    XtImmediate             /* constant */
    XtResourceString        /* resource name string */
    XtResourceQuark         /* resource name quark */
} XtAddressMode;
```

```
typedef struct {
    XtAddressMode address_mode;
    caddr_t address_id;
    Cardinal size;
} XtConvertArgRec, *XtConvertArgList;
```

The address_mode member specifies how to interpret the address_id member:

XtAddress   causes address_id to be interpreted as the address of the data.

XtBaseOffset   causes address_id to be interpreted as the offset from the widget
                   base.

XtImmediate   causes address_id to be interpreted as a constant.

XtResourceString   causes address_id to be interpreted as the name of a resource to be
                   converted into an offset from the widget base.

XtResourceQuark   means address_id is an internal compiled form of an Xt-
                   ResourceString. The size field specifies the length of the data in
                   bytes.

Assuming a routine called CvtStringToPixel (see XtConverter for an example of this
converter), the following code registers the routine as an official resource converter:

```
static XtConvertArgRec colorConvertArgs[] = {
    {XtBaseOffset, (caddr_t) XtOffset(Widget, core.screen),
        sizeof(Screen *)},
    {XtBaseOffset, (caddr_t) XtOffset(Widget, core.colormap),
        sizeof(Colormap)}
};

XtAddConverter(XtRString, XtRPixel, CvtStringToPixel,
    colorConvertArgs, XtNumber(colorConvertArgs));
```

The conversion argument descriptors colorConvertArgs and screenConvertArg are
predefined. The screenConvertArg descriptor puts the widget's screen field into
args[0]. The colorConvertArgs descriptor puts the widget's screen field into
args[0] and the widget's colormap field into args[1].

Conversion routines should not just put a descriptor for the address of the base of the widget
into args[0] and then use that in the routine. They should pass in the actual values that the
conversion depends on. By keeping the dependencies of the conversion procedure-specific, it
is more likely that subsequent conversions will find what they need in the conversion cache.
This way the cache is smaller and has fewer and more widely applicable entries.

XtAddConverter provides a simplified interface for programs using the default application
context.

XtConverter(2) explains the responsibilities and conventions of the converter function
itself; it also shows an example converter, CvtStringToPixel.

See Also

    XtAddConverter, XtDirectConvert,
    XtConverter(2)

XtAppAddInput

Name

XtAppAddInput — register a new file as an input source for a given application.

Synopsis

```
XtInputId XtAppAddInput(app_context, source, condition, proc,
        client_data)
    XtAppContext app_context;
    int source;
    caddr_t condition;
    XtInputCallbackProc proc;
    caddr_t client_data;
```

Arguments

app_context   Specifies the application context that identifies the application.

source   Specifies the source file descriptor (on a UNIX-based system) or other operating-system-dependent device specification.

condition   Specifies a mask that indicates a read, write, or exception condition or some operating-system-dependent condition.

proc   Specifies the procedure that is to be called when condition is true. See XtInputCallbackProc(2).

client_data   Specifies for argument source to be passed to proc when I/O is available.

Description

While most applications are driven only by X events, some applications need to incorporate other sources of input. XtAppAddInput allows an application to integrate notification of pending file data into the event mechanism. The application uses XtAppAddInput to register a file with the Intrinsics read routine. When I/O is pending on the file source, the registered callback procedure proc is invoked. source is usually file input but can also be file output. (Note that "file" means any sink or source of data.)

XtAppAddInput also specifies the condition under which source can generate events. The legal values for condition are operating-system-dependent. On a UNIX-based system, the possible values are XtInputReadMask, XtInputWriteMask, or XtInputExceptMask. The masks cannot be ORed together. These limit the invocation of proc to either a pending read, write, or exception condition on the source file. See the UNIX system select call for discussion of these conditions.

Callback procedures that are used when there are file events are of type XtInputCallbackProc.

Note that when reading from a socket, you should be careful not to close the end of the socket that is waiting before exiting the XtMainLoop. If you do this, you will get an infinite loop, in which the proc is called repeatedly, while the Intrinsics wait for an EOF to be read.

See Chapter 8, *More Input Techniques*, in Volume Four, *X Toolkit Intrinsics Programming Manual*, for a complete example using this function.

See Also
> XtAddInput, XtRemoveInput,
> XtInputCallbackProc(2)

XtAppAddTimeOut

Name

XtAppAddTimeOut — invoke a procedure after a specified timeout.

Synopsis

```
XtIntervalId XtAppAddTimeOut(app_context, interval, proc,
        client_data)
    XtAppContext app_context;
    unsigned long interval;
    XtTimerCallbackProc proc;
    caddr_t client_data;
```

Arguments

app_context   Specifies the application context for which the timer is to be set.

interval   Specifies the time interval in milliseconds.

proc   Specifies the procedure that is to be called when the time expires. See Xt-TimerCallbackProc(2).

client_data Specifies the argument to be passed to the specified procedure when it is called.

Description

While most applications are driven only by X events, some applications need to incorporate other types of events, such as timeouts or file data pending. XtAppAddTimeOut allows a program to have an event occur after a specified timeout. XtAppAddTimeOut creates the timeout and returns an identifier for it. The length of the timeout value is *interval* milliseconds.

The Intrinsics invoke the specified callback when *interval* elapses, and the timeout is removed from the event queue.

The return value XtIntervalID uniquely identifies the pending timer pseudo-event. The pending event can be deleted from the queue before the interval expires by calling Xt-RemoveTimeOut.

The callback procedure pointer that is invoked when timeouts expire is of type XtTimer-CallbackProc.

XtAppNextEvent and XtAppPeekEvent dispatch timer queue entries.

See Also

Section 1.4, "Events,"
XtAddTimeOut, XtAppNextEvent, XtAppPeekEvent, XtDispatchEvent,
XtRemoveTimeOut,
XtTimerCallbackProc(2).

XtAppAddWorkProc

Name
XtAppAddWorkProc — register a work procedure for a given application

Synopsis
```
XtWorkProcId XtAppAddWorkProc(app_context, proc, client_data)
    XtAppContext app_context;
    XtWorkProc proc;
    caddr_t client_data;
```

Arguments
app_context   Specifies the application context that identifies the application.

proc   Specifies the procedure that is to be called when the application is idle

client_data   Specifies the argument to be passed to the specified procedure when it is called.

Description
Xt supports a limited form of background processing. Most applications spend most of their time waiting for input, to do useful work during this idle time, you can register a work procedure that will run when the application would otherwise block in XtAppNextEvent or XtAppProcessEvent.

XtAppAddWorkProc adds the specified *proc* for the application identified by *app_context* XtWorkProcId is an opaque identifier unique to this work procedure. Multiple work procedures can be registered, and the most recently added one is always the one that is called However, if a work procedure itself adds another work procedure, the newly added one has lower priority than the current one

Passing the XtWorkProcId returned from the XtWorkProc to XtRemoveWorkProc causes *proc* to stop being called.

Work procedures are of type XtWorkProc. XtWorkProc discusses the responsibilities of the application's background processing routine XtAddWorkProc is a simplified interface to this function

See Also
XtAddWorkProc, XtAppNextEvent, XtAppProcessEvent, XtRemoveWorkProc, XtWorkProc(2).

XtAppCreateShell

Name

XtAppCreateShell — create additional top-level widget.

Synopsis

```
Widget XtAppCreateShell(application_name, application_class,
        widget_class, display, args, num_args)
    String application_name;
    String application_class;
    WidgetClass widget_class;
    Display *display;
    ArgList args;
    Cardinal num_args;
```

Arguments

application_name
Specifies the name of the application instance. If this argument is NULL, the application name passed to XtDisplayInitialize is used.

application_class
Specifies the class name of this application.

widget_class
Specifies the widget class that the application top-level widget should be (normally applicationShellWidgetClass).

display
Specifies the display from which to get the resources.

args
Specifies the argument list in which to set in the WM_COMMAND property.

num_args
Specifies the number of arguments in the argument list.

Description

An application can have multiple top-level widgets, which can potentially be on many different screens. An application uses XtAppCreateShell if it needs to have several independent windows. (A help system that stayed on the screen and could be moved and resized independently of the application is an example of such an independent top-level window.) The Xt-AppCreateShell function creates a top-level widget that is the root of a widget tree.

application_name and application_class become the left-most components in all widget resource names for this new application. They are used for qualifying all subsequent widget resource specifiers.

XtAppCreateShell should be used to create a new logical application within a program or to create a shell on another display. In the first case, XtAppCreateShell allows the specification of a new root in the resource hierarchy. If XtAppCreateShell is used to create shells on multiple displays, it uses the resource database associated with display.

There are two alternatives for creating multiple top-level shells within a single (logical) application.

- Designate one shell as the real top-level shell and create the others as pop-up children of it by using XtCreatePopupShell.

- Have all shells as pop-up children of an unrealized top-level shell.

The first method, which is best when there is a clear choice for what is the main window, leads to resource specifications like the following

```
xmail.geometry:  .   .        (the main window)
xmail.read.geometry. . . .    (the read window)
mail.compose.geometry: . . .  (the compose window)
```

The second method, which is best if there is no main window, leads to resource specifications like the following·

```
xmail.headers.geometry: .   .  (the headers window)
xmail read.geometry: . . .     (the read window)
xmail.compose.geometry: . .    (the compose window)
```

XtInitialize is a simplified interface to XtCreateApplicationContext, Xt-
DisplayInitialize, and XtAppCreateShell

See Also
Section 1 1, "Widget Lifecycle,"
XtCreateApplicationContext, XtCreatePopupShell, XtDisplay-
Initialize, XtInitialize

XtAppError

Name
XtAppError — call the installed fatal error procedure.

Synopsis
```
void XtAppError(app_context, message)
    XtAppContext app_context;
    String message;
```

Arguments

app_context   Specifies the application context.

message   Specifies the message to be reported.

Description

Xt provides two levels of error handling:

- A high-level interface that takes an error name and class and looks the error up in an error resource database.

- A low-level interface that takes a simple string, which is printed out as the error message.

Application-context-specific error handling is not implemented on many systems. Most implementations will have just one set of error handlers. If different handlers are set for different application contexts, the one set last will be used.

In theory, most programs should use XtAppErrorMsg (or XtErrorMsg if application contexts are not being used), not XtAppError or XtError, so that the programs can be easily customized to provide international or other custom error messages. However, the low-level handlers are much easier to use.

XtAppError calls the low-level fatal error handler. Fatal errors are assumed to be catastrophic and irrecoverable. A warning error handler also exists for errors that require attention but do not preempt a program running correctly to a normal successful completion. (XtApp-Warning calls the corresponding nonfatal error handler. XtAppErrorMsg and XtApp-WarningMsg call the corresponding high-level handlers.)

See Also
XtAppErrorMsg, XtAppSetErrorHandler, XtAppSetErrorMsgHandler, XtApp-SetWarningHandler, XtAppSetWarningMsgHandler, XtAppWarning, XtApp-WarningMsg, XtError, XtErrorHandler, XtErrorMsg, XtErrorMsgHandler, XtSetErrorHandler, XtSetErrorMsgHandler, XtSetWarningHandler, XtSet-WarningMsgHandler, XtWarning, XtWarningMsg.

Name

XtAppErrorMsg — call the high-level fatal error handler.

Synopsis

```
void XtAppErrorMsg(app_context, name, type, class, default,
        params, num_params)
    XtAppContext app_context;
    String name;
    String type;
    String class;
    String default,
    String *params;
    Cardinal *num_params;
```

Arguments

app_context	Specifies the application context.
name	Specifies the general kind of error; for example, InvalidParameter
type	Specifies the detailed name of the error This is specified using printf-like syntax, with the parameters and number of parameters specified by params and num_params.
class	Specifies the resource class.
default	Specifies the default message to use if no message is found in the database.
params	Specifies a pointer to a list of values to be stored in the type argument when the message is generated.
num_params	Specifies the number of values in the parameter list

Description

Xt provides two levels of error handling:

- A high-level interface that takes an error name and class and looks the error up in an error resource database

- A low-level interface that takes a simple string, which is printed out as the error message

The high-level functions construct a string to pass to the lower-level interface. The name and type arguments are concatenated to form the "name" that is used to look up a message in the error database On UNIX-based systems, the error database is usually /usr/lib/X11/XtErrorDB.

In theory, most programs should use XtAppErrorMsg (or XtErrorMsg if application contexts are not being used), not XtAppError or XtError, so that the programs can be easily customized to provide international or other custom error messages However, the low-level handlers are much easier to use.

XtAppError calls the low-level fatal error handler Fatal errors are assumed to be catastrophic and irrecoverable. A warning error handler also exists for errors that require attention but do not preempt a program running correctly to a normal successful completion.

(XtAppWarning calls the corresponding non-fatal error handler. XtAppErrorMsg and XtAppWarningMsg call the corresponding high-level handlers.)

The Intrinsics internal errors all have class XtToolkitError.

See Also

XtAppError, XtAppSetErrorHandler, XtAppSetErrorMsgHandler, XtAppSet-
WarningHandler, XtAppSetWarningMsgHandler, XtAppWarning, XtApp-
WarningMsg, XtError, XtErrorHandler, XtErrorMsg, XtErrorMsgHandler,
XtSetErrorHandler, XtSetErrorMsgHandler, XtSetWarningHandler, XtSet-
WarningMsgHandler, XtWarning, XtWarningMsg.

Name

XtAppGetErrorDatabase — obtain the error database

Synopsis

```
XrmDatabase *XtAppGetErrorDatabase(app_context)
    XtAppContext app_context,
```

Arguments

app_context Specifies the application context

Description

Xt's high-level error and warning message handlers use a resource-like database for storing error messages. On UNIX-based systems, the error database is usually stored in the file */usr/lib/X11/XtErrorDB* However, it is possible to have separate application-context-specific databases.

To obtain the error database (for example, to merge with an application or widget-specific database), use XtAppGetErrorDatabase.

The XtAppGetErrorDatabase function returns the address of the error database The Intrinsics do a lazy binding of the error database and do not merge in the database file until the first call to XtAppGetErrorDatabaseText.

Application-context-specific error handling is not implemented on many systems Most implementations will have just one set of error handlers. If they are set for different application contexts, the one performed last will prevail.

The high-level error and warning handler procedure pointers are of type XtErrorMsg-Handler(2) For a complete listing of all errors and warnings that can be generated by the Intrinsics, see Appendix D, *Standard Errors and Warnings*

Structures

The type XrmDatabase is opaque and should not be manipulated directly The return value can be manipulated with the Xlib functions XrmPutResource, XrmQPutResource, Xrm-GetResource, and XrmQGetResource.

See Also

XtAppGetErrorDatabaseText, XtGetErrorDatabase, XtGetErrorDatabase-Text,
XtErrorMsgHandler(2)

XtAppGetErrorDatabaseText

Name

XtAppGetErrorDatabaseText — obtain the error database text for an error or a warning.

Synopsis

```
void XtAppGetErrorDatabaseText(app_context, name, type, class,
        default, buffer_return, nbytes, database)
    XtAppContext app_context;
    char *name, *type, *class;
    char *default;
    char *buffer_return;
    int nbytes;
    XrmDatabase database;
```

Arguments

app_context Specifies the application context.

name, type   Specifies the name and type that are concatenated to form the resource name of the error message.

class   Specifies the resource class of the error message.

default   Specifies the default message to use if an error database entry is not found.

buffer_return
              Specifies the buffer into which the error message is to be returned.

nbytes   Specifies the size of the buffer in bytes.

database   Specifies the name of the alternative database to be used, or specifies NULL if the application's database is to be used.

Description

Xt's high-level error and warning message handlers use a resource-like database for storing messages. Messages are looked up by name and class, and the appropriate message retrieved from the database. A custom error message handler can obtain the error database text for an error or a warning by calling XtAppGetErrorDatabaseText.

XtAppGetErrorDatabaseText returns the appropriate message from the error database or returns the specified default message if one is not found in the error database.

On UNIX-based systems, the error database is usually stored in */usr/lib/X11/XtErrorDB*. Custom error or warning messages should be appended to this file.

The address of the loaded database can be returned by a call to XtAppGetErrorDatabase (or XtGetErrorDatabase). Note that application-context-specific error handling is not implemented on many systems. Most implementations will have just one set of error handlers. If they are set for different application contexts, the one performed last will prevail.

Typical usage of XtAppGetErrorDatabaseText() is deep in the X Toolkit error handling code. See the code below (slightly modified for clarity) for use of this function from the Xt

Intrinsics. The first four arguments to XtAppGetErrorDatabaseText() are just passed in from the XtErrorMsg() call in XtMalloc().

The XtMalloc() call assumes that the default error database (errorDB) has an error message for resource name allocError malloc of class XtToolkitError If not found, the default error message "Cannot perform malloc" will be used instead

You do not need to use this function unless you are writing an Xt error message handler of your own.

```
char *
XtMalloc(size)
       unsigned        size;
{
       char            *ptr;

       if ((ptr = malloc(size)) == NULL)
              XtErrorMsg("allocError", "malloc", "XtToolkitError",
                     "Cannot perform malloc", (String *) NULL,
                                   (Cardinal *) NULL),

       return (ptr),
}

void
XtErrorMsg(name, type, class, defaultp, params, num_params)
       String          name, type, class, defaultp;
       String          *params;
       Cardinal        *num_params;

       char            buffer[1000], message[1000],

       XtGetErrorDatabaseText(name, type, class, defaultp, buffer, 1000);

       /*
        * Need better solution here, perhaps use lower-level
         * printf primitives?
        */
       if (num_params == NULL)
              XtError(buffer),
       else {
              (void) sprintf(message, buffer, params[0], params[1],
                     params[2], params[3], params[4], params[5],
                     params[6], params[7], params[8], params[9]);
              _XtDefaultError(message),
       }
}

static void
_XtDefaultError(message)
       String message;
{
       extern void exit(),
```

```
        (void)fprintf(stderr, "X Toolkit Error: %s\n", message);
        exit(1);
}
void
XtGetErrorDatabaseText(name, type, class, defaultp, buffer, nbytes)
        register char *name, *type, *class;
        char          *defaultp;
        char          *buffer;
        int            nbytes;
{
        XtAppGetErrorDatabaseText(_XtDefaultAppContext(),
               name, type, class, defaultp, buffer, nbytes, NULL);
}
```

See Also

XtAppGetErrorDatabase, XtGetErrorDatabase, XtGetErrorDatabaseText,
XtErrorMsgHandler(2).

XtAppGetSelectionTimeout

Name
XtAppGetSelectionTimeout — get the current selection timeout value.

Synopsis
```
unsigned int XtAppGetSelectionTimeout(app_context)
    XtAppContext app_context;
```

Arguments
app_context Specifies the application context

Description
XtAppGetSelectionTimeout returns the current selection timeout value for the specified application context, in milliseconds (XtGetSelectionTimeout performs the same function for the default application context.) The selection timeout is the time within which the two communicating applications must respond to one another. The initial timeout value is set by the selectionTimeout application resource, or if selectionTimeout is not specified, it defaults to 5000 milliseconds (5 seconds). A new value can be set by a call to XtAppSet-SelectionTimeout or XtSetSelectionTimeout.

See Also
XtAppSetSelectionTimeout, XtGetSelectionTimeout, XtSetSelection-Timeout

XtAppMainLoop

Xt Functions and Macros

Name

XtAppMainLoop — process input from a given application.

Synopsis

```
void XtAppMainLoop(app_context)
    XtAppContext app_context;
```

Arguments

app_context Specifies the application context that identifies the application.

Description

XtAppMainLoop first reads the next incoming X event by calling XtAppNextEvent and dispatches it to the appropriate registered procedure by calling XtDispatchEvent. This constitutes the main loop of X Toolkit applications, and as such, it does not return. Applications are expected to exit in response to some user action.

There is nothing special about XtAppMainLoop; it is simply an infinite loop that calls XtAppNextEvent and then XtDispatchEvent. An application can provide its own version of this loop. For example, it might test an application-dependent global flag or other termination condition before looping back and calling XtAppNextEvent. For example, if the number of top-level widgets drops to zero, the application may be able to exit safely.

See XtAppAddWorkProc for information on how to spend idle time.

See Also

Section 1.1, "Widget Lifecycle,"
XtAppAddWorkProc, XtAppNextEvent, XtDispatchEvent, XtMainLoop.

XtAppNextEvent

Name

XtAppNextEvent — return next event from an application's input queue

Synopsis

```
void XtAppNextEvent(app_context, event_return)
    XtAppContext app_context;
    XEvent *event_return,
```

Arguments

app_context   Specifies the application context that identifies the application

event_return   Returns the event information from the dequeued event structure

Description

If a server has queued an event for the specified application, XtAppNextEvent removes the event from the queue and returns it to the caller.

If there are no events in the X input queue, XtAppNextEvent flushes the X output buffer and waits for an event from the X server or auxiliary input sources or for a timeout value to expire If a timer pseudo-event or auxiliary input event occurs, XtAppNextEvent dispatches the designated callbacks When an X event occurs, XtAppNextEvent removes it from the queue and returns it The events returned by XtAppNextEvent should be dispatched with Xt-DispatchEvent XtAppNextEvent dispatches XtWorkProcs and XtTimer-CallbackProcs directly that are registered for app_context. See XtAppAddWork-Proc and XtAppAddTimeOut

XtAppNextEvent blocks until an event occurs An application can instead use this wait time by interleaving background processing with calls to XtAppPending

Programs rarely need this much control over the event dispatching mechanism Most programs use XtAppMainLoop or XtMainLoop

See Also

XtAppAddWorkProc, XtAppMainLoop, XtAppPeekEvent, XtAppPending, XtApp-ProcessEvent, XtDispatchEvent, XtMainLoop, XtNextEvent, XtWorkProc

XtAppPeekEvent

Name

XtAppPeekEvent — nondestructively examine the head of an application's input queue.

Synopsis

```
Boolean XtAppPeekEvent(app_context, event_return)
    XtAppContext app_context;
    XEvent *event_return;
```

Arguments

app_context Specifies the application context that identifies the application.

event_return

Returns the event information from the head event structure in the queue.

Description

XtAppPeekEvent returns the value from the head of a given application's event queue without removing the value from the queue.

If a server has queued an event for the application, XtAppPeekEvent fills in the event and returns a nonzero value. It returns TRUE if the event returned is an X event and FALSE otherwise (i.e., if it is a Timer or alternate input event).

If there is no X event in the queue, XtAppPeekEvent flushes the output buffer and waits for an event from the X server or auxiliary input sources or for a timeout value to expire. If timer pseudo-events expire, it dispatches them itself, the same way XtAppNextEvent does. If the input is an event, XtAppPeekEvent fills in the event and returns a nonzero value. Otherwise, if input is from an alternate input source, XtAppPeekEvent returns NULL for the event.

Programs rarely need this much control over the event dispatching mechanism. Most programs use XtAppMainLoop or XtMainLoop.

However, all event sources depend on idle time in the application to return XtMainLoop where Xt can check to see if input is available from any of the various sources. If an application has long calculations to make, the progrm may not return to XtMainLoop frequently enough to detect important input in a timely fahsion. The application itself should, if possible, suspend important calculations for a moment to check whether input is available. Then it can determine whether to process the input before continuing or finish the calculation.

To detect whether input from any input source is available, you can call XtPending.

To find out what the first event in the queue contains, you can call XtPeekEvent. This function returns an event structure without removing the event from Xlib's queue.

It is also possible to remove and process a single event. XtProcessEvent combines some (but not all) of the functions from XtNextEvent and XtDispatchEvent. That is, while XtNextEvent takes the next event from the queue, whatever it is, XtProcessEvent allows you to specify as a mask a bitwise OR of the symbolic constants XtIMXEvent, XtIMTimer, and XtIMAlternateInput. This lets you select only some of these event types for processing In addition, XtProcessEvent actually calls XtDispatchEvent to dispatch X events, so only this one call is necessary

See Also

XtAppMainLoop, XtAppNextEvent, XtAppPending, XtAppProcessEvent, Xt-DispatchEvent, XtPeekEvent

XtAppPending

Name

XtAppPending — determine if there are any events in an application's input queue.

Synopsis

```
XtInputMask XtAppPending(app_context)
    XtAppContext app_context;
```

Arguments

app_context   Specifies the application context for the application to check.

Description

XtAppPending returns a nonzero value if there are pending events from the X server, timer, or other input sources. The return value is a bit mask that is the OR of XtIMXEvent (an X event), XtIMTimer (a timer event introduced onto the queue by a call to XtAppAddTime-Out), and XtIMAlternateInput (an alternate input event introduced onto the queue by a call to XtAppAddInput). As a convenience, the symbolic name XtIMAll is defined as the bitwise inclusive OR of all event types. If there are no events pending, XtAppPending flushes the output buffer and returns zero. This call is the Intrinsics equivalent to the Xlib call XPending.

Programs rarely need this much control over the event dispatching mechanism. Most programs use XtAppMainLoop or XtMainLoop.

However, all event sources depend on idle time in the application to return XtMainLoop where Xt can check to see if input is available from any of the various sources. If an application has long calculations to make, the progrm may not return to XtMainLoop frequently enough to detect important input in a timely fahsion. The application itself should, if possible, suspend important calculations for a moment to check whether input is available. Then it can determine whether to process the input before continuing or finish the calculation.

To detect whether input from any input source is available, you can call XtPending.

To find out what the first event in the queue contains, you can call XtPeekEvent. This function returns an event structure without removing the event from Xlib's queue.

It is also possible to remove and process a single event. XtProcessEvent combines some (but not all) of the functions from XtNextEvent and XtDispatchEvent. That is, while XtNextEvent takes the next event from the queue, whatever it is, XtProcessEvent allows you to specify as a mask a bitwise OR of the symbolic constants XtIMXEvent, Xt-IMTimer, and XtIMAlternateInput. This lets you select only some of these event types for processing. In addition, XtProcessEvent actually calls XtDispatchEvent to dispatch X events, so only this one call is necessary.

See Also

XtAppAddInput, XtAppAddTimeOut, XtAppMainLoop, XtAppNextEvent, XtAppPeekEvent, XtAppProcessEvent, XtDispatchEvent, XtPending.

XtAppProcessEvent

Name
XtAppProcessEvent — process one input event.

Synopsis
```
void XtAppProcessEvent(app_context, mask)
    XtAppContext app_context;
    XtInputMask mask;
```

Arguments
app_context Specifies the application context for which to process input.

mask Specifies what types of events to process The mask is the bitwise inclusive OR of XtIMXEvent (X event), XtIMTimer (timer events), or XtIMAlternateInput (alternate input events) The symbolic name XtIMAll is the bitwise inclusive OR of all event types

Description
While most widgets will use the Resource Manager to handle events, the X Toolkit does provide a mechanism for widgets or application code to handle X events directly. Every client interested in X events on a widget uses XtAddEventHandler to register which events it is interested in and a procedure (event handler) that is to be called when the event happens in that window The handler can then use XtAppProcessEvent to actually handle the events. XtAppProcessEvent processes an X event, a timer event, or an alternate input event If there is nothing to process, XtAppProcessEvent blocks until there is. If there is more than one type of event available, the one that will get processed is undefined.

XtAppProcessEvent processes timer events and alternate input events by calling the appropriate callbacks, the same way XtAppPeekEvent and XtAppNextEvent do. XtAppProcessEvent calls XtDispatchEvent to handle X events.

When an X event is received, it is passed to XtDispatchEvent, which calls the appropriate event handlers and passes them the widget, the event, and client-specific data registered with each procedure. If there are no handlers registered for that event, the event is ignored and the dispatcher simply returns. The order in which the handlers are called is undefined.

Programs rarely need this much control over the event dispatching mechanism. Most programs use XtAppMainLoop.

See Also
Section 1 5, "Translations and Actions,"
XtAppMainLoop, XtAppNextEvent, XtAppPeekEvent, XtAppPending, XtDispatchEvent, XtProcessEvent.

XtAppSetErrorHandler

Name

XtAppSetErrorHandler — register a procedure to be called on fatal error conditions.

Synopsis

```
void XtAppSetErrorHandler(app_context, handler)
    XtAppContext app_context;
    XtErrorHandler handler;
```

Arguments

`app_context` Specifies the application context.

`handler` Specifies the new fatal error procedure, which should not return.

Description

The default error handler provided by the Intrinsics is `_XtError`. On UNIX-based systems, it prints the message to standard error and terminates the application.

Using `XtAppSetErrorHandler` or `XtSetErrorHandler`, you can replace this default handler with one of your own.

Fatal error handlers should not return. If one does, subsequent X Toolkit behavior is undefined.

Note that application-context-specific error handling is not implemented on many systems. Most implementations will have just one set of error handlers. If they are set for different application contexts, the one performed last will prevail.

See Also

`XtAppError`, `XtAppErrorMsg`, `XtAppSetErrorMsgHandler`, `XtAppSetWarning-Handler`, `XtAppSetWarningMsgHandler`, `XtAppWarning`, `XtAppWarningMsg`, `XtError`, `XtErrorHandler`, `XtErrorMsg`, `XtErrorMsgHandler`, `XtSetError-Handler`, `XtSetErrorMsgHandler`, `XtSetWarningHandler`, `XtSetWarningMsg-Handler`, `XtWarning`, `XtWarningMsg`, `XtErrorHandler(2)`.

XtAppSetErrorMsgHandler

Name
XtAppSetErrorMsgHandler — register a procedure to be called on fatal error conditions

Synopsis
```
void XtAppSetErrorMsgHandler(app_context, msg_handler)
    XtAppContext app_context,
    XtErrorMsgHandler msg_handler,
```

Arguments
app_context Specifies the application context.

msg_handler Specifies the new fatal error message handling procedure, which should not
return.

Description
The default error handler provided by the Intrinsics constructs a string from the error resource
database (see `XtAppGetErrorDatabase`) and calls `XtError`.

Using `XtAppSetErrorMsgHandler` (or `XtSetErrorMsgHandler`), you can replace
the default handler with one of your own. Note that if you simply want to change the way the
message is displayed (rather than the way the message database is used), you should probably
replace the low-level error handler (using `XtAppSetErrorHandler`) instead.

Fatal error message handlers should not return. If one does, subsequent X Toolkit behavior is
undefined. See `XtErrorMsgHandler(2)` for details. Note that application-context-specific
error handling is not implemented on many systems. Most implementations will have just one
set of error handlers. If they are set for different application contexts, the one performed last
will prevail.

See Also
XtAppError, XtAppErrorMsg, XtAppSetErrorHandler, XtAppSetWarning-
Handler, XtAppSetWarningMsgHandler, XtAppWarning, XtAppWarningMsg,
XtError, XtErrorHandler, XtErrorMsg, XtErrorMsgHandler, XtSetError-
Handler, XtSetErrorMsgHandler, XtSetWarningHandler, XtSetWarningMsg-
Handler, XtWarning, XtWarningMsg.

XtAppSetSelectionTimeout

Name

XtAppSetSelectionTimeout — set the Intrinsics selection timeout.

Synopsis

```
void XtAppSetSelectionTimeout(app_context, timeout)
    XtAppContext app_context;
    unsigned long timeout;
```

Arguments

app_context   Specifies the application context.

timeout   Specifies the selection timeout in milliseconds.

Description

XtAppSetSelectionTimeout sets the Intrinsics selection timeout value for the specified application context. (XtSetSelectionTimeout performs the same function for the default application context.) The selection timeout is the time within which the two communicating applications must respond to one another. The initial timeout value is set by the selection-Timeout application resource, or if selectionTimeout is not specified, it defaults to 5000 milliseconds (5 seconds).

The current timeout value can be retrieved by a call to XtAppGetSelectionTimeout or XtGetSelectionTimeout.

See Also

XtAppGetSelectionTimeout, XtGetSelectionTimeout, XtSetSelection-Timeout.

XtAppSetWarningHandler

Name

XtAppSetWarningHandler — register a procedure to be called on nonfatal error conditions

Synopsis

```
void XtAppSetWarningHandler(app_context, handler)
    XtAppContext app_context,
    XtErrorHandler handler;
```

Arguments

app_context   Specifies the application context.

handler   Specifies the new nonfatal error procedure, which usually returns

Description

The default warning handler provided by the Intrinsics is _XtWarning On UNIX-based systems, it prints the message to standard error and returns to the caller. Using XtAppSet-WarningHandler, you can replace this default handler with one of your own

Note that application-context-specific error handling is not implemented on many systems. Most implementations will have just one set of error handlers. If they are set for different application contexts, the one performed last will prevail.

See Also

XtAppError, XtAppErrorMsg, XtAppSetErrorHandler, XtAppSetErrorMsg-Handler, XtAppSetWarningHandler, XtAppSetWarningMsgHandler, XtApp-Warning, XtAppWarningMsg, XtError, XtErrorHandler, XtErrorMsg, Xt-ErrorMsgHandler, XtSetErrorHandler, XtSetErrorMsgHandler, XtSet-WarningMsgHandler, XtWarning, XtWarningMsg

XtAppSetWarningMsgHandler

Name

XtAppSetWarningMsgHandler — register a procedure to be called on nonfatal error conditions.

Synopsis

```
void XtAppSetWarningMsgHandler(app_context, msg_handler)
    XtAppContext app_context;
    XtErrorMsgHandler msg_handler;
```

Arguments

app_context Specifies the application context.

msg_handler Specifies the new nonfatal error procedure, which usually returns.

Description

The default warning handler provided by the Intrinsics constructs a string from the error resource database and calls XtWarning. Using XtAppSetWarningMsgHandler, you can replace this default handler with one of your own. Note that if you simply want to change the way the message is displayed (rather than the way the message database is used), you should probably replace the low-level warning handler (using XtAppSetWarningHandler) instead.

Note that application-context-specific error handling is not implemented on many systems. Most implementations will have just one set of error handlers. If they are set for different application contexts, the one performed last will prevail.

See Also

XtAppError, XtAppErrorMsg, XtAppSetErrorHandler, XtAppSetErrorMsg-
Handler, XtAppSetWarningHandler, XtAppSetWarningMsgHandler, XtApp-
Warning, XtAppWarningMsg, XtError, XtErrorHandler, XtErrorMsg, Xt-
ErrorMsgHandler, XtSetErrorHandler, XtSetErrorMsgHandler, XtSet-
WarningHandler, XtWarning, XtWarningMsg.

XtAppWarning

Name
XtAppWarning — call the installed nonfatal error procedure

Synopsis
```
void XtAppWarning(app_context, message)
    XtAppContext app_context,
    String message;
```

Arguments
app_context   Specifies the application context.

message   Specifies the nonfatal error message that is to be reported.

Description
Xt provides two levels of error handling:

* A high-level interface that takes an error name and class and looks the error up in an error resource database.

* A low-level interface that takes a simple string, which is printed out as the error message

Application-context-specific error handling is not implemented on many systems Most implementations will have just one set of error handlers. If different handlers are set for different application contexts, the one set last will be used

In theory, most programs should use XtAppWarningMsg (or XtWarningMsg if application contexts are not being used), not XtAppWarning or XtWarning, so that programs can be easily customized to provide international or other custom error messages However, the low-level handlers are much easier to use.

XtAppError calls the low-level fatal error handler. Fatal errors are assumed to be catastrophic and irrecoverable. A warning error handler also exists for errors that require attention but do not preempt a program running correctly to a normal successful completion. (XtAppWarning calls the corresponding non-fatal error handler XtAppErrorMsg and XtAppWarningMsg call the corresponding high-level handlers)

See Also
XtAppError, XtAppErrorMsg, XtAppSetErrorHandler, XtAppSetErrorMsg-
Handler, XtAppSetWarningHandler, XtAppSetWarningMsgHandler, XtApp-
WarningMsg, XtError, XtErrorHandler, XtErrorMsg, XtErrorMsgHandler,
XtSetErrorHandler, XtSetErrorMsgHandler, XtSetWarningHandler, XtSet-
WarningMsgHandler, XtWarning, XtWarningMsg.

Name

XtAppWarningMsg — call the installed high-level warning handler.

Synopsis

```
void XtAppWarningMsg(app_context, name, type, class , default,
        params, num_params)
    XtAppContext app_context;
    String name;
    String type;
    String class;
    String default;
    String *params;
    Cardinal *num_params;
```

Arguments

app_context   Specifies the application context.

name   Specifies the general kind of error; for example, InvalidParameter.

type   Specifies the detailed name of the error. This is specified using printf-like
               syntax, with the parameters and number of parameters specified by params
               and num_params.

class   Specifies the resource class.

default   Specifies the default message to use if no message is found in the database.

params   Specifies a pointer to a list of values to be stored in the type argument when
               the message if generated.

num_params   Specifies the number of values in the parameter list.

Description

Xt provides two levels of error handling:

- A high-level interface that takes an error name and class and looks the error up in an error resource database.

- A low-level interface that takes a simple string, which is printed out as the error message.

The high-level functions construct a string to pass to the lower-level interface. The name and type arguments are concatenated to form the "name" that is used to look up a message in the error database. On UNIX-based systems, the error database is usually /usr/lib/X11/XtErrorDB. In theory, most programs should use XtAppErrorMsg (or XtErrorMsg if application contexts are not being used), not XtAppError or XtError, so that the programs can be easily customized to provide international or other custom error messages. However, the low-level handlers are much easier to use.

XtAppError calls the low level fatal error handler. Fatal errors are assumed to be catastrophic and irrecoverable. A warning error handler also exists for errors that require attention but do not preempt a program running correctly to a normal successful completion.

(XtAppWarning calls the corresponding non-fatal error handler. XtAppErrorMsg and XtAppWarningMsg call the corresponding high-level handlers)

See Also

XtAppError, XtAppErrorMsg, XtAppSetErrorHandler, XtAppSetErrorMsg-
Handler, XtAppSetWarningHandler, XtAppSetWarningMsgHandler, XtApp-
Warning, XtError, XtErrorHandler, XtErrorMsg, XtErrorMsgHandler, Xt-
SetErrorHandler, XtSetErrorMsgHandler, XtSetWarningHandler, XtSet-
WarningMsgHandler, XtWarning, XtWarningMsg

XtAugmentTranslations

Name

XtAugmentTranslations — nondestructively merge new translations with widget's existing ones.

Synopsis

```
void XtAugmentTranslations(w, translations)
    Widget w;
    XtTranslations translations;
```

Arguments

w Specifies the widget into which the new translations are to be merged.

translations Specifies the compiled translation table to merge in (must not be NULL).

Description

XtAugmentTranslations nondestructively merges *translations* into a widget's existing translations. If *translations* contains an event or event sequence that already exists in the widget's translations, then the new translation is ignored.

The translation table must be in compiled form, as produced by XtParseTranslationTable.

Translation tables can also be constructed by converting resources. To make it easy to modify translation tables in resource files, the string-to-translation-table resource type converter allows you to specify whether the table should replace, augment, or override any existing translation table in the widget. As an option, a pound sign (#) as the first character of the table followed by replace (default), augment, or override indicates how to treat existing translations (Release 3 and later only.)

To merge new translations but keep existing translations in case of conflict, use XtAugmentTranslations. To completely remove existing translations, use XtUninstallTranslations.

XtParseTranslationTable produces the binary form of the translation table from text. XtConvert can also do the conversion, specifying XtRTranslationTable as the destination resource type. A text translation table is automatically parsed in the Core widget structure when a widget class is initialized.

Release Information

In Release 2, a bug made it impossible to successfully call *XtAugmentTranslations* on a widget that had already been realized. This bug was fixed in Release 3.

The # syntax described above was new in Release 3. In addition, new syntax was added to support all keysym names in modifiers or detail fields, as well as case sensitivity, plus hooks for providing nonstandard case converters and nonstandard keycode-to-keysym converters.

See Also

Section 1.5, "Translations and Actions,"
XtConvert, XtOverrideTranslations, XtParseTranslationTable, Xt-
UninstallTranslations.

XtBuildEventMask

Name

XtBuildEventMask — retrieve a widget's event mask.

Synopsis

```
EventMask XtBuildEventMask(w)
    Widget w;
```

Arguments

w   Specifies the widget.

Description

XtBuildEventMask returns a widget's event mask. The mask reflects the events the widget is currently selecting. (If the widget is unrealized, then the mask reflects the events the widget will select when it is realized.) This event mask is the logical OR of all event masks selected by adding event handlers and event translations (including accelerators).

This event mask is stored in the XSetWindowAttributes structure by XtRealize-Widget and is sent to the server when event handlers and translations are installed or removed for the realized widget.

Structures

The event_mask is formed by combining the event mask symbols listed in the first column of the table below using the bitwise OR operator (|). Each mask symbol sets a bit in the event_mask.

The table also briefly describes the circumstances under which you would want to specify each symbol.

Event Mask Symbol	Circumstances
NoEventMask	No events
KeyPressMask	Keyboard down events
KeyReleaseMask	Keyboard up events
ButtonPressMask	Pointer button down events
ButtonReleaseMask	Pointer button up events
EnterWindowMask	Pointer window entry events
LeaveWindowMask	Pointer window leave events
PointerMotionMask	All pointer motion events
PointerMotionHintMask	Fewer pointer motion events
Button1MotionMask	Pointer motion while button 1 down
Button2MotionMask	Pointer motion while button 2 down
Button3MotionMask	Pointer motion while button 3 down
Button4MotionMask	Pointer motion while button 4 down
Button5MotionMask	Pointer motion while button 5 down
ButtonMotionMask	Pointer motion while any button down
KeymapStateMask	Any keyboard state change on EnterNotify, LeaveNotify, FocusIn or FocusOut

Event Mask Symbol	Circumstances
ExposureMask	Any exposure (except GraphicsExpose and NoExpose)
VisibilityChangeMask	Any change in visibility
StructureNotifyMask	Any change in window configuration.
ResizeRedirectMask	Redirect resize of this window
SubstructureNotifyMask	Notify about reconfiguration of children
SubstructureRedirectMask	Redirect reconfiguration of children
FocusChangeMask	Any change in keyboard focus
PropertyChangeMask	Any change in property
ColormapChangeMask	Any change in colormap
OwnerGrabButtonMask	Modifies handling of pointer events

See Also

Section 1.4, "Events," Section 1.5, "Translations and Actions,"
XtAddEventHandler, XtAddRawEventHandler, XtRealizeWidget.

XtCallAcceptFocus

Name
XtCallAcceptFocus — call a widget's `accept_focus` procedure.

Synopsis
```
Boolean XtCallAcceptFocus(w, time)
     Widget w;
     Time *time;
```

Arguments
w   Specifies the widget.

time   Specifies the X time of the event that is causing the accept focus.

Description
XtCallAcceptFocus calls the specified widget's `accept_focus` method, passing it the specified widget and time, and returns whatever the `accept_focus` method returns. If the `accept_focus` procedure is NULL, XtCallAcceptFocus returns FALSE.

XtCallAcceptFocus does not actually set the keyboard focus; it is used to determine if the widget would take the focus if offered. XtSetKeyboardFocus and the Xlib function XSetInputFocus actually pass the focus to a child.

The `accept_focus` method is part of the Core class structure.

See Also
XtSetKeyboardFocus,
XtAcceptFocusProc(2).

Name
XtCallbackExclusive — callback function to pop up a widget.

Synopsis
```
void XtCallbackExclusive(w, client_data, call_data)
    Widget w;
    caddr_t client_data;
    caddr_t call_data;
```

Arguments
w   Specifies the widget.

client_data   Specifies the pop-up shell.

call_data   Specifies the callback data, which is not used by this procedure.

Description
The XtCallback* routines are built in callback functions that pop up a pop-up shell widget. The suffixes *Exclusive*, *Nonexclusive*, and *None* refer to the grab types XtGrabExclusive, XtGrabNonexclusive, and XtGrabNone, respectively, to be applied to the pop-up shell. Callback XtExclusive and callback XtNonexclusive call XtAddGrab with the exclusive argument set to TRUE and FALSE respectively XtCallbackNone does not call XtAddGrab.

To pop up a shell from a callback list, it is sufficient to pass one of the above routines in a callback list and to the client_data field to be the pop-up shell. When the XtCallback routine is called, it invokes XtPopup with the designated grab type. Before XtPopup is called, the XtCallback routine uses XtSetSensitive to set the calling widget to be insensitive

These routines provide one strategy for popping up widgets—but you do not *have* to use them It may be better to write a custom routine to call XtPopup yourself In particular, an application may provide customized code to create pop-up shells dynamically or to perform additional processing. For example, XtCallbackExclusive does nothing to place the pop-up widget, so it pops up in the upper-left corner of the display A custom pop-up routine might move the pop-up shell to the location of the pointer, or the middle of the current window, before calling XtPopup. This can also be done in a separate callback function, added to the callback list before XtCallback*.

An example follows:
```
f()
{
    Widget pshell, button;
        .
        .

    pshell = XtCreatePopupShell(...);
    button = XtCreateWidget(...),
        XtAddcallback(button,XtCallbackNone,pshell),
    }
```

The callback list cb in Args is an argument to a widget. When the widget invokes XtCall-Callbacks on its XtNcallback resource, the pop-up shell pshell will be popped up.

A companion example to the one above is presented on XtCallbackPopdown.

See Also

Section 1.6, "Pop Ups,"
XtCallbackNone, XtCallbackPopdown, XtCallCallbacks, XtMoveWidget, Xt-Popdown, XtPopup, XtSetSensitive.

XtCallbackNone

—Xt – Pop Ups—

Name

XtCallbackNone — callback function to pop up a widget.

Synopsis

```
void XtCallbackNone(w, client_data, call_data)
    Widget w;
    caddr_t client_data;
    caddr_t call_data;
```

Arguments

w   Specifies the widget.

client_data Specifies the pop-up shell

call_data   Specifies the callback data, which is not used by this procedure

Description

See XtCallbackExclusive

XtCallbackNonexclusive

Name

XtCallbackNonexclusive — callback function to pop up a widget.

Synopsis

```
void XtCallbackNonexclusive(w, client_data, call_data)
    Widget w;
    caddr_t client_data;
    caddr_t call_data;
```

Arguments

w   Specifies the widget.

client_data Specifies the pop-up shell.

call_data   Specifies the callback data, which is not used by this procedure.

Description

See XtCallbackExclusive.

XtCallbackPopdown

Name
XtCallbackPopdown — pop down a widget from a callback routine

Synopsis
```
void XtCallbackPopdown(w, client_data, call_data)
    Widget w;
    caddr_t client_data;
    caddr_t call_data;
```

Arguments
w   Specifies the widget.

client_data   Specifies a pointer to the XtPopdownID structure

call_data   Specifies the callback data, which is not used by this procedure.

Description
XtCallbackPopdown pops down a pop-up shell widget. This function is suitable for popping down shells that were previously popped up with XtCallbackNone, XtCallbackNonexclusive, or XtCallbackExclusive. An XtPopdownID in the *client_data* field indicates which widget is to be popped down.

Structures
XtCallbackPopdown casts the client data parameter to an XtPopdownID pointer

```
typedef struct {
        Widget shell_widget;
        Widget enable_widget;
} XtPopdownIDRec, *XtPopdownID,
```

shell_widget is the pop-up shell to pop down, and enable_widget is the widget that was used to pop it up.

XtCallbackPopdown calls XtPopdown with the specified shell_widget and then calls XtSetSensitive to resensitize the enable_widget.

Here is an example·

```
Widget pshell, confirm,

XtPopdownIDRec pop_rec;

main() {
  confirm = XtCreateWidget(...);
  pshell = XtCreatePopupShell( ..),
  pop_rec shell_widget = pshell;
  pop_rec enable_widget = confirm,
  XtAddCallback(confirm,XtCallbackPopdown,pop_rec);
}
```

When the widget invokes `XtCallCallbacks` on its resource `XtNCallback`, the pop-up shell `pshell` will be popped down. See the companion example in `XtCallback-Exclusive`.

See Also

Section 1.6, "Pop Ups,"
`XtCallbackExclusive`, `XtCallCallbacks`, `XtPopdown`, `XtSetSensitive`.

XtCallCallbacks

Name

XtCallCallbacks — execute the procedures in a widget's callback list

Synopsis

```
void XtCallCallbacks(w, callback_name, call_data)
    Widget w;
    String callback_name;
    caddr_t call_data;
```

Arguments

w   Specifies the widget.

callback_name
         Specifies the resource name of the callback list to be executed

call_data   Specifies the value to pass to each callback procedure as its third argument.

Description

XtCallCallbacks is used to execute the callbacks in a given callback list

The call_data argument is a (32-bit) longword. The actual form of the data in the argument must be agreed on in advance by the callback function and the widget or application invoking it through XtCallCallbacks. The longword can be used to represent an address if more data is to be passed to the callback procedure.

If no data is needed, the call_data argument should be NULL (For example, the Xt-Ncallback callback list in the Athena Command widget needs only to notify its clients that the button has been activated. No data is passed in.)

XtCallCallbacks ensures that if a callback procedure itself *adds* callbacks (with XtAdd-Callbacks), no unwanted recursion ensues.

Callback lists are maintained in an internal compiled form. Callback lists can be accessed outside the widget as resources but cannot be added, deleted, or invoked except through one of the Intrinsics functions (such as XtAddCallback) provided to access them. The Intrinsics themselves make sure that resources of type Callback get compiled into this internal form

For more information on how to explicitly compile callbacks as resources of type Xt-RCallback, see XtConvert.

See Also

XtAddCallback, XtAddCallbacks, XtCallbackProc, XtConvert, XtRemove-AllCallbacks, XtRemoveCallbacks.

XtCalloc

Name
XtCalloc — allocate an array and initialize elements to zero.

Synopsis
```
char *XtCalloc(num, size);
    unsigned int num;
    unsigned int size;
```

Arguments
num   Specifies the number of array elements to allocate.

size   Specifies the size of an array element in bytes.

Description
XtCalloc allocates space for the specified number of array elements of the specified size and initializes the space to zero. If there is insufficient memory to allocate the new block, Xt-Calloc terminates by calling XtErrorMsg.

XtCalloc differs from XtMalloc in that it stores zero in all the array elements.

The function XtCalloc is implemented by the Toolkit independently of the particular environment, so programs ported to a system not supporting calloc will still work.

XtNew and XtNewString provide slightly higher-level approaches to memory allocation.

See Also
XtErrorMsg, XtFree, XtMalloc, XtNew, XtNewString, XtRealloc.

XtCheckSubclass

Name
XtCheckSubclass — in DEBUG mode, verify a widget's class

Synopsis
```
void XtCheckSubclass(w, widget_class, message)
    Widget w;
    WidgetClass widget_class;
    String message;
```

Arguments
w	Specifies the widget.
widget_class	Specifies the widget class to test against
message	Specifies the message to be used.

Description
XtCheckSubclass determines if widget w belongs to a subclass of the specified widget_class. (Note that two widgets of the same class belong to mutual subclasses) The widget can be any number of subclasses removed and need not be an immediate subclass of the specified widget class.

If the w is not a subclass, XtCheckSubclass constructs an error message from the supplied message, the widget's actual class, and the expected class, and it calls XtErrorMsg.

XtCheckSubclass should be used at the entry point of exported routines to ensure that the client has passed in a valid widget class for the exported operation.

XtCheckSubclass is a macro. It is only executed when the widget has been compiled with the compiler symbol DEBUG defined, otherwise, it is defined as the empty string and generates no code.

XtCheckSubclass uses the Core widget data structures to perform its checking.

See Also
XtClass, XtIsSubclass, XtSuperclass,
Core(3)

XtClass

Name

XtClass — obtain a widget's class.

Synopsis

```
WidgetClass XtClass(w)
    Widget w;
```

Arguments

w   Specifies the widget.

Description

XtClass returns a pointer to the widget's class structure.

The class is obtained by accessing the widget core field core.widget_class.

XtClass is a macro for programs that include *<X11/CoreP.h>*. It is a function for application programs that do not have access to the Core widget field names.

See Also

XtCheckSubclass, XtIsSubclass, XtSuperclass,
Core(3).

XtCloseDisplay

Name

XtCloseDisplay — close a display and remove it from an application context

Synopsis

```
void XtCloseDisplay(display)
    Display *display;
```

Arguments

display   Specifies the display.

Description

XtCloseDisplay closes the specified display as soon as it is safe to do so If called from within an event dispatch (for example, a callback procedure), XtCloseDisplay does not close the display until the dispatch is complete Note that applications need only call Xt-CloseDisplay if they are to continue executing after closing the display; otherwise, they should call XtDestroyApplicationContext or just exit

See Also

XtAppCreateShell, XtDestroyApplicationContext, XtInitialize.

XtConfigureWidget

Name
XtConfigureWidget — move and/or resize widget.

Synopsis
```
void XtConfigureWidget(w, x, y, width, height, border_width)
    Widget w;
    Position x;
    Position y;
    Dimension width;
    Dimension height;
    Dimension border_width;
```

Arguments

w   Specifies the widget.

x, y   Specify the widget's new x and y coordinates.

width, height, border_width
            Specify the widget's new dimensions.

Description
XtConfigureWidget moves and/or resizes a widget according to the specified width, height, and position values. It returns immediately if the specified geometry fields are the same as the old values. Otherwise, XtConfigureWidget writes the new x, y, width, height, and border_width values into the widget and, if the widget is realized, makes an Xlib XConfigureWindow call on the widget's window.

If either the new width or the new height is different from its old value, XtConfigure-Widget calls the widget's resize procedure to notify it of the size change.

A parent widget can use XtConfigureWidget to set the geometry of its children. It may also be used to reconfigure a sibling widget. A child widget can use XtMakeGeometry-Request and XtMakeResizeRequest to request more space from a parent.

If only the size of a widget is to be changed, XtResizeWidget is simpler to use; similarly, if only the location of a widget is to be changed, use XtMoveWidget.

The x and y coordinates are specified with respect to the origin in the upper-left corner of the screen. Widget coordinates can be converted to screen coordinates with XtTranslate-Coords.

Note that once a widget is resized or otherwise reconfigured by its parent, it may need to do additional processing in its own resize method. Widgets usually need to know when they have changed size so that they can lay out their displayed data again to match the new size. When a parent resizes a child, it calls XtResizeWidget, which updates the geometry fields in the widget, configures the window if the widget is realized, and calls the child's resize method to notify the child. The resize procedure pointer is of type XtWidgetProc(2).

If a class need not recalculate anything when a widget is resized, it can specify NULL for the resize field in its class record. This is an unusual case and should occur only for widgets with very trivial display semantics. The resize method takes a widget as its only argument

See Also

Section 1 8, "Geometry Management,"
XtMakeGeometryRequest, XtMakeResizeRequest, XtMoveWidget, XtResize-
Widget, XtTranslateCoords.

XtConvert

Name

XtConvert — convert resource type.

Synopsis

```
void XtConvert(w, from_type, from, to_type, to_return)
    Widget w;
    String from_type;
    XrmValuePtr from;
    String to_type;
    XrmValuePtr to_return;
```

Arguments

w	Specifies the widget to use for additional arguments (if any are needed).
from_type	Specifies the source type.
from	Specifies the value to be converted.
to_type	Specifies the destination type.
to_return	Returns the converted value.

Description

XtConvert looks up the appropriate resource converter registered to convert *from_type* to *to_type* and then calls XtDirectConvert to convert *from* to *to_return*. If the conversion is successful, *to_return.addr* will be non-NULL.

Xt recognizes and converts between the *from_types* and the *to_types* shown in the table below. In addition, it is possible to register custom converters using XtAddConverter.

from_type	to_type	Description
XtRString	XtRAcceleratorTable	Compiles a string accelerator table into internal accelerator table format (no need to call XtParseAcceleratorTable).
	XtRBoolean	Converts strings "true," "false," "yes," "no," "on," "off" to corresponding Boolean value (case insensitive).
	XtRBool	Same as for XtRBoolean.
	XtRCursor	Given a standard X cursor name, returns a cursor ID.
	XtRDimension	Converts a width or height value to a Dimension.
	XtRDisplay	Given a display name, opens the display and returns a Display structure.
	XtRFile	Given a filename, opens the file and returns the file descriptor.
	XtRFloat	Converts a numeric string to floating point.

from type	to type	Description
	XtRFont	Given a font name, loads the font (if it is not already loaded) and returns the font ID. See Appendix C, *Specifying Fonts and Colors*, for more information on legal values. The value XtDefaultFont will return the default font for the screen.
	XtRFontStruct	Given a font name, loads the font (if it is not already loaded) and returns a pointer to the FontStruct containing font metrics. The value XtDefaultFont will return the default font for the screen.
	XtRInt	Converts a numeric string to an integer.
	XtRPixel	Converts a color name string (e.g., "red" or "#FF0000") into the pixel value that will produce the closest color possible on the hardware. See Appendix C, *Specifying Fonts and Colors*, for more information on legal values. The two values XtDefault-Background and XtDefaultForeground are always guaranteed to exist, and to contrast, on any server.
	XtRPosition	Converts an x or y value to a Position.
	XtRShort	Converts a numeric string to a short integer.
	XtRTranslationTable	Compiles string translation table into internal translation table format (no need to call XtParse-TranslationTable).
	XtRUnsignedChar	Converts a string to an unsigned char.
XtRColor	XtRPixel	Converts an XColor structure to a pixel value.
XtRPixel	XtRColor	Converts a pixel value to an XColor structure.
XtRInt	XtRBoolean	Converts an int to a Boolean.
	XtRBool	Converts an int to a Bool.
	XtRColor	Converts an int to an XColor.
	XtRDimension	Converts an int to a Dimension.
	XtRFloat	Converts an int to a float.
	XtRFont	Converts an int to a Font.
	XtRPixel	Converts an int to a pixel value.
	XtRPixmap	Converts an int to a Pixmap.
	XtRPosition	Converts an int to a Position.
	XtRShort	Converts an int to a short.
	XtRUnsignedChar	Converts an int to an unsigned char.

In addition, the Xmu library (miscellaneous utilities) contains converters between XtRString and XtRBackingStore, XtRCursor, XtRJustify, XtROrientation, XtRPixmap, and XtRWidget and between XtRFunction and XtRCallback. See Chapter 9, *Resource Management and Type Conversion*, in Volume Four, *X Toolkit Intrinsics Programming Manual*, for details.

All resource-fetching routines (e.g., XtGetSubresources, XtGetApplication-Resources as well as the internal code that reads the resource database when a widget is created) call resource converters if the user-specified resource is represented in a different form from the desired representation. A widget seldom has to access resource converters explicitly with XtConvert or XtDirectConvert.

XtConvert accesses the widget *w* to obtain values for any additional arguments the resource converter needs. The computation of additional arguments is discussed with XtAppAdd-Converter. XtConvert invokes XtDirectConvert to perform the actual conversion. It is usually easier to access resource conversion indirectly through the resource mechanism.

Converters not only are a good labor-saving device, but also make it possible to hide the details of data structures in the resource converter. For example, a program can access fonts, files, and application-dependent data structures using resource conversions.

Structures

```
typedef struct {
    unsigned int    size;
    caddr_t         addr;
} XrmValue, *XrmValuePtr;
```

See Also

Section 1.7, "Resources,"
XtAppAddConverter, XtDirectConvert, XtGetApplicationResources, Xt-GetSubresources.

Name

XtConvertCase — determine upper-case and lower-case versions of a keysym.

Synopsis

```
void XtConvertCase(display, keysym, lower_return, upper_return)
    Display *display;
    KeySym keysym;
    KeySym *lower_return,
    KeySym *upper_return,
```

Arguments

display	Specifies the display that the keysym came from
keysym	Specifies the keysym to convert.
lower_return	Returns the lower-case equivalent of the keysym.
upper_return	Returns the upper-case equivalent of the keysym

Description

XtConvertCase is used to determine upper-case and lower-case equivalents for a keysym It calls the case converter that is currently registered to convert those keysyms and returns the results This procedure can perform application-specific shifting of characters

A user-supplied XtKeyProc may need to use this function

XtRegisterCaseConverter can be used to register a new case converter.

For a more detailed discussion of processing keyboard input, see Chapter 13, *Miscellaneous Toolkit Programming Techniques*, in Volume Four, *X Toolkit Intrinsics Programming Manual* See Chapter 9, *The Keyboard and the Pointer*, in Volume One, *Xlib Programming Manual*, for more information on keysyms.

See Also

XtRegisterCaseConverter, XtSetKeyTranslator, XtTranslateKey, Xt-TranslateKeycode,
XtCaseProc(2), XtKeyProc(2)

XtCreateApplicationContext

Name

XtCreateApplicationContext — create an application context.

Synopsis

```
XtAppContext XtCreateApplicationContext()
```

Description

XtCreateApplicationContext returns an application context, which is an opaque type.
Every application must have at least one application context. XtInitialize creates a
default application context.

XtInitialize is a simplified interface to XtToolkitInitialize, XtCreate-
ApplicationContext, XtDisplayInitialize, and XtAppCreateShell; if it is
not used, all four of these routines must be called.

Routines that use an implicit context (like XtMainLoop and XtAddTimeOut) depend on the
default context created by XtInitialize. You cannot use these routines if you initialize a
specific application context.

Structures

```
/*
 * Data structure for setting window attributes.
 */
typedef struct {
    Pixmap background_pixmap;       /* pixmap, None, or ParentRelative */
    unsigned long background_pixel; /* background pixel */
    Pixmap border_pixmap;           /* pixmap, None, or CopyFromParent */
    unsigned long border_pixel;     /* border pixel value */
    int bit_gravity;                /* one of bit gravity values */
    int win_gravity;                /* one of the window gravity values */
    int backing_store;              /* NotUseful, WhenMapped, Always */
    unsigned long backing_planes;   /* planes to be preseved if possible */
    unsigned long backing_pixel;    /* value to use in restoring planes */
    Bool save_under;                /* should bits under be saved (pop ups) */
    long event_mask;                /* set of events that should be saved */
    long do_not_propagate_mask;     /* set of events that should not propagate */
    Bool override_redirect;         /* override redirected config request */
    Colormap colormap;              /* colormap to be associated with window */
    Cursor cursor;                  /* cursor to be displayed (or None) */
} XSetWindowAttributes;

/* Definitions for valuemask argument of CreateWindow and ChangeWindowAttributes */

#define CWBackPixmap        (1L<<0)
#define CWBackPixel         (1L<<1)
#define CWBorderPixmap      (1L<<2)
#define CWBorderPixel       (1L<<3)
#define CWBitGravity        (1L<<4)
#define CWWinGravity        (1L<<5)
#define CWBackingStore      (1L<<6)
#define CWBackingPlanes     (1L<<7)
#define CWBackingPixel      (1L<<8)
```

```
#define CWOverrideRedirect        (1L<<9)
#define CWSaveUnder               (1L<<10)
#define CWEventMask               (1L<<11)
#define CWDontPropagate           (1L<<12)
#define CWColormap                (1L<<13)
#define CWCursor                  (1L<<14)
```

See Also

Section 1 1, "Widget Lifecycle"

XtCreateApplicationShell

Name

XtCreateApplicationShell — create an additional top-level widget.

Synopsis

```
Widget XtCreateApplicationShell(application_name, widget_class,
       args, num_args)
   String application_name; /*unused in Release 3*/
   WidgetClass widget_class;
   ArgList args;
   Cardinal num_args;
```

Arguments

application_name
> Specifies the name of the application instance.

widget_class
> Specifies the widget class that the application top-level widget should be.

args   Specifies the argument list in which to set in the WM_COMMAND property.

num_args   Specifies the number of arguments in the argument list.

Description

XtCreateApplicationShell creates a new logical application within a program. This function is a simplified interface to XtAppCreateShell. Since most applications have only one display, XtCreateApplicationShell does not require the application to pass the display explicitly. It also does not allow the caller to specify the resource class of the application. To take advantage of the more general functionality, use XtAppCreateShell.

See Also

Section 1.1, "Widget Lifecycle,"
XtAppCreateShell.

Name

XtCreateManagedWidget — create and manage a child widget.

Synopsis

```
Widget XtCreateManagedWidget(name, widget_class, parent, args,
        num_args)
    String name;
    WidgetClass widget_class;
    Widget parent;
    ArgList args;
    Cardinal num_args;
```

Arguments

name	Specifies the text name for the created shell widget.
widget_class	Specifies the widget class pointer for the created widget.
parent	Specifies the parent widget.
args	Specifies the argument list to override the resource defaults
num_args	Specifies the number of arguments in the argument list

Description

XtCreateManagedWidget combines creation and management of a widget into one routine It calls XtCreateWidget and XtManageChild consecutively XtCreateManagedWidget is the usual way to create new widget instances.

See Also

Section 1 1, "Widget Lifecycle,"
XtCreateWidget, XtManageChild, XtManageChildren.

XtCreatePopupShell

Name

XtCreatePopupShell — create a pop-up shell.

Synopsis

```
Widget XtCreatePopupShell(name, widget_class, parent, args,
        num_args)
    String name;
    WidgetClass widget_class;
    Widget parent;
    ArgList args;
    Cardinal num_args;
```

Arguments

name	Specifies the text name for the created shell widget.
widget_class	Specifies the widget class pointer for the created shell widget.
parent	Specifies the parent widget.
args	Specifies the argument list to override the resource defaults.
num_args	Specifies the number of arguments in the argument list.

Description

XtCreatePopupShell creates a pop-up shell widget, suitable for containing one composite or simple widget that is to be popped up. Pop-up widgets are used to create windows that are descendants of the root window (rather than the application's main window) so that the pop-up window can appear anywhere on the screen, not just with the application. Therefore, pop ups have their own shell widget parent.

For a widget to pop up, it must be the child of a pop-up widget shell. A pop-up shell is never allowed more than one child, referred to as the pop-up child. Both the shell and child taken together are referred to as the pop up.

XtCreateManagedWidget is used to create the pop up's child (which is the widget which will be visible to the user). After the pop-up shell and its child are created, the shell can be popped up with XtPopup and popped down with XtPopdown. It can also be popped up from a callback list with XtCallbackExclusive, et al.

There are currently two classes of pop-up shells. They are listed in the table below and defined in <X11/Shell.h>. Either can be passed to XtCreatePopupShell as the widget_class argument.

Shell Types	Purpose
`overrideShellWidgetClass`	Bypasses window management
`transientShellWidgetClass`	Does not bypass window management

The `overrideShellWidgetClass` window is created with the override-redirect window attribute set, thereby forcibly bypassing window management. `transientShellWidget-Class` hints to the window manager that it should not decorate the window as it would a general application and asks it to allow it to bypass its geometry management. The latter approach is preferred, but the former may be used for dropdown menus and other short-term windows.

`XtCreatePopupShell` ensures that the specified class is a subclass of Shell and attaches the shell to the parent's pop-up list. The pop-up shell is not a normal child of its parent—a pop-up child is kept on its parent's list of pop-up children.

The pop-up shell accepts a resource callback list named `XtNpopupCallback` that will get called back when the widget is popped up. There is an analogous resource, `XtNpopdown-Callback`, that is invoked when the widget is popped down. These callbacks provide the opportunity either to make last-minute changes to a pop-up child before it is popped up or to change it after it is popped down. Note that excessive use of pop-up callbacks can make popping up occur more slowly.

Once a pop-up shell is created, the single child of the pop-up shell can be created in one of three ways

- At startup, an application can create the child of the pop-up shell. This is appropriate for pop-ups that the user will need on every invocation of the application. Creating the pop-up child at this time means that pop-up time is minimized, especially if the application calls `XtRealizeWidget` on the pop-up shell at startup. When the menu is needed, all the widgets that make up the menu already exist and need only be mapped. The menu should pop up as quickly as the X server can respond

- An application can postpone the creation of the child until it is needed, which minimizes application startup time, but slows pop-up time.

- An application can use work procedures (`XtAddWorkProc`) to create the child during application idle time. This solves both the above problems, but may introduce random user response delays.

The pop-up shell accepts a resource function pointer (of type `XtRFunction`) that gets invoked when a widget is popped up. The resource is named `XtNcreatePopupChild-Proc`. It can be used to create the pop-up child, if one does not exist at the time the pop-up is invoked

Pop-up child creation does not map the pop up, even if you create the child and call `Xt-RealizeWidget` on the pop-up shell. Pop ups can be popped up through several mechanisms:

- A call to `XtPopup`.

- One of the supplied callback procedures (for example, `XtCallbackNone`, `Xt-CallbackNonexclusive`, or `XtCallbackExclusive`).

- The standard translation action `MenuPopup`.

Some of these routines take an argument of type `XtGrabKind`, which is defined as:

```
typedef enum {XtGrabNone, XtGrabNonexclusive, XtGrabExclusive} XtGrabKind;
```

For a general discussion of pop ups, see Section 1.6, "Pop Ups." Popping up a shell with the Resource Manager is discussed in Section 1.5, "Translations and Actions." For a discussion of the underlying concepts of override-redirection, see Chapter 4 of Volume One, *Xlib Programming Manual*.

See Also

`XtCallbackExclusive`, `XtCreateManagedWidget`, `XtNameToWidget`, `Xt-Popdown`, `XtPopup`.

Name

XtCreateWidget — create an instance of a widget.

Synopsis

```
Widget XtCreateWidget(name, widget_class, parent, args,
        num_args)
    String name,
    WidgetClass widget_class;
    Widget parent;
    ArgList args;
    Cardinal num_args;
```

Arguments

name   Specifies the resource name for the created widget, which is used for retriev-
          ing resources and, for that reason, should not be the same as any other widget
          that is a child of same parent.

widget_class
          Specifies the widget class pointer for the created widget.

parent   Specifies the parent widget.

args   Specifies the argument list to override the resource defaults.

num_args Specifies the number of arguments in the argument list (Note that you can
           determine the number of arguments in a static argument list using the Xt-
           Number macro)

Description

XtCreateWidget creates a new widget instance of class *widget_class*. The usual way
to access XtCreateWidget is to combine creation and management with XtCreate-
ManagedWidget; you will normally use XtCreateWidget and XtManageChild only in
cases where you wish to create a number of interrelated widgets, and bring them under parental
management at the same time.

XtCreateWidget creates a new widget instance structure and invokes the widget's initialization method XtCreateWidget resolves conflicts between values for the arguments supplied in the environment with those supplied in *args* in the new widget instance structure

XtCreateWidget performs many of the boilerplate operations of widget creation·

*   Checks to see if the class_initialize procedure has been called for this class and
    for all superclasses and, if not, calls those necessary, in a superclass-to-subclass order

*   Allocates memory for the widget instance.

*   If the parent is a subclass of constraintWidgetClass, memory is allocated for the
    parent's constraints, and stores the address of this memory into the *constraints* field
    of the widget.

- Initializes the core nonresource data fields (for example, parent and visible).

- Initializes the resource fields (for example, background_pixel) by using the resource lists specified for this class and all superclasses.

- If the parent is a subclass of constraintWidgetClass, initializes the resource fields of the constraint record by using the constraint resource list specified for the parent's class and all superclasses up to constraintWidgetClass.

- Calls the initialize procedures for the widget starting at the Core initialize procedure and descending to the widget's initialize procedure.

- If the parent is a subclass of compositeWidgetClass, puts the widget into its parent's children list by calling its parent's insert_child procedure.

- If the parent is a subclass of constraintWidgetClass, calls the constraint initialize procedures, starting at constraintWidgetClass and descending to the parent's constraint initialize procedure.

Note that the XtCreateWidget function gets resources as a superclass-to-subclass operation. That is, the resources specified in the Core resource list are fetched, then those in the subclass, and so on down to the resources specified for this widget's class. Within a class, resources are fetched in the order they are declared.

In general, if a widget resource field is declared in a superclass, that field is included in the superclass's resource list and need not be included in the subclass's resource list. For example, the Core class contains a resource entry for background_pixel. Consequently, the implementation of Label need not also have a resource entry for background_pixel. However, a subclass, by specifying a resource entry for that field in its own resource list, can override the resource entry for any field declared in a superclass. This is most often done to override the defaults provided in the superclass with new ones. At class initialization time, resource lists for that class are scanned from the superclass down to the class to look for resources with the same offset. A matching resource in a subclass will be reordered to override the superclass entry. (A copy of the superclass resource list is made to avoid affecting other subclasses of the superclass.)

Section 1.8, "Geometry Management," gives a more general account of the role of the widget parent. The Intrinsic-supplied classes are described in Core(3), Constraint(3), and Composite(3).

See Also

Section 1.1, "Widget Lifecycle,"
XtCreateManagedWidget.

XtCreateWindow

Name

XtCreateWindow — create widget's working window

Synopsis

```
void XtCreateWindow(w, window_class, visual, value_mask,
        attributes)
    Widget w,
    unsigned int window_class;
    Visual *visual,
    XtValueMask value_mask;
    XSetWindowAttributes *attributes;
```

Arguments

w	Specifies the widget that is used to set the x,y coordinates and so on
window_class	Specifies the Xlib window class (InputOutput, InputOnly, or CopyFromParent).
visual	Specifies the Xlib visual type (usually CopyFromParent).
value_mask	Specifies which attribute fields to use
attributes	Specifies the window attributes to use in the XCreateWindow call.

Description

A widget is responsible for creating its own window when its Core realize method is called Rather than call the Xlib XCreateWindow function explicitly, a realize method should call the Intrinsics analog XtCreateWindow, which simplifies the creation of windows for widgets XtCreateWindow calls the Xlib XCreateWindow function, merging values from the Core widget instance structure (see below) and attributes Then it assigns the created window to the widget's core window field.

XtCreateWindow evaluates the following fields of the Core widget structure.

- depth
- screen
- parent -> core.window
- x and y
- width and height
- border_width

Window attributes are documented more fully in Volume One, *Xlib Programming Manual*, and Volume Two, *Xlib Reference Manual*, see XSetWindowAttributes for a summary.

Structures

```
/* Definitions for valuemask argument.  These control which fields in
 * XSetWindowAttributes structure should be used.
 */

typedef struct {
    Pixmap background_pixmap;       /* background or None or ParentRelative * /
    unsigned long background_pixel;/* background pixel */
    Pixmap border_pixmap;           /* border of the window */
    unsigned long border_pixel;     /* border pixel value */
    int bit_gravity;                /* one of bit gravity values */
    int win_gravity;                /* one of the window gravity values */
    int backing_store;              /* NotUseful, WhenMapped, Always */
    unsigned long backing_planes;   /* planes to be preserved if possible */
    unsigned long backing_pixel;    /* value to use in restoring planes */
    Bool save_under;                /* should bits under be saved (popups) */
    long event_mask;                /* set of events that should be saved */
    long do_not_propagate_mask;     /* set of events that should not propagate */
    Bool override_redirect;         /* boolean value for override-redirect */
    Colormap colormap;              /* colormap to be associated with window */
    Cursor cursor;                  /* cursor to be displayed (or None) */
} XSetWindowAttributes;
```

See Also

Section 1.1, "Widget Lifecycle,"
XtRealizeProc(2).

XtDatabase

Name

XtDatabase — obtain the resource database for a particular display

Synopsis

```
XrmDatabase XtDatabase(display)
    Display *display;
```

Arguments

display   Specifies the display for which the resource database should be returned

Description

XtDatabase returns the complete resource database built by XtDisplayInitialize that
is associated with *display*. The contents of the database are fully merged from resource values on the server and command line arguments.

If *display* has not been initialized by XtDisplayInitialize, the results are not
defined

In general, the type XrmDatabase should be treated as opaque and should not be manipulated
directly   XrmDatabases can be manipulated safely with Xlib functions (XrmPut-
Resource, XrmQPutResource, XrmGetResource, XrmQGetResource, etc.).

XtInitialize, XtGetResourceList, and XtGetSubresources provide a more
manageable approach to obtaining resources.

Structures

Set the typedef of XrmDatabase to _XrmHashBucketRec. _XrmHashBucketRec is
defined within Xlib source with this structure:

```
typedef struct _XrmHashBucketRec {
    XrmHashBucket    next;       /* Next entry in this hash chain          */
    XrmQuark         quark,      /* Quark for string                       */
    XrmRepresentation type;      /* Representation of value (if any)        */
    XrmValue         value;      /* Value of this node (if any)             */
    XrmHashTable     tables[2],  /* Hash table pointers for tight, loose */
} XrmHashBucketRec,
```

These data structures should not be traversed by the uninitiated   If you have Xt source available, examine the code in *X11R3/core src/lib/X/Xrm c*

Command line arguments and a complete example using alternate command line parsing are
presented in Chapter 9, *Resource Management and Type Conversion*, in Volume Four, *X Toolkit
Intrinsics Programming Manual*

See Also

XtDisplayInitialize, XtGetResourceList, XtGetSubresources, Xt-
Initialize.

XtDestroyApplicationContext

Name

XtDestroyApplicationContext — destroy an application context and close its displays.

Synopsis

```
void XtDestroyApplicationContext(app_context)
    XtAppContext app_context;
```

Arguments

app_context Specifies the application context.

Description

XtDestroyApplicationContext destroys the specified application context as soon as it is safe to do so. If called from within an event handler or a callback procedure, XtDestroy-ApplicationContext does not destroy the application context until the dispatch is complete.

All X Toolkit applications should terminate by calling XtDestroyApplicationContext and then exiting using the standard method for their operating system (typically, by calling exit for UNIX-based systems). The quickest way to make the windows disappear while exiting is to call XtUnmapWidget on each top-level shell widget. The X Toolkit has no resources beyond those in the program image, and the X server will free its resources when its connection to the application is broken.

See Also

Section 1.1, "Widget Lifecycle,"
XtCreateApplicationContext.

XtDestroyGC

Name
XtDestroyGC — Release 2 compatible function to free up read-only GCs.

Synopsis
```
void XtDestroyGC(gc)
    GC gc;
```

Arguments
w   Specifies the widget.

gc   Specifies the GC to be deallocated

Description
XtDestroyGC deallocates a shared (read-only) Graphics Context References to shareable GCs are counted, and a free request is generated to the server when the last user of a given GC destroys it. Note that some earlier versions of XtDestroyGC had only a gc argument. Therefore, this function is not very portable. In addition, XtDestroyGC is only guaranteed to work properly if there is exactly one open display in the application

Programs running under Release 3 should be converted to use XtReleaseGC. Programs running under Release 2 can conditionally compile in code in expectation of Release 3.

See Also
XtGetGC, XtReleaseGC.

XtDestroyWidget

Name

XtDestroyWidget — destroy a widget instance.

Synopsis

```
void XtDestroyWidget(w)
    Widget w;
```

Arguments

w   Specifies the widget to be destroyed.

Description

Most applications simply exit, causing widgets to be destroyed automatically. XtDestroy-Widget destroys widgets explicitly. It can also be used by widgets that need to destroy themselves. It can be called at any time, including from an application callback routine of the widget being destroyed.

Widget destruction occurs in two phases to prevent dangling references to destroyed widgets.

In phase one, XtDestroyWidget performs the following:

- If the being_destroyed field of the widget is TRUE, it returns immediately;

- Otherwise, it recursively descends the widget tree and sets the being_destroyed field to TRUE for the widget and all children; and

- It adds the widget to a list of widgets (the destroy list) that should be destroyed when it is safe to do so.

For entries on the destroy list, if w2 occurs after w1 on the destroy list, then w2 is not a descendant of w1. (A descendant can be either a normal or a pop-up child.)

Phase two occurs when all procedures that should execute as a result of the current event have been called (including all procedures registered with the Event and Resource Managers). That is, when the current invocation of XtDispatchEvent is about to return (or immediately if not in XtDispatchEvent).

In phase two, XtDestroyWidget performs the following on each entry in the destroy list:

- Calls the destroy callback procedures registered on the widget (and all descendants). The calls happen in reverse order (children callbacks before parent callbacks).

- If the widget's parent is a subclass of compositeWidgetClass and if the parent is not being destroyed, XtDestroyWidget calls XtUnmanageChild on the widget and then calls the widget's parent's delete_child procedure.

- If the widget's parent is a subclass of constraintWidgetClass, it calls the constraint destroy procedure for the parent, then the parent's superclass, until finally it calls the constraint destroy procedure for constraintWidgetClass.

- Calls the destroy methods for the widget (and all descendants) in post-order For each such widget, it calls the destroy procedure declared in the widget class, then the destroy procedure declared in its superclass, until finally it calls the destroy procedure declared in the Core class record.

- Calls the Xlib function xDestroyWindow if the widget is realized (that is, has an X window). The server recursively destroys all descendant windows.

- Recursively descends the tree and deallocates all pop-up widgets, constraint records, callback lists and, if the widget is a subclass of compositeWidgetClass, children.

When an application needs to perform additional processing during the destruction of a widget, it should register a destroy callback procedure for the widget. The destroy callback list is identified by the resource name XtNdestroyCallback.

The following example adds an application-supplied destroy callback procedure Client-Destroy with client data to a widget:

```
XtAddCallback(w, XtNdestroyCallback, ClientDestroy, client_data)
```

Similarly, the following example removes the application-supplied destroy callback procedure ClientDestroy

```
XtRemoveCallback(w, XtNdestroyCallback, ClientDestroy, client_data)
```

The ClientDestroy procedure is of type XtCallbackProc:

```
typedef void (*XtCallbackProc)(Widget, caddr_t, caddr_t);
```

For further information, see XtCallbackProc(2).

A widget's windows can be removed from the display while leaving the widget data structures intact by calling XtUnrealizeWidget.

See Also
Section 1.1, "Widget Lifecycle,"
XtRemoveAllCallbacks, XtRemoveCallback, XtUnrealizeWidget,
Core(3).

XtDirectConvert

Name
XtDirectConvert — perform resource conversion and cache result.

Synopsis
```
void XtDirectConvert(converter, args, num_args, from, to_return)
    XtConverter converter;
    XrmValuePtr args;
    Cardinal num_args;
    XrmValuePtr from;
    XrmValuePtr to_return;
```

Arguments
converter	Specifies the conversion procedure to be called.
args	Specifies the argument list that contains the additional arguments needed to perform the conversion (often NULL).
num_args	Specifies the number of additional arguments (often zero).
from	Specifies the value to be converted.
to_return	Returns the converted value.

Description
XtDirectConvert looks in the converter cache to see if the named conversion procedure has been called with the specified arguments. If so, it returns a descriptor for information stored in the cache; otherwise, it calls converter and enters the result in the cache.

Before calling the specified converter, XtDirectConvert sets the return value size to zero and the return value address to NULL. If the conversion succeeds, to_return.address will be non-NULL.

It is usually easier to access resource conversion indirectly through XtGetSubresources and XtGetApplicationResources. XtConvert provides a higher-level interface to XtDirectConvert; XtAddConverter and XtAppAddConverter allow additional conversion arguments.

Structures
```
typedef struct {
    unsigned int    size;
    caddr_t         addr;
} XrmValue, *XrmValuePtr;
```

See Also
Section 1.7, "Resources,"
XtAppAddConverter, XtConvert, XtGetApplicationResources,
XtGetSubresources,
XtConverter(2).

Name

XtDisownSelection — indicate that selection data is no longer available.

Synopsis

```
void XtDisownSelection(w, selection, time)
    Widget w;
    Atom selection;
    Time time;
```

Arguments

w	Specifies the widget relinquishing selection ownership.
selection	Specifies which selection the widget is giving up (XA_PRIMARY or XA_SECONDARY).
time	Specifies the timestamp that indicates when the selection is relinquished

Description

Usually the Intrinsics selection mechanism informs an application when one of its widgets has lost ownership of the selection. However, in response to some user actions (for example, when a user deletes the information selected), the application should explicitly inform the Intrinsics that its widget no longer is to be the selection owner by using XtDisownSelection.

XtDisownSelection renounces ownership of a selection. It informs the Intrinsics that new requests for selection data should be directed elsewhere. No subsequent requests will be sent to the XtConvertProc registered when the widget called XtOwnSelection.

If the widget does not currently own selection, either because it lost the selection or because it never had the selection to begin with, XtDisownSelection does nothing.

After a widget has called XtDisownSelection, its XtConvertProc is not called even if a request arrives with a timestamp indicating the period that it owned the selection. However, its XtDoneProc will be called if a conversion that *started* before the call to XtDisownSelection finishes after the call to XtDisownSelection.

If the selection has changed hands because another client has claimed it (rather than as a result of a call to XtDisownSelection), the Intrinsics inform the application of the loss by calling its XtLoseSelectionProc.

An example widget that sends and receives data using selection is presented in Chapter 10, *Inter-Client Communications*, in Volume Four, *X Toolkit Intrinsics Programming Manual*.

See Also

XtGetSelectionValue, XtOwnSelection,
XtConvertProc(2), XtDoneProc(2), XtLoseSelectionProc(2)

XtDispatchEvent

Name

XtDispatchEvent — dispatch registered handlers for an event.

Synopsis

```
void XtDispatchEvent(event)
    XEvent *event;
```

Arguments

event   Specifies a pointer to the event structure to be dispatched to the appropriate event handler.

Description

XtDispatchEvent sends events to handler functions previously registered with XtAddEventHandler. XtDispatchEvent calls the appropriate handler functions and passes them the widget, the event, and client-specific data.

If no handlers for the event are registered, the event is ignored. If there are multiple handlers registered for an event, the order in which handlers are called is undefined.

XtDispatchEvent returns TRUE if it dispatched the event to some handler and FALSE if it found no handler to dispatch the event to. In most applications, XtMainLoop is used to dispatch events transparently. XtAddEventHandler and XtAddRawEventHandler are used to register event handlers.

The most common use of XtDispatchEvent is to dispatch an event acquired with XtAppNextEvent. However, it also can be used to dispatch user-constructed events. XtDispatchEvent does not handle the pseudo-events (timer interrupts and auxiliary input). Those are dispatched directly by XtAppNextEvent.

XtDispatchEvent is used to implement the grab semantics for XtAddGrab.

See Also

Section 1.4, "Events,"
XtAddEventHandler, XtAddGrab, XtAddRawEventHandler, XtAppNextEvent, XtEventHandler, XtMainLoop.

XtDisplay

Name
XtDisplay — return the display pointer for the specified widget.

Synopsis
```
Display *XtDisplay(w)
    Widget w;
```

Arguments
w   Specifies the widget for which the Display is to be returned

Description
XtDisplay returns the display pointer for the specified widget.

See Also
XtScreen

XtDisplayInitialize

Name

XtDisplayInitialize — initialize a display and add it to an application context.

Synopsis

```
void XtDisplayInitialize(app_context, display, application_name,
       application_class, options, num_options, argc, argv)
    XtAppContext app_context;
    Display *display;
    String application_name;
    String application_class;
    XrmOptionDescRec *options;
    Cardinal num_options;
    Cardinal *argc;
    String *argv;
```

Arguments

app_context   Specifies the application context.

display   Specifies the display. Note that a display can be in at most one application context.

application_name
              Specifies the name of the application instance.

application_class
              Specifies the class name of this application. This name is usually the generic name for all instances of this application.

options   Specifies how to parse the command line for any application-specific resources. The options argument is passed as a parameter to XrmParse-Command.

num_options   Specifies the number of entries in the options list.

argc   Specifies a pointer to the number of command line parameters.

argv   Specifies the command line parameters.

Description

XtDisplayInitialize builds the resource database, parses the command line using the Xlib XrmParseCommand function, and performs other per-display initialization. This function is not often used unless you are creating multiple application contexts, since Xt-Initialize provides a simplified interface to it (and the other two Toolkit initialize functions, XtCreateApplicationContext and XtAppCreateShell).

See XtInitialize for a complete description of how the arguments are used.

Structures

```
typedef enum {
                            /* Value is ... */
    XrmoptionNoArg,         /* specified in OptionDescRec.value */
    XrmoptionIsArg,         /* the option string itself */
    XrmoptionStickyArg,     /* characters immediately following option */
    XrmoptionSepArg,        /* next argument in argv */

                            /* Ignore this option and . . */
    XrmoptionSkipArg,       /* the next argument in argv */
    XrmoptionSkipLine       /* the rest of argv */
} XrmOptionKind;

typedef struct {
    char *option;           /* Option name in argv */
    char *specifier;        /* Resource name (without application name) */
    XrmOptionKind argKind,  /* Which style of option it is */
    caddr_t value;          /* Value to provide if XrmoptionNoArg */
} XrmOptionDescRec, *XrmOptionDescList;
```

See Also

XtAppCreateShell, XtCreateApplicationContext, XtDatabase, Xt-
Initialize.

Xt Functions
and Macros

Name
XtError — call the low-level fatal error handler.

Synopsis
```
void XtError(message)
    String message;
```

Arguments
message   Specifies the message to be reported.

Description
Xt provides two levels of error handling:

- A high-level interface that takes an error name and class and looks the error up in an error resource database.

- A low-level interface that takes a simple string, which is printed out as the error message.

Application-context-specific error handling is not implemented on many systems. Most implementations will have just one set of error handlers. If different handlers are set for different application contexts, the one set last will be used.

In theory, most programs should use XtAppErrorMsg (or XtErrorMsg if application contexts are not being used), not XtError or XtAppError, so that the programs can be easily customized to provide international or other custom error messages. However, the low-level handlers are much easier to use.

XtAppError calls the low-level fatal error handler. Fatal errors are assumed to be catastrophic and irrecoverable. A warning error handler also exists for errors that require attention but do not preempt a program running correctly to a normal successful completion. (XtAppWarning calls the corresponding nonfatal error handler. XtAppErrorMsg and XtAppWarningMsg call the corresponding high-level handlers.)

See Also
XtErrorMsg, XtSetErrorHandler, XtSetWarningMsg, XtWarning, XtWarningMsg.

Name

XtErrorMsg — call the high-level fatal error handler

Synopsis

```
void XtErrorMsg(name, type, class, default, params, num_params)
    String name;
    String type,
    String class;
    String default;
    String *params;
    Cardinal *num_params;
```

Arguments

name Specifies the general kind of error; for example, `InvalidParameter`.

type Specifies the detailed name of the error. This is specified using `printf`-like syntax, with the parameters and number of parameters specified by *params* and *num_params*.

class Specifies the resource class.

default Specifies the default message to use if no message is found in the database

params Specifies a pointer to a list of values to be stored in the *type* argument when the message is generated.

num_params Specifies the number of values in the parameter list.

Description

Xt provides two levels of error handling·

• A high-level interface that takes an error name and class and looks the error up in an error resource database

• A low-level interface that takes a simple string, which is printed out as the error message

The high-level functions construct a string to pass to the lower-level interface. The *name* and *type* arguments are concatenated to form the "name" that is used to look up a message in the error database   On UNIX-based systems, the error database is usually called */usr/lib/X11/XtErrorDB*

In theory, most programs should use `AppXtErrorMsg` (or `XtErrorMsg` if application contexts are not being used), not `AppXtError` or `XtError`, so that the programs can be easily customized to provide international or other custom error messages. However, the low-level handlers are much easier to use

`XtAppError` calls the low-level fatal error handler. Fatal errors are assumed to be catastrophic and irrecoverable. A warning error handler also exists for errors that require attention but do not preempt a program running correctly to a normal successful completion   (XtApp-

`Warning` calls the corresponding nonfatal error handler. `XtAppErrorMsg` and `XtApp-WarningMsg` call the corresponding high-level handlers.) The Intrinsics internal errors all have class `XtToolkitError`.

See Also

`XtError, XtSetErrorHandler, XtSetWarningHandler, XtWarning, Xt-WarningMsg`.

Name

XtFree — free an allocated block of storage

Synopsis

```
void XtFree(ptr);
    char *ptr;
```

Arguments

ptr   Specifies a pointer to the block of storage to be freed

Description

XtFree returns storage previously allocated by XtCalloc and XtMalloc and allows it to be reused If *ptr* is NULL, XtFree returns immediately

Calling the Toolkit's XtMalloc and XtFree is more portable than calling system-specific malloc and free Deallocating blocks of memory *not* allocated by XtMalloc would be disastrous.

XtNew and XtNewString provide slightly higher-level approaches to memory allocation

See Also

XtCalloc, XtErrorMsg, XtMalloc, XtNew, XtNewString, XtRealloc.

XtGetApplicationResources

Name

XtGetApplicationResources — update base-offset resource list (by application).

Synopsis

```
void XtGetApplicationResources(w, base, resources,
        num_resources, args, num_args)
    Widget w;
    caddr_t base;
    XtResourceList resources;
    Cardinal num_resources;
    ArgList args;
    Cardinal num_args;
```

Arguments

w	Specifies the widget that identifies the resource database to search. (The database is that associated with the display for this widget.)
base	Specifies the base address of the data structure where the resources should be written.
resources	Specifies the list of resources to be retrieved.
num_resources	Specifies the number of resources in the resource list.
args	Specifies the argument list to override resources obtained from the resource database.
num_args	Specifies the number of arguments in the argument list.

Description

XtGetApplicationResources can be used to retrieve resources that apply to an overall application, rather than to a particular widget. (Widget resources are automatically retrieved by XtCreateWidget.)

First, XtGetApplicationResources uses the passed widget, which is usually an application shell, to construct a resource name and class list. Then, it retrieves resources from the argument list, the resource database, or the resource list default values. After adding base to each address, XtGetApplicationResources copies the resource values into the corresponding base-offset address. num_args must be zero. However, if num_args is zero, the argument list is not referenced.

The portable and recommended way to specify application resources is to declare them as structure members and pass a pointer to such a structure as base; then XtOffset can be used to specify resource_offset. (XtOffset determines the relative address of a field.) This is how widget instance variables are accessed by the Resource Manager in widget instances.

Here is a short program that sets up a resource argument list and accesses it.

```
/* res.c - access application resources */
#include <stdio h>

#include <X11/Xlib.h>
#include <X11/StringDefs.h>
#include <X11/IntrinsicP h>
#include <X11/Intrinsic.h>
/*
 * fields to be filled in from resources
 * Note that instance_variables must be defined as a pointer...
 */
typedef struct _instance_variables {
    String label,
    XFontStruct *font_struct;
    long foreground;
} instance_variable_rec, *instance_variables;
instance_variables InstanceVariables;

static XtResource resources[] = {
    {
    XtNforeground,
    XtCForeground,
    XtRPixel, sizeof(Pixel),
    XtOffset(instance_variables, foreground),
    XtRString, "XtDefaultForeground"
    },
    {
    XtNfont,
    XtCFont,
    XtRFontStruct, sizeof(XFontStruct *),
    XtOffset(instance_variables, font_struct),
    XtRString, "XtDefaultFont"
    },
    {
    XtNlabel,
    XtCLabel,
    XtRString, sizeof(String),
    XtOffset(instance_variables, label),
    XtRString, "Default Label"
    },
},

Arg args[] = {
    XtNlabel, (XtArgVal) "Stuff",
},

main(ac, av)
int ac;
char **av,
{
    Widget toplevel,
```

```
instance_variable_rec iv;

toplevel = XtInitialize(av[0], "my-widget", NULL, 0, &ac, av);
XtGetApplicationResources(toplevel,       /* widget */
                          &iv,            /* base address */
                          resources,      /* resource */
                          XtNumber(resources),/* how many */
                          NULL, 0);       /* ArgList to merge */

printf("label=%s\n", iv.label);
}
```

All resource-fetching routines (for example, XtGetSubresources and XtGet-
ApplicationResources) call resource converters if the user specifies a resource that is a
different representation from the desired representation or if the widget's default resource value
representation is different from the desired representation.

Structures

A Resource is defined as follows in *<X11/Intrinsic.h>*:

```
typedef struct _XtResource {
    String   resource_name;   /* Resource name */
    String   resource_class;  /* Resource class */
    String   resource_type;   /* Representation type desired */
    Cardinal resource_size;   /* Size in bytes of representation */
    Cardinal resource_offset;/* Offset from base to put resource value */
    String   default_type;    /* Representation type of specified default */
    caddr_t  default_addr;    /* Address of resource default value */
} XtResource, *XtResourceList;
```

An Arg is defined as follows:

```
typedef struct {
    String name;
    XtArgVal value;
} Arg, *ArgList;
```

See Also

XtGetSubresources, XtOffset.

XtGetErrorDatabase

Name

XtGetErrorDatabase — obtain the error database.

Synopsis

```
XrmDatabase *XtGetErrorDatabase()
```

Description

Xt's high-level error and warning message handlers use a resource-like database for storing error messages. On UNIX-based systems, the database is usually stored in the file */usr/lib/X11/XtErrorDb* The XtGetErrorDatabase function returns the address of the error database The Intrinsics do a lazy binding of the error database and do not read in the database file until the first call to XtGetErrorDatabaseText.

For a complete listing of all errors and warnings that can be generated by the Intrinsics, see Appendix D

Structures

The type XrmDatabase is opaque and should not be manipulated directly. The return value can be manipulated with the Xlib functions XrmPutResource, XrmQPutResource, XrmGetResource, XrmQGetResource

See Also

XtAppGetErrorDatabase, XtAppGetErrorDatabaseText, XtDatabase, XtGetErrorDatabaseText,
XtErrorMsgHandler(2).

XtGetErrorDatabaseText

Name

XtGetErrorDatabaseText — obtain the error database text for an error or a warning.

Synopsis

```
void XtGetErrorDatabaseText(name, type, class, default, buf-
        fer_return, nbytes)

    char *name, *type, *class;
    char *default;
    char *buffer_return;
    int nbytes;
```

Arguments

name, type
: Specify the name and type that are concatenated to form the resource name of the error message.

class
: Specifies the resource class of the error message.

default
: Specifies the default message to use if an error database entry is not found.

buffer_return
: Specifies the buffer into which the error message is to be returned.

nbytes
: Specifies the size of the buffer in bytes.

Description

XtGetErrorDatabaseText returns the appropriate message from the error database for name and type. If no such entry exists, it returns the specified default message. On UNIX-based systems, the error database is usually stored in /usr/lib/X11/XtErrorDb. Custom error or warning messages should be appended to this file. The address of the loaded database can be returned by a call to XtGetErrorDatabase.

See Also

XtAppGetErrorDatabase, XtAppGetErrorDatabaseText, XtGetError-
Database,
XtErrorMsgHandler(2).

XtGetGC

XtGetGC

Name
XtGetGC — obtain a read-only, sharable GC

Synopsis
```
GC XtGetGC(w, value_mask, values)
    Widget w;
    XtGCMask value_mask;
    XGCValues *values;
```

Arguments
w   Specifies the widget with which the GC is to be associated.

value_mask Specifies which fields of the GC are to be filled in with widget data.

values   Returns the actual values for this GC.

Description
The Intrinsics provide a mechanism whereby cooperating clients can share a graphics context (GC), thereby reducing both the number of GCs created and the total number of server calls in any given application. The mechanism is a simple caching scheme, and all GCs obtained by means of this mechanism must be treated as read-only. If a changeable GC is needed, the Xlib XCreateGC function should be used instead

The XtGetGC function returns a sharable, read-only GC. The parameters to this function are the same as those for XCreateGC except that a widget is passed instead of a display

XtGetGC shares only GCs in which all values in the GC are the same. In particular, it does not use the *value_mask* provided to determine which fields of the GC a widget considers relevant. *value_mask* is used only to tell the server which fields should be filled in with widget data and which it should fill in with default values

For a more rigorous account of GCs, see Volume One, *Xlib Programming Manual*.

Structures
```
typedef unsigned long  XGCMask; /* Mask of values that are used by widget*/

typedef struct {
    int function;               /* logical operation */
    unsigned long plane_mask,   /* plane mask */
    unsigned long foreground,   /* foreground pixel */
    unsigned long background;   /* background pixel */
    int line_width;             /* line width */
    int line_style;             /* LineSolid, LineOnOffDash,
                                   LineDoubleDash */
    int cap_style;              /* CapNotLast, CapButt,
                                   CapRound, CapProjecting */
    int join_style;             /* JoinMiter, JoinRound, JoinBevel */
    int fill_style;             /* FillSolid, FillTiled,
                                   FillStippled, FillOpaqueStippled */
    int fill_rule;              /* EvenOddRule, WindingRule */
    int arc_mode;               /* ArcChord, ArcPieSlice */
```

```
    Pixmap tile;              /* tile pixmap for tiling operations */
    Pixmap stipple;          /* stipple 1 plane pixmap for stipping */
    int ts_x_origin;         /* offset for tile or
    int ts_y_origin;          * stipple operations */
    Font font;               /* default text font for text operations */
    int subwindow_mode;      /* ClipByChildren, IncludeInferiors */
    Bool graphics_exposures; /* should exposures be generated? */
    int clip_x_origin;       /* origin for clipping */
    int clip_y_origin;
    Pixmap clip_mask;        /* bitmap clipping; other calls for rects */
    int dash_offset;         /* patterned/dashed line information */
    char dashes;
} XGCValues;
```

See Also

```
XtReleaseGC
```

XtGetResourceList

—Xt – Resource Management—

Name
XtGetResourceList — retrieve default values for a resource list.

Synopsis
```
void XtGetResourceList(widget_class, resources_return,
     num_resources_return);
   WidgetClass widget_class;
   XtResourceList *resources_return;
   Cardinal *num_resources_return;
```

Arguments
widget_class
> Specifies the widget class for which you want the list.

resources_return
> Specifies a pointer to where to store the returned resource list The caller must free this storage using XtFree when done with it.

num_resources_return
> Specifies a pointer to the number of entries in the resource list.

Description
XtGetResourceList allocates and returns a list of resources used by *widget_class* (as opposed to XtGetApplicationResources, which obtains the resources from the actual widget instance). If the widget class has not been initialized (i e., no instances of the widget have been created), the resource list is a copy of the resource list in the widget class record If the resource class has been initialized, the resource list is merged with the resources from all the widget's superclasses

Here is an abbreviated version of the resource list in the Label widget:

```
/* Resources specific to Label */
static XtResource resources[] = {
{XtNforeground, XtCForeground, XtRPixel, sizeof(Pixel),
    XtOffset(LabelWidget, label.foreground), XtRString,
XtDefaultForeground},
{XtNfont, XtCFont, XtRFontStruct, sizeof(XFontStruct *),
    XtOffset(LabelWidget, label.font),XtRString, XtDefaultFont},
{XtNlabel, XtCLabel, XtRString, sizeof(String),
    XtOffset(LabelWidget, label.label), XtRString, NULL},
        .
        .
)
```

The complete resource name for a field of a widget instance is the concatenation of the application name (from argv[0]) or the *–name* command-line option (see XtDisplay-Initialize), the instance names of all the widget's parents, the instance name of the widget itself, and the resource name of the specified field of the widget. Likewise, the full resource

                                    X Toolkit Intrinsics Reference Manual

class of a field of a widget instance is the concatenation of the application class (from XtApp-CreateShell), the widget class names of all the widget's parents (not the superclasses), the widget class name of the widget itself, and the resource name of the specified field of the widget.

Structures

A Resource is defined as follows in *<X11/Intrinsic.h>*:

```
typedef struct _XtResource {
    String    resource_name;   /* Resource name */
    String    resource_class;  /* Resource class */
    String    resource_type;   /* Representation type desired */
    Cardinal  resource_size;   /* Size in bytes of representation */
    Cardinal  resource_offset;/* Offset from base to put resource value */
    String    default_type;    /* Representation type of specified default */
    caddr_t   default_addr;    /* Address of resource default value */
} XtResource, XtResourceList;
```

See Also

Section 1.7, "Resources,"
XtAppCreateShell, XtDisplayInitialize, XtFree, XtGetApplication-Resources.

Name

XtGetSelectionTimeout — get the current selection timeout value

Synopsis

```
unsigned int XtGetSelectionTimeout()
```

Description

XtGetSelectionTimeout returns the current value of the selection timeout in milliseconds The default value is 5000 milliseconds (five seconds).

The selection timeout is the time within which the two communicating applications must respond to one another If one of them does not respond within this interval, the Intrinsics abort the selection request.

Chapter 10, *Inter-Client Communications*, in Volume Four, *X Toolkit Intrinsics Programming Manual*, presents a complete example widget that both sends and receives data using selection

See Also

XtSetSelectionTimeout

XtGetSelectionValue

Name

XtGetSelectionValue —— obtain the complete selection data.

Synopsis

```
void XtGetSelectionValue(w, selection, target, callback, cli-
        ent_data, time)
    Widget w;
    Atom selection;
    Atom target;
    XtSelectionCallbackProc callback;
    opaque client_data;
    Time time;
```

Arguments

w	Specifies the widget that is making the request.
selection	Specifies the particular selection desired (either XA_PRIMARY or XA_SECON-DARY).
target	Specifies the type to which the sender should convert the selection.
callback	Specifies the callback procedure to be called when the selection value has been obtained. Note that this is how the selection value is communicated back to the client.
client_data	Specifies an argument to be passed to the specified procedure when it is called.
time	Specifies the timestamp that indicates when the selection is desired. This should be the timestamp of the event that triggered this request; the value CurrentTime is not acceptable.

Description

XtGetSelectionValue requests the selection owner to send the value of the selection, converted to the target type. callback will be called some time after XtGetSelection-Value is called; in fact, it may be called before or after XtGetSelectionValue returns.

If multiple calls to the server are required to get all the data, this will be transparent to the widget; the Intrinsics perform all the necessary fragmentation and reassembly of the selection.

To determine the actual target types that the selection owner will be willing to return, intern the string TARGETS using XInternAtom, and send the corresponding Atom as target.

See Also

XtGetSelectionValues, XtOwnSelection,
XtSelectionCallbackProc(2).

XtGetSelectionValues

Name
XtGetSelectionValues — obtain selection data in multiple formats.

Synopsis
```
void XtGetSelectionValues(w, selection, targets, count,
        callback, client_data, time)
    Widget w;
    Atom selection;
    Atom *targets;
    int count;
    XtSelectionCallbackProc callback;
    opaque client_data;
    Time time;
```

Arguments

w
: Specifies the widget that is making the request.

selection
: Specifies the particular selection desired (either XA_PRIMARY or XA_SECON-DARY).

targets
: Specifies the types to which the sender should convert the selection.

count
: Specifies the length of the targets and client_data lists.

callback
: Specifies the callback procedure to be called with each selection value obtained. Note that this is how the selection values are communicated back to the client.

client_data
: Specifies the client data (one for each target type) that is passed to the callback procedure when it is called for that target.

time
: Specifies the timestamp that indicates when the selection value is desired. This should be the timestamp of the event which triggered this request; the value CurrentTime is not acceptable.

Description

XtGetSelectionValues is similar to XtGetSelectionValue except that it takes a list of target types and a list of client data and obtains the current value of the selection converted to each of the targets. The effect is as if each target were specified in a separate call to Xt-GetSelectionValue. The callback is called once with the corresponding client data for each target. XtGetSelectionValues guarantees that all the conversions will use the same selection value because the ownership of the selection cannot change in the middle of the list, as would happen when calling XtGetSelectionValue repeatedly.

To determine the actual target types that the selection owner will be willing to return, intern the string TARGETS, and send the corresponding Atom as target.

Chapter 10, *Inter-Client Communications*, in Volume Four, *X Toolkit Intrinsics Programming Manual*, presents a complete example widget that both sends and receives data using selection.

See Also
XtGetSelectionValue, XtOwnSelection,
XtSelectionCallbackProc(2).

XtGetSubresources

Name

XtGetSubresources — update base-offset resource list (by name or class)

Synopsis

```
void XtGetSubresources(w, base, name, class, resources,
        num_resources, args, num_args)
    Widget w;
    caddr_t base;
    String name;
    String class;
    XtResourceList resources;
    Cardinal num_resources;
    ArgList args;
    Cardinal num_args;
```

Arguments

w	Specifies the widget that wants resources for a subpart.
base	Specifies the base address of the subpart data structure where the resources should be written.
name	Specifies the name of the subpart.
class	Specifies the class of the subpart.
resources	Specifies the resource list for the subpart
num_resources	Specifies the number of resources in the resource list.
args	Specifies the argument list to override resources obtained from the resource database.
num_args	Specifies the number of arguments in the argument list

Description

A widget does not do anything to get its own resources, instead, XtCreateWidget does this automatically before calling the class initialize procedure.

However, some widgets have subparts that are not widgets but for which the widget would like to fetch resources. For example, the Athena Text widget fetches resources for its source and sink. Such widgets call XtGetSubresources to accomplish this

XtGetSubresources constructs a name or class list from the application name or class, the names or classes of all its ancestors, and the widget itself Then, it appends to this list the name or class pair passed in. resources is fetched from the argument list, the resource database, or the default values in the resource list. Then, resources is copied into the subpart record. If args is NULL, num_args must be zero. However, if num_args is zero, the argument list is not referenced

With the exception of *name* and *class*, the arguments to XtGetSubresources are the same as those for XtGetApplicationResources. See XtGetApplicationResources for additional details.

All resource-fetching routines (for example, XtGetSubresources and XtGet-ApplicationResources) call resource converters if the desired representation differs from the resource the user specifies or from the widget's default resource value.

Structures

A Resource is defined as follows in *<X11/Intrinsic.h>*:

```
typedef struct _XtResource {
    String    resource_name;   /* Resource name */
    String    resource_class;  /* Resource class */
    String    resource_type;   /* Representation type desired */
    Cardinal  resource_size;   /* Size in bytes of representation */
    Cardinal  resource_offset;/* Offset from base to put resource value */
    String    default_type;    /* Representation type of specified default */
    caddr_t   default_addr;    /* Address of resource default value */
} XtResource, XtResourceList;
```

An Arg is defined as follows:

```
typedef struct {
    String name;
    XtArgVal value;
} Arg, *ArgList;
```

See Also

Section 1.7, "Resources,"
XtGetApplicationResources,
Volume Four, *X Toolkit Intrinsics Programming Manual*, Chapter 9, *Resource Management and Type Conversion*.

XtGetSubvalues

Name

XtGetSubvalues — copy from base-offset resource list to the argument list.

Synopsis

```
void XtGetSubvalues(base, resources, num_resources, args,
        num_args)
    caddr_t base;
    XtResourceList resources;
    Cardinal num_resources;
    ArgList args;
    Cardinal num_args;
```

Arguments

base   Specifies the base address from which resources should be read

resources   Specifies the nonwidget resources list.

num_resources

     Specifies the number of resources in the resource list and the address into which the resource value is to be stored.

args   Specifies the argument list of name/address pairs that contain the resource name The arguments and values passed in are dependent on the subpart The storage for argument values that are pointed to by the argument list must be deallocated by the application when no longer needed.

num_args   Specifies the number of arguments in the argument list

Description

XtGetSubvalues obtains resource values from the structure identified by base, and writes them in the provided argument list. XtGetSubvalues expects the contents of args to be pointers to locations where the actual values can be put.

The conjugate function XtSetSubvalues sets a widget's values.

XtGetSubvalues is used for obtaining resource data from entities that are not widgets. For further discussion of nonwidget subclass resources, see XtGetSubresources.

Structures

A Resource is defined as follows in <X11/Intrinsic h>.

```
typedef struct _XtResource {
    String   resource_name;  /* Resource name */
    String   resource_class; /* Resource class */
    String   resource_type;  /* Representation type desired */
    Cardinal resource_size;  /* Size in bytes of representation */
    Cardinal resource_offset;/* Offset from base to put resource value */
    String   default_type;   /* Representation type of specified default */
    caddr_t  default_addr;   /* Address of resource default value */
} XtResource, XtResourceList;
```

An `Arg` is defined as follows:

```
typedef struct {
    String name;
    XtArgVal value;
} Arg, *ArgList;
```

See Also

Section 1.7, "Resources,"
XtSetArg,
XtArgsProc(2).

XtGetValues

Name

XtGetValues — copy resources from a widget to the argument list.

Synopsis

```
void XtGetValues(w, args, num_args)
    Widget w;
    ArgList args;
    Cardinal num_args;
```

Arguments

w
: Specifies the widget whose values are to be read and the address into which the resource value is to be stored.

args
: Specifies the argument list of name/address pairs that contain the resource name The resource names are widget-dependent.

num_args
: Specifies the number of arguments in the argument list.

Description

XtGetValues retrieves the current value of a resource associated with a widget instance. The conjugate function XtSetValues sets a widget's values.

The name fields in args contain the names of resources. The value fields in args contain addresses into which XtGetValues stores the corresponding resource values. XtGet-Values expects the args.value fields to be pointers to locations where the actual values can be put. It is the caller's responsibility to allocate and deallocate this storage according to the size of the resource representation type used within the widget.

XtGetValues starts with the resources specified for the Core widget fields and descends the subclass chain to the widget. If the widget's parent is a subclass of constraintWidget-Class, XtGetValues then fetches the values for any Constraint resources requested It starts with the Constraint resources specified for constraintWidgetClass and proceeds down the subclass chain to the parent's Constraint resources If the argument list contains a resource name that is not found in any of the resource lists searched, the value at the corresponding address is not modified.

Finally, if the widget's get_values_hook methods are non-NULL, they are called in super-class-to-subclass order after all the resource values have been fetched by XtGetValues. get_values_hook methods are used by widgets that have nonwidget subparts to provide nonwidget resource data to XtGetValues.

Structures

An Arg is defined as follows in <X11/Intrinsic h>:

```
typedef struct {
    String name;
    XtArgVal value,
} Arg, *ArgList;
```

X Toolkit Intrinsics Reference Manual

See Also

Section 1.7, "Resources,"
XtSetArg, XtSetValues,
XtArgsProc(2).

XtHasCallbacks

Name

XtHasCallbacks — determine the status of a widget's callback list.

Synopsis

```
XtCallbackStatus XtHasCallbacks(w, callback_name)
    Widget w;
    String callback_name;
```

Arguments

w   Specifies the widget.

callback_name Specifies the callback list to be checked.

Description

XtHasCallbacks checks the widget for a resource named callback_name. If the resource does not exist or is not of type XtRCallback, XtHasCallbacks returns Xt-CallbackNoList. If the callback list exists but is empty, it returns XtCallbackHas-None. If the callback list contains at least one callback procedure, it returns XtCallback-HasSome.

Structures

```
typedef enum {
    XtCallbackNoList,
    XtCallbackHasNone,
    XtCallbackHasSome
} XtCallbackStatus;
```

See Also

Section 1.3, "Application Interface,"
XtAddCallbacks, XtCallCallbacks.

XtInitialize

Name

XtInitialize — initialize toolkit and display.

Synopsis

```
Widget XtInitialize(shell_name, application_class, options,
        num_options, argc, argv)
    char *shell_name; /*unused in R3*/
    char *application_class;
    XrmOptionDescRec options[];
    Cardinal num_options;
    Cardinal *argc;
    char *argv[];
```

Arguments

shell_name   Specifies the name of the application shell widget instance.

application_class
              Specifies the class name of this application.

options   Specifies how to parse the command line for any application-specific resources. The options argument is passed as a parameter to XrmParse-Command.

num_options   Specifies the number of entries in options list.

argc   Specifies a pointer to the number of command line parameters.

argv   Specifies the command line parameters.

Description

XtInitialize returns an application shell suitable for parenting the rest of the application, and consolidates other requisite Toolkit initialization. This is the initialization routine of choice for simple applications that use widgets.

XtInitialize calls XtToolkitInitialize to initialize the Toolkit internals, creates a default application context with XtCreateApplicationContext, XtOpenDisplay, and XtAppCreateShell, and returns the created shell. XtInitialize is generally more convenient than calling each of the routines individually.

The semantics of calling XtInitialize more than once are undefined.

Command Line Parsing

XtInitialize calls XtDisplayInitialize, which in turn calls the Xlib XrmParse-Command function to parse the command line.

The command line parser modifies argc and argv to contain only those parameters that were not in the standard option table or in the table specified by the options argument. If the resulting argc is not zero, then there were unexpected parameters declared on the user's command line. Most applications handle this by simply printing out the remaining contents of *argv* along with a message listing the allowable options, with the application name (On UNIX-based systems, the application name is usually the final component of *argv*[0].)

Note that the argc and argv arguments of XtInitialize are in the same order as in the call to main This is the opposite order of arrays and array lengths throughout other Xt and Xlib routine calls. Also note that the address of argc, not argc itself, is passed to Xt-Initialize. This is so that XtInitialize can decrement the count to reflect recognized options Watch out for these snags.

Loading the Resource Database

The XtDisplayInitialize function loads the application's resource database for this display/host/application combination from the following sources (in order):

- Application-specific class resource file on the local host.

- Application-specific user resource file on the local host.

- Resource property on the server or user preference resource file on the local host.

- Per-host user environment resource file on the local host.

- Application command line (argv)

Each resource database is kept on a per-display basis

The application-specific class resource file name is constructed from the class name of the application. It points to a site-specific resource file that usually is installed by the site manager when the application is installed. On UNIX-based systems, this file usually is */usr/lib/X11/app-defaults/class*, where *class* is the application class name. This file is expected to be provided by the developer of the application and may be required for the application to function properly

The application-specific user resource file name is constructed from the class name of the application and points to a user-specific resource file. This file is owned by the application and typically stores user customizations. On UNIX-based systems, this file name is constructed from the user's XAPPLRESDIR variable by appending *class* to it, where *class* is the application class name. (That is, XAPPLRESDIR specifies the name of a directory, and *class* the name of a file contained in it.) If XAPPLRESDIR is not defined, it defaults to the user's home directory. If the resulting resource file exists, it is merged into the resource database. This file may be provided with the application or constructed by the user

The server resource file is the contents of the X server's RESOURCE_MANAGER property that was returned by XOpenDisplay. If no such property exists for the display, the contents of the resource file in the user's home directory is used instead On UNIX-based systems, the usual name for the user preference resource file is *Xdefaults* If the resulting resource file exists, it is merged into the resource database. The server resource file is constructed entirely by the user and contains both display-independent and display-specific user preferences.

If one exists, a user's environment resource file is then loaded and merged into the resource database This file name is user and host specific. On UNIX-based systems, the user's environment resource file name is constructed from the value of the user's XENVIRONMENT variable for the full path of the file If this environment variable does not exist, XtDisplay-Initialize searches the user's home directory for the *Xdefaults*-host file, where *host* is the name of the machine on which the application is running. If the resulting resource file exists, it is merged into the resource database. The environment resource file is expected to contain system-specific resource specifications that are to supplement those user-preference specifications in the server resource file.

Parsing the Command Line

XtDisplayInitialize has a table of standard command line options for adding resources to the resource database, and it can accept application-specific resource abbreviations.

The format of this table is shown below in the Structures section of this man page. The standard table contains the following entries:

Option	Resource	Value	Sets
-bg	*background	next argument	background color
-background	*background	next argument	background color
-bd	*borderColor	next argument	border color
-bw	.borderWidth	next argument	width of border in pixels
-borderwidth	.borderWidth	next argument	width of border in pixels
-bordercolor	*borderColor	next argument	color of border
-display	.display	next argument	server to use
-fg	*foreground	next argument	foreground color
-fn	*font	next argument	font name
-font	*font	next argument	font name
-foreground	*foreground	next argument	foreground color
-geometry	.geometry	next argument	size and position
-iconic	.iconic	"on"	start as an icon
-name	.name	next argument	name of application
-reverse	*reverseVideo	"on"	reverse video
-rv	*reverseVideo	"on"	reverse video
+rv	*reverseVideo	"off"	No Reverse Video
-selectionTimeout	.selectionTimeout	Null	selection timeout
-synchronous	.synchronous	"on"	synchronous debug mode
+synchronous	.synchronous	"off"	synchronous debug mode
-title	.title	next argument	title of application
-xrm	value of argument	next argument	depends on argument

Note that any unique abbreviation for an option name in the standard table or in the application table is accepted.

The table above lists the complete set of standard options. Options for which the resource name is shown starting with a dot rather than an asterisk set that resource only in the application's top-level Shell.

If the user specifies synchronize TRUE on the command line, XtDisplayInitialize calls the Xlib XSynchronize function to put the Xlib display connection into synchronous mode. If reverseVideo is TRUE, the Intrinsics exchange XtDefaultForeground and XtDefaultBackground for widgets created on this display. (See Section 1.7, "Resources," for more information on default resources.)

The *-xrm* option provides a method of setting any resource in an application. The next argument should be a quoted string identical in format to a line in the user resources file For example, to give a red background to all command buttons in an application named xmh, you can start it up as.

```
xmh -xrm 'xmh*Command.background: red'
```

When it fully parses the command line, XtDisplayInitialize merges the application option table with the standard option table and then calls the Xlib XrmParseCommand function. An entry in the application table with the same name as an entry in the standard table overrides the standard table entry If an option name is a prefix of another option name, both names are kept in the merged table

Structures

You make XtInitialize understand additional command-line options by initializing a XrmOptionDescRec structure (called the *options table*) and passing it as an argument to XtInitialize.

```
typedef struct {
    char *option;/* Option name in argv */
    char *specifier;/* Resource name (without application name) */
    XrmOptionKind argKind;/* Which style of option it is */
    caddr_t value;/* Value to provide if XrmoptionNoArg */
} XrmOptionDescRec, *XrmOptionDescList;
```

Each options table entry consists of four fields·

- The option to be searched for on the command line As with standard command-line options, Xt will automatically accept any unique abbreviation of the option specified here. For example, the option -pixmapWidthInPixels will be recognized if typed on the command line as -pixmapW. However, if you wanted the option -pw to set the same resource, then you would need another entry, since pw is not the leading string of pixmapWidthInPixels.

- The resource specification. This must identify a widget resource or an application resource, but not provide a value. Since it has the same form as allowed in the resource databases, it may apply to a single widget or to many widgets If it applies to no widgets, no error message will be issued

- The argument style. This field is one of seven enumerated constants describing how the option is to be interpreted. These constants are described below.

- The value. This field is the value to be used for the resource if the argument style is XrmOptionNoArg. This field is not used otherwise Note that this value must already be converted to the value expected for the resource (often not a string). You may be able to use Xt's type converter routines explicitly to convert this data to the right type.

The `XrmOptionKind` enum constants that specify the various command-line argument styles are as shown in the table below:

Constant	Meaning
XrmoptionNoArg	Take the value in the `value` field of the options table. For example, this is used for Boolean fields, where the option might be –debug and the default value FALSE.
XrmoptionIsArg	The flag itself is the value without any additional information. For example, if the option were –on, the value would be "on." This constant is infrequently used, because the desired value such as "on" is usually not descriptive enough when used as an option (-on).
XrmoptionStickyArg	The value is the characters immediately following the option with no white space intervening. This is the style of arguments for some UNIX utilities such as *uucico* where *-sventure* means to call system *venture*.
XrmoptionSepArg	The next item after the white space after this flag is the value. For example, -fg blue would indicate that "blue" is the value for the resource specified by -fg.
XrmoptionResArg	The resource name and its value are the next argument in argv after the white space after this flag. For example, the flag might be -res basecalc*background:white; then the resource name/value pair would be used as is. This form is rarely used because it is equivalent to -xrm, and because the C shell requires that special characters such as * be quoted.
XrmoptionSkipArg	Ignore this option and the next argument in argv.
XrmoptionSkipLine	Ignore this option and the rest of argv.

The options table is passed to `XtInitialize` as its third argument, and the number of options table entries as the fourth. The `XtNumber` macro is a convenient way to count the number of entries (this is only one of many contexts in which you'll see this macro used).

Note that you *cannot* override the standard options by providing options with the same names in your own parsing table. If you try this, your options with the same names will simply not be set to the values specified on the command line. Instead, the standard options will be set to these values. This was a design decision in Xt, one of the few cases where a user-interface policy is enforced. Uniformity in this basic area was deemed more valuable than flexibility.

See Also

Section 1.1, "Widget Lifecycle,"
XtOpenDisplay, XtToolkitInitialize.

Name
XtInstallAccelerators — install a widget's accelerators on another widget.

Synopsis
```
void XtInstallAccelerators(destination, source)
    Widget destination;
    Widget source;
```

Arguments
destination   Specifies the widget whose translations are to be augmented.

source   Specifies the widget whose actions are to be executed.

Description
It is often convenient to be able to bind events in one widget to actions in another In particular, it is often useful to be able to invoke menu actions from the keyboard. The Intrinsics provide a facility, called accelerators, that let you accomplish this. Accelerators are simply translation tables that map event sequences in one widget into actions in another

Every widget includes an XtNaccelerators resource, which is defined by the Core widget class. The actual value of this resource can be hardcoded by the application or set in a resource file, just like any other resource.

However, in order for the XtNaccelerators resource to actually be used, the application must call XtInstallAccelerators (or XtInstallAllAccelerators). This call specifies two arguments. The destination widget is the widget whose translation table will be augmented with the accelerator table from the Source widget. In other terms, you could think of the source as "source of actions" and the destination as "source of events." That is, events occurring in the destination widget will trigger actions in the source. (From the event point of view, the terminology seems backwards! However, the terms source and destination do make sense in terms of what is actually happening to the translation table of the destinaition widget.)

For example, assume an application whose top-level shell widget was named topLevel, and which contained a Command widget instance named quit. Further assume that the quit widget had the following XtNaccelerators resource defined for it:

```
*quit.accelerators: \n\
   <KeyPress>q: Quit()
```

The call:

```
XtInitialize (topLevel, quit),
```

would allow a "q" typed in the application's top-level window to invoke the quit widget's Quit action

If the display_accelerator method in the Core part of the source widget class is non-NULL, XtInstallAccelerators calls it with the source widget and a string representation of the accelerator table. (The string representation of the accelerator table is a canonical translation table representation, not an exact replica of what was registered.) The method is invoked to inform the source widget that its accelerators have been installed on the destination widget so it can display them appropriately.

Core(3) describes the `display_accelerator` method. Volume Four, *X Toolkit Intrinsics Programming Manual*, has a complete accelerator programming example.

See Also

Section 1.5, "Translations and Actions,"
`XtInstallAllAccelerators.`

XtInstallAllAccelerators

Name

XtInstallAllAccelerators — install all accelerators from a widget and its descendants onto a destination.

Synopsis

```
void XtInstallAllAccelerators(destination, source)
    Widget destination;
    Widget source;
```

Arguments

destination   Specifies the widget whose translations are to be augmented.

source   Specifies the widget from which the accelerators are to come

Description

XtInstallAllAccelerators is a convenience function for installing all accelerators from a widget and all its descendants onto one destination widget. It recursively traverses the widget tree rooted at *source* and installs the accelerators of each widget onto *destination*. A common use is to call XtInstallAllAccelerators and pass the application main window as the source. This will allow the events occurring anywhere in the application to be sent to a particular destination widget.

Assuming the example shown under XtInstallAccelerators, the difference between

```
XtInstallAccelerators(topLevel, quit);
```

and

```
XtInstallAllAccelerators(topLevel, quit);
```

is that in the second case, the quit widget's accelerator table will actually be merged with the translation table of every widget in the application, while in the first case, it will only be merged with the translation table for topLevel. Because of event propagation, the effect may be indistinguishable to the user in many cases (By default, an event that is not selected in a widget will propagate through that widget to the widget's parent.) However, it may make a difference if there are conflicting translations in a given widget, and you want the accelerator to override the existing translations (using the #Override directive in the accelerator table resource specification).

See Also

Section 1 5, "Translations and Actions,"
XtInstallAccelerators.

XtIsComposite

Name
XtIsComposite — test whether a widget is a subclass of the Composite widget class.

Synopsis
```
Boolean XtIsComposite(w)
    Widget w;
```

Arguments
w   Specifies the widget whose class is to be tested.

Description
XtIsComposite tests whether a widget is a subclass of the Composite widget class. This is really just a convenience function equivalent to calling XtIsSubclass with composite-WidgetClass as the *class* argument. XtIsComposite is defined as a macro in *<X11/Intrinsic.h>*:

```
#define XtIsComposite(widget) XtIsSubclass(widget, (WidgetClass) \
    compositeWidgetClass)
```

See Also
Composite(3), Core(3).

XtIsConstraint

Name

XtIsConstraint — test whether a widget is a subclass of the Constraint widget class.

Synopsis

```
Boolean XtIsConstraint(w)
    Widget w;
```

Arguments

w   Specifies the widget whose class is to be tested

Description

XtIsConstraint tests whether a widget is a subclass of the Constraint widget class. This is really just a convenience function equivalent to calling XtIsSubclass with constraint-WidgetClass as the *class* argument. XtIsConstraint is defined as a macro in *<X11/Intrinsic.h>*:

```
#define XtIsConstraint(widget) XtIsSubclass(widget, (WidgetClass) \
    constraintWidgetClass)
```

See Also

Constraint(3), Core(3).

XtIsManaged

Name

XtIsManaged — determine whether a widget is managed by its parent.

Synopsis

```
Boolean XtIsManaged(w)
    Widget w;
```

Arguments

w	Specifies the widget whose state is to be tested.

Description

XtIsManaged returns TRUE if the specified child widget is currently being managed and FALSE if it is not.

XtIsManaged is a macro for programs that include <X11/InstrinsicP.h>. It is a function for application programs that do not have access to the Core widget field names.

XtIsManaged simply accesses the Core widget's managed field.

See Also

XtManageChildren, XtUnmanageChildren,
Core(3).

XtIsRealized

Name

XtIsRealized — determine whether a widget has been realized.

Synopsis

```
Boolean XtIsRealized(w)
    Widget w;
```

Arguments

w   Specifies the widget whose state is to be tested.

Description

XtIsRealized returns TRUE if the widget has been realized, and FALSE otherwise. A widget is realized if it has a nonzero X window ID in its Core field window.

XtIsRealized is a macro for programs that include *<X11/IntrinsicP.h>*. It is a function for application programs that do not have access to the Core widget field names. XtIsRealized accesses the window field from the Core widget structure, whose field definition is opaque from the point of view of application programmers. (Since the Core fields are opaque, they cannot be accessed by a macro.)

Some widget methods (for example, set_values) might wish to operate differently depending on whether or not the widget has been realized.

See Also

Section 1.1, "Widget Lifecycle"

XtIsSensitive

Name

XtIsSensitive — check the current sensitivity state of a widget.

Synopsis

```
Boolean XtIsSensitive(w)
    Widget w;
```

Arguments

w   Specifies the widget whose state is to be tested.

Description

XtIsSensitive returns TRUE or FALSE to indicate whether or not the widget is sensitive, (i.e., whether or not user input events are being dispatched). If both core.sensitive and core.ancestor_sensitive are TRUE, XtIsSensitive returns TRUE; otherwise, it returns FALSE.

A widget's sensitivity is often checked by its parent. For example the parent may wish to determine whether it should should pass the keyboard focus to the child, or it may choose to follow the lead of its children, and make itself insensitive.

See Also

XtCallAcceptFocus, XtSetSensitive,
Core(3).

XtIsShell

Name

XtIsShell — test whether a widget is a subclass of the Shell widget class

Synopsis

```
Boolean XtIsShell(w)
    Widget w;
```

Arguments

w   Specifies the widget whose class is to be tested.

Description

XtIsShell tests whether a widget is a subclass of the Shell widget class. This is really just a convenience function equivalent to calling XtIsSubclass with shellWidgetClass as the *class* argument. XtIsShell is defined as a macro in *<X11/Intrinsic.h>*:

```
#define XtIsShell(widget) XtIsSubclass(widget, (WidgetClass) \
    shellWidgetClass)
```

See Also

Shell(3), Core(3).

XtIsSubclass

Name

XtIsSubclass — determine whether a widget is a subclass of a class.

Synopsis

```
Boolean XtIsSubclass(w, widget_class)
    Widget w;
    WidgetClass widget_class;
```

Arguments

w   Specifies the widget whose class is to be tested.

widget_class   Specifies the widget class to test against.

Description

If w belongs to a derived class of widget_class, then it is a subclass. XtIsSubclass returns TRUE if the specified widget is a subclass of the given class.

A widget is trivially a subclass of its own widget class, or it can be any number of subclasses removed. XtIsSubclass starts with the widget_class field in the Core class part of w's widget structure and follows the superclass pointer until it reaches the top of the class hierarchy.

Composite widgets that restrict the class of widgets they will adopt as children can use XtIsSubclass to find out if a widget belongs to the desired widget class.

See Also

XtCheckSubclass, XtClass, XtSuperclass,
Composite(3), Core(3).

XtMainLoop

Name

XtMainLoop — continuously process events

Synopsis

```
void XtMainLoop()
```

Description

XtMainLoop obtains the default application context and reads the next incoming X event by calling XtAppNextEvent It then dispatches the appropriate registered procedure with Xt-DispatchEvent. This constitutes the main loop of Toolkit applications, and, as such, it does not return. Applications are expected to exit in response to some user action. (XtAppAdd-WorkProc provides a way of using an application's idle time.) There is nothing special about XtMainLoop; it is simply an infinite loop that calls XtAppNextEvent and then Xt-DispatchEvent

An application can provide its own version of this loop. For example, it might test an application-dependent global flag or other termination condition before looping back and calling Xt-AppNextEvent. Instead of exiting on a particular event (say a button press), it might exit if the number of top-level widgets drops to zero

See Also

Section 1 1, "Widget Lifecycle,"
XtAppAddWorkProc, XtAppMainLoop, XtAppNextEvent, XtDispatchEvent

XtMakeGeometryRequest

Name

XtMakeGeometryRequest — request parent to change child's geometry.

Synopsis

```
XtGeometryResult XtMakeGeometryRequest(w, request, reply_return)
    Widget w;
    XtWidgetGeometry *request;
    XtWidgetGeometry *reply_return;
```

Arguments

w   Specifies the child widget that is making the request.

request   Specifies the desired widget geometry (size, position, border width, and stacking order).

reply_return

Returns the allowed widget size or may be NULL if the requesting widget is not interested in handling XtGeometryAlmost.

Description

Child widgets are not allowed to change their own size or position. Instead, a child uses Xt-MakeGeometryRequest to ask its parent to change its geometry. XtMakeGeometry-Request returns XtGeometryYes or XtGeometryNo. (See below.)

XtMakeGeometryRequest performs the following tasks:

- If the widget is unmanaged or the widget's parent is not realized, it makes the changes to the widget's preferred geometry and returns XtGeometryYes.

- If the parent is not a subclass of compositeWidgetClass or the parent's geometry_manager method (the function pointed to by the geometry_manager field in the widget class record) is NULL, it issues an error.

- If the widget's being_destroyed field is TRUE, it returns XtGeometryNo.

- If the widget x, y, width, height and border_width fields are already equal to the requested values, it returns XtGeometryYes; otherwise, it calls the parent's geometry_manager method with the given parameters.

  - If the parent's geometry manager returns XtGeometryYes, XtCWQueryOnly is not set in request_mode (see Structures below for details) and if the widget is realized, XtMakeGeometryRequest calls the Xlib XConfigureWindow function to adjust the widget's window (setting its size, location, and stacking order as appropriate).

  - If the geometry manager returns XtGeometryDone, the change has been approved and actually has been done. In this case, XtMakeGeometryRequest does no configuring and returns XtGeometryYes. XtMakeGeometry-Request never returns XtGeometryDone.

Otherwise, XtMakeGeometryRequest returns the resulting value from the parent's geometry manager.

Children of primitive widgets are always unmanaged; thus, XtMakeGeometryRequest always returns XtGeometryYes when called by a child of a primitive widget

Structures

The return codes from geometry managers are:

```
typedef enum _XtGeometryResult {
    XtGeometryYes,    /* Request accepted */
    XtGeometryNo,     /* Request denied */
    XtGeometryAlmost, /* Request denied but willing to take reply */
    XtGeometryDone    /* Request accepted and done */
} XtGeometryResult;
```

The XtWidgetGeometry structure is similar to but not identical to the corresponding Xlib structure

```
typedef unsigned long XtGeometryMask,

typedef struct {
    XtGeometryMask request_mode;
    Position x, y;
    Dimension width, height,
    Dimension border_width;
    Widget sibling,
    int stack_mode;
} XtWidgetGeometry,
```

The request_mode definitions are from <X11/X h>:

```
#define  CWX            (1<<0)
#define  CWY            (1<<1)
#define  CWWidth        (1<<2)
#define  CWHeight       (1<<3)
#define  CWBorderWidth  (1<<4)
#define  CWSibling      (1<<5)
#define  CWStackMode    (1<<6)
```

The Xt Intrinsics also support the following value

```
#define XtCWQueryOnly  (1<<7)
```

XtCWQueryOnly indicates that the corresponding geometry request is only a query as to what would happen if this geometry request were made and that no widgets should actually be changed

XtMakeGeometryRequest, like the Xlib XConfigureWindow function, uses request_mode to determine which fields in the XtWidgetGeometry structure you want to specify

The stack_mode definitions are from *<X11/X.h>*:

```
#define    Above         0
#define    Below         1
#define    TopIf         2
#define    BottomIf      3
#define    Opposite      4
```

The Intrinsics also support the following value:

```
#define    XtSMDontChange    5
```

For precise definitions of Above, Below, TopIf, BottomIf, and Opposite, see the reference page for XtConfigureWindow in Volume Two, *Xlib Reference Manual.* XtSMDont-Change indicates that the widget wants its current stacking order preserved.

See Also
Section 1.8, "Geometry Management,"
XtMakeResizeRequest.

XtMakeResizeRequest

Name
XtMakeResizeRequest — request parent to change child's size.

Synopsis
```
XtGeometryResult XtMakeResizeRequest(w, width, height,
        width_return, height_return)
    Widget w;
    Dimension width, height;
    Dimension *width_return, *height_return
```

Arguments
w   Specifies the child widget making the request.

width, height   Specify the desired widget width and height

width_return, height_return
                        Return the allowed widget width and height.

Description
XtMakeResizeRequest is a simplified version of XtMakeGeometryRequest A child
uses XtMakeResizeRequest to ask its parent to change its size.

XtMakeResizeRequest creates an XtWidgetGeometry structure and specifies that
width and height should change The geometry manager is free to modify any of the other
window attributes (position or stacking order) to satisfy the resize request.

If the return value is XtGeometryAlmost, width_return and height_return contain
a compromise width and height. If these are acceptable, the widget should immediately make
another XtMakeResizeRequest and request that the compromise width and height be
applied. If the widget is not interested in XtGeometryAlmost replies, it can pass NULL for
width_return and height_return.

Structures
The return codes from geometry managers are.

```
typedef enum _XtGeometryResult {
    XtGeometryYes,   /* Request accepted */
    XtGeometryNo,    /* Request denied */
    XtGeometryAlmost,/* Request denied but willing to take reply */
    XtGeometryDone   /* Request accepted and done */
} XtGeometryResult;
```

See Also
Section 1 8, "Geometry Management,"
XtMakeGeometryRequest,
Volume Four, *X Toolkit Intrinsics Programming Manual*, Chapter 11, *Geometry Management*

XtMalloc

Name
XtMalloc — allocate storage.

Synopsis
```
char *XtMalloc(size);
    unsigned int size;
```

Arguments
size   Specifies the number of bytes desired.

Description
XtMalloc returns a pointer to a block of storage of at least the specified size bytes. If there is insufficient memory to allocate the new block, XtMalloc terminates by calling XtError-Msg.

If a widget is passed a pointer to resource data, it is expected to recopy the actual data into space of its own, so the application can do whatever it wants with its own data. The best way to preserve data is to allocate memory with XtMalloc and copy the data there.

XtMalloc makes no guarantee about the contents of the memory when it is allocated.

Memory allocated with XtMalloc must be deallocated with XtFree. The function Xt-Malloc is implemented by the Toolkit independently of the particular environment, so programs ported to a system not supporting malloc will still work.

XtNew and XtNewString provide slightly higher-level approaches to memory allocation.

See Also
XtCalloc, XtErrorMsg, XtFree, XtNew, XtNewString, XtRealloc.

XtManageChild

Name

XtManageChild — add a widget to its parent's list of managed children.

Synopsis

```
void XtManageChild(w)
    Widget w;
```

Arguments

w   Specifies the child widget to be managed

Description

XtManageChild brings a child widget created with XtCreateWidget under the geometry management of its parent. A widget cannot be made visible until it is managed

XtManageChild constructs a WidgetList of length one and calls XtManageChildren. Calling XtManageChild or XtManageChildren can be bypassed if widgets are created with XtCreateManagedWidget

Note that XtManageChild, XtManageChildren, XtUnmanageChild, and Xt-UnmanageChildren are low-level routines that are used by generic composite widget building routines. In addition, composite widgets can provide widget-specific, high-level convenience procedures to let applications create and manage children more easily.

See Also

Section 1 1, "Widget Lifecycle,"
XtCreateManagedWidget, XtIsManaged, XtManageChildren, XtSetMapped-WhenManaged, XtUnmanageChild, XtUnmanageChildren.

XtManageChildren

Name
XtManageChildren — add widgets to their parent's list of managed children.

Synopsis
```
void XtManageChildren(children, num_children)
    WidgetList children;
    Cardinal num_children;
```

Arguments

children   Specifies an array of child widgets.

num_children   Specifies the number of children in the array.

Description
XtManageChildren brings a list of widgets created with XtCreateWidget under the geometry management of their parent. A widget cannot be made visible until it is managed. (A widget can be created and managed at the same time by calling the convenience function Xt-CreateManagedWidget.)

XtManageChildren performs the following:

- Issues an error if the children do not all have the same parent or if the parent is not a sub-class of compositeWidgetClass. It returns immediately if the common parent is being destroyed.

- Marks each child viewable that is not already under management and not being destroyed.

- For each viewable child, if the parent is realized, XtManageChildren:

    - Calls the parent's change_managed routine.
    - Calls XtRealizeWidget if the child is unrealized.
    - Maps child if map_when_managed is TRUE.

Managing children is independent of their ordering and their creation and deletion. The parent should lay out only children whose managed field is TRUE and ignore all others. Note that some composite widgets, especially fixed boxes, call XtManageChild from their insert_child method.

If the parent widget is realized, its change_managed method is called to notify it that its set of managed children has changed. The parent can reposition and resize any of its children. It moves each child as needed by calling XtMoveWidget, which first updates the x and y fields and then calls the Xlib XMoveWindow function if the widget is realized.

If the composite widget wishes to change the size or border width of any of its children, it calls XtResizeWidget, which first updates the Core fields and then calls the Xlib XConfigureWindow function if the widget is realized.

Calling XtManageChild or XtManageChildren explicitly can be bypassed if widgets are created with the convenience function XtCreateManagedWidget. Note that

XtManageChild, XtManageChildren, XtUnmanageChild, and XtUnmanage-
Children are low-level routines that are used by generic composite widget building routines
In addition, composite widgets can provide widget-specific, high-level convenience procedures
to let applications create and manage children more easily.

Structures

    typedef Widget *WidgetList;

See Also

Section 1.1, "Widget Lifecycle," Section 1.8, "Geometry Management,"
XtCreateManagedWidget, XtIsManaged, XtManageChild, XtMoveWidget, Xt-
RealizeWidget, XtResizeWidget, XtSetMappedWhenManaged, XtUnmanage-
Child, XtUnmanageChildren.

XtMapWidget

Name

XtMapWidget — map a widget to its display.

Synopsis

```
XtMapWidget(w)
    Widget w;
```

Arguments

w   Specifies the widget to be mapped.

Description

XtMapWidget maps a widget's window to its display, causing it to become visible. A widget must be realized before it can be mapped.

If a widget's core map_when_managed field is set to TRUE, the widget is automatically mapped when it is managed. This is the case for most widgets. Widgets that are not must be mapped explicitly with XtMapWidget. The map_when_managed field can also be set through a call to XtSetMapWhenManaged.

See Also

Section 1.1, "Widget Lifecycle,"
XtSetMappedWhenManaged, XtUnmapWidget.

XtMergeArgLists

Name
XtMergeArgLists — merge two ArgList structures.

Synopsis
```
ArgList XtMergeArgLists(args1, num_args1, args2, num_args2)
    ArgList args1;
    Cardinal num_args1;
    ArgList args2;
    Cardinal num_args2;
```

Arguments

args1   Specifies the first ArgList.

num_args1   Specifies the number of arguments in the first argument list.

args2   Specifies the second ArgList.

num_args2   Specifies the number of arguments in the second argument list.

Description
XtMergeArgLists allocates a new ArgList large enough to hold args1 and args2 and copies both into it. It does not check for duplicate entries.

When the new ArgList is no longer needed, the application program can return it to the free pool with XtFree.

Structures
Arg is defined as follows in *<X11/Intrinsic.h>*:

```
typedef struct {
    String name;
    XtArgVal value;
} Arg, *ArgList;
```

See Also
XtFree, XtMalloc, XtSetArg.

XtMoveWidget

Name

XtMoveWidget —— move a widget on the display.

Synopsis

```
void XtMoveWidget(w, x, y)
    Widget w;
    Position x;
    Position y;
```

Arguments

w   Specifies the widget to be moved.

x, y   Specify the new widget x and y coordinates.

Description

XtMoveWidget returns immediately if the specified geometry fields for the widget are the same as the old values. Otherwise, XtMoveWidget writes the new x and y values into the widget and, if the widget is realized, issues an Xlib XMoveWindow call on the widget's window.

The XtConfigure widget resizes and moves a widget. A parent widget must use XtMove-Widget to rearrange its children on the display. It may also be used to relocate a sibling widget. A child widget must use XtMakeGeometryRequest and XtMakeResize-Request to ask its parent to move or resize it; it cannot move or resize itself.

The x and y coordinates are specified with respect to the origin in the upper left of the screen. Widget coordinates can be converted to screen coordinates with XtTranslateCoords.

See Also

Section 1.8, "Geometry Management,"
XtMakeGeometryRequest, XtMakeResizeRequest, XtTranslateCoords.

XtNameToWidget

Name

XtNameToWidget — translate a widget name to a widget instance.

Synopsis

```
Widget XtNameToWidget(reference, name);
    Widget reference;
    String name,
```

Arguments

reference   Specifies the widget from which the search is to start.

name   Specifies the fully qualified name of the desired widget.

Description

XtNameToWidget searches for a widget instance by name. *name* can refer to a child (either pop-up or normal) of the *reference* widget, or it can refer to a distant descendant. To look up a distant descendant, separate the names of ancestors with periods. There are no wildcard searches

The search for a fully specified name proceeds as follows. The first (leftmost) component of the name string is searched for as a direct descendant of the *reference* widget. If a widget with the given name is found, it is used as the *reference* widget and the search repeats for the next component.

A widget's name is given to it when it is created. If XtNameToWidget cannot find the specified widget, it returns NULL

The Intrinsics do not require widgets to have unique names. If more than one child of the reference widget matches a name, XtNameToWidget may select any of the matching widgets

If the specified names contain more than one component and if more than one child matches the first component, XtNameToWidget can return NULL if the single branch that it follows does not contain the named widget. That is, XtNameToWidget does not back up and follow other matching branches of the widget tree. A search involving an ambiguous component name is not guaranteed to succeed, even if a widget of the specified name exists

Chapter 12, *Menus, Gadgets, and Cascaded Pop Ups*, in Volume Four, *X Toolkit Intrinsics Programming Manual*, presents a discussion and an example of XtNameToWidget.

See Also

Section 1.5, "Translations and Actions," Section 1.6, "Pop Ups,"
XtCreateManagedWidget, XtCreatePopupShell, XtCreateWidget.

XtNew

Name

XtNew —allocate storage for one instance of a data type.

Synopsis

```
type *XtNew(type)
    type;
```

Arguments

type   Specifies a previously declared data type.

Description

XtNew is used to allocate storage for one instance of a data type. It returns a pointer to the allocated storage. For example, XtNew(XtCallbackList) allocates storage for one call-back list structure.

If there is insufficient memory to allocate the new block, XtErrorMsg terminates execution.

XtNew is a convenience macro that calls XtMalloc with the following arguments specified:

```
((type *) XtMalloc((unsigned) sizeof(type))
```

To copy an instance of a string, use XtNewString.

See Also

XtMalloc, XtNewString.

XtNewString

Name

XtNewString — copy an instance of a string.

Synopsis

```
String XtNewString(string)
    String string;
```

Arguments

string   Specifies a NULL-terminated string

Description

XtNewString is used to copy an instance of a string. It returns a pointer to the allocated storage. If there is insufficient memory to allocate the new block, XtNewString calls XtErrorMsg. For example, XtNew(XtCallbackList) allocates storage for one callback list structure. XtNewString is a macro that allocates storage for a string, copies the string into the new storage, and returns the pointer. For example, a string can be copied into new storage using the following:

```
static String buf[] = "How do you do?";
String p,

p = XtNewString(buf);
```

After this sequence, p points to a separate string that contains "How do you do?" Then buf can be changed without affecting p.

XtNewString is a convenience macro that calls XtMalloc with the following arguments specified

```
(strcpy(XtMalloc((unsigned) strlen(str) + 1), str))
```

See Also

XtMalloc, XtNew, XtFree.

XtNextEvent

Name

XtNextEvent — return next event from input queue.

Synopsis

```
void XtNextEvent(event_return)
    XEvent *event_return;
```

Arguments

event_return   Returns the event information from the dequeued event structure.

Description

XtNextEvent obtains the default application context, and invokes XtAppNextEvent. It is retained as a simplified interface to XtAppNextEvent. Since most applications have only one application context, this routine does not require the application to pass an application context explicitly.

Release Information

In Release 2, a bug prevented widgets from calling XtNextEvent recursively from input or timer callbacks. This bug was fixed in Release 3.

See Also

XtAppNextEvent

XtNumber

Name
XtNumber — determine the number of elements in a fixed-size array.

Synopsis
```
Cardinal XtNumber(array)
    array;
```

Arguments
array   Specifies a fixed-size array

Description
XtNumber returns the number of elements in the specified argument list, resource list, or other fixed-size array. It only works for objects whose total size is known at compile time.

It is a macro defined in <*X11/Xt Intrinsic h*> as:

```
#define XtNumber(arr)  ((Cardinal) (sizeof(arr) / sizeof(arr[0])))
```

Related Commands
XtOffset, XtSetArg.

Name
XtOffset — determine the byte offset of a field within a structure.

Synopsis
```
Cardinal XtOffset(pointer_type, field_name)
    Type pointer_type;
    Field field_name;
```

Arguments
pointer_type   Specifies a type that is declared as a pointer to the structure.

field_name   Specifies the name of the field for which to calculate the byte offset.

Description
XtOffset computes the relative address of a field in bytes, given a pointer to a structure.
Using XtOffset, a program can use field names, instead of numeric byte offsets, to specify
addresses in a structure relative to a base pointer. XtOffset can be used at compile time in
static initializations.

XtOffset is often used to determine the location of an instance variable in a widget record.
Resource fields are defined in terms of offsets from a base address from the beginning of a
widget. Thus, a resource value can be kept up to date by the Resource Manager without any
knowledge of the instance structure of the widget; it uses just a relative byte offset.

The following code uses XtOffset to define the foreground resource in the Athena Label
widget:

```
static XtResource resources[] = {
    {
    XtNforeground,         /* Resource name is foreground */
    XtCForeground,         /* Resource class is Foreground */
    XtRPixel,              /* Resource type is Pixel */
    sizeof(Pixel),         /* allocate enough space to hold a Pixel value */
    XtOffset(LabelWidget, label.foreground),/*where in instnce strct*/
    XtRString,             /*Default val is a String (will need conversion)*/
    XtDefaultForeground    /* Default address */
    },
        .
        .
        .

    {
    XtNlabel,
    XtCLabel,
    XtRString,
    NULL
    },
        .
        .
        .

}
```

XtOffset is a macro defined in *<X11/Xt Intrinsic h>* as follows:

```
#define XtOffset(type,field)   ((unsigned int) (((char *) \
     (&(((type)NULL)->field)))--((char *) NULL)))
```

See Also
Section 1.7, "Resources,"
XtGetResources.

XtOpenDisplay

Name

XtOpenDisplay — open, initialize, and add a display to an application context.

Synopsis

```
Display *XtOpenDisplay(app_context, display_name,
        application_name, application_class, options,
        num_options, argc, argv)
    XtAppContext app_context;
    String display_name;
    String application_name;
    String application_class;
    XrmOptionDescRec *options;
    Cardinal num_options;
    Cardinal *argc;
    String *argv;
```

Arguments

app_context   Specifies the application context.

display_name

Specifies the display. A display can be in at most one application context.

application_name

Specifies the name of the application instance.

application_class

Specifies the class name of this application, which is usually the generic name for all instances of this application.

options   Specifies how to parse the command line for any application-specific resources. The options argument is passed as a parameter to XrmParse-Command. For further information, see XtInitializeDisplay.

num_options Specifies the number of entries in the options list.

argc   Specifies a pointer to the number of command line parameters.

argv   Specifies the command line parameters.

Description

XtOpenDisplay can be used to open a display (possibly an additional display) and add it to an application context.

XtOpenDisplay first parses the command line for the following options:

–display   The display name to be passed to XOpenDisplay; overrides *display_name*.

–name   The resource name prefix; overrides *application_name*.

XtOpenDisplay then calls the Xlib function XOpenDisplay to open the display. If *display_string* was NULL, and no display was specified in *argv*, it uses the default display (on UNIX-based systems, this is the value of the DISPLAY environment variable)

If XOpenDisplay succeeds, XtOpenDisplay then calls XtDisplayInitialize with the opened display. If there was no *–name* option specified in *argv* and *application_name* is NULL, it uses the last component of argv[0].

XtOpenDisplay returns the newly opened display or NULL on failure.

See Section 1.1, "Widget Lifecycle," for more general discussion. XtInitialize is a convenience function that can be used if only one display is to be opened Application contexts are constructed with XtAppCreateContext. Parsing the command line is discussed in Section 1.7, "Resources," and in XtDisplayInitialize There is example code in Chapter 9, *Resource Management and Type Conversion*, in Volume Four, *X Toolkit Intrinsics Programming Manual*

See Also
XtDisplayInitialize, XtInitialize

XtOverrideTranslations

Name
XtOverrideTranslations — merge new translations, overwriting widget's existing ones.

Synopsis
```
void XtOverrideTranslations(w, translations)
    Widget w;
    XtTranslations translations;
```

Arguments
w   Specifies the widget into which the new translations are to be merged.

translations Specifies the compiled translation table to merge in (must not be NULL).

Description
XtOverrideTranslations merges new translations into the existing widget translations, overriding the translations for any event or event sequence that already exists in the widget's translations, and possibly adding new ones.

The translation table must be in compiled form, as produced by XtParseTranslation-Table. XtParseTranslationTable produces the binary form of the translation table from text. XtConvert can also do this, specifying XtRTranslationTable as the destination resource type. (A text translation table is automatically parsed in the Core widget structure when a widget class is initialized.)

Translation tables can also be constructed by converting resources with XtConvert. To make it easy to modify translation tables in resource files, the string-to-translation-table resource type converter allows you to specify whether the table should replace, augment, or override any existing translation table in the widget. As an option, a pound sign (#) as the first character of the table followed by replace (default), augment, or override indicates how to treat existing translations (Release 3 only).

To merge new translations, but keep existing translations in case of conflict, use XtAugment-Translations.

To replace a widget's translations completely and not just selectively overwrite some of them, use XtSetValues on the XtNtranslations resource and specify a compiled translation table as the value.

To completely remove existing translations, use XtUninstallTranslations.

See Also
Section 1.5, "Translations and Actions,"
XtAugmentTranslations, XtConvert, XtParseTranslationTable,
Core(3),
Text(4).

Name

XtOwnSelection — indicate that selection data is available.

Synopsis

```
Boolean XtOwnSelection(w, selection, time, convert_proc,
        lose_proc, done_proc)
    Widget w;
    Atom selection;
    Time time;
    XtConvertSelectionProc convert_proc;
    XtLoseSelectionProc lose_proc;
    XtSelectionDoneProc done_proc;
```

Arguments

w	Specifies the widget that wishes to become the owner
selection	Specifies an atom that describes the type of the selection (for example, XA_PRIMARY, XA_SECONDARY, these two are declared beforehand in <X11/Xatom h>).
time	Specifies the times when selection ownership should commence This should be the timestamp of the event that triggered ownership It should be the time field taken directly from an XEvent structure. The value Current-Time is not acceptable.
convert_proc	Specifies the procedure to call whenever someone requests the current value of the selection.
lose_proc	Specifies the procedure to call whenever the widget has lost selection owner-ship, or specifies NULL if the owner is not interested in being called back
done_proc	Specifies the procedure to call after the transfer completes, or specifies NULL if the owner is not interested in being called back

Description

Calling XtOwnSelection is a precursor to sending data through the selection mechanism XtOwnSelection informs the Intrinsics of its claim on the selection, and its readiness to send data on request. XtOwnSelection returns TRUE if the widget has successfully become the owner and FALSE otherwise.

The widget may fail to become the owner if some other widget has asserted ownership after this widget, as indicated by time. Widgets can lose selection ownership either because another client more recently asserted ownership of the selection, or because the widget voluntarily gave up ownership of the selection with XtDisownSelection.

The lose_proc procedure is invoked when another widget successfully claims the selection after w. The lose_proc procedure is not called if the widget fails to obtain selection owner-ship in the first place

If the widget successfully obtains the selection ownership, subsequent requests for data will be directed to `convert_proc`.

`XtConvertSelectionProc`(2) describes the responsibilities of the widget or application sending data and its conversion duties. Chapter 10, *Inter-Client Communications*, in Volume Four, *X Toolkit Intrinsics Programming Manual*, presents a complete example widget that both sends and receives data using selection.

See Also

`XtDisownSelection`, `XtGetSelectionValue`, `XtSelectionDone`,
`XtConvertSelectionProc`(2), `XtLoseSelectionProc`(2).

XtParent

Name

XtParent — return the parent widget for the specified widget.

Synopsis

```
Widget XtParent(w)
    Widget w;
```

Arguments

w   Specifies the widget whose parent is to be returned.

Description

XtParent returns the parent widget of the specified widget.

XtParseAcceleratorTable

Name

XtParseAcceleratorTable — compile an accelerator table into its internal representation.

Synopsis

```
XtAccelerators XtParseAcceleratorTable(table)
    String table;
```

Arguments

table   Specifies the accelerator table to compile.

Description

XtParseAcceleratorTable compiles the accelerator table into its opaque internal representation.

An accelerator is a translation table that is bound with its actions in the context of a particular widget. The accelerator table can then be installed on some destination widget. When an action in the destination widget would cause an accelerator action to be taken, rather than causing an action in the context of the destination, the actions are executed as though triggered by an action in the accelerator widget.

Each widget instance contains that widget's exported accelerator table. Each class of widget exports a method that takes a displayable string representation of the accelerators so that widgets can display their current accelerators. The representation is the accelerator table in canonical translation table form (see Appendix B, *X Toolkit Data Types*). The display_accelerator procedure pointer is of type XtStringProc.

The facility to parse accelerator tables can also be accessed by converting a string resource into a resource of type XtRAcceleratorTable.

Accelerators can be specified in defaults files, and the string representation is the same as for a translation table. However, the interpretation of the #augment and #override directives apply to what will happen when the accelerator is installed; that is, whether or not the accelerator translations will override the translations in the destination widget. The default is #augment, which means that the accelerator translations have lower priority than the destination translations. The #replace directive is ignored for accelerator tables.

An accelerator table must be stored in the Core widget structure in this compiled format, not as a string. Core(3) describes the display_accelerator method.

See Also

Section 1.5, "Translations and Actions,"
XtInstallAccelerators,
Volume Four, *X Toolkit Intrinsics Programming Manual*, Chapter 7, *Events, Translations, and Accelerators*.

XtParseTranslationTable

Name

XtParseTranslationTable — compile a translation table into its internal representation.

Synopsis

```
XtTranslations XtParseTranslationTable(table)
    String table;
```

Arguments

table   Specifies the translation table to compile.

Description

XtParseTranslationTable compiles *table* into its opaque internal representation of type XtTranslations.

A translation table is a string containing a list of translations from an event sequence into one or more action procedure calls. The translations are separated from one another by newline characters (ASCII LF). The complete syntax of translation tables is specified in Appendix F, *Translation Table Syntax*. All widget instance records contain a translation table, which is a resource with no default value. A translation table specifies what action procedures are invoked for an event or a sequence of events.

As an example, the default behavior of the Athena Command widget is:

- Highlight on enter window.

- Unhighlight on exit window.

- Invert on left button down.

- Call callbacks and reinvert on left button up.

The following illustrates the Command widget's default translation table:

```
static String defaultTranslations =
        "<EnterWindow>: Highlight()\n\
        <LeaveWindow>:  Unhighlight()\n\
        <Btn1Down>:     Set()\n\
        <Btn1Up>:       Notify() Unset()";
```

The tm_table field of the CoreClass record should be filled in at static initialization time with the string containing the class' default translations. If a class wants to inherit its superclass' translations, it can store the special value XtInheritTranslations into tm_table. After the class initialization procedures have been called, the Intrinsics compile this translation table into an efficient internal form. Then, at widget creation time, this default translation table is used for any widgets that have not had their core translations field set by the Resource Manager or the initialize procedures.

The resource conversion mechanism automatically compiles string translation tables that are resources. If a client uses translation tables that are not resources, it must compile them itself using XtParseTranslationTable.

The Intrinsics use the compiled form of the translation table to register the necessary events with the Event Manager. Widgets need do nothing other than specify the action and translation tables for events to be processed by the Resource Manager.

The facility to parse translation tables can also be accessed by converting a string resource into a resource of type XtRTranslationTable. If an empty translation table is required for any purpose, one can be obtained by calling XtParseTranslationTable and passing an empty string.

XtAugmentTranslations and XtOverrideTranslations both expect translations in this compiled form.

See Also

Section 1.5, "Translations and Actions,"
Volume Four, *X Toolkit Intrinsics Programming Manual*, Chapter 7, *Events, Translations, and Accelerators*.

XtPeekEvent

Name

XtPeekEvent — nondestructively examine the head of an application's input queue.

Synopsis

```
Boolean XtPeekEvent(event_return)
    XEvent *event_return;
```

Arguments

event_return   Returns the event information from the head event structure in the queue.

Description

XtPeekEvent obtains the default application context, and invokes XtAppPeekEvent. It is retained as a simplified interface to XtAppPeekEvent. Since most applications have only one application context, this function does not require the application to pass an application context explicitly

Programs rarely need this much control over the event dispatching mechanism. Most programs use XtMainLoop.

See Also

XtAppPeekEvent

XtPending

Name

XtPending — determine if there are any events in an application's input queue.

Synopsis

```
XtInputMask XtPending ()
```

Description

XtPending obtains the default application context, and invokes XtAppPending. It is retained as a simplified interface to XtAppPending. Since most applications have only one application context, XtPending does not require the application to pass an application context explicitly.

Programs rarely need this much control over the event dispatching mechanism. Most programs use XtMainLoop.

See Also

XtAppPending

XtPopdown

Name

XtPopdown — unmap a pop-up shell.

Synopsis

```
void XtPopdown(popup_shell)
    Widget popup_shell;
```

Arguments

popup_shell   Specifies the widget shell to pop down.

Description

XtPopdown pops down a pop-up shell that was popped up by XtPopup or by one of the built-in callback functions, XtCallbackExclusive, XtCallbackNonexclusive, or XtCallbackNone.

To perform a pop down from a callback list, use XtCallbackPopdown. To do so from a translation table, use MenuPopdown.

XtPopdown performs the following:

* Calls XtCheckSubclass to ensure *popup_shell* is a subclass of Shell.

* Checks that *popup_shell* is currently popped_up; otherwise, it generates an error.

* Unmaps *popup_shell*'s window.

* If *popup_shell*'s grab_kind is either XtGrabNonexclusive or XtGrab-Exclusive, it calls XtRemoveGrab. The grab kind is specified as an argument to XtPopup.

* Sets *popup_shell*'s popped_up field to FALSE.

* Calls the callback procedures on the shell's popdown_callback list, designated by the resource XtNpopdownCallback. (See XtCreatePopupShell.)

Pop-up widgets can be created and popped up with XtCreatePopupShell and XtPopup.

See Also

Section 1.6, "Pop Ups,"
XtCallbackExclusive, XtCallbackNone, XtCallbackNonexclusive, Xt-CheckSubclass, XtCreatePopupShell, XtPopup, XtRemoveGrab.
Volume Four, *X Toolkit Intrinsics Programming Manual*, Chapter 12, *Menus, Gadgets, and Cascaded Pop Ups*.

XtPopup

Name
XtPopup — map a pop-up shell.

Synopsis
```
void XtPopup(popup_shell, grab_kind)
    Widget popup_shell;
    XtGrabKind grab_kind;
```

Arguments

popup_shell   Specifies a widget shell returned by *XtCreatePopupShell*.

grab_kind   Specifies how user events should be constrained. (Can be one of `XtGrab-None`, `XtGrabNonexclusive`, `XtGrabExclusive`.)

Description

After creating a pop-up shell with `XtCreatePopupShell` and its managed child with `Xt-CreateManagedWidget`, the pop up is ready to be mapped to the display. The easiest way to map the pop up is with `XtPopup`.

`XtPopup` maps its window, by default, to the upper-left corner of the display. This can be circumvented by relocating the pop-up shell with `XtMoveWidget` before calling `XtPopup`.

`XtPopup` performs the following duties:

- Calls `XtCheckSubclass` to ensure *popup_shell* is a subclass of Shell.

- Generates a nonfatal error if the shell is already popped up.

- Calls the callback procedures on the shell's pop-up callback list, designated by the resource `XtNpopupCallback`. (See `XtCreatePopupShell`.)

- Sets the shell *popped_up* field to TRUE, the shell *spring_loaded* field to FALSE, and the shell *grab_kind* field to *grab_kind*. *grab_kind* specifies the grab type inserted in the modal cascade. (See `XtAddGrab`.)

- If the shell's `create_popup_child` field is non-NULL, `XtPopup` calls it with *popup_shell* as the parameter. This field is designated by the resource `XtNcreate-PopupChildProc`. (See `XtCreatePopupShell`).

- If *grab_kind* is either `XtGrabNonexclusive` or `XtGrabExclusive`, it calls:

      XtAddGrab(popup_shell, (grab_kind == XtGrabExclusive), FALSE)

- Calls `XtRealizeWidget` with *popup_shell*.

- Calls `XMapWindow` with the Core window field from *popup_shell*.

Widgets can be popped down with `XtPopdown`. For more specifics on how to relocate the pop-up shell before popping it up, see `XtMoveWidget` and `XtTranslateCoords`. To perform a pop up from a callback list, see `XtCallbackNone`, `XtCallbackNonexclusive`, and `XtCallbackExclusive`. To do so from a translation table, use `MenuPopup`. For details on how events are constrained to the pop up, see `XtAddGrab`.

See Also
Section 1 6, "Pop Ups,"
XtCheckSubclass, XtCreateManagedWidget, XtRealizeWidget
Volume Four, *X Toolkit Intrinsics Programming Manual*, Chapter 12, *Menus, Gadgets, and Cascaded Pop Ups.*

XtProcessEvent

Name

XtProcessEvent — process one input event.

Synopsis

```
void XtProcessEvent(mask)
    XtInputMask mask;
```

Arguments

mask   Specifies what types of events to process. The mask is the bitwise inclusive OR of XtIMXEvent (an X event), XtIMTimer (a timer event), or Xt-IMAlternateInput (an alternate input event). The symbolic name Xt-IMAll is the bitwise inclusive OR of all event types.

Description

XtProcessEvent obtains the default application context, and invokes XtAppProcess-Event. It is retained as a simplified interface to XtAppProcessEvent. Since most applications have only one application context, XtProcessEvent does not require the application to pass app_context explicitly.

Programs rarely need this much control over the event dispatching mechanism. Most programs use XtMainLoop.

See Also

XtAppProcessEvent

XtQueryGeometry

Name

XtQueryGeometry — query a child widget's preferred geometry.

Synopsis

```
XtGeometryResult XtQueryGeometry(w, intended, preferred_return)
    Widget w;
    XtWidgetGeometry *intended;
    XtWidgetGeometry *preferred_return,
```

Arguments

w   Specifies the widget whose geometry preferences are being queried

intended   Specifies any changes the parent plans to make to the child's geometry, or
                NULL.

preferred_return
                Returns the child widget's preferred geometry.

Description

Some parents may be willing to adjust their layouts to accommodate the preferred geometries
of their children They can use XtQueryGeometry to obtain the preferred geometry and, as
they see fit, can use or ignore any portion of the response

To discover a child's preferred geometry, the child's parent sets any changes that it intends to
make to the child's geometry in the corresponding fields of the intended structure, sets the
corresponding bits in intended.request_mode, and calls XtQueryGeometry.

XtQueryGeometry clears all bits in the preferred_return->request_mode and
checks the query_geometry field of the specified widget's class record. If the widget's
query_geometry method is not NULL, XtQueryGeometry calls the query_geometry
method and passes w, intended, and preferred_return as arguments. If intended is
NULL, XtQueryGeometry replaces it with a pointer to an XtWidgetGeometry structure
with request_mode=0 before calling query_geometry.

The query_geometry procedure pointer is of type XtGeometryHandler(2).

The query_geometry procedure is expected to examine the bits set in
request->request_mode, evaluate the preferred geometry of the widget, and store the
result in geometry_return (setting the bits in geometry_return->request_mode
corresponding to those geometry fields that it cares about). If the proposed geometry change is
acceptable without modification, the query_geometry procedure should return Xt-
GeometryYes If at least one field in geometry_return is different from the corresponding field in request or if a bit was set in geometry_return that was not set in request, the
query_geometry procedure should return XtGeometryAlmost If the preferred
geometry is identical to the current geometry, the query_geometry procedure should return
XtGeometryNo.

After calling the query_geometry procedure or if the query_geometry field is NULL,
XtQueryGeometry examines all the unset bits in geometry_return->request_mode

and sets the corresponding fields in `geometry_return` to the current values from the widget instance. If the `request_mode` field is not set to `CWStackMode`, the `stack_mode` field is set to `XtSMDontChange`. `XtQueryGeometry` returns the value returned by the `query_geometry` procedure or `XtGeometryYes` if the `query_geometry` field is `NULL`.

Therefore, the caller can interpret a return of `XtGeometryYes` as not needing to evaluate the contents of the reply and, more importantly, not needing to modify its layout plans. A return of `XtGeometryAlmost` means either that both the parent and the child expressed interest in at least one common field and the child's preference does not match the parent's intentions or that the child expressed interest in a field that the parent might need to consider. A return value of `XtGeometryNo` means that both the parent and the child expressed interest in a field and that the child suggests that the field's current value is its preferred value. In addition, whether or not the caller ignores the return value or the reply mask, it is guaranteed that the reply structure contains complete geometry information for the child.

Parents are expected to call `XtQueryGeometry` in their layout routine and wherever other information is significant after `change_managed` has been called. The `change_managed` method may assume that the child's current geometry is its preferred geometry. Thus, the child is still responsible for storing values into its own geometry during its initialize method.

Structures

The return codes from geometry managers are:

```
typedef enum {
    XtGeometryYes,     /* Request accepted */
    XtGeometryNo,      /* Request denied */
    XtGeometryAlmost,/* Request denied but willing to take reply */
    XtGeometryDone    /* Request accepted and done */
} XtGeometryResult;
```

The `XtWidgetGeometry` structure is similar to but not identical to the corresponding Xlib structure:

```
typedef unsigned long XtGeometryMask;

typedef struct {
    XtGeometryMask request_mode;
    Position x, y;
    Dimension width, height;
    Dimension border_width;
    Widget sibling;
    int stack_mode;
} XtWidgetGeometry;
```

The `request_mode` definitions are from *<X11/X.h>*:

```
#define   CWX            (1<<0)
#define   CWY            (1<<1)
#define   CWWidth        (1<<2)
#define   CWHeight       (1<<3)
```

```
#define   CWBorderWidth    (1<<4)
#define   CWSibling        (1<<5)
#define   CWStackMode      (1<<6)
```

The Xt Intrinsics also support the following value.

```
#define   XtCWQueryOnly    (1<<7)
```

XtCWQueryOnly indicates that the corresponding geometry request is only a query as to what would happen if this geometry request were made and that no widgets should actually be changed.

XtMakeGeometryRequest, like the Xlib XConfigureWindow function, uses request_mode to determine which fields in the XtWidgetGeometry structure you want to specify.

The stack_mode definitions are from <*X11/X h*>·

```
#define   Above       0
#define   Below       1
#define   TopIf       2
#define   BottomIf    3
#define   Opposite    4
```

The Intrinsics also support the following value:

```
#define   XtSMDontChange   5
```

For precise definitions of Above, Below, TopIf, BottomIf, and Opposite, see Volume Two, *Xlib Reference Manual* XtSMDontChange indicates that the widget wants its current stacking order preserved

See Also

Section 1.8, "Geometry Management,"
XtMakeGeometryRequest,
Core(3), Composite(3)

XtRealizeWidget

Name
XtRealizeWidget — realize a widget instance.

Synopsis
```
void XtRealizeWidget(w)
    Widget w;
```

Arguments
w   Specifies the widget to be realized.

Description
XtRealizeWidget causes widgets to create their windows on the display, and perform their final initializations. XtRealizeWidget is called just prior to calling XtMainLoop to process events. The argument to XtRealizeWidget is usually the top-level widget returned from XtInitialize.

If the widget is already realized, XtRealizeWidget simply returns. Otherwise, it performs the following:

- Binds all action names in the widget's translation table to procedures. (See Section 1.5, "Translations and Actions.")

- Makes a post-order traversal of the widget tree rooted at the specified widget and calls the change_managed procedure of each composite widget that has one or more managed children.

- Constructs an XSetWindowAttributes structure filled in with information derived from the Core widget fields and calls the realize procedure for the widget, which adds any widget-specific attributes and creates the X window.

- If the widget is not a subclass of compositeWidgetClass, XtRealizeWidget returns; otherwise, it performs the following:

  - Descends recursively to each of the widget's managed children and calls the realize procedures. Primitive widgets that instantiate children are responsible for realizing those children themselves.

  - Maps all of the managed child windows that have mapped_when_managed TRUE. (If a widget is managed but mapped_when_managed is FALSE, the widget is allocated visual space but is not displayed.)

If the widget is a top-level shell widget. (that is, it has no parent), and mapped_when_managed is TRUE, XtRealizeWidget maps the widget window.

XtCreateWidget, XtRealizeWidget, XtManageChildren, XtUnmanage-Children, and XtDestroyWidget maintain the following invariants

- If a widget is realized, then all its managed children are realized
- If a widget is realized, then all its managed children that are also mapped_when_managed are mapped.

Functions should take special care to work correctly with both realized and unrealized widgets.

See Also
Section 1 1, "Widget Lifecycle,"
XtInitialize, XtIsRealized, XtRealizeProc, XtUnrealizeWidget, Core(3).

XtRealloc

Name

XtRealloc — change the size of an allocated block of storage.

Synopsis

```
char *XtRealloc(ptr, num);
    char *ptr;
    unsigned int num;
```

Arguments

ptr   Specifies a pointer to the old storage.

num   Specifies the number of bytes desired in new storage.

Description

XtRealloc changes the size of a block of storage, possibly moving it. Then, it copies the old contents (or as much as will fit) into the new block and frees the old block. If there is insufficient memory to allocate the new block, XtRealloc terminates by calling XtErrorMsg.

If ptr is NULL, XtRealloc allocates the new storage without copying the old contents. That is, it simply calls XtMalloc.

The function XtRealloc is implemented by the Toolkit independently of the particular environment, so programs ported to a system not supporting realloc will still work.

See Also

XtAlloc, XtErrorMsg, XtFree, XtMalloc, XtNew, XtNewString.

Name

XtRegisterCaseConverter — register a case converter.

Synopsis

```
void XtRegisterCaseConverter(display, proc, start, stop)
    Display *display;
    XtCaseProc proc;
    KeySym start;
    KeySym stop;
```

Arguments

display	Specifies the display from which the key events are to come.
proc	Specifies the XtCaseProc that is to do the conversions
start	Specifies the first keysym for which this converter is valid.
stop	Specifies the last keysym for which this converter is valid.

Description

XtRegisterCaseConverter registers the specified case converter (see XtCase-Proc(2)). start and stop provide the inclusive range of keysyms for which this converter is to be called. The new converter overrides any previous converters for keysyms in that range.

The only way to remove a converter is to register a new one. For example, the default key translator (_XtConvertCase) can be explicitly reinstalled

The default converter understands case conversion for all keysyms defined in the X11 protocol The keysyms defining a keysym range are defined in <X11/keysym h>.

A related keyboard example is presented in Chapter 13, *Miscellaneous Toolkit Programming Techniques*, in Volume Four, *X Toolkit Intrinsics Programming Manual*.

Structures

```
typedef XID KeySym;
```

See Also

XtSetKeyTranslator, XtTranslateKeycode,
XtCaseProc(2), XtKeyProc(2)

XtReleaseGC

Name

XtReleaseGC — deallocate a shared GC when it is no longer needed.

Synopsis

```
void XtReleaseGC(w, gc)
    Widget w;
    GC gc;
```

Arguments

w   Specifies the widget that no longer needs the specified GC.

gc   Specifies the GC to be deallocated.

Description

XtReleaseGC disassociates an application from a GC allocated with XtGetGC. It *must* be used instead of XtDestroyGC if the application is using XtGetGC on multiple displays.

The Intrinsics maintain reference counts of sharable GCs allocated by XtGetGC. The Intrinsics do not actually pass a free request to the server until the last user of a GC in an application releases it.

The Intrinsics use a caching mechanism for sharable read-only GCs. This is explained in Chapter 6, *Basic Widget Methods*, in Volume Four, *X Toolkit Intrinsics Programming Manual*.

See Also

XtDestroyGC, XtGetGC.

Name

XtRemoveAllCallbacks — delete all procedures from a callback list.

Synopsis

```
void XtRemoveAllCallbacks(w, callback_name)
    Widget w;
    String callback_name;
```

Arguments

w   Specifies the widget whose callbacks are to be deleted.

callback_name Specifies the callback list to be removed.

Description

XtRemoveAllCallbacks removes all the widget's callback procedures identified by callback_name, regardless of the value of its client_data. This is in contrast to XtRemoveCallback and XtRemoveCallbacks, which remove the specified callback only if a specified client_data argument also matches.

Calling any of these routines implicitly frees all storage associated with the Intrinsics' internal representation of the callback list.

See Also

Section 1.3, "Application Interface,"
XtAddCallbacks, XtCallCallbacks, XtRemoveCallback, XtRemove-Callbacks.

XtRemoveCallback

Name

XtRemoveCallback — delete a procedure from a callback list.

Synopsis

```
void XtRemoveCallback(w, callback_name, callback, client_data)
    Widget w;
    String callback_name;
    XtCallbackProc callback;
    caddr_t client_data;
```

Arguments

w   Specifies the widget.

callback_name
         Specifies the callback list from which the procedure is to be deleted.

callback   Specifies the callback procedure which is to be deleted.

client_data Specifies the client data to match on the registered callback procedure.

Description

XtRemoveCallback removes a callback procedure identified by callback_name.

The procedure is removed only if both the procedure callback and client_data match a callback on the list. No warning message is generated if a procedure to be removed fails to match a callback on the list. Use XtRemoveAllCallbacks if you want to remove a particular callback regardless of the value of its client_data.

See Also

Section 1.3, "Application Interface."

XtAddCallbacks, XtCallCallbacks, XtRemoveAllCallbacks, XtRemove-
Callbacks.

XtRemoveCallbacks

Name

XtRemoveCallbacks — delete a list of procedures from a callback list.

Synopsis

```
void XtRemoveCallbacks(w, callback_name, callbacks)
    Widget w;
    String callback_name;
    XtCallbackList callbacks;
```

Arguments

w   Specifies the widget.

callback_name
                    Specifies the callback list from which the procedure is to be deleted.

callbacks   Specifies the NULL-terminated list of callback procedures and corresponding
                    client data to be deleted.

Description

XtRemoveCallbacks removes a list of procedures from the callback list identified by the
resource callback_name.

The procedure is removed only if both the procedure callback and client_data match a
callback on the list. No warning message is generated if a procedure to be removed fails to
match a callback on the list. Use XtRemoveAllCallbacks if you want to remove a particular callback regardless of the value of its client_data.

Structures

```
typedef struct _XtCallbackRec* XtCallbackList;
```

See Also

Section 1.3, "Application Interface,"
XtAddCallbacks, XtCallCallbacks, XtRemoveAllCallbacks, XtRemove-
Callback.

XtRemoveEventHandler

Name

XtRemoveEventHandler — remove a previously registered event handler.

Synopsis

```
void XtRemoveEventHandler(w, event_mask, nonmaskable, proc,
        client_data)
    Widget w;
    EventMask event_mask;
    Boolean nonmaskable;
    XtEventHandler proc;
    caddr_t client_data;
```

Arguments

w	Specifies the widget for which this handler is registered.
event_mask	Specifies the events for which to unregister this handler.
nonmaskable	Specifies a Boolean value that indicates whether this handler should be unregistered for nonmaskable events (GraphicsExpose, NoExpose, SelectionClear, SelectionRequest, SelectionNotify, ClientMessage, and MappingNotify).
proc	Specifies the handler procedure to be removed.
client_data	Specifies the client data to match on the registered handler.

Description

XtRemoveEventHandler stops the specified procedure from receiving any more of the specified events.

A handler is removed only if both the procedure proc and client_data match a previously registered handler. If a handler to be removed fails to match a procedure, or if it has been registered with a different value of client_data, XtRemoveEventHandler returns without reporting an error.

If the widget is realized, XtRemoveEventHandler calls XSelectInput, if necessary, to prevent the client from receiving further events of that type.

To keep a procedure from receiving *any* events, and to remove it from the widget's event_table entirely, call XtRemoveEventHandler with an event_mask of XtAll-Events with nonmaskable TRUE, and the client_data registered in a previous call to Xt-AddEventHandler.

Structures

The event_mask is formed by combining the event mask symbols listed in the first column of the table below using the bitwise OR operator (|). Each mask symbol sets a bit in the event_mask.

The table also describes briefly the circumstances under which you would want to specify each symbol.

Event Mask Symbol	Circumstances
NoEventMask	No events
KeyPressMask	Keyboard down events
KeyReleaseMask	Keyboard up events
ButtonPressMask	Pointer button down events
ButtonReleaseMask	Pointer button up events
EnterWindowMask	Pointer window entry events
LeaveWindowMask	Pointer window leave events
PointerMotionMask	All pointer motion events
PointerMotionHintMask	Fewer pointer motion events
Button1MotionMask	Pointer motion while button 1 down
Button2MotionMask	Pointer motion while button 2 down
Button3MotionMask	Pointer motion while button 3 down
Button4MotionMask	Pointer motion while button 4 down
Button5MotionMask	Pointer motion while button 5 down
ButtonMotionMask	Pointer motion while any button down
KeymapStateMask	Any keyboard state change on EnterNotify, LeaveNotify, FocusIn or FocusOut
ExposureMask	Any exposure (except GraphicsExpose and NoExpose)
VisibilityChangeMask	Any change in visibility
StructureNotifyMask	Any change in window configuration.
ResizeRedirectMask	Redirect resize of this window
SubstructureNotifyMask	Notify about reconfiguration of children
SubstructureRedirectMask	Redirect reconfiguration of children
FocusChangeMask	Any change in keyboard focus
PropertyChangeMask	Any change in property
ColormapChangeMask	Any change in colormap
OwnerGrabButtonMask	Modifies handling of pointer events

See Also

Section 1.4, "Events,"
XtAddEventHandler, XtRemoveRawEventHandler,
XtEventHandler(2).

XtRemoveGrab

Name
XtRemoveGrab — redirect user input from modal widget back to normal destination.

Synopsis
```
void XtRemoveGrab(w)
    Widget w;
```

Arguments
w   Specifies the widget to remove from the modal cascade. XtRemoveGrab does not terminate a grab requested through the server; it simply changes Xt's event dispatching.

Description
XtRemoveGrab removes widgets from the *modal cascade* (a set of widgets that lock out user input to the application except through themselves). It issues an error if the specified widget was not in the modal cascade.

The modal cascade is a data structure used by XtDispatchEvent when it tries to dispatch a user event. It is a list of widgets which have issued a request, from the Intrinsics, for events that would ordinarily be outside their jurisdiction.

When the modal cascade is not empty, XtDispatchEvent delivers the event to the most recent modal cascade entry, with the exclusive parameter TRUE.

XtPopup uses XtAddGrab and XtRemoveGrab to constrain user events to a modal cascade. It is unusual to call XtAddGrab or XtRemoveGrab explicitly.

See Also
XtAddGrab, XtDispatchEvent, XtPopup.

XtRemoveInput

Name

XtRemoveInput — cancel source of alternate input events.

Synopsis

```
void XtRemoveInput(id)
    XtInputId id;
```

Arguments

id   Specifies the ID returned from the corresponding XtAddInput call.

Description

XtRemoveInput causes the Intrinsics to stop watching for events from an alternate input source registered with XtAddInput. Alternate input events are usually operating system reads, but they can be any I/O operation supported by the operating system.

For more general discussion of alternate input events, see Chapter 13, *Miscellaneous Toolkit Programming Techniques*, in Volume Four, *X Toolkit Intrinsics Programming Manual*.

See Also

XtAddInput, XtAppAddInput.

XtRemoveRawEventHandler

Name

XtRemoveRawEventHandler — remove a raw event handler.

Synopsis

```
void XtRemoveRawEventHandler(w, event_mask, nonmaskable, proc,
        client_data)
    Widget w;
    EventMask event_mask;
    Boolean nonmaskable;
    XtEventHandler proc;
    caddr_t client_data;
```

Arguments

w   Specifies the widget for which this handler is registered.

event_mask   Specifies the events for which to unregister this handler.

nonmaskable Specifies a Boolean value that indicates whether this procedure should be unregistered for the nonmaskable events (GraphicsExpose, NoExpose, SelectionClear, SelectionRequest, SelectionNotify, ClientMessage, and MappingNotify).

proc   Specifies the procedure to be registered.

client_data Specifies the client data to match on the registered event handler.

Description

XtRemoveRawEventHandler stops the specified procedure from receiving any more of the specified events.

A handler is removed only if both the procedure proc and client_data match a previously registered handler. If a handler to be removed fails to match a procedure, or if it has been registered with a different value of client_data, XtRemoveEventHandler returns without reporting an error.

Because the procedure is a raw event handler, it does not affect the widget's mask and never calls the Xlib XSelectInput function.

Structures

The event_mask is formed by combining the event mask symbols listed in the first column of the table below using the bitwise OR operator (|). Each mask symbol sets a bit in the event_mask.

The table also describes briefly the circumstances under which you would want to specify each symbol.

Event Mask Symbol	Circumstances
NoEventMask	No events
KeyPressMask	Keyboard down events
KeyReleaseMask	Keyboard up events
ButtonPressMask	Pointer button down events
ButtonReleaseMask	Pointer button up events
EnterWindowMask	Pointer window entry events
LeaveWindowMask	Pointer window leave events
PointerMotionMask	All pointer motion events
PointerMotionHintMask	Fewer pointer motion events
Button1MotionMask	Pointer motion while button 1 down
Button2MotionMask	Pointer motion while button 2 down
Button3MotionMask	Pointer motion while button 3 down
Button4MotionMask	Pointer motion while button 4 down
Button5MotionMask	Pointer motion while button 5 down
ButtonMotionMask	Pointer motion while any button down
KeymapStateMask	Any keyboard state change on EnterNotify, LeaveNotify, FocusIn or FocusOut
ExposureMask	Any exposure (except GraphicsExpose and NoExpose)
VisibilityChangeMask	Any change in visibility
StructureNotifyMask	Any change in window configuration.
ResizeRedirectMask	Redirect resize of this window
SubstructureNotifyMask	Notify about reconfiguration of children
SubstructureRedirectMask	Redirect reconfiguration of children
FocusChangeMask	Any change in keyboard focus
PropertyChangeMask	Any change in property
ColormapChangeMask	Any change in colormap
OwnerGrabButtonMask	Modifies handling of pointer events

See Also

Section 1.4, "Events,"
XtRemoveEventHandler.
XtEventHandler(2).

XtRemoveTimeOut

Name

XtRemoveTimeOut — clear a timeout value.

Synopsis

```
void XtRemoveTimeOut(id)
    XtIntervalId id;
```

Arguments

id   Specifies the ID for the timeout request to be destroyed.

Description

XtRemoveTimeOut removes the timeout specified by *id*. *id* is the value returned by either XtAppAddTimeOut or XtAddTimeOut.

Note that timeouts are automatically removed once they expire and the callback has been delivered.

See Also

Section 1.4, "Events,"
XtAddTimeOut, XtAppAddTimeOut.

XtRemoveWorkProc

Name

XtRemoveWorkProc — remove a work procedure.

Synopsis

```
void XtRemoveWorkProc (id)
    XtWorkProcId id,
```

Arguments

id   Specifies which work procedure to remove

Description

XtRemoveWorkProc explicitly removes the specified background work procedure. The Xt-WorkProcId is returned from a corresponding XtAddWorkProc call.

An XtWorkProc is removed automatically once it returns TRUE.

See Also

XtAddWorkProc, XtAppAddWorkProc,
XtWorkProc(2).

XtResizeWidget

Name

XtResizeWidget — resize a child or sibling widget.

Synopsis

```
void XtResizeWidget(w, width, height, border_width)
    Widget w;
    Dimension width;
    Dimension height;
    Dimension border_width;
```

Arguments

w   Specifies the widget to be resized.

width, height, border_width
          Specify the new widget size and border width.

Description

XtResizeWidget is customarily used by a parent to resize widgets that are its children. It can also be used on siblings.

XtResizeWidget returns immediately if the specified geometry fields are the same as the old values. Otherwise, XtResizeWidget writes the new width, height, and border_width values into the widget and, if the widget is realized, issues an Xlib XConfigureWindow call on the widget's window.

XtResizeWidget calls the widget's resize procedure to notify it of the size change.

Note that once a widget is resized or otherwise reconfigured by its parent, it may need to do additional processing in its own resize procedure. Widgets usually need to know when they have changed size so that they can lay out their displayed data again to match the new size. When a parent resizes a child, it calls XtResizeWidget, which updates the geometry fields in the widget, configures the window if the widget is realized, and calls the child's resize procedure to notify the child. The resize procedure pointer is of type XtWidgetProc.

If a class need not recalculate anything when a widget is resized, it can specify NULL for the resize field in its class record. This is an unusual case and should occur only for widgets with very trivial display semantics. The resize procedure takes a widget as its only argument.

See Also

Section 1.8, "Geometry Management,"
XtConfigureWidget, XtMakeGeometryRequest, XtResizeWindow.

XtResizeWindow

Name

XtResizeWindow — resize a widget according to the values of its core dimensions.

Synopsis

```
void XtResizeWindow(w)
    Widget w;
```

Arguments

w   Specifies the widget.

Description

XtResizeWindow calls the XConfigureWindow Xlib function to make the window of the specified widget match its Core $width$, $height$, and $border\_width$.

The call to XConfigureWindow is done unconditionally because there is no way to tell if these values match the current values

XtResizeWindow does not cause the widget's resize method to be called

There are very few occasions when you need to use XtResizeWindow; it is more diplomatic to use XtResizeWidget.

See Also

Section 1.8, "Geometry Management,"
XtResizeWidget.

XtScreen

Name

XtScreen — return the screen pointer for the specified widget.

Synopsis

```
Screen *XtScreen(w)
    Widget w;
```

Arguments

w   Specifies the widget.

Description

XtScreen returns a pointer to the screen the specified widget is on.

See Also

XtDisplay

XtSetArg

Name

XtSetArg — construct or modify an argument list dynamically.

Synopsis

```
void XtSetArg(arg, resource_name, value)
    Arg arg;
    String resource_name;
    XtArgVal value;
```

Arguments

arg   Specifies the argument to set.

resource_name
         Specifies the name of the resource .

value   Specifies the value of the resource, or else its address   (If the size of the resource is less than or equal to the size of an XtArgVal, the resource value is stored directly in value; otherwise, a pointer to it is stored in value.)

Description

Many Intrinsics functions need to be passed pairs of resource names and values   These are passed as an ArgList (see the Structures section below) To dynamically change values in an existing ArgList, use XtSetArg.

XtSetArg sets the value of the arg structure. Arg structures are passed to widgets and resource routines setting or overriding resource values.

Note that XtSetArg is a macro. Expressions involving autoincrement and autodecrement operations are unsafe in its argument list, since XtSetArg evaluates its first argument twice

XtSetArg is usually used in a highly stylized manner to minimize the probability of making a mistake; for example:

```
Arg args[20];
int n;

n = 0;
XtSetArg(args[n], XtNheight, 100),      n++;
XtSetArg(args[n], XtNwidth, 200);       n++;
XtSetValues(widget, args, n);
```

Volume Four, *X Toolkit Intrinsics Programming Manual*, presents several examples using Args, setting them both with values initialized at compile time and using XtSetArg.

Structures

Arg is defined as follows in <*X11/Intrinsic h*>:

```
typedef struct {
    String name;
    XtArgVal value;
} Arg, *ArgList,
```

The definition of XtArgVal differs depending on architecture—its purpose is precisely to make code portable between architectures with different byte sizes.

The macro itself, from the same file, is listed below:

```
#define XtSetArg(arg, n, d)  ( (arg) .name = (n), (arg) .value = (XtArgVal) (d) )
```

See Also
Section 1.7, "Resources,"
XtMergeArgLists, XtNumber.

XtSetErrorHandler

Name

XtSetErrorHandler — register a procedure to be called on fatal error conditions.

Synopsis

```
void XtSetErrorHandler(handler)
    XtErrorHandler handler;
```

Arguments

handler   Specifies the new low-level fatal error procedure, which should not return.

Description

The Intrinsics let a client register procedures that are to be called whenever a fatal or nonfatal error occurs. These facilities are intended for both error reporting and logging and for error correction or recovery.

Two levels of interface are provided:

* A high-level interface that takes an error name and class and looks the error up in an error resource database. The high-level fatal error handler is invoked by a call to XtErrorMsg or XtAppErrorMsg; the high-level nonfatal error handler is invoked by a call to XtWarningMsg or XtAppWarningMsg. A new handler can be registered by calling XtSetErrorMsgHandler or XtSetWarningMsgHandler.

* A low-level interface that takes a simple string, which is printed out as the error message. The low-level fatal error handler is invoked by a call to XtError or XtAppError; the low-level nonfatal error handler is invoked by a call to XtWarning or XtAppWarning. A new handler can be registered by calling XtSetErrorHandler or XtSetWarningHandler.

The high-level functions construct a string to pass to the lower-level interface. On UNIX-based systems, the error database is usually /usr/lib/X11/XtErrorDB.

To obtain the error database (for example, to merge with an application or widget-specific database), use XtAppGetErrorDatabase.

Application-context-specific error handling is not implemented on many systems. Most implementations will have just one set of error handlers. If they are set for different application contexts, the one performed last will prevail.

The default low-level fatal error handler provided by the Intrinsics is _XtError. On UNIX-based systems, it prints the message to standard error and terminates the application. Using XtSetErrorHandler, you can replace this default error handler with one of your own.

Fatal error message handlers should not return. If one does, subsequent Toolkit behavior is indeterminate. See XtSetErrorHandler(2) for more details.

See Also

XtSetErrorMsgHandler, XtSetWarningHandler,
XtErrorHandler(2).

XtSetErrorMsgHandler

Name

XtSetErrorMsgHandler — register a procedure to be called on nonfatal error conditions.

Synopsis

```
void XtSetErrorMsgHandler(msg_handler)
    XtErrorMsgHandler msg_handler;
```

Arguments

msg_handler Specifies the new high-level fatal error procedure, which should not return.

Description

The Intrinsics let a client register procedures that are to be called whenever a fatal or nonfatal error occurs. These facilities are intended for both error reporting and logging and for error correction or recovery.

Two levels of interface are provided:

* A high-level interface that takes an error name and class and looks the error up in an error resource database. The high-level fatal error handler is invoked by a call to Xt-ErrorMsg or XtAppErrorMsg; the high-level nonfatal error handler is invoked by a call to XtWarningMsg or XtAppWarningMsg. A new handler can be registered by calling XtSetErrorMsgHandler or XtSetWarningMsgHandler.

* A low-level interface that takes a simple string, which is printed out as the error message. The low-level fatal error handler is invoked by a call to XtError or XtAppError; the low-level nonfatal error handler is invoked by a call to XtWarning or XtApp-Warning. A new handler can be registered by calling XtSetErrorHandler or Xt-SetWarningHandler.

The high-level functions construct a string to pass to the lower level interface. On UNIX-based systems, the error database is usually */usr/lib/X11/XtErrorDB*.

To obtain the error database (for example, to merge with an application or widget-specific database), use XtAppGetErrorDatabase.

Application-context-specific error handling is not implemented on many systems. Most implementations will have just one set of error handlers. If they are set for different application contexts, the one performed last will prevail.

The default error handler provided by the Intrinsics constructs a string from the error resource database and calls XtError. Using XtSetErrorMsgHandler, you can replace this with your own handler.

See Also

XtSetErrorHandler, XtSetWarningMsgHandler,
XtErrorMsgHandler(2).

XtSetKeyboardFocus

Name

XtSetKeyboardFocus — redirect keyboard input to a child widget.

Synopsis

```
void XtSetKeyboardFocus(subtree, descendant)
    Widget subtree, descendant;
```

Arguments

subtree   Specifies the widget to be considered the root of the subtree for which the
           keyboard focus is to be set. (For example, a composite widget that is turning
           over all keyboard input to one of its children)

descendant Specifies either the widget in the subtree structure which is to receive the
           keyboard event, or NULL. Note that it is not an error to specify NULL when no
           input focus was previously set.

Description

XtSetKeyboardFocus directs subsequent keyboard events that occur within *subtree* or
one of its descendants to one specified *descendant* widget. (This routine can be used
instead of calling the Xlib XSetInputFocus routine) *subtree* presumably specifies a
composite widget that is turning over all the keyboard input to one of its children.

If a future KeyPress or KeyRelease event occurs within the specified subtree (i e , in the
subtree widget or one of its descendants), XtSetKeyboardFocus causes Xt-
DispatchEvent to remap and send the event to the specified *descendant* widget.

When there is no modal cascade, keyboard events can occur within a widget *W* in one of three
ways:

* *W* has the X keyboard focus

* *W* has the keyboard focus of one of its ancestors, and the event occurs within the ancestor
  or one of the ancestor's descendants.

* No ancestor of *W* has a descendant within the keyboard focus, and the pointer is within
  W.

When there is a modal cascade (see XtAddGrab), a widget *W* receives keyboard events if an
ancestor of *W* is in the active subset of the modal cascade and one or more of the previous conditions is TRUE.

When *subtree* or one of its *descendants* acquires the X keyboard focus, or the pointer
moves into the subtree such that keyboard events would now be delivered to *subtree*, a
FocusIn event is generated for *descendant* if FocusNotify events have been selected
by *descendant*. Similarly, when *W* loses the X keyboard focus or the keyboard focus for one
of its ancestors, a FocusOut event is generated for *descendant* if FocusNotify events
have been selected by *descendant*.

Note that every widget exports an accept_focus procedure to allow outside agents to cause
a widget to get the keyboard focus. To call a widget's accept_focus procedure, use Xt-
CallAcceptFocus The widget returns whether it actually took the focus or not, so that the

parent can give the focus to another widget. Widgets that need to know when they lose the keyboard focus must use the Xlib focus notification mechanism explicitly (typically by specifying translations for FocusIn and FocusOut events). Widgets that need the keyboard focus can call XSetInputFocus explicitly. Widgets that never want the keyboard focus should set their accept_focus procedure pointer to NULL.

See Also

XtAcceptFocusProc, XtAddGrab, XtCallAcceptFocus, XtDispatchEvent, Composite(3).

Name
XtSetKeyTranslator — register a key translator.

Synopsis
```
void XtSetKeyTranslator(display, proc)
    Display *display;
    XtKeyProc proc;
```

Arguments
display   Specifies the display from which to translate the events.

proc   Specifies the procedure that is to perform key translations.

Description
XtSetKeyTranslator registers the specified procedure as the current key translator. The default translator is XtTranslateKey, an XtKeyProc that uses Shift and Lock modifiers with the interpretations defined by the X11 protocol. XtSetKeyTranslator is provided so that new translators can call it to get default keycode-to-keysym translations and so that the default translator can be reinstalled.

The only way to remove a converter is to register a new one. For example, the default key translator (XtTranslateKey) can be explicitly reinstalled. Another approach to deleting a converter would be for an application to register an *identity* converter that simply copied the input keysym to both output keysyms.

For a more detailed discussion of processing keyboard input, see Volume Four, *X Toolkit Intrinsics Programming Manual*.

See Also
XtRegisterCaseConverter, XtTranslateKeycode,
XtTranslateKey, XtKeyProc(2).

XtSetMappedWhenManaged

Name

XtSetMappedWhenManaged — change the value of a widget's map_when_managed field.

Synopsis

```
void XtSetMappedWhenManaged(w, map_when_managed)
    Widget w;
    Boolean map_when_managed;
```

Arguments

w   Specifies the widget.

map_when_managed

                  Specifies a Boolean value that indicates the new value of the map_
                  when_managed field.

Description

After a widget is realized, it must be mapped before it can become visible. XtSetMapped-
WhenManaged controls whether this mapping occurs automatically or not.

If the widget is realized and managed and if the new value of map_when_managed is TRUE,
XtSetMappedWhenManaged maps the window. If the widget is realized and managed and
if the new value of map_when_managed is FALSE, it unmaps the window.

XtSetMappedWhenManaged is a convenience function that is equivalent to (but slightly
faster than) calling XtSetValues and setting the new value for the MappedWhenManaged
resource. As an alternative to using XtSetMappedWhenManaged to control mapping, a client may set mapped_when_managed to FALSE and use XtMapWidget and XtUnmap-
Widget explicitly.

A widget is normally mapped if it is managed. However, this behavior can be overridden by
setting the Core XtNmappedWhenManaged resource for the widget when it is created or by
setting the map_when_managed field to FALSE.

The mapped_when_managed field can be altered in several ways. A widget can control
whether it is mapped when managed by setting its core map_when_managed field. This
field, normally TRUE, can be set to FALSE explicitly. At the application level, the
mapped_when_managed attribute can be disabled by setting the XtNmappedWhen-
Managed resource to false in the argument list specified at widget creation time.

See Also

Section 1.1, "Widget Lifecycle,"
XtCreateManagedWidget, XtManageChildren, XtMapWidget, XtSetValues,
XtUnmapWidget.

XtSetSelectionTimeout

Name

XtSetSelectionTimeout — set value of selection timeout.

Synopsis

```
void XtSetSelectionTimeout(timeout)
    unsigned long timeout;
```

Arguments

timeout   Specifies the selection timeout in milliseconds.

Description

timeout is the time within which the two communicating applications must respond to one another. If one of them does not respond within this interval, Xt aborts the selection request. The default value of *timeout* is 5000 milliseconds (five seconds).

Chapter 10, *Inter-Client Communications*, in Volume Four, *X Toolkit Intrinsics Programming Manual*, presents a complete example widget that both sends and receives data using selections.

See Also

XtGetSelectionTimeout

Name

XtSetSensitive — set the sensitivity state of a widget.

Synopsis

```
void XtSetSensitive(w, sensitive)
    Widget w;
    Boolean sensitive;
```

Arguments

w   Specifies the widget.

sensitive   Specifies a Boolean value that indicates whether the widget should receive
                keyboard and pointer events.

Description

Many widgets have a mode in which they assume a different appearance (for example, grayed out or stippled), do not respond to user events, and become dormant.

When dormant, a widget is *insensitive*. This means the Event Manager does not dispatch any events to the widget with an event type of KeyPress, KeyRelease, ButtonPress, ButtonRelease, MotionNotify, EnterNotify, LeaveNotify, FocusIn, or FocusOut.

Widget sensitivity is controlled by the sensitive and ancestor_sensitive fields in the Core class record. A widget can be insensitive because its sensitive field is FALSE or because one of its ancestors is insensitive; therefore, the widget's ancestor_sensitive field is also FALSE (sensitive is always set to FALSE if ancestor_sensitive is FALSE). A widget can, but does not need to, distinguish these two cases visually.

XtSetSensitive first calls XtSetValues on the current widget with an argument list specifying that the sensitive field should change to the new value. It then recursively propagates the new value down the managed children tree by calling XtSetValues on each child to set ancestor_sensitive to the new value if the new values for *sensitive* and the child's ancestor_sensitive are not the same.

XtSetSensitive calls XtSetValues to change the sensitive and ancestor_sensitive fields in Core. Therefore, when one of these changes, the widget's set_values procedure should take whatever display actions are needed (for example, graying or stippling the widget).

XtSetSensitive ensures that if a parent has either sensitive or ancestor_sensitive set to FALSE, then all children have ancestor_sensitive set to FALSE.

Both *sensitive* and the ancestor_sensitive field are maintained as Booleans in the Core instance record, defined in <*X11/CoreP.h*>.

See Also

XtGetValues, XtIsSensitive, XtSetValues.

Name

XtSetSubvalues — copy from ArgList to base-offset resource list.

Synopsis

```
void XtSetSubvalues(base, resources, num_resources, args,
        num_args)
    caddr_t base;
    XtResourceList resources;
    Cardinal num_resources;
    ArgList args,
    Cardinal num_args;
```

Arguments

base   Specifies the base address to which the resources should be written.

resources   Specifies the current nonwidget resources values

num_resources
     Specifies the number of resources in the resource list

args   Specifies the argument list of name/value pairs that contain the resources to be modified The resources and values passed are dependent on the subpart of the widget being modified

num_args   Specifies the number of arguments in the argument list.

Description

XtSetSubvalues stores resources into the structure identified by base In particular, Xt-SetSubvalues writes the values of args into resources. The location of the resources to write are determined from the resources array and the base address.

This is used for explicitly writing resource data in entities that are not widgets.

The conjugate function XtGetSubvalues gets a widget's values

Structures

A Resource is defined as follows in <X11/Instrinsic h>

```
typedef struct _XtResource {
    String    resource_name;   /* Resource name */
    String    resource_class,  /* Resource class */
    String    resource_type;   /* Representation type desired */
    Cardinal resource_size,   /* Size in bytes of representation */
    Cardinal resource_offset;/* Offset from base to put resource value */
    String    default_type;    /* Representation type of specified default */
    caddr_t  default_addr,    /* Address of resource default value */
} XtResource, XtResourceList;
```

Arg is defined as follows in *<X11/Intrinsic.h>*:

```
typedef struct {
    String name;
    XtArgVal value;
} Arg, *ArgList;
```

See Also

Section 1.7, "Resources,"
XtSetArg,
XtArgsFunc (2).

XtSetValues

Name

XtSetValues — copy resources from ArgList to widget.

Synopsis

```
void XtSetValues(w, args, num_args)
    Widget w;
    ArgList args;
    Cardinal num_args;
```

Arguments

w   Specifies the widget whose values are to be written and their new values.

args   Specifies the argument list of name/value pairs that contain the resources to be modified. The resources and values passed are dependent on the widget being modified.

num_args   Specifies the number of arguments in the argument list

Description

XtSetValues modifies the current state of resources associated with a widget instance. (Actually, the widget decides what changes it will actually allow and updates all derived fields appropriately.)

The name fields in args contain the names of resources. The value fields in args contain the new values of resources.

XtSetValues starts with the resources specified for the Core widget fields and descends the subclass chain to the widget. At each stage, it writes the new value (if specified by one of the arguments) or the existing value (if no new value is specified) to a new widget data record. XtSetValues then calls the set_values methods for the widget in superclass-to-subclass order. If the widget has any non-NULL set_values_hook fields, these methods are called immediately after the corresponding set_values method. This permits access to nonwidget resource data from XtSetValues

If the widget's parent is a subclass of constraintWidgetClass, XtSetValues also updates the widget's constraints. It starts with the constraint resources specified for constraintWidgetClass and proceeds down the subclass chain to the parent's class At each stage, it writes the new value or the existing value to a new constraint record. It then calls the constraint set_values methods from constraintWidgetClass down to the parent's class. The constraint set_values methods are called with widget arguments, as for all set_values methods, not just the constraint record arguments, so that they can make adjustments to the desired values based on full information about the widget.

XtSetValues determines if a geometry request is needed by comparing the current widget to the new widget. If any geometry changes are required, it makes the request, and the geometry manager returns XtGeometryYes, XtGeometryAlmost, or XtGeometryNo. If XtGeometryYes is returned, XtSetValues calls the widget's resize method. If XtGeometryNo is returned, XtSetValues resets the geometry fields to their original values. If XtGeometryAlmost is returned, XtSetValues calls the set_values_almost method, which determines what should be done and writes new values for the geometry fields into the new widget. XtSetValues then repeats this process, deciding once more whether the geometry manager should be called.

Finally, if any of the set_values methods returned TRUE, XtSetValues causes the widget's expose procedure to be invoked by calling the Xlib XClearArea function on the widget's window.

The conjugate function XtGetValues retrieves a widget's values.

Structures

Arg is defined as follows in *<X11/Intrinsic.h>*:

```
typedef struct {
    String name;
    XtArgVal value;
} Arg, *ArgList;
```

See Also

Section 1.7, "Resources,"
XtSetArg,
XtArgsFunc(2).

XtSetWarningHandler

Name
XtSetWarningHandler — register a procedure to be called on nonfatal error conditions.

Synopsis
```
void XtSetWarningHandler(handler)
    XtErrorHandler handler;
```

Arguments
handler   Specifies the new low-level nonfatal error procedure, which usually returns

Description
The Intrinsics let a client register procedures that are to be called whenever a fatal or nonfatal error occurs. These facilities are intended for both error reporting and logging and for error correction or recovery.

Two levels of interface are provided:

- A high-level interface that takes an error name and class and looks the error up in an error resource database The high-level fatal error handler is invoked by a call to XtErrorMsg or XtAppErrorMsg, the high-level nonfatal error handler is invoked by a call to XtWarningMsg or XtAppWarningMsg. A new handler can be registered by calling XtSetErrorMsgHandler or XtSetWarningMsgHandler.

- A low-level interface that takes a simple string, which is printed out as the error message The low-level fatal error handler is invoked by a call to XtError or XtAppError, the low-level nonfatal error handler is invoked by a call to XtWarning or XtAppWarning. A new handler can be registered by calling XtSetErrorHandler or XtSetWarningHandler.

The high-level functions construct a string to pass to the lower-level interface On UNIX-based systems, the error database is usually */usr/lib/X11/XtErrorDB*.

To obtain the error database (for example, to merge with an application or widget-specific database), use XtAppGetErrorDatabase.

Application-context-specific error handling is not implemented on many systems. Most implementations will have just one set of error handlers. If they are set for different application contexts, the one performed last will prevail.

The default warning handler provided by the Intrinsics is _XtWarning. On UNIX-based systems, it prints the message to standard error and returns to the caller Using XtSetWarningHandler, you can replace this handler with one of your own

Warning message handlers should return If an error is non-recoverable, an application should generate a fatal error.

See Also
XtErrorMsgHandler, XtSetErrorHandler, XtSetWarningMsgHandler, XtWarning,
XtWarningHandler(2).

XtSetWarningMsgHandler

Name

XtSetWarningMsgHandler — register a high-level procedure to be called on nonfatal error conditions.

Synopsis

```
void XtSetWarningMsgHandler(msg_handler)
    XtErrorMsgHandler msg_handler;
```

Arguments

msg_handler   Specifies the new high-level nonfatal error procedure, which usually returns.

Description

The Intrinsics let a client register procedures that are to be called whenever a fatal or nonfatal error occurs. These facilities are intended for both error reporting and logging and for error correction or recovery.

Two levels of interface are provided:

- A high-level interface that takes an error name and class and looks the error up in an error resource database. The high-level fatal error handler is invoked by a call to XtErrorMsg or XtAppErrorMsg; the high-level nonfatal error handler is invoked by a call to XtWarningMsg or XtAppWarningMsg. A new handler can be registered by calling XtSetErrorMsgHandler or XtSetWarningMsgHandler.

- A low-level interface that takes a simple string, which is printed out as the error message. The low-level fatal error handler is invoked by a call to XtError or XtAppError; the low-level nonfatal error handler is invoked by a call to XtWarning or XtAppWarning. A new handler can be registered by calling XtSetErrorHandler or XtSetWarningHandler.

The high-level functions construct a string to pass to the lower-level interface. On UNIX-based systems, the error database is usually */usr/lib/X11/XtErrorDB*.

To obtain the error database (for example, to merge with an application or widget-specific database), use XtAppGetErrorDatabase.

Application-context-specific error handling is not implemented on many systems. Most implementations will have just one set of error handlers. If they are set for different application contexts, the one performed last will prevail.

The default warning handler provided by the Intrinsics constructs a string from the error resource database and calls XtWarning. Using XtSetWarningMsgHandler, you can replace this default handler with one of your own.

See Also

XtSetErrorHandler, XtSetErrorMsgHandler, XtSetWarningHandler, XtWarningMsg,
XtWarningMsgHandler(2).

Name

XtStringConversionWarning — emit boilerplate string conversion error message.

Synopsis

```
void XtStringConversionWarning(src, dst_type)
    String src, dst_type;
```

Arguments

src   Specifies the string that could not be converted.

dst_type   Specifies the name of the type to which the string could not be converted.

Description

XtStringConversionWarning is a convenience routine for use in new resource converters that convert from strings. It issues a warning message with the name conversionError, type string, class XtToolkitError, and default message string

"Cannot convert *src* to type *dst_type*"

It can be used by a conversion routine to announce a nonfatal conversion error.

See Also

XtWarning, XtWarningMsgHandler.

XtSuperclass

Name

XtSuperclass — obtain a widget's superclass.

Synopsis

```
WidgetClass XtSuperclass(w)
     Widget w;
```

Arguments

w   Specifies the widget whose superclass is to be checked.

Description

XtSuperclass returns a pointer to the class structure of the widget's superclass.

See Also

XtCheckSubclass, XtClass, XtIsSubclass,
Core(3).

XtToolkitInitialize

Name
XtToolkitInitialize — initialize the X Toolkit internals.

Synopsis
```
void XtToolkitInitialize()
```

Description
XtToolkitInitialize initializes internal Toolkit data structures. It does not set up an application context or open a display.

XtInitialize calls XtToolkitInitialize in the course of its initialization. Programs too sophisticated to use XtInitialize (such as those that create multiple application contexts) need to call XtToolkitInitialize explicitly.

The semantics of calling XtToolkitInitialize more than once are undefined

See Also
Section 1.1, "Widget Lifecycle,"
XtInitialize

XtTranslateCoords

Name

XtTranslateCoords — translate an x-y coordinate pair from widget coordinates to root coordinates.

Synopsis

```
void XtTranslateCoords(w, x, y, rootx_return, rooty_return)
    Widget w;
    Position x, y;
    Position *rootx_return, *rooty_return;
```

Arguments

w   Specifies the widget.

x, y   Specify the widget-relative x and y coordinates.

rootx_return, rooty_return
           Return the root-relative x and y coordinates.

Description

XtTranslateCoords converts widget-relative coordinates to display-relative coordinates. This is useful in moving and resizing widgets, since those routines work with display-relative coordinates.

The display height and width can be obtained in pixels with the Xlib macros XDisplay-Height and XDisplayWidth, and in millimeters with the Xlib macros XDisplay-HeightMM and XDisplayWidthMM.

These macros require a display and screen, which can be returned by Intrinsics functions. An example might be:

```
height = XDisplayHeight(XtDisplay(w), XtScreen(w));
```

XtTranslateCoords is similar to the Xlib XTranslateCoordinates function, which also translates window-relative coordinates to display-relative coordinates. But Xt-TranslateCoords does not generate a server request because the required information is already in the widget's data structures.

Availability

As of Release 3, the Intrinsics define Position as short rather than as int. This saves space in widget instance records, but may break Release 2 programs that pass pointers to ints.

See Also

Core(3)

XtTranslateKey

Name

XtTranslateKey — invoke the currently registered keycode-to-keysym translator.

Synopsis

```
void XtTranslateKey(display, keycode, modifiers,
        modifiers_return, keysym_return)
    Display *display;
    KeyCode keycode;
    Modifiers modifiers;
    Modifiers *modifiers_return;
    KeySym *keysym_return;
```

Arguments

display	Specifies the display that the keycode is from
keycode	Specifies the keycode to translate
modifiers	Specifies the modifiers to be applied to the keycode

modifiers_return

Returns a mask that indicates the modifiers actually used to generate the keysym (an AND of modifiers and any default modifiers applied by the currently registered translator)

keysym_return

Returns the resulting keysym.

Description

XtTranslateKey is the default XtKeyProc. It takes a keycode and returns the corresponding KeySym, recognizing Shift and Lock modifiers. It is provided so that new translators with more expanded functionality can call it to get default KeyCode-to-KeySym translations in addition to whatever they add, and so that the default translation can be reinstalled.

The default key translator can be invoked directly by calling XtTranslateKeyCode. A new translator can be registered by calling XtSetKeyTranslator. There is no way to remove a translator; to reinstall the default behavior, call XtSetKeyTranslator with XtTranslateKey as the proc argument.

Structures

```
typedef unsigned int Modifiers;
```

Modifiers will be made up of the bitwise OR of the following masks

ShiftMask	Shift key was depressed
LockMask	Caps Lock key was depressed.
ControlMask	Control key was depressed.

`Mod1Mask`	Key defined as Mod1 was depressed.
	.
	.
	.
`Mod5Mask`	Key defined as Mod5 was depressed.
`StandardMask`	(`ShiftMask | LockMask`).

See Also

`XtRegisterCaseConverter`, `XtSetKeyTranslator`,
`XtKeyProc`(2).

Name

XtTranslateKeycode — invoke the currently registered keycode-to-keysym translator.

Synopsis

```
void XtTranslateKeycode(display, keycode, modifiers, modifi-
        ers_return, keysym_return)
    Display *display;
    KeyCode keycode;
    Modifiers modifiers;
    Modifiers *modifiers_return;
    KeySym *keysym_return;
```

Arguments

display   Specifies the display that the keycode is from

keycode   Specifies the keycode to translate.

modifiers   Specifies the modifiers to be applied to the keycode

modifiers_return
Returns a mask that indicates the modifiers actually used to generate the keysym (an AND of modifiers and any default modifiers applied by the currently registered translator)

keysym_return
Returns the resulting keysym

Description

XtTranslateKeycode is used to invoke the currently registered keycode-to-keysym translator (XtTranslateKey by default). It passes its arguments directly to that converter. The translator is registered by a call to XtSetKeyTranslator.

A related keyboard example is presented in Chapter 13, *Miscellaneous Toolkit Programming Techniques*, in Volume Four, *X Toolkit Intrinsics Programming Manual*.

Structures

```
typedef unsigned int Modifiers;
```

Modifiers will be made up of the bitwise OR of the following masks:

ShiftMask   Shift key was depressed.

LockMask   Caps Lock key was depressed

ControlMask   Control key was depressed.

Mod1Mask   Key defined as Mod1 was depressed.

Mod5Mask	Key defined as Mod5 was depressed.
StandardMask	(ShiftMask | LockMask).

See Also

XtRegisterCaseConverter, XtSetKeyTranslator, XtTranslateKey, XtKeyProc(2).

XtUninstallTranslations

Name
XtUninstallTranslations — remove existing translations.

Synopsis
```
void XtUninstallTranslations(w)
    Widget w;
```

Arguments
w   Specifies the widget from which the translations are to be removed

Description
XtUninstallTranslations removes a widget's translation table. This might be useful to eliminate all of a widget's translations, perhaps for debugging or testing.

To replace a widget's translations completely and not just selectively overwrite some of them, use XtSetValues on the XtNtranslations resource and specify a compiled translation table as the value.

To merge new translations, but keep existing translations in case of conflict, use XtAugmentTranslations.

To completely remove existing translations, use XtUninstallTranslations.

See Also
Section 1.5, "Translations and Actions,"
XtAugmentTranslations, XtOverrideTranslations, XtParseTranslationTable, XtSetValues.

XtUnmanageChild

Name

XtUnmanageChild — remove a widget from its parent's managed list.

Synopsis

```
void XtUnmanageChild(w)
    Widget w;
```

Arguments

w   Specifies the child widget to be unmanaged.

Description

XtUnmanageChild constructs a widget list containing one element and calls Xt-UnmanageChildren.

Note that XtManageChild, XtManageChildren, XtUnmanageChild, and Xt-UnmanageChildren are low-level routines that are used by generic composite widget building routines. In addition, composite widgets can provide widget-specific, high-level convenience procedures to let applications create and manage children more easily.

See Also

Section 1.1, "Widget Lifecycle,"
XtDestroyWidget, XtIsManaged, XtManageChild, XtManageChildren, Xt-UnmanageChildren.

XtUnmanageChildren

Name
XtUnmanageChildren — remove a list of children from a parent widget's managed list.

Synopsis
```
void XtUnmanageChildren(children, num_children)
    WidgetList children;
    Cardinal num_children;
```

Arguments
children   Specifies a list of child widgets

num_children   Specifies the number of children.

Description
XtUnmanageChildren removes a list of widgets from a parent widget's geometry management list It performs the following:

- Issues an error if children do not all have the same parent or if the parent is not a subclass of compositeWidgetClass.

- Returns immediately if the common parent is being destroyed, otherwise, for each unique child on the list, XtUnmanageChildren performs the following:

  - Marks children viable if they are not being destroyed and are currently managed. For each viable child, if the child is realized, it makes it invisible by unmapping it.

  - If the parent is realized, it calls the change_managed routine of the widgets' parent.

XtUnmanageChildren does not destroy children. Removing widgets from a parent's managed set is often a temporary banishment—some time later, they may be managed again To destroy widgets entirely, see XtDestroyWidget.

Note that XtManageChild, XtManageChildren, XtUnmanageChild, and XtUnmanageChildren are low-level routines that are used by generic composite widget building routines In addition, composite widgets can provide widget-specific, high-level convenience procedures to let applications create and manage children more easily.

Structures
```
typedef widget *WidgetList;
```

See Also
Section 1 1, "Widget Lifecycle,"
XtDestroyWidget, XtIsManaged, XtManageChild, XtManageChildren, XtUnmanageChild.

XtUnmapWidget

Name

XtUnmapWidget — unmap a widget explicitly.

Synopsis

```
XtUnmapWidget(w)
    Widget w;
```

Arguments

w   Specifies the widget to be unmapped.

Description

XtUnmapWidget unmaps a widget's window from its display, causing it to become invisible.

Most widgets are mapped when they are managed. Widgets that are not must be mapped explicitly by calling XtMapWidget. XtUnmapWidget takes a widget off the display without deleting it.

See Also

Section 1.1, "Widget Lifecycle,"
XtManageChild, XtMapWidget, XtSetMappedWhenManaged.

XtUnrealizeWidget

Name
XtUnrealizeWidget — destroy the windows associated with a widget and its descendants

Synopsis
```
void XtUnrealizeWidget(w)
    Widget w;
```

Arguments
w   Specifies the widget.

Description
XtUnrealizeWidget destroys the windows of a widget and its children. It traverses the widget tree in *pre-order traversal*, unrealizing children before it unrealizes the parent.

Note that this call simply destroys the windows associated with the widget(s) The widget instances themselves remain intact To recreate the windows at a later time, call XtRealize-Widget again Compare XtDestroyWidget, which destroys the widget(s) themselves

If the widget was managed, it will be unmanaged automatically before its window is freed.

See Also
Section 1.1, "Widget Lifecycle,"
XtDestroyWidget, XtRealizeWidget.

XtWarning

Name

XtWarning — call the installed low-level warning handler.

Synopsis

```
void XtWarning(message)
    String message;
```

Arguments

message   Specifies the nonfatal error message to be reported.

Description

XtWarning calls the existing low-level warning error procedure. Warning errors are nonfatal. The default low-level warning handler provided by the Intrinsics is _XtWarning. On UNIX-based systems, it prints the message to standard error and returns to the caller.

Most programs should use the more elaborate XtWarningMsg, to print customized error messages from an error database. XtWarningMsg allows an application to be more easily customized by site, and allows for international considerations in reporting errors.

A custom warning handler can be installed by calling XtSetWarningHandler.

See Also

XtSetErrorHandler, XtSetErrorMsgHandler, XtSetWarningHandler, XtSet-WarningMsgHandler, XtWarningMsg.

XtWarningMsg

Name
XtWarningMsg — call the installed high-level warning handler

Synopsis
```
void XtWarningMsg(name, type, class, default, params,
        num_params)
    String name;
    String type;
    String class;
    String default;
    String *params;
    Cardinal *num_params;
```

Arguments

name	Specifies the general kind of error
type	Specifies the detailed name of the error
class	Specifies the resource class.
default	Specifies the default message to use
params	Specifies a pointer to a list of values to be stored in the message.
num_params	Specifies the number of values in the parameter list.

Description
XtWarningMsg calls the currently installed high-level warning handler. This is the preferred method of delivering warning messages. The error handler that gets invoked can be customized on a per site basis, and can manage details like international considerations and system-wide error logging

Warning errors are assumed to be informative and recoverable. Fatal error handlers should be used for errors that require attention, fatal error handlers prevent a program from completing successfully.

The Intrinsic internal errors all have class XtToolkitError.

See Also
XtWarning

XtWidgetToApplicationContext

Name

XtWidgetToApplicationContext — get the application context for a given widget.

Synopsis

```
XtAppContext XtWidgetToApplicationContext(w)
    Widget w;
```

Arguments

w   Specifies the widget for which you want the application context .

Description

XtWidgetToApplicationContext returns the application context for the specified widget.

It locates the application context by following the chain of Core widget Parent structures until it finds one that is a subclass of the fundamental widget class windowObjClass. Then it accesses the application context associated with the display for that widget.

See Also

XtCreateApplicationContext

XtWindow

Name

XtWindow — return the window of the specified widget.

Synopsis

```
Window XtWindow(w)
    Widget w;
```

Arguments

w   Specifies the widget.

Description

XtWindow returns the window of the specified widget.

XtWindowToWidget

Name

XtWindowToWidget — translate a window and display pointer into a widget instance.

Synopsis

```
Widget XtWindowToWidget(display, window)
    Display *display;
    Window window;
```

Arguments

display   Specifies the display on which the window is defined.

window   Specify the window for which you want the widget.

Description

XtWindowToWidget takes a display pointer and a window and returns the associated widget. The widget must be within the same application as the caller.

On failure, XtWindowToWidget returns NULL.

See Also

XtNameToWidget, XtWindow.

Prototype Procedures

This section contains alphabetically-organized reference pages for function proto-types (typedefs) used for widget methods and other handlers.

Each page contains a synopsis of the routine's calling sequence, its arguments, a description of its function, and a reference to related routines.

XtAcceptFocusProc

Name

XtAcceptFocusProc — prototype procedure to accept or reject keyboard focus.

Synopsis

```
typedef Boolean (*XtAcceptFocusProc)(Widget, Time);
    Widget w;
    Time *time;
```

Arguments

w	Specifies the widget.
time	Specifies the X time of the event causing the accept focus.

Description

When the keyboard focus is given to a widget, Xt invokes the widget's accept_focus procedure. The procedure should return a Boolean to indicate whether or not it will accept the focus, so that the parent can give the focus to another widget if necessary.

The accept_focus procedure is part of the Core class structure. A widget that never wants the keyboard focus should set its accept_focus procedure to NULL when it initializes its class record.

A widget can usurp the keyboard focus by calling the Xlib function XSetInputFocus explicitly. Similarly, widgets can be notified of the loss of keyboard focus by specifying translations or event handlers for FocusIn and FocusOut events.

XtSetKeyboardFocus and the Xlib XSetInputFocus must be used to actually pass the focus to a child.

See Also

XtCallAcceptFocus, XtSetKeyboardFocus.

XtActionProc

Name

XtActionProc — prototype procedure for registering action tables.

Synopsis

```
typedef void (*XtActionProc)(Widget, XEvent *, String *,
        Cardinal *);
    Widget w;
    XEvent *event;
    String *params;
    Cardinal *num_params;
```

Arguments

w	Specifies the widget that caused the action to be called.
event	Specifies the event that caused the action to be called. If the action is called after a sequence of events, then the last event in the sequence is used.
params	Specifies a pointer to the list of strings that were specified in the translation table as arguments to the action.
num_params	Specifies the number of arguments specified in the translation table.

Description

All widget class records contain an action table. In addition, using XtAddActions, an application can register its own action tables with the Resource Manager. An action table consists of a list of string names (which can be used in translation tables to associate an action with one or more events) and corresponding function pointers (often spelled the same as the string). The function pointer is of type XtActionProc.

An XtActionProc is just a function with four arguments: a widget, an event, a string containing any arguments specified for the action, and the number of arguments contained in the string. In most cases, the last two arguments are unused. When you don't pass any arguments, you can call your action function with only the first two arguments, or, if the additional arguments are declared but not used, you should be sure to include the *lint* comment /*ARGUSED*/.

Another major difference between an action function and a callback function is that action functions are called with an event as an argument, while actions do not have the client_data or call_data arguments present for callback functions. This means the only way to pass application data into an action function is through global variables. On the other hand, the presence of the event argument means that you can use the contents of the event structure in the action function.

Many action routines are intentionally written not to depend on the detailed information inside any particular type of event, so that the user uses the translation table to call the action in response to different types of events. For example, it is useful for an action routine normally triggered by a pointer click to work when called in response to a key instead. Such an action should not depend on the event structure fields unique to button events.

However, many other action routines, and most event handlers, do use the detailed information inside event structures. The first member of the event structure, type, identifies the type of event this structure represents, and hence implies what other fields are present in the structure.

To access event structure fields other than type, you need to cast XEvent into the appropriate event structure type. If you are expecting only one type of event to trigger this action, then you can simply declare the argument as the appropriate type, as show below.

```
static void
Turn(w, event)
TetrisWidget w;
XButtonEvent *event;
{
    /* we must now use only the fields in XButtonEvent */
    if (event->type != ButtonPress)
        XtWarning("TetrisWidget: Turn action invoked\
            by wrong event type.");
        .
        .
}
```

If the data in the event structure is important to an action, it is usually better to write the action so that it is called in response to only one type of event. If you want the same code called for two event types, then you would do better to create two separate translations and two separate actions that each call a common routine. However, it is sometimes more convenient to have an action called by two different events. The example below shows the ToggleCell action from the BitmapEdit widget, developed in Volume Four, *X Toolkit Intrinsics Programming Manual*, which is called in response to either MotionNotify or ButtonPress events. This action inverts a pixel in the bitmap either if the pointer is clicked on a cell in the widget, or if it is dragged across the cell with the pointer buttons held down.

```
static void
ToggleCell(w, event)
BitmapEditWidget w;
XEvent *event;
{
    static int oldx = -1, oldy = -1;
    GC gc;
    int mode;
    int newx, newy;

    if (event->type == ButtonPress) {
        newx = (w->bitmapEdit.cur_x + ((XButtonEvent *)event)->x) /
    w->bitmapEdit.cell_size_in_pixels;
        newy = (w->bitmapEdit.cur_y + ((XButtonEvent *)event)->y) /
    w->bitmapEdit.cell_size_in_pixels;
    }
    else if (event->type == MotionNotify) {
        newx = (w->bitmapEdit.cur_x + ((XMotionEvent *)event)->x) /
    w->bitmapEdit.cell_size_in_pixels;
```

```
        newy = (w->bitmapEdit.cur_y + ((XMotionEvent *)event)->y) /
    w->bitmapEdit.cell_size_in_pixels;
    }
    else
        XtWarning("BitmapEdit. ToggleCell called with wrong
                event type\n"),

        .


        .

}
```

Notice that some code is repeated to cast the event structure to the two different event types With the current MIT implementation of Xlib, the positions of the x and y fields in the XButtonEvent and XMotionEvent structures are the same, and therefore this casting is unnecessary However, it is improper to depend on any particular implementation of Xlib The order of the fields in one of these events could be different in a vendor's implementation of Xlib

XtAlmostProc

Name

XtAlmostProc — prototype set_values_almost method.

Synopsis

```
typedef void (*XtAlmostProc)(Widget, Widget, XtWidgetGeometry *,
        XtWidgetGeometry *);
    Widget w;
    Widget new_widget_return;
    XtWidgetGeometry *request;
    XtWidgetGeometry *reply;
```

Arguments

w
: Specifies the widget for which the geometry change is requested.

new_widget_return
: Specifies the new widget into which the geometry changes are to be stored.

request
: Specifies the original geometry request that was sent to the geometry manager that returned XtGeometryAlmost.

reply
: Specifies the compromise geometry that was returned by the geometry manager that returned XtGeometryAlmost.

Description

The purpose of an XtAlmostProc is to negotiate geometry requests. The set_values_almost procedure pointer in a widget class is of type XtAlmostProc.

A widget's set_values_almost method is called when a client tries to set a widget's geometry by means of a call to XtSetValues and the geometry manager cannot satisfy the request but instead returns XtGeometryAlmost and a compromise geometry. The set_values_almost method takes the original geometry and the compromise geometry and determines whether the compromise is acceptable or a different compromise might work. It returns its results in the new_widget_return parameter, which is then sent back to the geometry manager for another try.

Most classes inherit this operation from their superclass by specifying XtInheritSet-ValuesAlmost in the class initialization. The Core set_values_almost method always accepts the compromise suggested.

See Chapter 11, *Geometry Management*, in Volume Four, *X Toolkit Intrinsics Programming Manual*.

Structures

The XtWidgetGeometry structure is similar to but not identical to the corresponding Xlib structure:

```
typedef unsigned long XtGeometryMask;

typedef struct {
    XtGeometryMask request_mode;
```

```
        Position x, y;
        Dimension width, height;
        Dimension border_width;
        Widget sibling,
        int stack_mode;
   } XtWidgetGeometry;
```

The `request_mode` definitions are from *<X11/X h>*.

```
#define    CWX                (1<<0)
#define    CWY                (1<<1)
#define    CWWidth            (1<<2)
#define    CWHeight           (1<<3)
#define    CWBorderWidth      (1<<4)
#define    CWSibling          (1<<5)
#define    CWStackMode        (1<<6)
```

The Xt Intrinsics also support the following value·

```
#define    XtCWQueryOnly      (1<<7)
```

`XtCWQueryOnly` indicates that the corresponding geometry request is only a query as to what would happen if this geometry request were made and that no widgets should actually be changed.

`XtMakeGeometryRequest`, like the Xlib `XConfigureWindow` function, uses `request_mode` to determine which fields in the `XtWidgetGeometry` structure you want to specify.

The `stack_mode` definitions are from *<X11/X.h>*

```
#define    Above              0
#define    Below              1
#define    TopIf              2
#define    BottomIf           3
#define    Opposite           4
```

The Intrinsics also support the following value·

```
#define    XtSMDontChange     5
```

For precise definitions of `Above`, `Below`, `TopIf`, `BottomIf`, and `Opposite`, see the reference page for `ConfigureWindow` in Volume Two, *Xlib Reference Manual*. `XtSMDontChange` indicates that the widget wants its current stacking order preserved

See Also
Core(3)

XtArgsFunc

Name

XtArgsFunc — prototype set_values_hook method.

Synopsis

```
typedef Boolean (*XtArgsFunc)(Widget, ArgList, Cardinal *);
    Widget w;
    ArgList args;
    Cardinal *num_args;
```

Arguments

w   Specifies the widget whose nonwidget resource values are to be changed.

args   Specifies the argument list that was passed to XtCreateWidget.

num_args   Specifies the number of arguments in the argument list.

Description

An XtArgsFunc procedure returns a Boolean indicating whether, based on the values passed
in args, the widget needs to be redrawn. Widgets can set subpart resource values when the
application calls XtSetValues by supplying an XtArgsFunc procedure in the core widget
class set_values_hook method. To set the actual subvalues of the nonwidget data, the
widget should call XtSetSubvalues and pass the appropriate resource list.

The set_values_hook method is similar to the set_values method, except that it is
passed only the current widget instance structure and the arglist, instead of the old and new
copies of the widget instance structure which are passed to set_values. As a result,
set_values_hook needs to use a different technique for comparing the current subresource
values with the values set by XtSetValues.

There are two ways to do this. One is to loop through the widget's resource list, using strcmp
to compare each resource name in the argument list with the subresource names, and then comparing each argument value with the current value of the subresource.

The other way is to copy the instance structure passed in using bcopy (after allocating memory for the new copy with XtNew, described in Chapter 13, *Miscellaneous Toolkit Programming Techniques*, in Volume Four, *X Toolkit Intrinsics Programming Manual*). Then call Xt-
SetSubvalues to set the actual values to those in the argument list. After this process, you
can compare the old and new values the same way this is done in the set_values method.

As of Release 4, the initialize_hook and set_values_hook methods are still called
for backwards compatibility but are obsolete because the same information (the argument lists)
has been added as arguments to the initialize and set_values methods.

Structures

Arg is defined as follows in *<X11/Intrinsic.h>*:

```
typedef struct {
    String name;
    XtArgVal value;
} Arg, *ArgList;
```

See Also
Section 1.7, "Resources,"
XtCreateWidget, XtSetSubvalues, XtSetValues,
Core(3).

XtArgsProc

Name

XtArgsProc — prototype procedure for get_values_hook method.

Synopsis

```
typedef void (*XtArgsProc)(Widget, ArgList, Cardinal *);
    Widget w;
    ArgList args;
    Cardinal *num_args;
```

Arguments

w   Specifies the widget whose nonwidget resource values are to be retrieved.

args   Specifies the argument list that was passed to XtCreateWidget.

num_args   Specifies the number of arguments in the argument list.

Description

Widgets can return resource values from subparts for XtGetValues by supplying a pointer to an XtArgsProc procedure in the Core widget class get_values_hook field. To obtain the actual subvalues of the nonwidget data, the widget should call XtGetSubvalues and pass the appropriate resource list.

The initialize_hook method is also of type XtArgsProc. The initialize_hook method allows a widget instance to initialize nonwidget data using information from the specified argument list. For example, the Text widget has subparts that are not widgets, yet these subparts have resources that can be specified by means of the resource file or an argument list.

The hook methods are called with different arguments than their nonhook counterparts. They are passed a single copy of the widget instance structure (the new copy already modified in the nonhook methods), and the argument list passed to the Xt routine that triggered the method. The set_values_hook and get_values_hook methods simply take this widget ID and argument list and pass them to XtSetSubvalues or XtGetSubvalues respectively. The initialize_hook method uses the contents of the argument list to validate resource settings for subparts and set nonresource subpart data.

As of Release 4, the initialize_hook and set_values_hook methods are still called for backwards compatibility but are obsolete because the same information (the argument lists) has been added as arguments to the initialize and set_values methods. However, get_values_hook is still necessary. The example below shows the get_values_hook method for the AsciiSrc subpart of the Text widget (somewhat simplified to show only the essential elements).

```
static void
GetValuesHook(src, args, num_args)
XawTextSource src;
ArgList args;
Cardinal * num_args;
{
```

```
        .
        .
    XtGetSubvalues((caddr_t) src,
    sourceResources,
    XtNumber(sourceResources),
    args,
    *num_args);
}
```

See Also
Section 1 7, "Resources,"
XtCreateWidget, XtGetSubvalues, XtGetValues,
Core(3).

XtCallbackProc

Name

XtCallbackProc — prototype callback procedure.

Synopsis

```
typedef void (*XtCallbackProc)(Widget, caddr_t, caddr_t);
    Widget w;
    caddr_t client_data;
    caddr_t call_data;
```

Arguments

w   Specifies the widget for which the callback is registered.

client_data Specifies the data that the widget should pass to the client's procedure when
                   the widget performs the callback.

call_data   Specifies callback-specific data that the widget passes to the client.

Description

Generally speaking, a widget expecting to interact with an application will declare one or more
callback lists as resources; the application adds functions to these callback lists, which will be
invoked whenever the predefined callback conditions are met. Callback lists are resources, so
that the application can set or change the function that will be invoked.

Callbacks are not necessarily invoked in response to any event; a widget can call the specified
routines at any arbitrary point in its code, whenever it wants to provide a "hook" for application
interaction. For example, all widgets provide an XtNdestroyCallback resource to allow
applications to interpose a routine to be executed when the widget is destroyed.

Whenever a client wants to pass a callback list as an argument in an XtCreateWidget, Xt-
SetValues, or XtGetValues call, it should specify the address of a NULL-terminated array
of type XtCallbackList (see the Structures section below). Callback procedure fields for
use in callback lists are of type XtCallbackProc.

When a callback procedure, or list of callback procedures, is passed as a resource argument, Xt
constructs an internal data structure for the callback list. Subsequently, callback lists must be
referred to with strings representing the name of the resource in the widget. Because Xt doesn't
support a string to Callback resource converter, callbacks cannot be specified in resource files.
The internal form can only be accessed by the Intrinsics functions XtAddCallbacks, Xt-
DeleteCallbacks, XtCallCallbacks, etc. Furthermore, since callback lists are handled specifically by the Intrinsics, widget procedures should not allocate memory for callback
lists passed as resources. Unlike other resources, a widget's initialize method should not
attempt to make copies of resources of type XtRCallback.

An XtCallbackProc takes three arguments

- The first argument is the widget that triggered the callback, as specified as the first argument in XtAddCallback. You would use the value of this argument in your callback function if you registered the same function as a callback for two different widgets, and if you wanted to distinguish in the callback which widget called it.

- The second argument, *client_data*, is the value passed as the last argument of Xt-AddCallback. *client_data* provides a way for the client registering the callback also to register client-specific data (for example, a pointer to additional information about the widget, a reason for invoking the callback, and so on) *client_data* should be NULL if all necessary information is in the widget.

- The third argument, *call_data*, is a piece of data passed from the widget. Some classes of widget set this argument, but others do not. The documentation for the widget will specify the contents of this data if it is used. The Athena Command widget doesn't provide any *call_data*, but the Athena Scroll widget, for example, passes back the current position of the thumb.

call_data is a convenience to avoid having simple cases where the client could otherwise call XtGetValues or a widget-specific function to retrieve data from the widget. Widgets should generally avoid putting complex state information in *call_data* The client can use the more general data retrieval methods, if necessary.

Structures

```
typedef struct {
    XtCallbackProc callback;
    caddr_t closure;
} XtCallbackRec, *XtCallbackList;
```

For example, the callback list for procedures A and B with client data clientDataA and clientDataB, respectively, is

```
static XtCallbackRec callbacks[] = {
    {A, (caddr_t) clientDataA},
    {B, (caddr_t) clientDataB},
    {(XtCallbackProc) NULL, (caddr_t) NULL}
};
```

See Also

Section 1 3, "Application Interface,"
XtAddCallback, XtAddCallbacks, XtCallCallbacks, XtCreateWidget, Xt-GetValues, XtHasCallbacks, XtRemoveCallback, XtRemoveCallbacks, Xt-SetValues.

Name

XtCaseProc — prototype procedure called to convert the case of keysyms.

Synopsis

```
typedef void (*XtCaseProc)(KeySym *, KeySym *, KeySym *);
    KeySym *keysym;
    KeySym *lower_return;
    KeySym *upper_return;
```

Arguments

keysym	Specifies the keysym to convert.
lower_return	Specifies the lower-case equivalent for the keysym.
upper_return	Specifies the upper-case equivalent for the keysym.

Description

To handle capitalization of nonstandard keysyms, the Intrinsics allow clients to register case conversion routines. Case converter procedure pointers are of type XtCaseProc.

An XtCaseProc allows an application to specify its own upper-case and lower-case translations for keyboard keys.

If there is no case distinction, the procedure should store the input keysym into both return values. The case converter can be registered with XtRegisterCaseConverter.

Here is the default case converter from the R3 Intrinsics:

```
/* ARGSUSED */
void _XtConvertCase(dpy, keysym, lower_return, upper_return)

    Display *dpy;
    KeySym keysym;
    KeySym *lower_return;
    KeySym *upper_return;

{
    if ((keysym >= XK_a && keysym <= XK_z) ||
        (keysym >= XK_ssharp && keysym <= XK_odiaeresis) ||
        (keysym >= XK_oslash && keysym <= XK_ydiaeresis)) {
        *lower_return = keysym;
        *upper_return = keysym-0x20;
        return;
    }
    if ((keysym >= XK_A && keysym <= XK_Z) ||
        (keysym >= XK_Agrave && keysym <= XK_Odiaeresis) ||
        (keysym >= XK_Ooblique && keysym <= XK_Thorn)) {
        *upper_return = keysym;
        *lower_return = keysym+0x20;
        return;
        }
```

```
    *lower_return = keysym;
    *upper_return = keysym;

}
```

A related keyboard example is presented in Chapter 13, *Miscellaneous Toolkit Programming Techniques*, in Volume Four, *X Toolkit Intrinsics Programming Manual*.

See Also

XtRegisterCaseConverter, XtTranslateKeycode.

Name

XtConvertSelectionProc — prototype procedure to return selection data.

Synopsis

```
typedef Boolean (*XtConvertSelectionProc)(Widget, Atom *, Atom
      *, Atom *, caddr_t *, unsigned long *, int *);
   Widget w;
   Atom *selection;
   Atom *target;
   Atom *type_return;
   caddr_t *value_return;
   unsigned long *length_return;
   int *format_return;
```

Arguments

w	Specifies the widget that currently owns this selection.
selection	Specifies the atom that describes the type of selection requested (for example, XA_PRIMARY or XA_SECONDARY).
target	Specifies the target type of the selection that has been requested, which indicates the desired information about the selection (for example, File Name, Text, Window).
type_return	Specifies a pointer to an atom into which the property type of the converted value of the selection is to be stored. For instance, either file name or text might have the property type XA_STRING.
value_return	Specifies a pointer into which a pointer to the converted value of the selection is to be stored. The selection owner is responsible for allocating this storage. If the selection owner has provided an XtSelection-DoneProc for the selection, this storage is owned by the selection owner; otherwise, it is owned by the Intrinsics selection mechanism, which frees it by calling XtFree when it is done with it.
length_return	Specifies a pointer into which the number of elements in value (each of size indicated by format) is to be stored.
format_return	Specifies a pointer into which the size in bits of the data elements of the selection value is to be stored.

Description

Arbitrary widgets (possibly not all in the same application) can communicate with each other by means of the Toolkit global selection mechanism, which is defined in the *Inter-Client Communications Manual* (see Volume Two, *Xlib Reference Manual*). The Intrinsics provide functions for providing and receiving selection data in one logical piece (atomic transfers). The actual transfer between the selection owner and the Intrinsics is not required to be atomic; the Intrinsics will break a too-large selection into smaller pieces for transport if necessary.

The Intrinsics call the selection owner's XtConvertSelectionProc to obtain selection data when another client requests it. The XtConvertSelectionProc is registered when the selection owner asserts its ownership

The XtConvertSelectionProc should return TRUE if the owner successfully converted the selection to the target type or FALSE otherwise If the procedure returns FALSE, the values of the return arguments are undefined

Each XtConvertSelectionProc should respond to target value TARGETS by returning a value containing the list of the targets they are prepared to convert their selection into This is used by the selection owner The list of targets should be an array of interned Atoms, and return_type should be XA_ATOM.

Most type Atoms are defined in *<X11/Xatom h>*. Those that are not (for example, TARGETS) must be interned explicitly as Atoms by calling the Xlib function XInternAtom.

See Also

XtFree, XtGetSelectionValue, XtOwnSelection, XtSelectionDoneProc.

The example below shows code to handle standard selection targets This code is taken from the BitmapEdit widget developed in Volume Four, *X Toolkit Intrinsics Programming Manual*; however, this portion of it is adapted from the standard client *xclipboard*, and can be copied almost directly into your widget.

```
static Boolean
convert_proc(w, selection, target, type_return, value_return,
    length_return, format_return)
BitmapEditWidget w,
Atom *selection;
Atom *target;
Atom *type_return;
caddr_t *value_return,
unsigned long *length_return,
int *format_return,
{
    int x, y;
    int width, height;

    /* handle TARGETS target */
    if (*target == XA_TARGETS(XtDisplay(w))) {
    Atom* targetP;
    Atom* std_targets;
    unsigned long std_length,
    XmuConvertStandardSelection(w, CurrentTime, selection,
    target, type_return,
    (caddr_t*)&std_targets,
    &std_length, format_return),
    *value_return = XtMalloc(sizeof(Atom)*(std_length + 1));
    targetP = *(Atom**)value_return;
    *length_return = std_length + 1,
    *targetP++ = w->bitmapEdit.target_atom;
```

```
bcopy((char*)std_targets, (char*)targetP,
                    sizeof(Atom)*std_length);
XtFree((char*)std_targets);
*type_return = XA_ATOM;
*format_return = sizeof(Atom) * 8;
return(TRUE);
}

/* Xt already handles MULTIPLE, no branch needed */

/* Handle expected selection target */
else if (*target == w->bitmapEdit.target_atom) {
    /* code shown and described in Volume 4, Chapter 10 */
.

.

.
}
else {
/* Handle other standard targets defined by Xmu */
if (XmuConvertStandardSelection(w, CurrentTime,
                            selection, tarrget, type_return,
value_return, length_return,
                            format_return))
return TRUE;
else {
fprintf(stderr,
                        "bitmapEdit: requestor is requesting",
                        "unsupported selection target type.\n");
return(FALSE);
}
}
}
```

Overall, this code handles the TARGETS atom in the first branch, the expected selection target in the second, and any remaining standard atoms and any unknown atoms as two cases in the third branch. For ICCCM-compliant code, you can copy this entire function into your widget and then write just the second branch. Note that branches that successfully provide the requested data return TRUE, and ones that don't return FALSE. The ICCCM also specifies that functions implementing selections must be able to respond to a MULTIPLE target value, which is used to handle selections too large to fit into a single property. However, the necessary handling is done by the Intrinsics. Your procedures do not need to worry about responding to the MULTIPLE target value; a selection request with this target type will be transparently transformed into a series of smaller transfers.

In the first branch you will also need to change the reference to the instance part field that stores the target atom used for selections, bitmapEdit.target_atom. If your widget uses a predefined atom or one supported by the Xmu facility, you would reference that atom here instead of the instance part field. If you called XInternAtom in initialize and stored the result in an instance part field, you specify that here.

XtConverter

Name

XtConverter — prototype of a resource converter procedure

Synopsis

```
typedef void (*XtConverter)(XrmValue *, Cardinal *, XrmValue *,
        XrmValue *);
    XrmValue *args;
    Cardinal *num_args;
    XrmValue *from;
    XrmValue *to;
```

Arguments

args
: Specifies a list of additional XrmValue arguments to the converter if additional context is needed to perform the conversion, or specifies NULL For example, a string-to-font converter needs the widget's screen, or a string-to-pixel converter needs the widget's screen and colormap

num_args
: Specifies the number of additional XrmValue arguments, or specifies zero

from
: Specifies the value to convert

to
: Specifies the descriptor to use to return the converted value

Description

The Intrinsics provide a mechanism for registering converters that are automatically invoked by the resource-fetching routines The Intrinsics additionally provide and register several commonly used converters. This resource conversion mechanism serves several purposes

- It permits user and application resource files to contain ASCII representations of non-textual values.

- It allows textual or other representations of default resource values that are dependent on the display, screen, or colormap and thus must be computed at run time.

- It caches all conversion source and result data Conversions that require much computation or space (for example, string to translation table) or that require round trips to the server (for example, string to font or color) are performed only once

The Intrinsics define all the representations used in the Core, Composite, Constraint, and Shell widgets. The following resource converters are registered with the Intrinsics:

From XtRString to:

> XtRAcceleratorTable, XtRBoolean, XtRBool, XtRCursor, XtRDimension, XtRDisplay, XtRFile, XtRFloat, XtRFont, XtRFontStruct, XtRInt, Xt-RPixel, XtRPosition, XtRShort, XtRTranslationTable, and Xt-RUnsignedChar.

From XtRColor to:

    XtRPixel.

From XRInt to:

    XtRBoolean, XtRBool, XtRColor, XtRDimension, XtRFloat, XtRFont, Xt-
    RPixel, XtRPixmap, XtRPosition, XtRShort, and XtRUnsignedChar.

From XtRPixel to:

    XtRColor.

The string-to-pixel conversion has two predefined constants that are guaranteed to work and contrast with each other and with XtDefaultBackground. They evaluate the black and white pixel values of the widget's screen, respectively. For applications that run with reverse video, however, they evaluate the white and black pixel values of the widget's screen, respectively. Similarly, the string to font and font structure converters recognize the constant Xt-DefaultFont and evaluate this to the font in the screen's default graphics context.

Type converters use pointers to XrmValue structures (defined in *<X11/Xresource.h>*) for input and output values.

```
typedef struct {
    unsigned int size;
    caddr_t addr;
} XrmValue, *XrmValuePtr;
```

A resource converter procedure pointer is of type XtConverter.

Type converters should perform the following actions:

- Check to see that the number of arguments passed is correct.

- Attempt the type conversion.

- If successful, return a pointer to the data in the to parameter; otherwise, call Xt-WarningMsg and return without modifying to.

Most type converters just take the data described by the specified *from* argument and return data by writing into the specified *to* argument. A few need other information, which is available in the specified argument list.

A type converter can invoke another type converter, which allows differing sources that may convert into a common intermediate result to make maximum use of the type converter cache.

Note that the address written in to->addr cannot be that of a local variable of the converter because this is not valid after the converter returns. It should be a pointer to a static variable, as in the example below in which screenColor is returned.

All type converters should define some set of conversion values that they are guaranteed to succeed on so these can be used in the resource defaults. This might be problematic with particular conversions, such as fonts and colors, where there is no string representation that all server implementations will necessarily recognize. For resources like these, the converter should

define a symbolic constant (for example, XtDefaultForeground, XtDefault-
Background, or XtDefaultFont)

The following example shows a converter that takes a string and converts it to a pixel value

```
static void CvtStringToPixel(args, num_args, fromVal, toVal)
    XrmValuePtr    args,
    Cardinal       *num_args;
    XrmValuePtr    fromVal,
    XrmValuePtr    toVal;
{
    static XColor screenColor;
    XColor        exactColor;
    Screen        *screen,
    Colormap      colormap,
    Status        status;
    char          message[1000],
    XrmQuark      q;
    String        params[1];
    Cardinal      num_params = 1,

    if (*num_args != 2)
        XtErrorMsg("cvtStringToPixel","wrongParameters",
            "XtToolkitError",
        "String to pixel conversion needs screen and
            colormap arguments",
        (String *)NULL, (Cardinal *)NULL);

    screen = *((Screen **) args[0].addr),
    colormap = *((Colormap *) args[1].addr);

    LowerCase((char *) fromVal->addr, message);
    q = XrmStringToQuark(message),

    if (q == XtQExtdefaultbackground) { done(&screen->white_pixel, Pixel);
        return, }
    if (q == XtQExtdefaultforeground) { done(&screen->black_pixel, Pixel),
        return; }

    if ((char) fromVal->addr[0] == '#') {  /* some color rgb definition */

        status = XParseColor(DisplayOfScreen(screen), colormap,
            (String) fromVal->addr, &screenColor),
        if (status != 0) status = XAllocColor(DisplayOfScreen
            (screen), colormap, &screenColor);

    } else  /* some color name */

        status = XAllocNamedColor(DisplayOfScreen(screen), colormap,
            (String) fromVal->addr, &screenColor, &exactColor);

    if (status == 0) {

        params[0]=(String)fromVal->addr;
        XtWarningMsg("cvtStringToPixel","noColormap",
            "XtToolkitError",
```

```
        "Cannot allocate colormap entry for \\"%s\\"", params, &num_params);
    } else {
        done(&(screenColor.pixel), Pixel)
    }
};
```

See Also
Section 1.7, "Resources,"
XtAppAddConverter, XtConvert, XtDirectConvert, XtStringConversion-
Warning.

XtErrorHandler

Name
XtErrorHandler — prototype for low-level error and warning handlers.

Synopsis
```
typedef void (*XtErrorHandler) (String);
    String message;
```

Arguments
message   Specifies the error message

Description
The error handler should display the message string in some appropriate fashion Some applications may wish to log errors to a file as well.

The default handlers simply print a message to standard error, and exit (for errors) or return (for warnings), as shown below:

```
static void _XtDefaultError(message)
    String message;
{
    extern void exit();

    (void)fprintf(stderr, "X Toolkit Error  %s\n", message);
    exit(1);
}
static void _XtDefaultWarning(message)
    String message;
{
        (void)fprintf(stderr, "X Toolkit Warning  %s\n", message);
    return;
}
```

See Also
XtError, XtSetErrorHandler, XtSetWarningHandler, XtWarning.

Name
XtErrorMsgHandler — prototype for high-level error and warning handlers.

Synopsis
```
typedef void (*XtErrorMsgHandler)(String, String, String,
        String, String *, Cardinal *);
    String name;
    String type;
    String class;
    String defaultp;
    String *params;
    Cardinal *num_params;
```

Arguments

name	Specifies the name that is concatenated with the specified type to form the resource name of the error message.
type	Specifies the type that is concatenated with the name to form the resource name of the error message.
class	Specifies the resource class of the error message.
defaultp	Specifies the default message to use if no error database entry is found.
params	Specifies a pointer to a list of values to be substituted in the message.
num_params	Specifies the number of values in the parameter list.

Description
Application-supplied error handling functions, for both warnings and fatal errors, are of type XtErrorMsgHandler.

The specified name can be a general kind of error, like invalidParameters or invalid-Window, and the specified type gives extra information. Standard printf notation is used to substitute the parameters into the message.

The default Toolkit-supplied XtErrorMsgHandler routines construct a string and pass the result to XtError and XtWarning, respectively. Low-level handlers are of type XtError-Handler(2).

The error handler should make a call to XtGetErrorDatabase or XtAppGetError-Database to retrieve the address of the loaded error database (if a database other than the default is being used), and XtGetErrorDatabaseText or XtAppGetErrorDatabase-Text to actually retrieve the message from the database.

The example below shows the default error message handler from the MIT R3 Intrinsics.

```
static void _XtDefaultErrorMsg (name,type,class,defaultp,params,num_params)
    String name,type,class,defaultp;
    String* params;
    Cardinal* num_params;
{
```

```
char buffer[1000],message[1000],
XtGetErrorDatabaseText(name,type,class,defaultp, buffer, 1000);
if (num_params == NULL) XtError(buffer);
else {
    (void) sprintf(message, buffer, params[0], params[1], params[2],
            params[3], params[4], params[5], params[6], params[7],
            params[8], params[9]);
    XtError(message),
}
}
```

See Also

XtSetErrorHandler, XtSetMsgHandler.

XtEventHandler

Name

XtEventHandler — prototype procedure to handle input events.

Synopsis

```
typedef void (*XtEventHandler)(Widget, caddr_t, XEvent *);
    Widget w;
    caddr_t client_data;
    XEvent *event;
```

Arguments

w	Specifies the widget for which to handle events.
client_data	Specifies the client-specific information registered with the event handler, which is usually NULL if the event handler is registered by the widget itself.
event	Specifies the triggering event for this handler.

Description

Event handlers are of type XtEventHandler. A widget expresses interest in an event by calling XtAddEventHandler, specifying as the handler argument a pointer to a procedure of this type.

Most widgets need not use event handlers explicitly. Instead they use the Xt Resource Manager to accept events and invoke procedures based on the interpretation of multiple events.

The example below shows the code from *xterm* that registers an event handler for FocusIn and FocusOut events, and a gutted version of the event handler itself.

```
extern void HandleFocusChange();

static void VTInitialize (request, new)
XtermWidget request, new;
{
      .
      .
      .

    XtAddEventHandler(topLevel,/* widget */
    FocusChangeMask, /* event mask */
    FALSE,/* non-maskable events */
    HandleFocusChange,/* event handler */
    (Opaque)NULL);/* client_data */

      .
      .
      .

}

/*ARGSUSED*/
void HandleFocusChange(w, unused, event)
Widget w;
register XFocusChangeEvent *event;
```

```
caddr_t unused,/* client_data */
{
        if(event->type == FocusIn)
    /* process FocusIn */
      .
      .
      .
      else {
    /* process FocusOut */
      .
      .
      .
        }
}
```

See Also
Section 1.4, "Events," Section 1 5, "Translations and Actions,"
XtAddEventHandler.

Name

XtExposeProc — prototype expose method used in Core widget class.

Synopsis

```
typedef void (*XtExposeProc)(Widget, XEvent *, Region);
    Widget w;
    XEvent *event;
    Region region;
```

Arguments

w   Specifies the widget instance requiring redisplay.

event   Specifies the exposure event giving the rectangle requiring redisplay.

region   Specifies the union of all rectangles in this exposure sequence.

Description

The expose method is responsible for initially drawing into a widget's window and for redrawing the window every time a part of the window becomes exposed. This redrawing is necessary because the X server does not maintain the contents of windows when they are obscured. When a window becomes visible again, it must be redrawn.

The expose method usually needs to modify its drawing based on the geometry of the window and other instance variables set in other methods. For example, the Label widget will left-justify, center, or right-justify its text according to the XtNjustify resource, and the actual position to draw the text depends on the widget's current size.

Another factor to consider when writing the expose method is that many widgets also draw from action routines, in response to user events. For example, BitmapEdit toggle bitmap cells in action routines. The expose method must be capable of redrawing the current state of the widget at any time. This means that action routines usually set instance variables when they draw so that the expose method can read these instance variables and draw the right thing.

BitmapEdit uses a slightly unusual exposure handling strategy. Most widgets keep track of what they draw in some form of arrays or display lists. When they need to redraw, they simply replay the saved drawing commands in the original order to redraw the window. For example, BitmapEdit keeps track of the state of each bitmap cell in a character array. It could easily traverse this array and redraw each cell that is set in the array.

However, BitmapEdit does not use this strategy. In order to improve its scrolling performance, the expose method copies an off-screen pixmap into the window whenever redisplay is required. The actions draw into this off-screen pixmap, and then call the expose method directly to have the pixmap copied to the window.

The expose method is passed an event that contains the bounding box of the area exposed. To achieve maximum performance it copies only this area from the pixmap to the window. The

BitmapEdit widgets take advantage of this, too They manufacture an artificial event contain-ing the bounding box of the cell to be toggled, and pass it when they call `expose`. This causes the expose method to copy only that one cell that was just updated to the window.

The example below shows the `expose` method from the BitmapEdit widget described in Vol-ume Four, *X Toolkit Intrinsics Programming Manual*

```
/* ARGSUSED */
static void
Redisplay(cw, event)
BitmapEditWidget cw;
XExposeEvent *event,
{
    register int x, y;
    unsigned int width, height;
    if (!XtIsRealized(cw))
    return;

    if (event) {  /* called from btn-event */
    x = event->x,
        y = event->y;
    width = event->width;
    height = event->height,
    }
    else {        /* called because of expose */
    x = 0;
        y = 0;
    width = cw->bitmapEdit pixmap_width_in_pixels;
    height = cw->bitmapEdit.pixmap_height_in_pixels;
    }

    if (DefaultDepthOfScreen(XtScreen(cw)) == 1)
    XCopyArea(XtDisplay(cw), cw->bitmapEdit.big_picture,
            XtWindow(cw),
                cw->bitmapEdit.copy_gc, x + cw->bitmapEdit.cur_x, y +
                cw->bitmapEdit.cur_y, width, height, x, y),
    else
    XCopyPlane(XtDisplay(cw), cw->bitmapEdit.big_picture,
            XtWindow(cw),
                cw->bitmapEdit copy_gc, x + cw->bitmapEdit.cur_x, y +
                cw->bitmapEdit.cur_y, width, height, x, y, 1);

}
```

Note that the `expose` method first checks to see that the widget is realized using `Xt-IsRealized`. This is a precaution against the unlikely event that an instance of this widget is suddenly destroyed or unrealized by an application while `Expose` events are still pending If this did happen, drawing on the nonexistent window would cause an X protocol error.

Next, BitmapEdit's expose method sets the rectangle it will redraw based on the event passed in by Xt. We also call this method directly from the action that processes button presses That action routine creates a pseudo-event to pass to expose to describe the area to be drawn.

If the compress_exposures field of the class structure is initialized to TRUE, as it is in BitmapEdit, Xt automatically merges the multiple Expose events that may occur because of a single user action into one Expose event. In this case, the Expose event contains the bounding box of the areas exposed. BitmapEdit redraws everything in this bounding box. For widgets that are very time-consuming to redraw, you might want to use the third argument of the expose method, which is a region. The Region type is opaquely defined by Xlib (internally a linked list of rectangles). The Region passed into expose describes the union of all the areas exposed by a user action. You can use this region to clip output to the exposed region, and possibly calculate which drawing primitives affect this area. Xlib provides region mathematics routines (such as XRectInRegion) to compare the regions in which your widget needs to draw with the region needing redrawing. If certain areas do not require redrawing, you can skip the code that redraws them, thereby saving valuable time. However, if this calculation is complicated, its cost/benefit ratio should be examined.

Each of these exposure handling techniques may be the best for certain widgets. For a widget like BitmapEdit, any of the three methods will work, but the bounding box method is the most efficient and convenient. For a complete description of Expose event handling strategies, see Chapter 8, *Events*, in Volume One, *Xlib Programming Manual*.

The remainder of BitmapEdit's expose method shown in the example above consists of a single Xlib call to copy from a pixmap into the widget's window. As described in Chapter 4, *An Example Application*, in Volume Four, *X Toolkit Intrinsics Programming Manual*, Bitmap-Edit makes a large pixmap that is one plane deep and draws the current bitmap into it. When needed in the expose method, this pixmap just has to be copied into the window. This approach was chosen for its simplicity. When scrollbars are added, the widget is able to pan around in the large bitmap quickly and efficiently. Note that one of two Xlib routines is called based on the depth of the screen. This is because XCopyArea is slightly more efficient than XCopyPlane and should be used when running on a monochrome screen.

Note that instance variables are used for the arguments of the Xlib routines in the example above. Don't worry about exactly what each Xlib routine does or the meaning of each argument. See the reference page for each routine in Volume Two, *Xlib Reference Manual* when you need to call them in your code.

See Chapters 5, 6, and 7 in Volume One, *Xlib Programming Manual*, for more information on the GC, drawing graphics, and color, respectively.

Structures

The definition of a region is given in *<X11/Xutil.h>*:

```
typedef struct _XRegion *Region;
```

This is an opaque definition pointing to a file in the library source file *X11R3/lib/X/region.h*. (*X11R3* is the name of the directory where the X11 source is rooted.)

```
typedef struct {
    short x1, x2, y1, y2;
} Box, BOX, BoxRec, *BoxPtr,

typedef struct _XRegion {
    long size;
    long numRects;
    BOX *rects,
    BOX extents,
} REGION;
```

See Also
Core(3)

XtGeometryHandler

Name

XtGeometryHandler — prototype procedure to handle geometry requests.

Synopsis

```
typedef XtGeometryResult (*XtGeometryHandler)(Widget, XtWidget-
        Geometry *, XtWidgetGeometry *);
    Widget w;
    XtWidgetGeometry *request;
    XtWidgetGeometry *geometry_return;
```

Arguments

w   Specifies the widget that is making the request.

request   Specifies the desired widget geometry (size, position, border width, and stacking order.)

geometry_return

                  Returns the allowed widget size or may be null if the requesting widget is not interested in handling XtGeometryAlmost.

Description

Procedures of type XtGeometryHandler are used to negotiate geometry requests.

The Core query_geometry method and the Composite geometry_manager method are both of type XtGeometryHandler. See Composite(3) for additional details.

The query_geometry procedure pointer is of type XtGeometryHandler:

```
typedef XtGeometryResult (*XtGeometryHandler)(Widget, XtWidgetGeometry *,\
        XtWidgetGeometry *);
    Widget w;
    XtWidgetGeometry *request;
    XtWidgetGeometry *geometry_return;
```

The query_geometry procedure is expected to examine the bits set in request->request_mode, evaluate the preferred geometry of the widget, and store the result in geometry_return (setting the bits in geometry_return->request_mode corresponding to those geometry fields that it cares about). If the proposed geometry change is acceptable without modification, the query_geometry procedure should return Xt-GeometryYes. If at least one field in geometry_return is different from the corresponding field in request or if a bit was set in geometry_return that was not set in request, the query_geometry procedure should return XtGeometryAlmost. If the preferred geometry is identical to the current geometry, the query_geometry procedure should return Xt-GeometryNo.

Structures

The return codes from geometry managers are:

```
typedef enum _XtGeometryResult {
    XtGeometryYes,    /* Request accepted */
    XtGeometryNo,     /* Request denied */
    XtGeometryAlmost,/* Request denied but willing to take reply */
    XtGeometryDone   /* Request accepted and done */
} XtGeometryResult;
```

The XtWidgetGeometry structure is similar to but not identical to the corresponding Xlib structure:

```
typedef unsigned long XtGeometryMask;

typedef struct {
    XtGeometryMask request_mode;
    Position x, y,
    Dimension width, height,
    Dimension border_width;
    Widget sibling;
    int stack_mode,
} XtWidgetGeometry,
```

The request_mode definitions are from <*X11/X h*>

```
#define    CWX              (1<<0)
#define    CWY              (1<<1)
#define    CWWidth          (1<<2)
#define    CWHeight         (1<<3)
#define    CWBorderWidth    (1<<4)
#define    CWSibling        (1<<5)
#define    CWStackMode      (1<<6)
```

The Xt Intrinsics also support the following value.

```
#define    XtCWQueryOnly    (1<<7)
```

XtCWQueryOnly indicates that the corresponding geometry request is only a query as to what would happen if this geometry request were made and that no widgets should actually be changed

XtMakeGeometryRequest, like the Xlib XConfigureWindow function, uses request_mode to determine which fields in the XtWidgetGeometry structure you want to specify.

The stack_mode definitions are from <*X11/X h*>·

```
#define    Above        0
#define    Below        1
#define    TopIf        2
#define    BottomIf     3
#define    Opposite     4
```

The Intrinsics also support the following value:

```
#define    XtSMDontChange    5
```

For precise definitions of Above, Below, TopIf, BottomIf, and Opposite, see the reference page for XConfigureWindow in Volume Two, *Xlib Reference Manual*. XtSMDont-Change indicates that the widget wants its current stacking order preserved.

See Also
Section 1.8, "Geometry Management,'"
Chapter 11, *Geometry Management*, in Volume 4, *X Toolkit Intrinsics Programming Manual*.

Name

XtInitProc — prototype initialize procedure for a widget class

Synopsis

```
typedef void (*XtInitProc)(request, new);
    Widget request, new;
```

Arguments

request   Specifies the widget with resource values as requested by the argument list,
           the resource database, and the widget defaults

new   Specifies a widget with the new values, both resource and nonresource, as
           modified by the initialize procedure

Description

An initialization procedure performs the following.

- Allocates space for and copies any resources that are referenced by address For example, if a widget has a field that is a `String`, it cannot depend on the characters at that address remaining constant but must dynamically allocate space for the string and copy it to the new space. (Note that you should not allocate space for or copy callback lists)

- Computes values for unspecified resource fields. For example, if width and height are zero, the widget should compute an appropriate width and height based on other resources. This is the only time that a widget should ever directly assign its own width and height.

- Computes values for uninitialized nonresource fields that are derived from resource fields. For example, graphics contexts (GCs) that the widget uses are derived from resources like background, foreground, and font.

An initialization procedure also can check certain fields for internal consistency For example, it makes no sense to specify a color map for a depth that does not support that color map

Initialization procedures are called in superclass-to-subclass order. Most of the initialization code for a specific widget class deals with fields defined in that class and not with fields defined in its superclasses.

If a subclass does not need an initialization procedure because it does not need to perform any of the above operations, it can specify NULL for the initialize field in the class record.

Sometimes a subclass may want to overwrite values filled in by its superclass. In particular, size calculations of a superclass are often incorrect for a subclass and in this case, the subclass must modify or recalculate fields declared and computed by its superclass

As an example, a subclass can visually surround its superclass display In this case, the width and height calculated by the superclass initialize procedure are too small and need to be incremented by the size of the surround The subclass needs to know if its superclass' size was calculated by the superclass or was specified explicitly All widgets must place themselves into whatever size is explicitly given, but they should compute a reasonable size if no size is requested.

The `request` and `new` arguments provide the necessary information for how a subclass knows the difference between a specified size and a size computed by a superclass. The `request` widget is the widget as originally requested. The `new` widget starts with the values in the request, but it has been updated by all superclass initialization procedures called so far. A subclass initialize procedure can compare these two to resolve any potential conflicts.

In the above example, the subclass with the visual surround can see if the width and height in the `request` widget are zero. If so, it adds its surround size to the width and height fields in the `new` widget. If not, it must make do with the size originally specified.

The `new` widget will become the actual widget instance record. Therefore, the initialization procedure should do all its work on the `new` widget (the `request` widget should never be modified), and if it needs to call any routines that operate on a widget, it should specify `new` as the widget instance.

See Also
Section 1.1, "Widget Lifecycle,"
Core(3).

Prototype
Procedures

XtInputCallbackProc

Name
XtInputCallbackProc — prototype procedure called to handle file events

Synopsis
```
typedef void (*XtInputCallbackProc)(caddr_t, int *, XtInputId *),
    caddr_t client_data;
    int *source;
    XtInputId *id;
```

Arguments
client_data Specifies the client data that was registered for this procedure in XtApp-
             AddInput.

source   Specifies the source file descriptor generating the event.

id   Specifies the ID returned from the corresponding XtAppAddInput call.

Description
An XtInputCallbackProc is registered by calling XtAddInput or XtAppAddInput
id is the return value from the procedure that registered it.

An XtInputCallbackProc is called when there is activity in file source A procedure of
this type is called to handle the type of file activity (input, output) it was registered for.

The example below shows an XtInputCallbackProc named get_file_input together
with the application used to register it.

```
/* header files */
    .
    .
    .

/* ARGSUSED */
get_file_input(client_data, fid, id)
caddr_t client_data,/* unused */
int *fid;
XtInputId *id,
{
    char buf[BUFSIZ];
    int nbytes,
    int i;

    if ((nbytes = read(*fid, buf, BUFSIZ)) == -1)
    perror("get_file_input");

    if (nbytes)
    for (i = 0; i < nbytes, i++)
    putchar(buf[i]),
}

main(argc, argv)
int argc,
```

```
char **argv;
{
    Widget topLevel, goodbye;
    FILE *fid;
    String filename;

    topLevel = XtInitialize(argv[0], "XFileInput", NULL,
    0, &argc, argv);

    if (argv[1] == NULL) {
    fprintf(stderr, "xfileinput: filename must be specified on\
                     command line.\n");
    exit(1);
    }
    filename = argv[1];
        .
        .
        .

    /* open file */
    if ((fid = fopen(filename, "r")) == NULL)
    fprintf(stderr, "xfileinput: couldn't open input file");

    /* register function to handle that input, NULL arg is client_data */
    XtAddInput(fileno(fid), XtInputReadMask, get_file_input, NULL);

    XtRealizeWidget(topLevel);

    XtMainLoop();
}
```

See Also

XtAddInput, XtAppAddInput.

XtKeyProc

Xt – Keyboard Handling

Name

XtKeyProc — prototype procedure to translate a key

Synopsis

```
typedef void (*XtKeyProc)(Display *, KeyCode *, Modifiers *,
Modifiers *, KeySym *);
    Display *display;
    KeyCode *keycode;
    Modifiers *modifiers;
    Modifiers *modifiers_return;
    KeySym *keysym_return;
```

Arguments

display   Specifies the display from which to translate the events.

keycode   Specifies the keycode that is to be translated.

modifiers   Specifies the mask that indicates what modifier keys (Shift, Meta, Control, etc.) are pressed

modifiers_return
                 Specifies the mask of modifier keys that the function actually evaluated in making the conversion.

keysym_return
                 Specifies the resulting keysym

Description

The Resource Manager provides support for automatically translating keycodes in incoming key events into keysyms. Keycode-to-keysym translator procedure pointers are of type Xt-KeyProc

This procedure takes a keycode and modifiers and produces a keysym For any given key translator function, *modifiers_return* will be a constant that indicates the subset of all modifiers that are examined by the key translator

The default translator is XtTranslateKey, an XtKeyProc that uses Shift and Lock modifiers with the interpretations defined by the core protocol. The MIT R3 code for Xt-TranslateKey and associated internal routines is shown below

```
void _XtBuildKeysymTable(dpy,pd)
    Display* dpy,
    XtPerDisplay pd;
{
    int count,
    KeySym lower_return, upper_return,nbd, *bd;

    count = dpy->max_keycode-dpy->min_keycode+1;
    pd->keysyms = XGetKeyboardMapping(
        dpy,dpy->min_keycode,count,&pd->keysyms_per_keycode);
    if (pd->keysyms_per_keycode > 1)
```

306   *Xt Intrinsics Reference Manual*

```
        nbd = (dpy->max_keycode - dpy->min_keycode + 1)
            * pd->keysyms_per_keycode;
        for (bd = pd->keysyms; bd < (pd->keysyms + nbd);
             bd += pd->keysyms_per_keycode) {
            if ((*(bd+1)) == NoSymbol) {
                XtConvertCase(dpy,*bd, &lower_return, &upper_return);
                *bd = lower_return;
                *(bd+1) = upper_return;
            }
        }
}

KeySym _XtKeyCodeToKeySym(dpy,pd,keycode,col)
    Display* dpy;
    XtPerDisplay pd;
    KeyCode keycode;
    int col;
{
/* copied from Xlib */
    int ind;
    if (pd->keysyms == NULL) {
        _XtBuildKeysymTable(dpy,pd); /* pd->keysyms*/
    }
    if (col < 0 || col >= pd->keysyms_per_keycode) return (NoSymbol);
    if (keycode < dpy->min_keycode || keycode > dpy->max_keycode)
      return(NoSymbol);

    ind = (keycode - dpy->min_keycode) * pd->keysyms_per_keycode + col;
    return (pd->keysyms[ind]);
}

void XtTranslateKey(dpy, keycode, modifiers,
                            modifiers_return, keysym_return)
    Display *dpy;
    KeyCode keycode;
    Modifiers modifiers;
    Modifiers *modifiers_return;
    KeySym *keysym_return;

{
    XtPerDisplay perDisplay;
    perDisplay = _XtGetPerDisplay(dpy);
    *modifiers_return = StandardMask;
    if ((modifiers & StandardMask) == 0)
        *keysym_return = _XtKeyCodeToKeySym(dpy,perDisplay,keycode,0);
    else if ((modifiers & (ShiftMask | LockMask)) != 0)
        *keysym_return = _XtKeyCodeToKeySym(dpy,perDisplay,keycode,1);
    else
        *keysym_return = NoSymbol;
}
```

Prototype Procedures

The XtPerDisplay structure referenced in the example is an internal structure used to keep track of variables that may differ on a display-by-display basis

Structures

```
typedef unsigned int Modifiers,
```

Modifiers will be made up of the bitwise OR the following masks

ShiftMask	Shift key was depressed
LockMask	Caps Lock key was depressed.
ControlMask	Control key was depressed.
Mod1Mask	Key defined as Mod1 was depressed

.

.

Mod5Mask	Key defined as Mod5 was depressed.
StandardMask	(ShiftMask | LockMask).

For a more detailed discussion of processing keyboard input, see Chapter 13, *Miscellaneous Toolkit Programming Techniques*, in Volume Four, *X Toolkit Intrinsics Programming Manual*

See Also

XtSetKeyTranslator, XtTranslateKeycode, XtTranslateKey

Name

XtLoseSelectionProc — prototype procedure called by the Intrinsics when another client claims the selection.

Synopsis

```
typedef void (*XtLoseSelectionProc)(Widget, Atom *);
    Widget w;
    Atom *selection;
```

Arguments

w   Specifies the widget that has lost selection ownership.

selection   Specifies the atom that describes the selection type.

Description

This procedure is called by the Intrinsics when the specified widget loses the selection. The XtLoseSelectionProc is registered when a widget asserts selection ownership with Xt-OwnSelection.

The Intrinsics use this procedure to inform the former selection owner after the selection changes hands. Note that this procedure does not ask the widget to lose the selection ownership.

Chapter 10, *Inter-Client Communications*, in Volume Four, *X Toolkit Intrinsics Programming Manual*, presents a complete example widget that both sends and receives data using selections.

See Also

XtDisownSelection, XtGetSelectionValues, XtOwnSelection.

XtOrderProc

Name

XtOrderProc — prototype procedure for ordering the children of composite widget instances.

Synopsis

```
typedef Cardinal (*XtOrderProc)(Widget);
    Widget w;
```

Arguments

w   Specifies the widget.

Description

Instances of composite widgets need to specify about the order in which their children are kept. For example, an application may want a set of command buttons in some logical order grouped by function, and it may want buttons that represent file names to be kept in alphabetical order.

The `insert_position` method in a composite widget instance is of type `XtOrderProc`

Composite widgets that allow clients to order their children (usually homogeneous boxes) can call their widget instance's `insert_position` method from the class' `insert_child` method to determine where a new child should go in its children array Thus, a client of a composite class can apply different sorting criteria to widget instances of the class, passing in a different `insert_position` method when it creates each composite widget instance.

The return value of the `insert_position` method indicates how many children should go before the widget. Returning zero indicates that the widget should go before all other children, and returning `num_children` indicates that it should go after all other children. The default `insert_position` method returns `num_children` and can be overridden by a specific composite widget's resource list or by the argument list provided when the composite widget is created.

XtProc

Name

XtProc — prototype procedure to initialize data for a widget class.

Synopsis

```
typedef void (*XtProc);
```

Description

An XtProc is a procedure to initialize data at program startup time. One-time initialization can be performed here, such as parsing accelerator tables, registering type converters, run-time alterations to data structures, or other actions that cannot be performed at compile time.

The Core class_init method is of this type.

See Also

Core(3)

Prototype
Procedures

XtRealizeProc

Name

XtRealizeProc — prototype procedure called when widget is realized.

Synopsis

```
typedef void (*XtRealizeProc)(Widget, XtValueMask, XSetWindow-
        Attributes *);
    Widget w;
    XtValueMask value_mask;
    XSetWindowAttributes *attributes;
```

Arguments

w   Specifies the widget.

value_mask   Specifies which fields in the attributes structure to use.

attributes   Specifies the window attributes to use in the XCreateWindow call.

Description

The Intrinsics invoke the Core realize method when the application calls XtRealize-Widget on the application's top-level widget.

The Core realize method must create the widget's window. The value mask indicates what values in the XSetWindowAttributes structure are used.

The generic XtRealizeWidget function fills in a mask and a corresponding XSet-WindowAttributes structure. It sets the following fields based on information in the widget Core structure:

- The background_pixmap (or background_pixel if background_pixmap is NULL) is filled in from the corresponding field.

- The border_pixmap (or border_pixel if border_pixmap is NULL) is filled in from the corresponding field

- The event_mask is filled in based on the event handlers registered, the event translations specified, whether expose is non-NULL, and whether visible_interest is TRUE

- The bit_gravity is set to NorthWestGravity if the expose field is NULL

- The do_not_propagate_mask is set to propagate all pointer and keyboard events up the window tree. A composite widget can implement functionality caused by an event anywhere inside it (including on top of children widgets) as long as children do not specify a translation for the event.

All other fields in attributes (and the corresponding bits in value_mask) can be set by the realize method

Note that because realize is not a chained operation, the widget class realize method must update the XSetWindowAttributes structure with all the appropriate fields from non-Core superclasses.

A widget class can inherit its `realize` method from its superclass during class initialization. The `realize` method defined for Core calls `XtCreateWindow` with the passed `value_mask` and attributes and with `windowClass` and `visual` set to `CopyFrom-Parent`. Both `CompositeWidgetClass` and `ConstraintWidgetClass` inherit this `realize` method, and most new widget subclasses can do the same.

The most common noninherited `realize` methods set `bit_gravity` in the mask and attributes to the appropriate value and then create the window. For example, depending on its justi-fication, Label sets `bit_gravity` to `WestGravity`, `CenterGravity`, or `East-Gravity`. Consequently, shrinking it just moves the bits appropriately, and no `Expose` event is needed for repainting.

If a composite widget's children should be realized in a particular order (typically to control the stacking order), the widget should call `XtRealizeWidget` on its children itself in the appropriate order from within its own `realize` method.

Widgets that have children and that are not a subclass of `compositeWidgetClass` are responsible for calling `XtRealizeWidget` on their children, usually from within the `realize` method.

Structures

```
/* Definitions for valuemask argument.  These control which fields in
 * XSetWindowAttributes structure should be used.
 */

typedef struct {
    Pixmap background_pixmap;        /* background or None or ParentRelative * /
    unsigned long background_pixel;  /* background pixel */
    Pixmap border_pixmap;            /* border of the window */
    unsigned long border_pixel;      /* border pixel value */
    int bit_gravity;                 /* one of bit gravity values */
    int win_gravity;                 /* one of the window gravity values */
    int backing_store;               /* NotUseful, WhenMapped, Always */
    unsigned long backing_planes;    /* planes to be preserved if possible */
    unsigned long backing_pixel;     /* value to use in restoring planes */
    Bool save_under;                 /* should bits under be saved (popups) */
    long event_mask;                 /* set of events that should be saved */
    long do_not_propagate_mask;      /* set of events that should not propagate */
    Bool override_redirect;          /* boolean value for override-redirect */
    Colormap colormap;               /* colormap to be associated with window */
    Cursor cursor;                   /* cursor to be displayed (or None) */
} XSetWindowAttributes;
```

See Also

Section 1.1, "Widget Lifecycle,"
`XtCreateWindow`, `XtRealizeWidget`,
`Core`(3).

Name

XtResourceDefaultProc — prototype procedure passed as a resource converter of type Xt-RCallProc

Synopsis

```
typedef void (*XtResourceDefaultProc)(Widget, int, XrmValue *)
    Widget w,
    int offset;
    XrmValue *value,
```

Arguments

w	Specifies the widget whose resource is to be obtained
offset	Specifies the offset of the field in the widget record.
value	Specifies the resource value to fill in.

Description

Every resource has a representation type There are 26 types defined by the Intrinsics, and additional user types can be created by registering a type converter for them (see XtAddConverter).

Two special representation types (XtRImmediate and XtRCallProc) are usable only as default resource types. XtRImmediate indicates that the value in the default_address field of the XtResource structure is the actual value of the resource rather than the address of the value The value must be in correct representation type for the resource No conversion is possible since there is no source representation type XtRCallProc indicates that the value in the default_address field of the XtResource structure is a procedure variable This procedure is automatically invoked with the widget, resource_offset, and a pointer to the XrmValue in which to store the result and is an XtResourceDefaultProc.

The XtResourceDefaultProc procedure should fill in the addr field of the value with a pointer to the default data in its correct type.

The default_address field in the resource structure is declared as a caddr_t On some machine architectures, this may be insufficient to hold procedure variables.

The example below shows an XtResourceDefaultProc used to obtain a pointer to the current screen at runtime.

```
/*ARGSUSED*/
void XtCopyScreen(widget, offset, value)
    Widget      widget,
    int         offset;
    XrmValue    *value;
{
    value->addr = (caddr_t)(&widget->core screen);
}
```

See Also
 Section 1.7, "Resources"

Prototype
Procedures

XtSelectionCallbackProc

Name

XtSelectionCallbackProc — prototype procedure called when requested selection data arrives.

Synopsis

```
typedef void (*XtSelectionCallbackProc)(Widget, caddr_t, Atom *,
        Atom *, caddr_t, unsigned long *, int *),
    Widget w;
    caddr_t client_data;
    Atom *selection;
    Atom *type;
    caddr_t value;
    unsigned long *length;
    int *format;
```

Arguments

w	Specifies the widget that requested the selection value.
client_data	Specifies a value passed in by the widget when it requested the selection
selection	Specifies the type of selection that was requested
type	Specifies the representation type of the selection value (for example, XA_STRING) Note that it is not the target that was requested but the type that is used to represent the target. The special X Toolkit atom XT_CONVERT_FAIL is used to indicate that the selection conversion failed because the selection owner did not respond within the Intrinsics' selection timeout interval
value	Specifies a pointer to the selection value. The requesting client owns this storage and is responsible for freeing it by calling XtFree when it is done with it.
length	Specifies the number of elements in value
format	Specifies the size in bits of the data elements of value.

Description

This procedure is called by the Intrinsics selection mechanism to deliver the requested selection to the requestor Data transfer proceeds as follows data is requested from the owner of the selection with XtGetSelectionValue or XtGetSelectionValues; when it finally arrives, the SelectionCallbackProc is invoked with the actual data

Data delivery is done by callback, since the Intrinsics may have to perform multiple server requests to get data, and other events may require processing ahead of the data transfer Therefore, actual data delivery must occur asynchronously with respect to XtGetSelection-Value or XtGetSelectionValues

Chapter 10, *Inter-Client Communications*, in Volume Four, *X Toolkit Intrinsics Programming Manual*, presents a complete example widget that both sends and receives data using selections.

See Also

XtDisownSelection, XtGetSelectionValue, XtGetSelectionValues, XtOwn-Selection.

Name

XtSelectionDoneProc — prototype procedure called after a data transfer completes.

Synopsis

```
typedef void (*XtSelectionDoneProc)(Widget, Atom *, Atom *);
    Widget w;
    Atom *selection;
    Atom *target;
```

Arguments

w	Specifies the widget that owns the converted selection.
selection	Specifies the atom that describes the selection type that was converted.
target	Specifies the target type to which the conversion was done

Description

The Intrinsics call the XtSelectionDoneProc specified in the call to XtGet-SelectionValue or XtGetSelectionValues when the data transfer is actually complete.

If the selection owner has registered an XtSelectionDoneProc, it will be called once for each conversion that it performs after the converted value has been successfully transferred to the requestor

If the selection owner has registered an XtSelectionDoneProc, it also owns the storage containing the converted selection value. XtSelectionDoneProc can be used by the selection owner to deallocate memory allocated in ConvertSelectionProc.

Chapter 10, *Inter-Client Communications*, in Volume Four, *X Toolkit Intrinsics Programming Manual*, presents a complete example widget that both sends and receives data using selections.

See Also

XtDisownSelection, XtGetSelectionValue, XtGetSelectionValues, XtOwn-Selection.

XtSetValuesFunc

Name

XtSetValuesFunc — prototype procedure for various set_values methods.

Synopsis

```
typedef Boolean (*XtSetValuesFunc)(Widget, Widget, Widget);
    Widget current;
    Widget request;
    Widget new;
```

Arguments

current   Specifies a copy of the widget as it was before the XtSetValues call.

request   Specifies a copy of the widget with all values changed as asked for by the XtSetValues call before any class set_values procedures have been called.

new   Specifies the widget with the new values that are actually allowed.

Description

The Core set_values method and Constraint set_values method are both of type Xt-SetValuesFunc. The Constraint set_values method operates in the context of the child. This means its widget arguments are instances of the child, not the parent, even though they are class fields of the (Constraint) Parent.

current, request, and new are widget instance records of the appropriate widget class. new reflects values that have been modified by superclass set_values methods. request reflects changes made only by the XtSetValues call itself. current was the widget instance at the time of the call, reflecting no changes. A widget can refer to request, to resolve conflicts between current and new. Any changes that the widget needs to make should be made to new.

An XtSetValuesFunc returns a Boolean indicating TRUE if the widget should be redisplayed and FALSE otherwise. set_values methods should not do any work in response to anticipated changes in geometry because XtSetValues will eventually perform a geometry request. The request might be denied. If the widget actually changes size in response to an XtSetValues, its resize method is called. Widgets should make geometry-related changes there.

An XtSetValuesFunc cannot assume that the widget is realized, since it is permissible for an application to call XtSetValues before a widget is realized.

See Also

XtSetValues,
Constraint(3), Core(3).

XtStringProc

Name
XtStringProc — prototype procedure for `display_accelerator` method.

Synopsis
```
typedef void (*XtStringProc)(Widget, String)
    Widget w;
    String string;
```

Arguments
w   Specifies the widget instance requiring redisplay

string   Provides the string representation of the accelerators currently registered for the widget.

Description
This is the type of the `display_accelerator` method in the Core class

The string may not be an exact replica of the event it was registered with Instead, it represents a translation in canonical form.

See Also
`XtDisplayAccelerator`

XtTimerCallbackProc

Name

XtTimerCallbackProc — prototype callback procedure invoked when timeouts expire.

Synopsis

```
typedef void (*XtTimerCallbackProc)(caddr_t, XtIntervalId *);
    caddr_t client_data;
    XtIntervalId *id;
```

Arguments

client_data   Specifies the client data that was registered for this procedure in XtApp-
           AddTimeOut.

id   Specifies the ID returned from the corresponding XtAppAddTimeOut call.

Description

An XtTimerCallbackProc is invoked in response to an expired timing interval, as set by
XtAddTimeOut.

For a periodic wakeup, the callback procedure must call XtAddTimeOut again from this procedure.

See Also

XtAddTimeOut, XtAppAddTimeOut,
Chapter 8, *More Input Techniques*, in Volume Four, *X Toolkit Intrinsics Programming Manual*.

XtWidgetProc

Name

XtWidgetProc — common prototype procedure for widget methods.

Synopsis

```
typedef void (*XtWidgetProc)(Widget);
    Widget w;
```

Arguments

w   Specifies the widget.

Description

Several widget methods are of type XtWidgetProc. These include the Core and Constraint destroy methods, and the Composite insert_child, delete_child, and change_managed methods.

Since there are no additional arguments, methods of this type must access the widget instance data structures. For example, the change_managed method must access the child array from the Composite structures in the instance record.

See Also

Section 1.1, "Widget Lifecycle, "Section 1.8, "Geometry Management,"
Composite(3), Constraint(3), Core(3).

322   X Toolkit Intrinsics Reference Manual

XtWorkProc

Name

XtWorkProc — perform background processing.

Synopsis

```
typedef Boolean (*XtWorkProc)(caddr_t);
    caddr_t client_data;
```

Arguments

client_data   Represents the client data specified when the work procedure was registered.

Description

A work procedure is an application-supplied function that is executed while an application is idle waiting for an event. Work procedures are registered with XtAddWorkProc. They can perform any calculation that is short enough that the routine will return in a small fraction of a second. If the work procedure is too long, the user's response time will suffer.

If a work procedure returns TRUE, then Xt will remove it and it will not be called again. But if one returns FALSE, it will be called repeatedly every time there is idle time, until the application calls XtRemoveWorkProc. A work procedure would return TRUE if it performs a one-time setup such as creating a pop-up widget. It would return FALSE if it were continuously updating a disk file as security against a system crash or server connection failure.

You can register multiple work procedures, and they will be performed one at a time. The most recent work procedure added has the highest priority. Therefore, for example, if you want to create ten pop-up widgets during idle time, you should add ten work procedures. The pop up that you expect to need first should be added in the last work procedure registered.

Work procedures should be judicious about how much processing they consume each time they are called. If they run for more than a fraction of a second, an application's interactive response time is likely to suffer.

The example below shows a work procedure to create a pop-up widget.

```
Widget pshell;

/* work procedure */
Boolean
create_popup(parent)
Widget parent;
{
    Widget dialog, dialogDone;

        pshell = XtCreatePopupShell(
                "pshell",
                transientShellWidgetClass,
                parent,
                NULL,
                0
                );

        dialog = XtCreateManagedWidget(
```

```
            "dialog",/* widget name    */
            dialogWidgetClass,/* widget class */
            pshell,/* parent widget*/
            NULL,/* argument list*/
            0/* arglist size */
            );

    dialogDone = XtCreateManagedWidget(
            "dialogDone",/* widget name    */
            commandWidgetClass,/* widget class */
            dialog,/* parent widget*/
            NULL,/* argument list*/
            0/* arglist size */
            );

    XtAddCallback(dialogDone, XtNcallback, DialogDone, dialog);

    return(TRUE);/* makes Xt remove this work proc automatically */
}
```

Remember that Xt cannot interrupt a work procedure while it is running; the procedure must voluntarily give up control by returning, and it must do so quickly to avoid slowing user response

See Also
XtAppAddWorkProc

Intrinsics-mandated
Widget Classes

This section contains reference pages for the Intrinsics-mandated widget classes: Core, Composite, Constraint, and Shell. It describes the class and instance records for these widget classes, and provides a detailed description of each of their methods.

As an exception to the general rule that reference pages are organized alphabetically, in this section they are presented in order of inheritance: Core, Composite, Constraint, and Shell.

Core

Name
Core Widget Class — fundamental, top-level widget.

Synopsis
```
#include StringDefs.h
#include Intrinsic.h
```

Description
The Core widget class is the most fundamental type of widget. All other widgets are subclasses of it. Widgets consist of two data structures: a class record (CoreClassPart) and an instance record (CorePart). Both records are defined in *<X11/CoreP.h>*. Volume Four, *X Toolkit Intrinsics Programming Manual*, discusses how Intrinsics support object-oriented programming. The Core widget itself is described there also, as is a template widget.

The Release 3 data structures are described here. They differ only in minor ways from the Release 2 structures.

The class and instance structure are defined in *<X11/CoreP.h>*.

The ClassPart is defined below:

```
typedef struct _CoreClassPart {
    WidgetClass superclass;           /* pointer to superclass ClassRec */
    String class_name;                /* widget resource class name */
    Cardinal widget_size;             /* size in bytes of widget record */
    XtProc class_initialize;          /* class initialization proc */
    XtWidgetClassProc class_part_initialize;
                                      /* dynamic initialization */
    Boolean class_inited;             /* has class been initialized? */
    XtInitProc initialize;            /* initialize subclass fields */
    XtArgsProc initialize_hook;       /* notify that initialize called */
    XtRealizeProc realize;            /* XCreateWindow for widget */
    XtActionList actions;             /* widget semantics name to proc map */
    Cardinal num_actions;             /* number of entries in actions */
    XtResourceList resources;         /* resources for subclass fields */
    Cardinal num_resources;           /* number of entries in resources */
    XrmClass xrm_class;               /* resource class quarkified */
    Boolean compress_motion;          /* compress MotionNotify for widget */
    Boolean compress_exposure;        /* compress Expose events for widget*/
    Boolean compress_enterleave;      /* compress enter and leave events */
    Boolean visible_interest;         /* select for VisibilityNotify */
    XtWidgetProc destroy;             /* free data for subclass pointers */
    XtWidgetProc resize;              /* geom manager changed widget size */
    XtExposeProc expose;              /* redisplay window */
    XtSetValuesFunc set_values;       /* set subclass resource values */
    XtArgsFunc set_values_hook;       /* notify that set_values called */
    XtAlmostProc set_values_almost;   /* set_values got "Almost" geo reply */
    XtArgsProc get_values_hook;       /* notify that get_values called */
    XtAcceptFocusProc accept_focus;   /* assign input focus to widget */
    XtVersionType version;            /* version of Intrinsics used */
```

```
    struct _XtOffsetRec *callback_private;
                                /* list of callback offsets */
    String tm_table,            /* state machine */
    XtGeometryHandler query_geometry;
                                /* return preferred geometry */
    XtStringProc display_accelerator,
                                /* display your accelerator */
    caddr_t extension;          /* pointer to extension record */
} CoreClassPart,
```

The core instance record is defined as follows

```
typedef struct _CorePart {
    Widget self;                    /* pointer to widget itself */
    WidgetClass widget_class,       /* pointer to widget's ClassRec */
    Widget parent,                  /* parent widget */
    XrmName xrm_name;               /* widget resource name quarkified */
    Boolean being_destroyed,        /* marked for destroy */
    XtCallbackList destroy_callbacks,/* who to call when widget destroyed */
    caddr_t constraints;            /* constraint record */
    Position x, y,                  /* window position */
    Dimension width, height,        /* window dimensions */
    Dimension border_width;         /* window border width */
    Boolean managed;                /* is widget geometry managed? */
    Boolean sensitive;              /* is widget sensitive to user events */
    Boolean ancestor_sensitive;     /* are all ancestors sensitive? */
    XtEventTable event_table;       /* private to event dispatcher */
    XtTMRec tm,                     /* translation management */
    XtTranslations accelerators,    /* accelerator translations */
    Pixel border_pixel;             /* window border pixel */
    Pixmap border_pixmap;           /* window border pixmap or NULL */
    WidgetList popup_list;          /* list of pop ups */
    Cardinal num_popups;            /* how many pop ups */
    String name,                    /* widget resource name */
    Screen *screen,                 /* window's screen */
    Colormap colormap;              /* colormap */
    Window window;                  /* window ID */
    Cardinal depth;                 /* number of planes in window */
    Pixel background_pixel;         /* window background pixel */
    Pixmap background_pixmap;       /* window background pixmap or NULL */
    Boolean visible;                /* is window mapped and not occluded? */
    Boolean mapped_when_managed;    /* map window if it is managed? */
} CorePart;
```

The default values for the core fields, which are filled in by the Core resource list and the Core
initialize method, are

Field	Default Value
self	Address of the widget structure (may not be changed).
widget_class	*widget_class* argument to XtCreateWidget (may not be changed).
parent	*parent* argument to XtCreateWidget (may not be changed).
xrm_name	Encoded *name* argument to XtCreateWidget (may not be changed).
being_destroyed	Parent's *being_destroyed* value.
destroy_callbacks	NULL
constraints	NULL
x	0
y	0
width	0
height	0
border_width	1
managed	FALSE
sensitive	TRUE
ancestor_sensitive	Bitwise AND of parent's *sensitive* and *ancestor_sensitive*.
event_table	Initialized by the Event Manager.
tm	Initialized by the Resource Manager.
accelerators	NULL
border_pixel	XtDefaultForeground
border_pixmap	NULL
popup_list	NULL
num_popups	0
name	*name* argument to XtCreateWidget (may not be changed).
screen	Parent's screen; top-level widget gets it from display specifier (may not be changed).
colormap	Default colormap for the screen.
window	NULL
depth	Parent's depth; top-level widget gets root window depth.
background_pixel	XtDefaultBackground
background_pixmap	NULL
visible	TRUE
mapped_when_managed	TRUE

Core Methods

Core methods can often be inherited from a superclass. This is done by specifying Xt-Inherit*procname* in the class field. For example, XtInheritRealize will inherit the realize method

Initialize

initialize methods are of type XtInitProc. initialize is called once for each widget instance that is created. A minimum initialize method is shown below.

```
static XtInitProc Initialize(request, new)
Widget request, new;
{
 new->core.height = 100;
 new->core width = 100,
 }
```

request is a copy of the widget instance with resources supplied by the caller. new is the widget after it has been initialized by the superclasses of the widget. new will endure beyond the initialization as the actual widget instance record. request is a template and will be destroyed when initialization is complete, it should not be modified. Using request and new, a class can determine whether a value was computed by the superclass or was specified by the widget creator explicitly.

As an example, a subclass can visually surround its superclass display In this case, the width and height calculated by the superclass initialize procedure are too small and need to be incremented by the size of the surrounding border.

At a minimum, the initialize method must compute values for core width and height, if they have not been computed by a superclass This is the only time that a widget should ever directly assign its own width and height

Additionally, an initialization procedure may perform the following

- Allocate space and copy the actual value of any resource that is passed by pointer For example, if a widget is passed a pointer to a String, the widget must dynamically allocate space for a new string and copy it—the application's copy of the String may not remain intact after the call Note that you should not allocate space for, or copy, callback lists Any resource of type XtRCallback should be treated as opaque Callback lists can be manipulated by specific Intrinsic routines (See XtAddCallbacks, XtCall-Callbacks, XtRemoveCallbacks, etc.)

- Compute values for instance variables and resources For example, the widget must ensure that core width and height are nonzero

- Compute instance variables that are derived from resources For example, graphics contexts (GCs) that the widget uses are derived from resources like background, foreground, and font.

- Supersede values in the superclass Initialization procedures are called in superclass-to-subclass order The main purpose of a subclass may be to change non-resource data in a superclass, since the subclass has direct access to the instance record

In particular, size calculations of a superclass are often incorrect for a subclass, and the subclass must modify or recalculate fields declared and computed by its superclass.

- Check fields for internal consistency. For example, the user may specify a colormap for a display depth that cannot support it.

If a subclass does not need an initialization procedure, it can specify NULL for the initialize field in the class record.

class_part_initialize and class_initialize

class_part_initialize and class_initialize are of types XtInitProc and XtProc, respectively.

class_initialize is called by the Intrinsics only once per program lifetime. It can be used to supply aggregate initialization of data.

It can perform Toolkit operations that are not dependent on a particular widget. For example, it can register converters and can cache strings into quarks for speedier subsequent use.

The class_part_initialize procedure is called once per class. For example, suppose a widget is part of several other classes. The class initialize will be called for each class record that the Intrinsics construct which contain this class.

Thus, if there are initialization operations dependent on the class record, it can perform those. For example, it may set the insert_position method in the composite instance record.

realize_proc

The realize method is of type XtRealizeProc. The realize method must create the widget's window. A minimum realize method is given below. (See also XtCreate-Window.)

```
static XtRealizeProc Realize(w, mask, attr)
GenericWidget w;
Mask *mask;
XSetWindowAttributes *attr;
{
   XtCreateWindow(w,
                  InputOutput,
                  (Visual *) CopyFromParent,
                  *mask,
                  attr);
}
```

The realize method defined for Core calls XtCreateWindow with the passed value_mask and attributes and with windowClass and visual set to CopyFromParent. Both CompositeWidgetClass and ConstraintWidgetClass inherit this realize method, and most new widget subclasses can do the same.

The most common noninherited realize methods set bit_gravity in the mask and attributes to the appropriate value and then create the window. For example, depending on its justification, Label sets bit_gravity to CenterGravity, EastGravity, or West-

Gravity. Consequently, shrinking the widget just moves the bits appropriately, and no Expose event is needed for repainting (See Volume One, *Xlib Programming Manual*, for additional details)

If a composite widget's children should be realized in a particular order (typically to control the stacking order), it should call its children's XtRealizeWidget in the appropriate order from within its own realize method.

Widgets that have children and are not subclasses of compositeWidgetClass are responsible for realizing their own children These children would usually be realized from their parent's realize method

destroy

The destroy method is of type XtWidgetProc.

The destroy methods are called in subclass-to-superclass order A widget's destroy method should only deallocate storage originally allocated by it and should not deallocate memory allocated by its superclasses If a widget does not need to deallocate any storage, the destroy procedure pointer in its widget class record can be NULL.

To reclaim memory, at least the following deallocations should be performed

- Call XtFree on dynamic storage allocated with XtCalloc, XtMalloc, etc

- Call XFreePixmap on pixmaps created with direct Xlib calls.

- Call XtDestroyGC on GCs allocated with XtGetGC.

- Call XFreeGC on GCs allocated with direct Xlib calls

- Call XtRemoveEventHandler on event handlers added with XtAddEvent-Handler

- Call XtRemoveTimeOut on timers created with XtAppAddTimeOut.

- Call XtDestroyWidget for each child if the widget has children and is not a subclass of compositeWidgetClass

expose

The expose method, responsible for all display and redisplay, is of type XtExposeProc If a widget has no display semantics, it can specify NULL for the expose field Many composite widgets serve only as containers for their children and have no expose method

If the expose method is NULL, XtRealizeWidget fills in a default bit gravity of North-WestGravity before it calls the widget's realize method

If the widget's compress_exposure field is FALSE, the region passed to the expose method is always NULL. If the widget's compress_exposure field is TRUE, the event contains the bounding box for region.

A small simple widget can ignore the bounding box information in the event and redisplay the entire window. A more complicated widget can use the bounding box to minimize the amount of calculation and redisplay it does. A very complex widget might use the region as a clip list in a GC and ignore the event information. The expose method is responsible for exposure of all superclass data as well as its own.

Sometimes it is possible to anticipate the display needs of several levels of subclass widgets. For example, rather than maintaining separate display procedures for the widgets Command, Label, and Toggle, they could share a single redisplay routine that uses display state information as follows:

```
Boolean invert
Boolean highlight
Dimension highlight_width
```

Label would have `invert` and `highlight` always FALSE and have `highlight_width` zero. Command would dynamically set `highlight` and `highlight_width`, but it would leave `invert` always FALSE. Finally, Toggle would dynamically set all three. In this case, the `expose` methods for Command and Toggle inherit their superclass' `expose` method.

Some widgets may use substantial computing resources to display data. However, this effort is wasted if the widget is not actually visible on the screen and is obscured by another application or is iconified.

The `visible` field in the Core widget instance structure provides a hint to the widget that it need not display data. This field is guaranteed TRUE by the time an `Expose` event is processed if the widget is visible but is usually FALSE if the widget is not visible.

Widgets can use or ignore the `visible` hint. If they ignore it, they should have `visible_interest` in their widget class record set FALSE. In such cases, the `visible` field is initialized TRUE and never changes. If `visible_interest` is TRUE, the Event Manager asks for `VisibilityNotify` events for the widget and updates the `visible` field accordingly.

resize

The `resize` method is of type `XtWidgetProc`. It takes a widget as its only argument. The `x, y, width, height` and `border_width` fields of the widget contain the new values. The `resize` method should recalculate the layout of internal data as needed.

If a widget simply draws itself from whatever size is placed in the core `height` and `width` instance variables, it does not need a `resize` method. If nothing needs to be recalculated, it can specify NULL for the `resize` field in its class record.

Other widgets need to know when they have changed size so that they can change the layout of their displayed data to match the new size. (For example, a widget may choose a new smaller font, if its size has been diminished.) The widget must treat `resize` as a command, not as a request. Nor can a widget appeal by issuing an `XtMakeGeometryRequest` or `XtMake-ResizeRequest` from its `resize` method.

When a parent widget is resized, it should reconfigure its children. When a parent resizes a child, it updates the geometry fields in the widget, configures the window if the widget is realized, and calls the child's `resize` method to notify the child. (See `XtConfigureWidget`.)

set_values

The set_values method is of type XtSetValuesFunc. It is called whenever the values within the widget structure are modified by a call to XtSetValues or a change in the widget's geometry (see XtConfigureWidget) The function should return a Boolean indicating whether the widget's redisplay method should be invoked

It should recompute any field derived from changed resources, for example, many GCs depend on foreground and background If no recomputation is ever necessary and if none of the resources specific to a subclass require the window to be redisplayed when their values are changed, you can specify NULL for the set_values field in the class record.

Like the initialize method, set_values is primarily concerned with the fields defined in the class, but it may have to resolve conflicts with its superclass, especially over width and height.

Sometimes a subclass may want to overwrite values filled in by its superclass In particular, size calculations of a superclass are often incorrect for a subclass, and in this case, the subclass must modify or recalculate fields declared and computed by its superclass.

As an example, a subclass can visually surround its superclass display. In this case, the width and height calculated by the superclass set_values method are too small and need to be incremented by the size of the surround The subclass needs to know if its superclass' size was calculated by the superclass or was specified explicitly. All widgets must place themselves into whatever size is explicitly given, but they should compute a reasonable size if no size is requested. How does a subclass know the difference between a specified size and a size computed by a superclass?

The request and new parameters provide the necessary information to resolve conflicts

```
static Boolean SetValues(current, request, new)
Widget current, request, new,
{ . . }
```

In the above example, the subclass with the visual surround can see if the width and height in the request widget are zero. If so, it adds its surround size to the width and height fields in the new widget. If not, it must make do with the size originally specified.

The request widget is the widget as originally requested. The new widget starts with the values in the request, after it has been updated by all the superclass set_values methods Subsequent subclass set_values methods can compare these two to resolve any conflicts Namely, if request fields are of the default value (height and width will be zero, for example), then the XtSetValues request did not affect those field, the fields in new are the result of the superclass' update

new is the actual widget instance record. Therefore, the set_values method should do all its work on the new widget (the request widget should never be modified), and if it needs to call any routines that operate on a widget, it should specify new as the widget instance. A widget need not refer to request, unless it must resolve conflicts between the current and new widgets. Any changes that the widget needs to make, including geometry changes, should be made in the new widget.

Note that a change in the geometry fields alone does not require the set_values method to return TRUE, thereby forcing a redisplay. The X server will eventually generate an Expose event, if necessary. After calling all the set_values methods, XtSetValues forces a redisplay by calling the Xlib XClearArea function if any of the set_values methods returned TRUE. Therefore, a set_values method should not try to do its own redisplay.

set_values methods should not do any work in response to changes in geometry because XtSetValues eventually will perform a geometry request, and that request might be denied. If the widget actually changes size in response to a XtSetValues, its resize method is called. Widgets should do any geometry-related work in their resize method.

Note that it is permissible to call XtSetValues before a widget is realized. Therefore, the set_values method must not assume that the widget is realized.

get_values_hook

Some widgets maintain data structures that have resource values. If so, these data structures can be updated after an XtSetValues or size request using the get_values_hook method. The get_values_hook method is of type XtArgsProc. The widget should call XtGetSubvalues and pass its subresource list. If the get_values_hook methods are non-NULL, they are called in superclass-to-subclass order after all the resource values have been fetched by XtGetValues. This permits a subclass to provide nonwidget resource data to XtGetValues.

XtGetValues expects the contents of arguments to be *pointers* to locations where the actual values can be put.

See Section 1.7, "Resources," and XtArgsProc(2).

set_values_hook

Widgets that have a subpart can set the resource values by using XtSetValues and supplying a set_values_hook method. The set_values_hook procedure pointer for a widget class is of type XtArgsFunc(2).

It returns a Boolean indicating whether or not XtSetValues should force the widget to be re-exposed.

set_values_almost

This method is of type XtAlmostProc. Most classes inherit this operation from their superclass by specifying XtInheritSetValuesAlmost in the class initialization. The Core set_values_almost method accepts the compromise suggested.

The set_values_almost method is called when a client tries to set a widget's geometry by means of a call to XtSetValues and the geometry manager cannot satisfy the request but instead returns XtGeometryAlmost and a compromise geometry. The set_values_almost method takes the original geometry and the compromise geometry and determines whether the compromise is acceptable or whether a different compromise might work. It returns its results in the new widget parameter, which is then sent back to the geometry manager for another try.

initialize_hook

This method is of type XtArgsProc It is passed the new created widget instance, the Arg-List passed to XtCreateWidget, and its size.

If this method is not NULL, it is called immediately after the corresponding initialize method or in its place if the initialize method is NULL

The initialize_hook method allows a widget instance to initialize nonwidget data using information from the specified argument list For example, the Text widget has subparts that are not widgets, yet these subparts have resources that can be specified by means of the resource file or an argument list

display_accelerator

The display_accelerator method is of type XtStringProc. The display_accelerator method is used to notify the widget that the Intrinsics have augmented another widget's translations with its accelerators

The accelerators themselves are specified as a translation table in the class accelerators field They must refer to actions that either are global or are valid in the context of the widget.

When the Intrinsics invoke the display_accelerator method, it is passed the accelerator table in an internal canonical form. This form is still text, but it differs from the original source of the accelerator table itself

query_geometry

The query_geometry procedure pointer is of type XtGeometryHandler:

```
typedef XtGeometryResult (*XtGeometryHandler) (Widget,
    XtWidgetGeometry *, XtWidgetGeometry *);
        Widget w,
        XtWidgetGeometry *request,
        XtWidgetGeometry *geometry_return,
```

The query_geometry method is expected to examine the bits set in request->request_mode, evaluate the preferred geometry of the widget, and store the result in geometry_return (setting the bits in geometry_return->request_mode corresponding to those geometry fields that it cares about). If the proposed geometry change is acceptable without modification, the query_geometry method should return Xt-GeometryYes If at least one field in geometry_return is different from the corresponding field in request or if a bit was set in geometry_return that was not set in request, the query_geometry method should return XtGeometryAlmost. If the preferred geometry is identical to the current geometry, the query_geometry method should return Xt-GeometryNo.

After calling the query_geometry method or if the query_geometry field is NULL, Xt-QueryGeometry examines all the unset bits in geometry_return->request_mode and sets the corresponding fields in geometry_return to the current values from the widget instance If CWStackMode is not set, the stack_mode field is set to XtSMDontChange. XtQueryGeometry returns the value returned by the query_geometry method or Xt-GeometryYes if the query_geometry field is NULL

Therefore, the caller can interpret a return of XtGeometryYes as not needing to evaluate the contents of reply and, more importantly, not needing to modify its layout plans. A return of XtGeometryAlmost means either that both the parent and the child expressed interest in at least one common field and the child's preference does not match the parent's intentions or that the child expressed interest in a field that the parent might need to consider. A return value of XtGeometryNo means that both the parent and the child expressed interest in a field and that the child suggests that the field's current value is its preferred value. In addition, whether or not the caller ignores the return value or the reply mask, it is guaranteed that the geometry_return structure contains complete geometry information for the child.

Parents are expected to call XtQueryGeometry in their layout routine and wherever other information is significant after change_managed has been called. The change_managed method may assume that the child's current geometry is its preferred geometry. Thus, the child is still responsible for storing values into its own geometry during its initialize method.

Name

Composite Widget Class — defines methods for geometry management

Synopsis

```
#include StringDefs h
#include Intrinsic.h
```

Description

The Composite widget defines methods for geometry management. Any widget that is capable of managing child widgets should be a subclass of the Composite widget. (See also Section 1 8, "Geometry Management.")

The class and instance structures are defined in <X11/CompositeP h>.

The composite class part is defined as follows:

```
typedef struct _CompositeClassPart {
    XtGeometryHandler geometry_manager;/* geometry manager for children */
    XtWidgetProc change_managed;      /* change managed state of child */
    XtWidgetProc insert_child;        /* physically add child to parent */
    XtWidgetProc delete_child;        /* physically remove child */
    caddr_t extension;                /* pointer to extension record */
} CompositeClassPart,*CompositePartPtr;
```

The composite instance record is defined as follows:

```
typedef struct _CompositePart {
    WidgetList  children;           /* array of ALL widget children */
    Cardinal    num_children;       /* total number of widget children */
    Cardinal    num_slots;          /* number of slots in children array */
    XtOrderProc insert_position;    /* compute position of new child */
} CompositePart,*CompositePtr;
```

Note that this instance record contains a method (Methods are generally kept in the *class* record, but many different subclasses of Composite may need a private XtOrderProc, so it is kept in the instance record)

The predefined class record and pointer for CompositeClassRec are:

```
extern CompositeClassRec compositeClassRec;
extern WidgetClass compositeWidgetClass,
```

The opaque types CompositeWidget and CompositeWidgetClass and the opaque variable compositeWidgetClass are defined for generic operations on widgets that are a subclass of CompositeWidget.

Field	Default Value
children	NULL
num_children	0
num_slots	0
insert_position	Internal function InsertAtEnd

Composite Methods

Detailed discussions and example programs performing geometry management are contained in Chapter 11, *Geometry Management*, in Volume Four, *X Toolkit Intrinsics Programming Manual*.

insert_child

To add a child to the parent's list of children, the XtCreateWidget function calls the parent's insert_child method. The insert_child procedure pointer in a composite widget is of type XtWidgetProc:

```
typedef void (*XtWidgetProc)(Widget);
```

Most composite widgets inherit this method from their superclass by specifying XtInherit-InsertChild for the insert_child field in the class record. Composite's insert_child method calls the insert_position method and inserts the child at the specified position.

Some composite widgets define their own insert_child method so that they can order their children in some convenient way, create companion controller widgets for a new widget, or limit the number or type of their children widgets.

This method can also be inherited dynamically and modified if the subclass widget wants to use it but wants to perform additional processing when the child is inserted. The example InsertChild method shown below does this:

```
static XtArgsProc InsertChild(w, args, num_args)
Widget w;
ArgList args;
Cardinal *num_args;
{
    CompositeWidgetClass superclass;

    /*
     * Satisfy parental responsibilities
     */
    superclass = (CompositeWidgetClass) compositeWidgetClass;
    (*superclass->composite_class.insert_child)(w,args,num_args);
}
```

If there is not enough room to insert a new child in the children array (that is, num_children = num_slots), the insert_child method must first reallocate the array and update num_slots. The insert_child method then places the child wherever it wants and increments the num_children field.

delete_child

To remove the child from the parent's children array, the XtDestroyWidget function eventually causes a call to the composite parent's class delete_child method The delete_child procedure pointer is of type XtWidgetProc.

```
typedef void (*XtWidgetProc)(Widget),
```

Most widgets inherit the delete_child method from their superclass. Composite widgets that create companion widgets define their own delete_child method to remove these companion widgets.

Note that the insert_child and delete_child methods exploit internal common data structures, so it would be unwise to inherit one and not the other

change_managed

The change_managed method is invoked when the application brings the child under its parent's management This happens automatically when the application uses XtCreate-ManagedWidget to create the widget change_managed is also invoked when the application removes a widget from the parent's managed list Children can be managed explicitly with XtManageChild, XtManageChildren, XtUnmanageChild, and XtUnmanage-Children The change_managed procedure pointer is of type XtWidgetProc:

```
static void ChangeManaged(w)
Widget w;
{  .  }
```

geometry_manager

The geometry_manager method actually lays out the children for display Only a subclass of a well-developed class of geometry manager can inherit this method, there is no default geometry manager defined by Composite that can manage multiple children

```
static XtGeometryResult GeometryManager(w, request, reply)
Widget w;
XtWidgetGeometry *request,
XtWidgetGeometry *reply,
{  .  }
```

A bit set to zero in the request's mask field means that the child widget does not care about the value of the corresponding field Then the geometry manager is free to set it as it wishes A bit set to 1 means that the child wants that geometry element changed to the value in the corresponding field

If the geometry manager can satisfy all changes requested and if XtCWQueryOnly is not specified, it updates the widget's x, y, width, height and border_width values appropriately Then it returns XtGeometryYes, and the value of the geometry_return argument is undefined The widget's window is moved and resized automatically by XtMake-GeometryRequest

Homogeneous composite widgets often find it convenient to treat the widget making the request the same as any other widget, possibly reconfiguring it as part of its layout process, unless XtCWQueryOnly is specified If it does this, it should return XtGeometryDone to inform `XtMakeGeometryRequest` that it does not need to do the configuration itself. Although `XtMakeGeometryRequest` resizes the widget's window, it does not call the widget class' resize procedure if the geometry manager returns `XtGeometryYes`. The requesting widget must perform whatever resizing calculations are needed explicitly.

If the geometry manager chooses to disallow the request, the widget cannot change its geometry. The value of the `reply` parameter is undefined, and the geometry manager returns `XtGeometryNo`.

Sometimes the geometry manager cannot satisfy the request exactly, but it may be able to satisfy a similar request. That is, it could satisfy only a subset of the requests (for example, size but not position) or a lesser request (for example, it cannot make the child as big as the request but it can make the child bigger than its current size). In such cases, the geometry manager fills in `reply` with the actual changes it is willing to make, including an appropriate mask, and returns `XtGeometryAlmost`. If a bit in `reply.request_mode` is zero, the geometry manager does not change the corresponding value if the `reply` is used immediately in a new request. If a bit is one, the geometry manager does change that element to the corresponding value in `geometry_return`. More bits may be set in `reply.request_mode` than in the original request if the geometry manager intends to change other fields should the child accept the compromise.

When `XtGeometryAlmost` is returned, the widget must decide if the compromise suggested in `reply` is acceptable. If it is, the widget must not change its geometry directly; rather, it must make another call to `XtMakeGeometryRequest`.

If the next geometry request from this child uses the `reply` filled in by an `XtGeometryAlmost` return and if there have been no intervening geometry requests on either its parent or any of its other children, the geometry manager must grant the request, if possible. That is, if the child asks immediately with the returned geometry, it should get an answer of `XtGeometryYes`. However, the user's window manager may affect the final outcome.

To return an `XtGeometryYes`, the geometry manager frequently rearranges the position of other managed children by calling `XtMoveWidget`. However, a few geometry managers may sometimes change the size of other managed children by calling `XtResizeWidget` or `XtConfigureWidget`. If `XtCWQueryOnly` is specified, the geometry manager must return how it would react to this geometry request without actually moving or resizing any widgets.

Geometry managers must not assume that the `request` and `reply` arguments point to independent storage. The caller is permitted to use the same field for both, and the geometry manager must allocate its own temporary storage, if necessary.

insert_position
Instances of composite widgets need to specify information about the order in which their children are kept. For example, an application may want a set of command buttons in some logical order grouped by function, and it may want buttons that represent file names to be kept in alphabetical order.

The insert_position method pointer in a composite widget instance is of type Xt-OrderProc

```
typedef Cardinal (*XtOrderProc)(Widget);
    Widget w,
```

w specifies the widget

Composite widgets that allow clients to order their children (usually homogeneous boxes) can call their widget instance's insert_position method from the class' insert_child method to determine where a new child should go in its children array Thus, a client of a composite class can apply different sorting criteria to widget instances of the class, passing in a different insert_position method when it creates each composite widget instance

The return value of the insert_position method indicates how many children should go before the widget. Returning zero indicates that the widget should go before all other children, and returning num_children indicates that it should go after all other children The default insert_position method returns num_children and can be overridden by a specific composite widget's resource list or by the argument list provided when the composite widget is created

See Also
Core(3)

Constraint

Name

Constraint Widget Class — provides data structures for a widget's parent.

Synopsis

```
#include StringDefs.h
#include Intrinsic.h
```

Description

Constraint widgets are a subclass of `compositeWidgetClass`. Their name is derived from the fact that they may manage the geometry of their children based on constraints associated with each child. These constraints can be as simple as the maximum width and height the parent will allow the child to occupy or as complicated as how other children should change if this child is moved or resized. Constraint widgets let a parent define resources that are supplied for their children. For example, if the Constraint parent defines the maximum sizes for its children, these new size resources are retrieved for each child as if they were resources that were defined by the child widget. Accordingly, constraint resources may be included in the argument list or resource file just like any other resource for the child.

Constraint widgets have all the responsibilities of normal composite widgets and, in addition, must process and act upon the constraint information associated with each of their children.

To make it easy for widgets and the Intrinsics to keep track of the constraints associated with a child, every widget has a constrains field, which is the address of a parent-specific structure that contains constraint information about the child. If a child's parent is not a subclass of `constraintWidgetClass`, then the child's constraints field is NULL.

Note that the constraint data structures are transparent to the child; that is, when a child is managed by a parent that is a subclass of a constraint widget, there is no difference, as far as the child is concerned, from being managed by a normal composite widget.

The values passed to the parent's constraint `set_values` method are the same as those passed to the child's class `set_values` method. A class can specify NULL for the `set_values` field of the `ConstraintPart` if it need not compute anything.

The constraint `set_values` method should recompute any constraint fields derived from constraint resources that are changed. Further, it should modify the widget fields as appropriate. For example, if a constraint for the maximum height of a widget is changed to a value smaller than the widget's current height, the constraint `set_values` method should reset the height field in the widget.

The class and instance structures are defined in <X11/ConstraintP.h>.

The class record defines the actual data in the form of resources

```
typedef struct _ConstraintClassPart {
    XtResourceList resources,         /* constraint resource list */
    Cardinal num_resources;           /* number of constraints in list */
    Cardinal constraint_size;         /* size of constraint record */
    XtInitProc constraint_initialize;/* constraint initialization */
    XtWidgetProc constraint_destroy, /* constraint destroy proc */
    XtSetValuesFunc set_values,       /* constraint set_values proc */
    caddr_t extension,                /* pointer to extension record */
} ConstraintClassPart;
```

The instance record defines no new fields, other than a dummy field to satisfy the C compiler

```
typedef struct _ConstraintPart {
    caddr_t dummy,                    /* No new fields, keep C compiler happy */
} ConstraintPart;
```

Subclasses of a Constraint widget can add additional constraint fields to their superclass To allow this, widget writers should define the constraint records in their private *h* file by using the same conventions as used for widget records For example, a widget that needs to maintain a maximum width and height for each child might define its constraint record as follows:

```
typedef struct {
    Dimension max_width,max_height;
} MaxConstraintPart;

typedef struct {
    MaxConstraintPart max,
} MaxConstraintRecord, *MaxConstraint;
```

A subclass of this widget that also needs to maintain a minimum size would define its constraint record as follows:

```
typedef struct {
    Dimension min_width,min_height;
} MinConstraintPart,

typedef struct {
    MaxConstraintPart max;
    MinConstraintPart min,
} MaxMinConstraintRecord, *MaxMinConstraint,
```

Constraints are allocated, initialized, deallocated and otherwise maintained insofar as possible by the Intrinsics The constraint class record part has several entries that facilitate this All entries in ConstraintClassPart are information and procedures that are defined and implemented by the parent, but they are called whenever actions are performed on the parent's children

The XtCreateWidget function uses the constraint_size field to allocated a constraint record when a child is created The constraint_size field gives the number of bytes occupied by a constraint record XtCreateWidget also uses the constraint resources to fill in resource fields in the constraint record associated with a child. It then calls the constraint initialize methods so that the parent can compute constraint fields that are derived from constraint resources and can possibly move or resize the child to conform to the given constraints.

The XtGetValues and XtSetValues functions use the constraint resources to get the values or set the values of constraint associated with a child. XtSetValues then calls the constraint set_values methods so that a parent can recompute derived constraint fields and move or resize the child as appropriate.

The XtDestroyWidget function calls the constraint destroy method to deallocate any dynamic storage associated with a constraint record. The constraint record itself must not be deallocated by the constraint destroy method; XtDestroyWidget does this automatically.

Methods

constraint_destroy

The constraint_destroy method identified in the ConstraintClassPart structure is called for a widget whose parent is a subclass of constraintWidgetClass. This constraint destroy procedure pointer is of type XtWidgetProc. The constraint destroy methods are called in subclass-to-superclass order, starting at the widget's parent and ending at constraintWidgetClass. Therefore, a parent's constraint destroy method only should deallocate storage that is specific to the constraint subclass and not the storage allocated by any of its superclasses.

If a parent does not need to deallocate any constraint storage, the constraint destroy method entry in its class record can be NULL.

constraint_initialize

The constraint_initialize procedure pointer is of type XtInitProc. The values passed to the parent constraint_initialize method are the same as those passed to the child's class_initialize method.

The constraint_initialize method should compute any constraint fields derived from constraint resources. It can make further changes to the widget to make the widget conform to the specified constraints; for example, changing the widget's size or position.

If a constraint class does not need a constraint_initialize method, it can specify NULL for the initialize field of the ConstraintClassPart in the class record.

See Also

Core(3)

Shell

Name
Shell Widget Class — application resources linking window managers.

Synopsis
```
#include StringDefs.h
#include Intrinsic.h
```

Description
Widgets negotiate their size and position with their parent widget, that is, the widget that directly contains them. Widgets at the top of the hierarchy do not have parent widgets Instead, they must deal with the outside world. To provide for this, each top-level widget is encapsulated in a special widget, called a Shell.

Shell widgets, a subclass of the Composite widget, encapsulate other widgets and can allow a widget to avoid the geometry clipping imposed by the parent/child window relationship. They also can provide a layer of communication with the window manager.

Shells have been designed to be as nearly invisible as possible. Clients have to create them (the top-level widget returned by a call to XtInitialize or XtCreateApplication-Context is a Shell widget, as is a pop-up widget created with XtPopup), but they should never have to worry about their sizes

If a shell widget is resized from the outside (typically by a window manager), the shell widget also resizes its child widget automatically. Similarly, if the shell's child widget needs to change size, it can make a geometry request to the shell, and the shell negotiates the size change with the outer environment. Clients should never attempt to change the size of their shells directly

There are seven different types of shells. Only four of these are public (i.e., should be instantiated by applications).

OverrideShell	Used for shell windows that completely bypass the window manager (for example, pop-up menu shells) A subclass of Shell (see below)
TransientShell	Used for shell windows that can be manipulated by the window manager but are not allowed to be iconified separately (for example, Dialog boxes that make no sense without their associated application) They are iconified by the window manager only if the main application shell is iconified A subclass of VendorShell (see below).
TopLevelShell	Used for normal top-level windows (for example, any additional top-level widgets an application needs). A subclass of VendorShell (see below)
ApplicationShell	Used by the window manager to define a separate application instance, which is the main top-level window of the application. A subclass of TopLevelShell

Three classes of shells are internal and should not be instantiated or subclassed:

Shell   Provides the base class for shell widgets and the fields needed for all
                         types of shells. Shell is a direct subclass of Composite.

WMShell   Contains fields needed by the common window manager protocol
                         and is a subclass of Shell.

VendorShell   Contains fields used by vendor-specific window managers and is a
                         subclass of WMShell.

The actual definitions are in *<X11/Shell.h>*, *<X11/ShellP.h>*, *<X11/Vendor.h>* and
<X11/VendorP.h>. Only *<X11/Shell.h>* needs to be routinely included in application code,
since it defines the class variables `applicationShellWidgetClass`, `override-
ShellWidgetClass`, `topLevelShellWidgetClass` and `transientShell-
WidgetClass`.

By using the Shell widget classes, any routine communication with the window manager that
an application would want to perform can be done by setting resources when the Shell widget is
created. For example, using `XtNiconPixmap`, the application can set a program-supplied
pixmap to be the application's icon. (See Chapter 10, *Inter-Client Communications*, in Volume
Four, *X Toolkit Intrinsics Programming Manual*, for a complete example that sets the application's icon.)

For more information on pop-up windows with `XtPopup`, see Chapter 12, *Menus, Gadgets,
and Cascaded Pop Ups*, in Volume Four, *X Toolkit Intrinsics Programming Manual*.

ShellClassPart Definitions

None of the shell widget classes has any additional fields:

```
typedef struct { caddr_t extension; } ShellClassPart, OverrideShellClassPart,
        WMShellClassPart, VendorShellClassPart, TransientShellClassPart,
        TopLevelShellClassPart, ApplicationShellClassPart;
```

Shell widget classes have the (empty) shell fields immediately following the composite fields:

```
typedef struct _ShellClassRec {
        CoreClassPart core_class;
        CompositeClassPart composite_class;
        ShellClassPart shell_class;
} ShellClassRec;

typedef struct _OverrideShellClassRec {
        CoreClassPart core_class;
        CompositeClassPart composite_class;
        ShellClassPart shell_class;
        OverrideShellClassPart override_shell_class;
} OverrideShellClassRec;

typedef struct _WMShellClassRec {
        CoreClassPart core_class;
        CompositeClassPart composite_class;
        ShellClassPart shell_class;
```

```
        WMShellClassPart wm_shell_class;
} WMShellClassRec;

typedef struct _VendorShellClassRec {
        CoreClassPart core_class;
        CompositeClassPart composite_class;
        ShellClassPart shell_class,
        WMShellClassPart wm_shell_class;
        VendorShellClassPart vendor_shell_class;
} VendorShellClassRec;

typedef struct _TransientShellClassRec {
        CoreClassPart core_class;
        CompositeClassPart composite_class;
        ShellClassPart shell_class;
        WMShellClassPart wm_shell_class;
        VendorShellClassPart vendor_shell_class;
        TransientShellClassPart transient_shell_class;
} TransientShellClassRec,

typedef struct _ApplicationShellClassRec {
        CoreClassPart core_class;
        CompositeClassPart composite_class;
        ShellClassPart shell_class;
        WMShellClassPart wm_shell_class;
        VendorShellClassPart vendor_shell_class;
        TopLevelShellClassPart top_level_shell_class;
        ApplicationShellClassPart application_shell_class;
} ApplicationShellClassRec;
```

The predefined class records and pointers for shells are:

```
extern ShellClassRec            shellClassRec;
extern OverrideShellClassRec    overrideShellClassRec;
extern WMShellClassRec wm       ShellClassRec,
extern VendorShellClassRec      vendorShellClassRec;
extern TransientShellClassRec   transientShellClassRec;
extern TopLevelShellClassRec    topLevelShellClassRec;
extern ApplicationShellClassRec applicationShellClassRec;

extern WidgetClass shellWidgetClass;
extern WidgetClass overrideShellWidgetClass;
extern WidgetClass wmShellWidgetClass;
extern WidgetClass vendorShellWidgetClass;
extern WidgetClass transientShellWidgetClass;
extern WidgetClass topLevelShellWidgetClass;
extern WidgetClass applicationShellWidgetClass;
```

The following opaque types and opaque variables are defined for generic operations on widgets that are a subclass of `ShellWidgetClass`:

Types	Variables
`ShellWidget`	`shellWidgetClass`
`OverrideShellWidget`	`overrideShellWidgetClass`
`WMShellWidget`	`wmShellWidgetClass`
`VendorShellWidget`	`vendorShellWidgetClass`
`TransientShellWidget`	`transientShellWidgetClass`
`TopLevelShellWidget`	`topLevelShellWidgetClass`
`ApplicationShellWidget`	`applicationShellWidgetClass`
`ShellWidgetClass`	
`OverrideShellWidgetClass`	
`WMShellWidgetClass`	
`VendorShellWidgetClass`	
`TransientShellWidgetClass`	
`TopLevelShellWidgetClass`	
`ApplicationShellWidgetClass`	

ShellPart Definition

The various shells have the following additional fields defined in their widget records:

```
typedef struct {
        String geometry;
        XtCreatePopupChildProc create_popup_child_proc;
        XtGrabKind grab_kind;
        Boolean spring_loaded;
        Boolean popped_up;
        Boolean allow_shell_resize;
        Boolean client_specified;
        Boolean save_under;
        Boolean override_redirect;
        XtCallbackList popup_callback;
        XtCallbackList popdown_callback;
} ShellPart;

typedef struct { int empty; } OverrideShellPart;

typedef struct {
        String title;
        int wm_timeout;
        Boolean wait_for_wm;
        Boolean transient;
        XSizeHints size_hints;
        XWMHints wm_hints;
} WMShellPart;

typedef struct {
```

```
         int vendor_specific;
} VendorShellPart;

typedef struct { int empty; } TransientShellPart;

typedef struct {
         String icon_name;
         Boolean iconic;
} TopLevelShellPart;

typedef struct {
         char *class;
         XrmClass xrm_class;
         int argc;
         char **argv;
} ApplicationShellPart;
```

The full definitions of the various shell widgets have shell fields following composite fields:

```
typedef struct {
         CorePart core;
         CompositePart composite;
         ShellPart shell;
} ShellRec, *ShellWidget;

typedef struct {
         CorePart core;
         CompositePart composite;
         ShellPart shell;
         OverrideShellPart override;
} OverrideShellRec, *OverrideShellWidget;

typedef struct {
         CorePart core;
         CompositePart composite;
         ShellPart shell;
         WMShellPart wm;
} WMShellRec, *WMShellWidget;

typedef struct {
         CorePart core,
         CompositePart composite;
         ShellPart shell,
         WMShellPart wm;
         VendorShellPart vendor;
} VendorShellRec, *VendorShellWidget,

typedef struct {
         CorePart core;
         CompositePart composite;
         ShellPart shell,
         WMShellPart wm;
         VendorShellPart vendor;
         TransientShellPart transient;
```

```
} TransientShellRec, *TransientShellWidget;

typedef struct {
        CorePart core;
        CompositePart composite;
        ShellPart shell;
        WMShellPart wm;
        VendorShellPart vendor;
        TopLevelShellPart topLevel;
} TopLevelShellRec, *TopLevelShellWidget;

typedef struct {
        CorePart core;
        CompositePart composite;
        ShellPart shell;
        WMShellPart wm;
        VendorShellPart vendor;
        TopLevelShellPart topLevel;
        ApplicationShellPart application;
} ApplicationShellRec, *ApplicationShellWidget;
```

ShellPart Default Values

The default values for fields common to all classes of public shells (filled in by the Shell resource lists and the Shell initialize procedures) are:

Field	Default Value
geometry	NULL
create_popup_child_proc	NULL
grab_kind	(internal)
spring_loaded	(internal)
popped_up	(internal)
allow_shell_resize	FALSE
client_specified	(internal)
save_under	TRUE for OverrideShell and TransientShell, FALSE otherwise
override_redirect	TRUE for OverrideShell, FALSE otherwise
popup_callback	NULL
popdown_callback	NULL

The geometry resource specifies the size and position and is usually done only from a command line or a defaults file. The create_popup_child_proc is called by the XtPopup procedure and is usually NULL. The allow_shell_resize field controls whether or not the widget contained by the shell is allowed to try to resize itself. If allow_shell_resize is FALSE, any geometry requests always return XtGeometryNo. Setting save_under instructs the server to attempt to save the contents of windows obscured by the shell when it is mapped and to restore its contents automatically later. It is useful for pop-up menus. Setting override_redirect determines whether or not the shell window is visible to the window manager. If it is TRUE, the window is immediately mapped without the manager's intervention. The pop-up and pop-down callbacks are called during XtPopup and XtPopdown.

The default values for shell fields in WMShell and its subclasses are:

Field	Default Value
title	Icon name, if specified, otherwise the application's name
wm_timeout	Five seconds
wait_for_wm	TRUE
transient	TRUE for TransientShell, FALSE otherwise
min_width	None
min_height	None
max_width	None
max_height	None
width_inc	None
height_inc	None
min_aspect_x	None
min_aspect_y	None
max_aspect_x	None
min_aspect_y	None
max_aspect_x	None
max_aspect_y	None
input	FALSE
initial_state	Normal
icon_pixmap	None
icon_window	None
icon_x	None
icon_y	None
icon_mask	None
window_group	None

The title is a string to be displayed by the window manager. The wm_timeout resource limits the amount of time a shell is to wait for confirmation of a geometry request to the window manager. If none comes back within that time, the shell assumes the window manager is not functioning properly and sets wait_for_wm to be FALSE (later events may reset this value). The wait_for_wm resource sets the initial state for this flag. When the flag is FALSE, the shell does not wait for a response but relies on asynchronous notification. All other resources are for fields in the window manager hints and the window manager size hints.

`TopLevel` shells have the the following additional resources:

Field	Default Value
icon_name	Shell widget's name
iconic	FALSE

The `icon_name` field is the string to display in the shell's icon, and the iconic field is an alternative way to set the initialState resource to indicate that a shell should be initially displayed as an icon.

`Application` shells have the following additional resources:

Field	Default Value
argc	0
argv	NULL

The `argc` and `argv` fields are used to initialize the standard property WM_COMMAND.

Athena Widgets

This section contains alphabetically-organized reference pages for the Athena widgets. This widget set is not part of the Intrinsics but was developed by MIT's Project Athena to demonstrate their use. It is documented here, since the Athena Widgets are used in the examples for Volume Four.

Each reference page provides a description of the widget class and documents the include files for the widget, its class hierarchy, resources, translations and actions, and its programmatic interface, including both the Intrinsics calls to create or manage the widget and any functions the widget itself exports.

Box

Name
boxWidgetClass — geometry-managing box widget.

Synopsis
```
#include <X11/StringDefs.h>
#include <X11/Intrinsic.h>
#include <X11/XawMisc.h>          /* <X11/Misc.h> in R2 */
#include <X11/Box.h>
widget = XtCreateWidget(widget, boxWidgetClass, ...);
```

Class Hierarchy
Core → Composite → Box

Description
The Box widget provides geometry management of arbitrary widgets in a box of a specified dimension. The children are rearranged when resizing events occur either on the Box or when children are added or deleted. The Box widget always attempts to pack its children as closely as possible within the geometry allowed by its parent.

Box widgets are commonly used to manage a related set of Command widgets and are frequently called ButtonBox widgets, but the children are not limited to buttons.

The children are arranged on a background that has its own specified dimensions and color.

Resources
When creating a Box widget instance, the following resources are retrieved from the argument list or from the resource database:

Name	Type	Default	Description
XtNbackground	Pixel	XtDefault-Background	Window background color
XtNbackground-Pixmap	Pixmap	None	Window background pixmap
XtNborderColor	Pixel	XtDefault-Foreground	Window border color
XtNborderPixmap	Pixmap	None	Window border pixmap
XtNborderWidth	Dimension	1	Border width on button box
XtNdestroy-Callback	XtCallbackList	NULL	Callbacks for XtDestroyWidget
XtNhSpace	Dimension	4	Pixel distance left and right of children
XtNheight	Dimension	See below	Viewing height of inner window
XtNmappedWhen-Managed	Boolean	TRUE	Whether XtMapWidget is automatic
XtNtranslations	TranslationTable	None	Event-to-action translations
XtNvSpace	Dimension	4	Pixel distance top and bottom of children

Name	Type	Default	Description
XtNwidth	Dimension	width of widest child	Viewing width of inner window
XtNx	Position	0	Widget location x coordinate
XtNy	Position	0	Widget location y coordinate

The Box widget positions its children in rows with XtNhSpace pixels to the left and right of each child and XtNvSpace pixels between rows. If the Box width is not specified, the Box widget uses the width of the widest child. Each time a child is managed or unmanaged, the Box widget will attempt to reposition the remaining children to compact the box. Children are positioned in order left to right, top to bottom When the next child does not fit on the current row, a new row is started If a child is wider than the width of the box, the box will request a larger width from its parent and will begin the layout process from the beginning if a new width is granted After positioning all children, the Box widget attempts to shrink its own size to the minimum dimensions required for the layout.

Programmatic Interface

- To create a Box widget instance, use XtCreateWidget and specify the class variable boxWidgetClass.

- To add a child to the Box, use XtCreateWidget and specify the widget ID of the Box as the parent of the new widget.

- To remove a child from a Box, use XtUnmanageChild or XtDestroyWidget and specify the widget ID of the child.

- To destroy a Box widget instance, use XtDestroyWidget and specify the widget ID of the Box widget. All the children of this box are automatically destroyed at the same time

See Also

Core(3), Composite(3), Command(4)

Command

Name

commandWidgetClass — command button activated by pointer click.

Synopsis

```
#include <X11/StringDefs.h>
#include <X11/Intrinsic.h>
#include <X11/XawMisc.h>          /* <X11/Misc.h> in R2 */
#include <X11/Command.h>
widget = XtCreateWidget(widget, commandWidgetClass, ...);
```

Class Hierarchy

Core → Simple → Label → Command

Description

The Command widget is a rectangular button that contains a text or pixmap label. When the
pointer cursor is on the button, the button border is highlighted to indicate that the button is
available for selection. Then, when a pointer button is pressed and released, the button is
selected, and the application's callback routine (specified by the XtNcallback resource) is
invoked.

Resources

When creating a Command widget instance, the following resources are retrieved from the
argument list or from the resource database:

Name	Type	Default	Description
XtNbackground	Pixel	XtDefault-Background	Window background color
XtNbackground-Pixmap	Pixmap	None	Window background pixmap
XtNbitmap	Pixmap	None	Pixmap to display in place of the label
XtNborderColor	Pixel	XtDefault-Foreground	Window border color
XtNborderPixmap	Pixmap	None	Window border pixmap
XtNborderWidth	Dimension	1	Width of button border
XtNcallback	XtCallbackList	NULL	Callback for button select
XtNcursor	Cursor	None	Pointer cursor
XtNdestroy-Callback	XtCallbackList	NULL	Callbacks for XtDestroyWidget
XtNfont	XFontStruct*	XtDefaultFont	Label font
XtNforeground	Pixel	XtDefault-Foreground	Foreground color
XtNheight	Dimension	Text height	Button height
XtNhighlight-Thickness	Dimension	2	Width of border to be highlighted
XtNinsensitive-Border	Pixmap	Gray	Border when not sensitive

Name	Type	Default	Description
XtNinternal- Height	Dimension	2	Internal border height for highlighting
XtNinternalWidth	Dimension	4	Internal border width for highlighting
XtNjustify	XtJustify	XtJustifyCenter	Type of text alignment
XtNlabel	String	Button name	Button label
XtNmappedWhen- Managed	Boolean	TRUE	Whether XtMapWidget is automatic
XtNresize	Boolean	TRUE	Whether to auto-resize in SetValues
XtNsensitive	Boolean	TRUE	Whether widget receives input
XtNtranslations	Translation- Table	See below	Event-to-action translations
XtNwidth	Dimension	Text width	Button width
XtNx	Position	0	x coordinate
XtNy	Position	0	y coordinate

Note that the Command widget supports two callback lists: XtNdestroyCallback and XtNcallback. The notify action executes the callbacks on the XtNcallback list. The *call_data* argument is unused.

The new resources (not inherited from superclasses) associated with the Command widget are:

XtNbitmap   Specifies a bitmap to display in place of the text label. See the description of this resource in the Label widget for further details.

XtNheight   Specifies the height of the Command widget. The default value is the minimum height that will contain:

       XtNinternalheight + height of XtNlabel + XtNinternalHeight

       If the specified height is larger than the minimum, the label string is centered vertically.

XtNInternalHeight

       Represents the distance in pixels between the top and bottom of the label text or bitmap and the horizontal edges of the Command widget. HighlightThickness can be larger or smaller than this value.

XtNInternalWidth

       Represents the distance in pixels between the ends of the label text or bitmap and the vertical edges of the Command widget. Highlight-Thickness can be larger or smaller than this value.

XtNjustify   Specifies left, center, or right alignment of the label string within the Command widget. If it is specified within an ArgList, one of the values XtJustifyLeft, XtJustifyCenter, or XtJustifyRight can be specified. In a resource of type string, one of the values *left*, *center*, or *right* can be specified.

XtNlabel   Specifies the text string that is to be displayed in the Command widget if
                    no bitmap is specified. The default is the widget name of the Command
                    widget.

XtNresize   Specifies whether the Command widget should attempt to resize to its pre-
                    ferred dimensions whenever XtSetValues is called for it. The default
                    is TRUE.

XtNsensitive   If set to FALSE, the Command widget will change its window border to
                    XtNinsensitiveBorder and will stipple the label string.

XtNwidth   Specifies the width of the Command widget. The default value is the min-
                    imum width that will contain:

                    XtNinternalWidth + width of XtNlabel + XtNinternalWidth

                    If the width is larger or smaller than the minimum, XtNjustify deter-
                    mines how the label string is aligned.

Translations and Actions

The following are the default translation bindings that are used by the Command widget:

```
<EnterWindow>:highlight()
<LeaveWindow>:reset()
<Btn1Down>:set()
<Btn1Up>:notify() unset()
```

With these bindings, the user can cancel the action before releasing the button by moving the
pointer out of the Command widget.

The Command widget supports the following actions:

*   Switching the button between the foreground and background colors with set and
    unset.

*   Processing application callbacks with notify.

*   Switching the internal border between highlighted and unhighlighted states with high-
    light and unhighlight.

The full list of actions supported by Command is:

highlight()   Displays the internal highlight border in the XtNforeground color.

unhighlight()   Displays the internal highlight border in the XtNbackground color.

set()   Enters the set state, in which notify is possible and displays the inter-
                    ior of the button, including the highlight border, in the foreground color.
                    The label is displayed in the background color.

unset()   Cancels the set state and displays the interior of the button, including the
                    highlight border, in the background color. The label is displayed in the
                    foreground color.

Athena
Widgets

reset()   Cancels any set or highlight and displays the interior of the button in the background color, with the label displayed in the foreground color

notify()   Executes the XtNcallback callback list if executed in the set state. The value of the *call_data* argument is undefined

Programmatic Interface

- To create a Command widget instance, use XtCreateWidget and specify the class variable commandWidgetClass

- To destroy a Command widget instance, use XtDestroyWidget and specify the widget ID of the Command widget.

See Also
Box(4), Label(4).

Dialog

Name
dialogWidgetClass — dialog box widget.

Synopsis
```
#include <X11/StringDefs.h>
#include <X11/Intrinsic.h>
#include <X11/XawMisc.h>            /* <X11/Misc.h> in R2 */
#include <X11/Dialog.h>
widget = XtCreateWidget(widget, dialogWidgetClass,...);
```

Class Hierarchy
Core → Composite → Constraint → Form → Dialog

Description
The Dialog widget implements a commonly used interaction semantic to prompt for auxiliary input from a user. For example, you can use a Dialog widget when an application requires a small piece of information, such as a filename, from the user. A Dialog widget is simply a special case of the Form widget that provides a convenient way to create a *preconfigured form*.

The typical Dialog widget contains three areas. The first line contains a description of the function of the Dialog widget, for example, the string *Filename:*. The second line contains an area into which the user types input. The third line can contain buttons that let the user confirm or cancel the Dialog input.

Resources
When creating a Dialog widget instance, the following resources are retrieved from the argument list or from the resource database:

Name	Type	Default	Description
XtNbackground	Pixel	XtDefault-Background	Window background color
XtNbackground-Pixmap	Pixmap	None	Window background pixmap
XtNborderColor	Pixel	XtDefault-Foreground	Window border color
XtNborderPixmap	Pixmap	None	Window border pixmap
XtNborderWidth	Dimension	1	Width of border in pixels
XtNdestroy-Callback	XtCallbackList	NULL	Callbacks for XtDestroyWidget
XtNheight	Dimension	Computed at create	Height of dialog
XtNlabel	String	Label name	String to be displayed
XtNmappedWhen-Managed	Boolean	TRUE	Whether XtMapWidget is automatic
XtNmaximumLength	int	256	Maximum number of input characters
XtNsensitive	Boolean	TRUE	Whether widget receives input
XtNtranslations	TranslationTable	None	Event-to-action translations

Name	Type	Default	Description
XtNvalue	char*	NULL	Pointer to default string
XtNwidth	Dimension	Computed at create	Width of dialog
XtNx	Position	NULL	x position of dialog
XtNy	Position	NULL	y position of dialog

The instance name of the label widget within the Dialog widget is *label*, and the instance name of the Dialog value widget is *value*.

Programmatic Interface

- To create a Dialog widget instance, use XtCreateWidget and specify the class variable dialogWidgetClass.

- To add a child button to the Dialog box, use XtCreateWidget and specify the widget ID of the previously created Dialog box as the parent of each child. When creating buttons, you do not have to specify form constraints. The Dialog box will automatically add the constraints.

- To return the character string in the text field, use:

```
char *XtDialogGetValueString(w)
    Widget w;
```

where *w* specifies the widget ID of the Dialog box.

If a string was specified in the XtNvalue resource, the Dialog widget will store the input directly into the string.

- To remove a child button from the Dialog box, use XtUnmanageChild or Xt-DestroyWidget and specify the widget ID of the child.

- To destroy a Dialog widget instance, use XtDestroyWidget and specify the widget ID of the Dialog widget. All children of the Dialog are automatically destroyed at the same time.

See Also

Command(4), Form(4), Text(4).

Form

Name

formWidgetClass —— geometry-managing widget implementing constraints on children.

Synopsis

```
#include <X11/StringDefs.h>
#include <X11/Intrinsic.h>
#include <X11/XawMisc.h>          /* <X11/Misc.h> in R2 */
#include <X11/Form.h>
widget = XtCreateWidget(widget, formWidgetClass, ...);
```

Class Hierarchy

Core → Composite → Constraint → Form

Description

The Form widget can contain an arbitrary number of children or subwidgets. The Form provides geometry management for its children, which allows individual control of the position of each child. Any combination of children can be added to a Form. The initial positions of the children may be computed relative to the positions of other children. When the Form is resized, it computes new positions and sizes for its children. This computation is based upon information provided when a child is added to the Form.

Resources

When creating a Form widget instance, the following resources are retrieved from the argument list or from the resource database:

Name	Type	Default	Description
XtNbackground	Pixel	XtDefault-Background	Window background color
XtNbackground-Pixmap	Pixmap	None	Window background pixmap
XtNborderColor	Pixel	XtDefault-Foreground	Window border color
XtNborderPixmap	Pixmap	None	Window border pixmap
XtNborderWidth	Dimension	1	Width of border in pixels
XtNdefault-Distance	int	4	Default value for XtNhorizDistance and XtNvertDistance
XtNdestroy-Callback	XtCallbackList	NULL	Callbacks for XtDestroyWidget
XtNheight	Dimension	Computed at realize	Height of form
XtNmappedWhen-Managed	Boolean	TRUE	Whether XtMapWidget is automatic
XtNsensitive	Boolean	TRUE	Whether widget receives input

Name	Type	Default	Description
XtNtranslations	TranslationTable	None	Event-to-action translations
XtNwidth	Dimension	Computed at realize	Width of form
XtNx	Position	NULL	x position of form
XtNy	Position	NULL	y position of form

Constraints

When creating children to be added to a Form, the following additional resources are retrieved from the argument list or from the resource database. Note that these resources are maintained by the Form widget, even though they are stored in the child.

Name	Type	Default	Description
XtNbottom	XtEdgeType	XtRubber	See text
XtNfromHoriz	Widget	NULL	See text
XtNfromVert	Widget	NULL	See text
XtNhorizDistance	int	XtdefaultDistance	See text
XtNleft	XtEdgeType	XtRubber	See text
XtNresizable	Boolean	FALSE	TRUE if allowed to resize
XtNright	XtEdgeType	XtRubber	See text
XtNtop	XtEdgeType	XtRubber	See text
XtNvertDistance	int	XtdefaultDistance	See text

These resources are called constraints, and can be specified to the Form to indicate where the child should be positioned within the Form.

The resources XtNhorizDistance and XtNfromHoriz let the widget position itself a specified number of pixels horizontally away from another widget in the form. As an example, XtNhorizDistance could equal 10 and XtNfromHoriz could be the widget ID of another widget in the Form. The new widget will be placed 10 pixels to the right of the widget defined in XtNfromHoriz. If XtNfromHoriz equals NULL, then XtNhorizDistance is measured from the left edge of the Form.

Similarly, the resources XtNvertDistance and XtNfromVert let the widget position itself a specified number of pixels vertically away from another widget in the Form. If Xt-NfromVert equals NULL, then XtNvertDistance is measured from the top of the Form. Form provides a StringToWidget conversion procedure. Using this procedure, the resource database may be used to specify the XtNfromHoriz and XtNfromVert resources by widget name rather than widget ID. The string value must be the name of a child of the same Form widget parent.

The XtNtop, XtNbottom, XtNleft, and XtNright resources tell the Form where to position the child when the Form is resized. XtEdgeType is defined in <X11/Form.h> and is one of XtChainTop, XtChainBottom, XtChainLeft, XtChainRight, or XtRubber.

The values XtChainTop, XtChainBottom, XtChainLeft, and XtChainRight specify that a constant distance from an edge of the child to the top, bottom, left, and right edges respectively of the Form is to be maintained. The value XtRubber specifies that a proportional distance from the edge of the child to the left or top edge of the Form is to be maintained when the form is resized. The proportion is determined from the initial position of the child and the initial size of the Form. Form provides a StringToEdgeType conversion procedure to allow the resize constraints to be easily specified in a resource file.

The default width of the Form is the minimum width needed to enclose the children after computing their initial layout, with a margin of XtNdefaultDistance at the right and bottom edges. If a width and height is assigned to the Form that is too small for the layout, the children will be clipped by the right and bottom edges of the Form.

Programmatic Interface

* To create a Form widget instance, use XtCreateWidget and specify the class variable formWidgetClass.

* To add a new child to a Form, use XtCreateWidget and specify the widget ID of the previously created Form as the parent of the child.

* To remove a child from a Form, use XtUnmanageChild or XtDestroyWidget and specify the widget ID of the child widget.

* To destroy a Form widget instance, use XtDestroyWidget and specify the widget ID of the Form. All children of the Form are automatically destroyed at the same time.

    When a new child becomes managed or an old child unmanaged, the Form widget will recalculate the positions of its children according to the values of the XtNhoriz-Distance, XtNfromHoriz, XtNvertDistance, and XtNfromVert constraints at the time the change is made. No re-layout is performed when a child makes a geometry request.

* To force or defer a re-layout of the Form widget, use XtFormDoLayout:

```
void XtFormDoLayout(w, do_layout)
    Widget w;
    Boolean do_layout;
```

where:

    w   Specifies the Form widget.

    do_layout   Enables (if TRUE) or disables (if FALSE) layout of the Form widget.

When making several changes to the children of a Form widget after the Form has been realized, it is a good idea to disable re-layout until all changes have been made, then allow the layout. The Form widget increments an internal count each time XtFormDoLayout is called with do_layout FALSE and decrements the count when do_layout is TRUE. When the count reaches 0, the Form widget performs a re-layout.

Grip

— Xt – Athena Widgets —

Name

gripWidgetClass — attachment point for dragging other widgets.

Synopsis

```
#include <X11/StringDefs.h>
#include <X11/Intrinsic.h>
#include <X11/XawMisc.h>          /* <X11/Misc.h> in R2 */
#include <X11/Grip.h>
widget = XtCreateWidget(widget, gripWidgetClass, ...);
```

Class Hierarchy

Core → Simple → Grip

Description

The Grip widget provides a small region in which user input events (such as ButtonPress or
ButtonRelease) may be handled. The most common use for the grip is as an attachment
point for visually repositioning an object, such as the pane border in a VPaned widget.

Resources

When creating a Grip widget instance, the following resources are retrieved from the argument
list or from the resource database:

Name	Type	Default	Description
XtNborderColor	Pixel	XtDefault- Foreground	Window border color
XtNborderPixmap	Pixmap	None	Window border pixmap
XtNborderWidth	Dimension	0	Width of the border in pixels
XtNcallback	XtCallbackList	None	Action routine
XtNcursor	Cursor	None	Cursor for the grip
XtNdestroy- Callback	XtCallbackList	NULL	Callback for XtDestroyWidget
XtNforeground	Pixel	XtDefault- Foreground	Window background color
XtNheight	Dimension	8	Height of the widget
XtNmappedWhen- Managed	Boolean	TRUE	Whether XtMapWidget is automatic
XtNsensitive	Boolean	TRUE	Whether widget should receive input
XtNtranslations	TranslationTable	None	Event-to-action translations
XtNwidth	Dimension	8	Width of the widget
XtNx	Position	0	x coordinate within parent
XtNy	Position	0	y coordinate within parent

Note that the Grip widget displays its region with the foreground pixel only.

Translations and Actions

The Grip widget does not declare any default event translation bindings, but it does declare a single action routine named `GripAction` in its action table. The client specifies an arbitrary event translation table giving parameters to the `GripAction` routine.

The `GripAction` action executes the callbacks on the `XtNcallback` list, passing as `call_data` a pointer to a `GripCallData` structure, defined in *<X11/Grip.h>*:

```
typedef struct _GripCallData {
    XEvent *event;
    String *params;
    Cardinal num_params;
} GripCallDataRec, *GripCallData;
```

In this structure, the event field is a pointer to the input event that triggered the action, and *params* and *num_params* give the string parameters specified in the translation table for the particular event binding.

The following is an example of a `GripAction` translation table:

```
<Btn1Down>:GripAction(press)
<Btn1Motion>:GripAction(move)
<Btn1Up>:GripAction(release)
```

Programmatic Interface

- To create a Grip widget instance, use `XtCreateWidget` and specify the class variable `gripWidgetClass`.

- To destroy a Command button widget instance, use `XtDestroyWidget` and specify the ID of the Grip widget.

See Also

Vpaned(4)

Label

Name

labelWidgetClass — widget to display a non-editable string.

Synopsis

```
#include <X11/StringDefs.h>
#include <X11/Intrinsic.h>
#include <X11/XawMisc.h>        /* <X11/Misc.h> in R2 */
#include <X11/Label.h>
widget = XtCreateWidget(widget, labelWidgetClass, ...);
```

Class Hierarchy

Core → Simple → Label

Description

A Label is an noneditable text string or pixmap that is displayed within a window. The string is
limited to one line and can be aligned to the left, right, or center of its window. A Label can
neither be selected nor directly edited by the user.

Resources

When creating a Label widget instance, the following resources are retrieved from the argument list or from the resource database:

Name	Class Type	Default	Description
XtNbackground	Pixel	XtDefault-Background	Window background color
XtNbackground-Pixmap	Pixmap	None	Window background pixmap
XtNbitmap	Pixmap	None	Pixmap to display in place of the label
XtNborderColor	Pixel	XtDefault-Foreground	Window border color
XtNborderPixmap	Pixmap	None	Window border pixmap
XtNborderWidth	Dimension	1	Border width in pixels
XtNcursor	Cursor	None	Pointer cursor
XtNdestroy-Callback	XtCallbackList	NULL	Callbacks for XtDestroyWidget
XtNfont	XFontStruct*	XtDefaultFont	Label font
XtNforeground	Pixel	XtDefault-Foreground	Foreground color
XtNheight	Dimension	Text height	Height of widget
XtNinsensitive-Border	Pixmap	Gray	Border when not sensitive
XtNinternal-Height	Dimension	2	See note
XtNinternalWidth	Dimension	4	See note
XtNjustify	XtJustify	XtJustifyCenter	Type of text alignment
XtNlabel	String	Label name	String to be displayed

Name	Class Type	Default	Description
XtNmappedWhen- Managed	Boolean	TRUE	Whether XtMapWidget is auto-matic
XtNresize	Boolean	TRUE	Whether to auto-resize in Set-Values
XtNsensitive	Boolean	TRUE	Whether widget receives input
XtNwidth	Dimension	Text width	Width of widget
XtNx	Position	0	x coordinate in pixels
XtNy	Position	0	y coordinate in pixels

Note that the Label widget supports only the XtNdestroyCallback callback list.

The new resources associated with Label are:

XtNbitmap   Specifies a bitmap to display in place of the text label. The bitmap can be specified as a string in the resource data base. The StringToPixmap converter will interpret the string as the name of a file in the bitmap utility format that is to be loaded into a pixmap. The string can be an absolute or a relative filename. If a relative filename is used, the directory specified by the resource name bitmapFilePath or the resource class BitmapFile-Path is added to the beginning of the specified filename. If the bitmap-FilePath resource is not defined, the default directory on a UNIX-based system is */usr/include/X11/bitmaps*.

XtNheight   Specifies the height of the Label widget. The default value is the minimum height that will contain:

XtNinternalheight + height of XtNlabel + XtNinternalHeight

If the specified height is larger than the minimum, the label string is centered vertically.

XtNinternalHeight

     Represents the distance in pixels between the top and bottom of the label text or bitmap and the horizontal edges of the Label widget.

XtNinternalWidth

     Represents the distance in pixels between the ends of the label text or bitmap and the vertical edges of the Label widget.

XtNjustify   Specifies left, center, or right alignment of the label string within the Label widget. If it is specified within an ArgList, one of the values Xt-JustifyLeft, XtJustifyCenter, or XtJustifyRight can be specified. In a resource of type string, one of the values *left*, *center*, or *right* can be specified.

XtNlabel   Specifies the text string that is to be displayed in the button if no bitmap is specified. The default is the widget name of the Label widget.

XtNresize   Specifies whether the Label widget should attempt to resize to its preferred
               dimensions whenever XtSetValues is called for it

XtNsensitive   If set to FALSE, the Label widget will change its window border to Xt-
               NinsensitiveBorder and will stipple the label string

XtNwidth   Specifies the width of the Label widget. The default value is the minimum
               width that will contain·

               XtNinternalWidth + width of XtNlabel + XtNinternalWidth

               If the width is larger or smaller than the minimum, XtNjustify deter-
               mines how the label string is aligned

Programmatic Interface

- To create a Label widget instance, use XtCreateWidget and specify the class variable
  labelWidgetClass.

- To destroy a Label widget instance, use XtDestroyWidget and specify the widget ID
  of the label

Name

listWidgetClass — widget for managing row-column geometry.

Synopsis

```
#include <X11/StringDefs.h>
#include <X11/Intrinsic.h>
#include <X11/XawMisc.h>          /* <X11/Misc.h> in R2 */
#include <X11/List.h>
widget = XtCreateWidget(widget, listWidgetClass, ...);
```

Class Hierarchy

Core → Simple → Grip

Description

The List widget is a rectangle that contains a list of strings formatted into rows and columns. When one of the strings is selected, it is highlighted, and an application callback routine is invoked.

Resources

When creating a List widget instance, the following resources are retrieved from the argument list or from the resource database:

Name	Type	Default	Description
XtNbackground	Pixel	XtDefault-Background	Window background color
XtNbackground-Pixmap	Pixmap	None	Window background pixmap
XtNborderColor	Pixel	XtDefault-Foreground	Window border color
XtNborderPixmap	Pixmap	None	Window border pixmap
XtNborderWidth	Dimension	1	Width of border
XtNcallback	XtCallbackList	NULL	Selection callback function
XtNcolumnSpacing	Dimension	6	Space between columns in the list
XtNcursor	Cursor	left_ptr	Pointer cursor
XtNdefaultColumns	int	2	Number of columns to use
XtNdestroy-Callback	XtCallbackList	NULL	Callbacks for XtDestroyWidget
XtNfont	XFontStruct*	XtDefaultFont	Font for list text
XtNforceColumns	Boolean	FALSE	Force the use of XtNdefault-Columns
XtNforeground	Pixel	XtDefault-Foreground	Foreground (text) color
XtNheight	Dimension	Contains list exactly	Height of widget
XtNinsensitive-Border	Pixmap	Gray	Border when not sensitive

Athena
Widgets

Name	Type	Default	Description
XtNinternalHeight	Dimension	2	Spacing between list and widget edges
XtNinternalWidth	Dimension	4	Spacing between list and widget edges
XtNlist	String *	List name	An array of strings that is the list
XtNlongest	int	Longest item	Length of the longest list item in pixels
XtNmappedWhen-Managed	Boolean	TRUE	Whether XtMapWidget is automatic
XtNnumberStrings	int	Number of strings	Number of items in the list
XtNpasteBuffer	Boolean	FALSE	Copy the selected item to cut buffer 0
XtNrowSpacing	Dimension	4	Space between rows in the list
XtNsensitive	Boolean	TRUE	Whether widget receives input
XtNtranslations	Translation-Table	None	Event-to-action translations
XtNverticalList	Boolean	FALSE	Specify the layout of list items
XtNwidth	Dimension	Contains list exactly	Width of widget
XtNx	Position	0	Widget x coordinate
XtNy	Position	0	Widget y coordinate

The new resources associated with the List widget are:

XtNcolumnSpacing XtNrowSpacing	Specify the amount of space between each of the rows and columns in the list.
XtNdefaultColumns	Specifies the default number of columns, which is used when neither the width nor the height of the List widget is specified or when Xt-NforceColumns is TRUE.
XtNforceColumns	Specifies that the default number of columns is to be used no matter what the current size of the List widget is.
XtNheight	Specifies the height of the List widget. The default value is the minimum height that will contain the entire list with the spacing values specified. If the specified height is larger than the minimum, the list is put in the upper left corner.
XtNinternalHeight	Represents a margin, in pixels, between the top and bottom of the list and the edges of the List widget.
XtNinternalWidth	Represents a margin, in pixels, between the left and right edges of the list and the edges of the List widget.
XtNlist	Specifies the array of text strings that is to displayed in the List widget. If the default for XtNnumberStrings is used, the list must

be NULL-terminated. If a value is not specified for the list, the number of strings is set to 1, and the name of the widget is used as the list.

XtNlongest — Specifies the length of the longest string in the current list in pixels. If the client knows the length, it should specify it. The List widget will compute a default length by searching through the list.

XtNnumberStrings — Specifies the number of strings in the current list. If a value is not specified, the list must be NULL-terminated.

XtNpasteBuffer — If this is TRUE, then the value of the string selected will be put into X cut buffer 0.

XtNsensitive — If set to FALSE, the List widget will change its window border to Xt-NinsensitiveBorder and display all items in the list as stippled strings. While the List widget is insensitive, no item in the list can be selected or highlighted.

XtNverticalList — If this is TRUE, the elements in the list are arranged vertically; if FALSE, the elements are arranged horizontally.

XtNwidth — Specifies the width of the List widget. The default value is the minimum width that will contain the entire list with the spacing values specified. If the specified width is larger than the minimum, the list is put in the upper left corner.

Translations and Actions

The List widget has three predefined actions: Set, Unset, and Notify. Set and Unset allow switching the foreground and background colors for the current list item. Notify allows processing application callbacks.

The following is the default translation table used by the List Widget:

```
<Btn1Down>,<Btn1Up>:Set() Notify()
```

Programmatic Interface

- To create a List widget instance, use XtCreateWidget and specify the class variable listWidgetClass.

- To destroy a List widget instance, use XtDestroyWidget and specify the widget ID of the List widget.

- The List widget supports two callback lists:

  — XtNdestroyCallback
  — XtNcallback

The notify action executes the callbacks on the the XtNcallback list.

The call_data argument passed to callbacks on the XtNcallback list is a pointer to an XtListReturnStruct structure, defined in <*X11/List.h*>:

```
typedef struct _XtListReturnStruct {
    String string;      /* string shown in the list */
```

Athena Widgets

```
    int index;          /* index of the item selected */
} XtListReturnStruct;
```

- To change the list of strings that is displayed, use

```
void XtListChange(w, list, nitems, longest, resize)
    Widget w;
    String * list;
    int nitems, longest;
    Boolean resize,
```

where·

     w   Specifies the widget ID.

     list   Specifies the new list for the list widget to display.

     nitems   Specifies the number of items in the list If a value less than 1 is specified, list must be NULL-terminated

     longest   Specifies the length of the longest item in the list in pixels If a value less than 1 is specified, the List widget calculates the value for you

     resize   Specifies a Boolean value that indicates whether the List widget should try to resize itself (TRUE) or not (FALSE) after making the change Note that the constraints of the parent of this widget are always enforced, regardless of the value specified

- To highlight an item in the list, use·

```
void XtListHighlight(w, item),
    Widget w,
    int item;
```

where

     w   Specifies the widget ID

     item   Specifies the index into the current list that indicates the item to be highlighted

Only one item can be highlighted at a time If an item is already highlighted when Xt-ListHighlight is called, the highlighted item is immediately unhighlighted and the new item is highlighted

- To unhighlight the currently highlighted item in the list, use:

```
void XtListUnhightlight(w);
    Widget w;
```

where *w* specifies the widget ID

- To retrieve an item in the list, use

```
XtListReturnStruct *XtListShowCurrent(w),
    Widget w;
```

where *w* specifies the widget ID

- The XtListShowCurrent function returns a pointer to an XtListReturnStruct structure that contains the currently highlighted item. If the value of the index member is XT_LIST_NONE, the string member is undefined, which indicates that no item is currently selected.

Scrollbar

Name

scrollbarWidgetClass — widget to control scrolling of viewing area in another widget

Synopsis

```
#include <X11/StringDefs.h>
#include <X11/Intrinsic.h>
#include <X11/XawMisc.h>          /* <X11/Misc.h> in R2 */
#include <X11/Scroll.h>
widget = XtCreateWidget(widget, scrollbarWidgetClass, ..),
```

Class Hierarchy

Core → Simple → Scroll

Description

The Scrollbar widget is a rectangular area that contains a slide region and a thumb (slide bar). A Scrollbar can be used alone, as a valuator, or within a composite widget (for example, a Viewport) A Scrollbar can be aligned either vertically or horizontally

When a Scrollbar is created, it is drawn with the thumb in a contrasting color The thumb is normally used to scroll client data and to give visual feedback on the percentage of the client data that is visible.

Each pointer button invokes a specific scrollbar action That is, given either a vertical or horizontal alignment, the pointer button actions will scroll or return data as appropriate for that alignment Pointer buttons 1 and 3 do not perform scrolling operations by default. Instead, they return the pixel position of the cursor on the scroll region When pointer button 2 is clicked, the thumb moves to the current pointer position When pointer button 2 is held down and the pointer is moved, the thumb follows the pointer.

The cursor in the scroll region changes depending on the current action When no pointer button is pressed, the cursor appears as an arrow that points in the direction that scrolling can occur. When pointer button 1 or 3 is pressed, the cursor appears as a single-headed arrow that points in the logical direction that the client will move the data. When pointer button 2 is pressed, the cursor appears as an arrow that points to the thumb

While scrolling is in progress, the application receives notification from callback procedures For both scrolling actions, the callback returns the Scrollbar widget ID, *client_data*, and the pixel position of the pointer when the button was released For smooth scrolling, the callback routine returns the scroll bar window, *client_data*, and the current relative position of the thumb When the thumb is moved using pointer button 2, the callback procedure is invoked continuously. When either button 1 or 3 is pressed, the callback procedure is invoked only when the button is released and the client callback procedure is responsible for moving the thumb

Resources

When creating a Scrollbar widget instance, the following resources are retrieved from the argument list or from the resource database:

Name	Type	Default	Description
XtNbackground	Pixel	White	Window background color
XtNbackground-Pixmap	Pixmap	None	Window background pixmap
XtNborderColor	Pixel	XtDefault-Foreground	Window border color
XtNborderPixmap	Pixmap	None	Window border pixmap
XtNborderWidth	Dimension	1	Width of button border
XtNdestroy-Callback	XtCallbackList	NULL	Callbacks for XtDestroyWidget
XtNforeground	Pixel	Black	Thumb color
XtNheight	Dimension	See below	Height of scroll bar
XtNjumpProc	XtCallbackList	NULL	Callback for thumb select
XtNlength	Dimension	None	Major dimension (height of XtorientVertical)
XtNmappedWhen-Managed	Boolean	TRUE	Whether XtMapWidget is automatic
XtNorientation	XtOrientation	XtorientVertical	Orientation (vertical or horizontal)
XtNscrollDCursor	Cursor	XC_sb_down_arrow	Cursor for scrolling down
XtNscrollHCursor	Cursor	XC_sb_h_double_arrow	Idle horizontal cursor
XtNscrollLCursor	Cursor	XC_sb_left_arrow	Cursor for scrolling left
XtNscrollProc	XtCallbackList	NULL	Callback for the slide region
XtNscrollRCursor	Cursor	XC_sb_right_arrow	Cursor for scrolling right
XtNscrollUCursor	Cursor	XC_sb_up_arrow	Cursor for scrolling up
XtNscrollVCursor	Cursor	XC_sb_v_double_arrow	Idle vertical cursor
XtNsensitive	Boolean	TRUE	Whether widget receives input
XtNshown	float	NULL	Percentage the thumb covers
XtNthickness	Dimension	14	Minor dimension (height if XtorientHorizontal)
XtNthumb	Pixmap	Gray	Thump pixmap
XtNtop	float	NULL	Position on scroll bar
XtNtranslations	Translation-Table	See below	Event-to-action translations
XtNwidth	Dimension	See below	Width of scroll bar
XtNx	Position	NULL	x position of scroll bar
XtNy	Position	NULL	y position of scroll bar

The class for all cursor resources is XtCCursor.

You can set the dimensions of the Scrollbar two ways. As for all widgets, you can use the Xt-Nwidth and XtNheight resources. In addition, you can use an alternative method that is independent of the vertical or horizontal orientation:

XtNlength	Specifies the height for a vertical Scrollbar and the width for a horizontal Scrollbar.
XtNthickness	Specifies the width for a vertical Scrollbar and the height for a horizontal Scrollbar.

Translations and Actions

The actions supported by the Scrollbar widget are·

StartScroll(*value*)

> The possible values are *Forward*, *Backward*, or *Continuous* This must be the first action to begin a new movement.

NotifyScroll(*value*)

> The possible values are *Proportional* or *FullLength* If the argument to StartScroll was *Forward* or *Backward*, NotifyScroll executes the XtNscrollProc callbacks and passes either the position of the pointer if its argument is *Proportional* or the full length of the scroll bar if its argument is *FullLength*. If the argument to StartScroll was *Continuous*, NotifyScroll returns without executing any callbacks

EndScroll()   This must be the last action after a movement is complete.

MoveThumb()   Repositions the scroll bar thumb to the current pointer location

NotifyThumb()

> Calls the XtNjumpProc callbacks and passes the relative position of the pointer as a percentage of the scroll bar length.

The default bindings for Scrollbar are

```
<Btn1Down>·StartScroll(Forward)
<Btn2Down> StartScroll(Continuous) MoveThumb() NotifyThumb()
<Btn3Down> StartScroll(Backward)
<Btn2Motion>·MoveThumb() NotifyThumb()
<BtnUp>:NotifyScroll(Proportional) EndScroll()
```

Examples of additional bindings a user might wish to specify in a resource file are·

```
*Scrollbar.Translations  \\e
    ˜Meta<KeyPress>space:StartScroll(Forward) NotifyScroll(FullLength) \\e
    Meta<KeyPress>space:StartScroll(Backward) NotifyScroll(FullLength) \\e
EndScroll()
```

Programmatic Interface

- To create a Scrollbar widget instance, use XtCreateWidget and specify the class variable scrollbarWidgetClass

- To destroy a Scrollbar widget instance, use XtDestroyWidget and specify the widget ID for the Scrollbar.

- The XtNscrollProc callback is used for incremental scrolling and is called by the NotifyScroll action XtNscrollProc looks like this:

```
void ScrollProc(scrollbar, client_data, position)
    Widget scrollbar;
    caddr_t client_data;
    caddr_t position;      /* int */
```

where:

>   *scrollbar*   Specifies the ID of the Scrollbar.
>
>   *client_data* Specifies the client data.
>
>   *position*   Returns the pixel position of the thumb in integer form.

position is a signed quantity and should be cast to an int when used. Using the default button bindings, button 1 returns a positive value, and button 3 returns a negative value. In both cases, the magnitude of the value is the distance of the pointer in pixels from the top (or left) of the Scrollbar. The value will never be less than zero or greater than the length of the Scrollbar.

• The XtNjumpProc callback is used for jump scrolling and is called by the Notify-Thumb action. The XtNjumpProc callback procedure looks like this:

```
void JumpProc(scrollbar, client_data, percent)
    Widget scrollbar;
    caddr_t client_data;
    caddr_t percent_ptr;      /* float* */
```

where:

>   *scrollbar*   Specifies the ID of the scroll bar window.
>
>   *client_data* Specifies the client data.
>
>   *percent_ptr* Specifies the floating point position of the thumb (0.0 — 1.0).

The XtNjumpProc callback is used to implement smooth scrolling and is called by the NotifyThumb action. *percent_ptr* must be cast to a pointer to float before use:

>   float percent = *(float*)percent_ptr;

With the default button bindings, button 2 moves the thumb interactively, and the Xt-NjumpProc is called on each new position of the pointer.

An older interface used XtNthumbProc and passed the percentage by value rather than by reference. This interface is not portable across machine architectures; therefore, it is no longer supported. This interface is still implemented for those (nonportable) applications that used it.

• To set the position and length of a Scrollbar thumb, use XtScrollbarSetThumb:

```
void XtScrollbarSetThumb(w, top, shown)
    Widget w;
    float top;
    float shown;
```

where:

w   Specifies the Scrollbar widget ID

top   Specifies the position of the top of the thumb as a fraction of the length
             of the Scrollbar.

shown   Specifies the length of the thumb as a fraction of the total length of the
             Scrollbar.

XtScrollbarThumb moves the visible thumb to position (0.0 — 1 0) and length (0 0 –
1 0) Either top or shown can be specified as –1 0, in which case the current value is left
unchanged   Values greater than 1 0 are truncated to 1 0

If called from XtNjumpProc, XtScrollbarSetThumb has no effect.

Template

Name

templateWidgetClass — widget to create a custom widget.

Synopsis

```
#include <X11/StringDefs.h>
#include <X11/Intrinsic.h>
#include <X11/XawMisc.h>          /* <X11/Misc.h> in R2 */
#include <X11/Template.h>
```

Description

Although the task of creating a new widget may at first appear a little daunting, there is a basic pattern that all widgets follow. The Athena widget library contains three files that are intended to assist in writing a custom widget: *Template.h*, *TemplateP.h*, and *Template.c*.

Reasons for wishing to write a custom widget include:

- Convenient access to resource management procedures to obtain fonts, colors, etc., even if user customization is not desired.

- Convenient access to user input dispatch and translation management procedures.

- Access to callback mechanism for building higher-level application libraries.

- Customizing the interface or behavior of an existing widget to suit a special application need.

- Desire to allow user customization of resources such as fonts, colors, etc., or to allow convenient re-binding of keys and buttons to internal functions.

- Converting a non-Toolkit application to use the Toolkit.

In each of these cases, the operation needed to create a new widget is to "subclass" an existing one. If the desired semantics of the new widget are similar to an existing one, then the implementation of the existing widget should be examined to see how much work would be required to create a subclass that will then be able to share the existing class methods. Much time will be saved in writing the new widget if an existing widget class `Expose`, `Resize` and/or `GeometryManager` method can be shared by the subclass.

Note that some trivial uses of a "bare-bones" widget may be achieved by simply creating an instance of the Core widget. The class variable to use when creating a Core widget is `widgetClass`. The geometry of the Core widget is determined entirely by the parent widget.

It is very often the case that an application will have a special need for a certain set of functions and that many copies of these functions will be needed. For example, when converting an older application to use the Toolkit, it may be desirable to have a "Window widget" class that might have the following semantics:

- Allocate two drawing colors in addition to a background color.

- Allocate a text font.

- Execute an application-supplied function to handle exposure events
- Execute an application-supplied function to handle user input events.

It is obvious that a completely general-purpose WindowWidgetClass could be constructed that would export all class methods as callback lists, but such a widget would be very large and would have to choose some arbitrary number of resources such as colors to allocate An application that used many instances of the general-purpose widget would therefore unnecessarily waste many resources

In this section, an outline will be given of the procedure to follow to construct a special-purpose widget to address the items listed above The reader should refer to the appropriate sections of Volume Four, *X Toolkit Intrinsics Programming Manual*, for complete details of the material outlined here

All Athena widgets have three separate files associated with them:

- A *public* header file containing declarations needed by applications programmers
- A *private* header file containing additional declarations needed by the widget and any subclasses.
- A source code file containing the implementation of the widget

This separation of functions into three files is suggested for all widgets, but nothing in the Toolkit actually requires this format In particular, a private widget created for a single application may easily combine the *public* and *private* header files into a single file, or merge the contents into another application header file Similarly, the widget implementation can be merged into other application code

In the following example, the public header file *<X11/Template h>*, the private header file *<X11/TemplateP h>* and the source code file *<X11/Template c>* will be modified to produce the Window widget described above. In each case, the files have been designed so that you can make a global string replacement of *Template* and *template* with the name of your new widget, using the appropriate case.

Public Header File

The public header file contains declarations that will be required by any application module that needs to refer to the widget, whether to create an instance of the class, to perform an Xt-SetValues operation, or to call a public routine implemented by the widget class

The contents of the Template public header file, *< X11/Template h>*, are

```
#include <X11/copyright.h>

/* XConsortium: Template h,v 1 2 88/10/25 17 22 09 swick Exp $ */
/* Copyright Massachusetts Institute of Technology 1987, 1988 */

#ifndef _Template_h
#define _Template_h

/************************************************************
 *
 * Template widget
```

```
        *
        ***************************************************************/

/* Resources:

Name                    Class                   RepType         Default Value
----                    -----                   -------         -------------
background              Background              Pixel           XtDefaultBackground
border                  BorderColor             Pixel           XtDefaultForeground
borderWidth             BorderWidth             Dimension       1
destroyCallback         Callback                Pointer         NULL
height                  Height                  Dimension       0
mappedWhenManaged       MappedWhenManaged       Boolean         TRUE
sensitive               Sensitive               Boolean         TRUE
width                   Width                   Dimension       0
x                       Position                Position        0
y                       Position                Position        0

*/

/* define any special resource names here *
 * that are not in <X11/StringDefs.h> */

#define XtNtemplateResource             "templateResource"

#define XtCTemplateResource             "TemplateResource"

/* declare specific TemplateWidget class and instance datatypes */

typedef struct _TemplateClassRec*       TemplateWidgetClass;
typedef struct _TemplateRec*            TemplateWidget;

/* declare the class constant */

extern WidgetClass templateWidgetClass;

#endif  _Template_h
```

You will notice that most of this file is documentation. The crucial parts are the last 8 lines where macros for any private resource names and classes are defined and where the widget class datatypes and class record pointer are declared.

For the Window widget, we want two drawing colors, a callback list for user input and an Xt‑NexposeCallback callback list, and we will declare three convenience procedures, so we need to add:

```
/* Resources:
                        . . .
callback                Callback                Callback        NULL
drawingColor1           Color                   Pixel           XtDefaultForeground
drawingColor2           Color                   Pixel           XtDefaultForeground
exposeCallback          Callback                Callback        NULL
font                    Font                    XFontStruct*    XtDefaultFont
                        . . .
*/
```

```
#define XtNdrawingColor1    "drawingColor1"
#define XtNdrawingColor2    "drawingColor2"
#define XtNexposeCallback   "exposeCallback"

extern Pixel WindowColor1(/* Widget */),
extern Pixel WindowColor2(/* Widget */),
extern Font  WindowFont(/* Widget */),
```

Note that we have chosen to call the input callback list by the generic name, XtNcallback, rather than a specific name If widgets that define a single user-input action all choose the same resource name then there is greater possibility for an application to switch between widgets of different types

Private Header File

The private header file contains the complete declaration of the class and instance structures for the widget and any additional private data that will be required by anticipated subclasses of the widget Information in the private header file is normally hidden from the application and is designed to be accessed only through other public procedures, such as Xt Set Values.

The contents of the Template private header file, *<X11/TemplateP h>*, are

```
#include <X11/copyright h>

/* XConsortium: TemplateP.h,v 1.2 88/10/25 17.31.47 swick Exp $ */
/* Copyright Massachusetts Institute of Technology 1987, 1988 */

#ifndef _TemplateP_h
#define _TemplateP_h

#include "Template h"
/* include superclass private header file */
#include <X11/CoreP.h>

/* define unique representation types not found in <X11/StringDefs h> */

#define XtRTemplateResource      "TemplateResource"

typedef struct {
      int empty,
} TemplateClassPart,

typedef struct _TemplateClassRec {
      CoreClassPart core_class,
      TemplateClassParttemplate_class;
} TemplateClassRec;

extern TemplateClassRec templateClassRec;

typedef struct {
      /* resources */
      char* resource;
      /* private state */
} TemplatePart,

typedef struct _TemplateRec {
```

```
        CorePart      core;
        TemplatePart  template;
} TemplateRec;

#endif _TemplateP_h
```

The private header file includes the private header file of its superclass, thereby exposing the entire internal structure of the widget. It may not always be advantageous to do this; your own project development style will dictate the appropriate level of detail to expose in each module.

The Window widget needs to declare two fields in its instance structure to hold the drawing colors, a resource field for the font and a field for the expose and user input callback lists:

```
typedef struct {
        /* resources */
        Pixel color_1;
        Pixel color_2;
        XFontStruct* font;
        XtCallbackList expose_callback;
        XtCallbackList input_callback;
        /* private state */
        /* (none) */
} WindowPart;
```

Widget Source File

The source code file implements the widget class itself. The unique part of this file is the declaration and initialization of the widget class record structure and the declaration of all resources and action routines added by the widget class.

The contents of the Template implementation file, *<X11/Template.c>*, are:

```
#include <X11/copyright.h>

/* XConsortium: Template.c,v 1.2 88/10/25 17:40:25 swick Exp $ */
/* Copyright Massachusetts Institute of Technology 1987, 1988 */

#include <X11/IntrinsicP.h>
#include <X11/StringDefs.h>
#include "TemplateP.h"

static XtResource resources[] = {
#define offset(field) XtOffset(TemplateWidget, template.field)
    /* {name, class, type, size, offset, default_type, default_addr}, */
    { XtNtemplateResource, XtCTemplateResource, XtRTemplateResource, \\e
          sizeof(char*), offset(resource), XtRString, "default" },
#undef offset
};

static void TemplateAction(/* Widget, XEvent*, String*, Cardinal* */);

static XtActionsRec actions[] =
{
    /* {name, procedure}, */
```

```
     {"template", TemplateAction},
},
static char translations[] =
"   <Key>· template() \\en\\e
",
TemplateClassRec templateClassRec = {
    {   /* core fields */
        /* superclass */               (WidgetClass) &widgetClassRec,
        /* class_name */               "Template",
        /* widget_size */              sizeof(TemplateRec),
        /* class_initialize */         NULL,
        /* class_part_initialize */    NULL,
        /* class_inited */             FALSE,
        /* initialize */               NULL,
        /* initialize_hook */          NULL,
        /* realize */                  XtInheritRealize,
        /* actions */                  actions,
        /* num_actions */              XtNumber(actions),
        /* resources */                resources,
        /* num_resources */            XtNumber(resources),
        /* xrm_class */                NULLQUARK,
        /* compress_motion */          TRUE,
        /* compress_exposure */        TRUE,
        /* compress_enterleave */      TRUE,
        /* visible_interest */         FALSE,
        /* destroy */                  NULL,
        /* resize */                   NULL,
        /* expose */                   NULL,
        /* set_values */               NULL,
        /* set_values_hook */          NULL,
        /* set_values_almost */        XtInheritSetValuesAlmost,
        /* get_values_hook */          NULL,
        /* accept_focus */             NULL,
        /* version */                  XtVersion,
        /* callback_private */         NULL,
        /* tm_table */                 translations,
        /* query_geometry */           XtInheritQueryGeometry,
        /* display_accelerator */      XtInheritDisplayAccelerator,
        /* extension */                NULL
    },
    { /* template fields */
        /* empty */                    0
    }
};

WidgetClass templateWidgetClass = (WidgetClass)&templateClassRec;
```

The resource list for the Window widget might look like the following:

```
static XtResource resources[] = {
#define offset(field) XtOffset(WindowWidget, window.field)
    /* {name, class, type, size, offset, default_type, default_addr}, */
    { XtNdrawingColor1, XtCColor, XtRPixel, sizeof(Pixel),
        offset(color_1), XtRString, XtDefaultForeground },
    { XtNdrawingColor2, XtCColor, XtRPixel, sizeof(Pixel),
        offset(color_2), XtRString, XtDefaultForeground },
    { XtNfont, XtCFont, XtRFontStruct, sizeof(XFontStruct*),
        offset(font), XtRString, XtDefaultFont },
    { XtNexposeCallback, XtCCallback, XtRCallback, sizeof(XtCallbackList),
        offset(expose_callback), XtRCallback, NULL },
    { XtNcallback, XtCCallback, XtRCallback, sizeof(XtCallbackList),
        offset(input_callback), XtRCallback, NULL },
#undef offset
};
```

The user input callback will be implemented by an action procedure that passes the event
pointer as *call_data*. The action procedure is declared as:

```
    /* ARGSUSED */
    static void InputAction(w, event, params, num_params)
        Widget w;
        XEvent *event;
        String *params;/* unused */
        Cardinal *num_params;/* unused */
    {
        XtCallCallbacks(w, XtNcallback, (caddr_t)event);
    }

    static XtActionsRec actions[] =
    {
        /* {name, procedure}, */
        {"input", InputAction},
    };
```

and the default input binding will be to execute the input callbacks on KeyPress and
ButtonPress:

```
    static char translations[] =
    "    <Key>:input() \\en\\e
        <BtnDown>:input() \\e
    ";
```

In the class record declaration and initialization, the only field that is different from the Template is the expose procedure:

```
/* ARGSUSED */
static void Redisplay(w, event, region)
    Widget w;
    XEvent *event;   /* unused */
    Region region;
```

```
{
    XtCallCallbacks(w, XtNexposeCallback, (caddr_t)region);
}
WindowClassRec windowClassRec = {
    . .
    /* expose */ Redisplay,
```

The Window widget will also declare three public procedures to return the drawing colors and the font ID, saving the application the effort of constructing an argument list for a call to Xt-GetValues.

```
Pixel WindowColor1(w)
    Widget w,
{
    return ((WindowWidget)w)->window.color_1;
}

Pixel WindowColor2(w)
    Widget w,
{
    return ((WindowWidget)w)->window color_2,
}

Font WindowFont(w)
    Widget w,
{
    return ((WindowWidget)w)->window.font->fid,
}
```

The Window widget is now complete The application can retrieve the two drawing colors from the widget instance by calling either XtGetValues, or the WindowColor functions, The actual window created for the Window widget is available by calling the XtWindow function

Text

Name

textWidgetClass — text-editing widget.

Synopsis

```
#include <X11/StringDefs.h>
#include <X11/Intrinsic.h>
#include <X11/XawMisc.h>          /* <X11/Misc.h> in R2 */
#include <X11/Text.h>
widget = XtCreateWidget(widget, textWidgetClass,...);
widget = XtCreateWidget(widget, asciiStringWidgetClass,...);
widget = XtCreateWidget(widget, asciiDiskWidgetClass,...);
```

Class Hierarchy

Core → Simple → Text → asciiString

Core → Simple → Text → asciiDisk

Description

A Text widget is a window that provides a way for an application to display one or more lines of text. The displayed text can reside in a file on disk or in a string in memory. An option also lets an application display a vertical Scrollbar in the Text window, letting the user scroll through the displayed text. Other options allow an application to let the user modify the text in the window.

The Text widget is divided into three parts:

- Source
- Sink
- Text widget

The idea is to separate the storage of the text (source) from the painting of the text (sink). The Text widget proper coordinates the sources and sinks. There are subclasses of the Text widget that automatically create the source and sink for the client. Widgets of class asciiString-WidgetClass use a string in memory as the source; asciiDiskWidgetClass widgets use a disk file. Both use a single-font, single-color ASCII sink. A client can, if it so chooses, explicitly create the source and sink before creating the Text widget.

The source stores and manipulates the text, and determines what editing functions may be performed on the text.

The sink obtains the fonts and the colors in which to paint the text. The sink also computes what text can fit on each line.

If a disk file is used as the source, two edit modes are available:

- Append
- Read-only

Append mode lets the user enter text into the window, while read-only mode does not. Text may only be entered if the insertion point is after the last character in the window.

If a string in memory is used as the source, the application must allocate the amount of space needed. Three types of edit mode are available:

- Append-only
- Read-only
- Editable

The first two modes are the same as displaying text from a disk file. Editable mode lets the user place the cursor anywhere in the text and modify the text at that position. The text cursor position can be modified by using the keystrokes or pointer buttons defined by the event bindings. (See Translations and Actions below.)

Resources

When creating a Text widget instance, the following resources are retrieved from the argument list or from the resource database:

Name	Type	Default	Description
XtNbackground	Pixel	XtDefault-Background	Window background color
XtNbackground-Pixmap	Pixmap	None	Window background pixmap
XtNborderColor	Pixel	XtDefault-Foreground	Window border color
XtNborderPixmap	Pixmap	None	Window border pixmap
XtNborderWidth	Dimension	4	Border width in pixels
XtNcursor	Cursor	XC_xterm	Pointer cursor
XtNdialogHOffset	int	10	Offset of insert file dialog
XtNdialogVOffset	int	10	Offset of insert file dialog
XtNdestroy-Callback	XtCallbackList	NULL	Callbacks for XtDestroyWidget
XtNdisplayPosition	int	0	Character position of first line
XtNeditType	XtEditType	XttextRead	Edit mode (see note)
XtNfile	char*	tmpnam()	File for asciiDiskWidgetClass
XtNforeground	Pixel	Black	Foreground color
XtNfont	XFontStruct*	Fixed	Fontname
XtNheight	Dimension	Font height	Height of widget
XtNinsertPosition	int	0	Character position of caret
XtNleftMargin	Dimension	2	Left margin in pixels
XtNlength	int	String length	Size of the string buffer
XtNmappedWhen-Managed	Boolean	TRUE	Whether XtMapWidget is automatic
XtNselectTypes	XtTextSelectType*	See below	Selection units for multi-click
XtNsensitive	Boolean	TRUE	Whether widget receives input
XtNstring	char*	Blank	String for asciiStringWidgetClass
XtNtextOptions	int	None	See below
XtNtextSink	XtTextSink	None	See below

Name	Type	Default	Description
XtNtextSource	XtTextSource	None	See below
XtNtranslations	TranslationTable	See above	event-to-action translations
XtNwidth	Dimension	100	Width of widget (pixels)
XtNx	Position	0	x coordinate in pixels
XtNy	Position	0	y coordinate in pixels

Note that:

1. You cannot use XtNeditType, XtNfile, XtNlength, and XtNfont with the Xt-TextSetValues and the XtTextGetValues calls.

2. The XtNeditType attribute has one of the values XttextAppend, XttextEdit, or XttextRead.

3. If asciiStringWidgetClass is used, the resource XtNstring specifies a buffer containing the text to be displayed and edited. asciiStringWidget does not copy this buffer but uses it in place.

Text Options

The options for the XtNtextOptions attribute are:

editable	Whether or not the user is allowed to modify the text.
resizeHeight	Makes a request to the parent widget to lengthen the window if all the text cannot fit in the window.
resizeWidth	Makes a request to the parent widget to widen the window if the text becomes too long to fit on one line.
scrollHorizontal	Puts a scroll bar on the top of the window.
scrollOnOverflow	Automatically scrolls the text up when new text is entered below the bottom (last) line.
scrollVertical	Puts a scroll bar on the left side of the window.
wordBreak	Starts a new line when a word does not fit on the current line.

These options can be ORed together to set more than one at the same time.

Selections

XtNselectionTypes is an array of entries of type XtTextSelectType and is used for multiclick. As the pointer button is clicked in rapid succession, each click highlights the next "type" described in the array.

XtselectAll	Selects the contents of the entire buffer.
XtselectChar	Selects text characters as the pointer moves over them.
XtselectLine	Selects the entire line.
XtselectNull	Indicates the end of the selection array.

XtselectParagraph	Selects the entire paragraph (delimited by newline characters)
XtselectPosition	Selects the current pointer position.
XtselectWord	Selects whole words (delimited by Whitespace) as the pointer moves onto them

The default selectType array is

```
{XtselectPosition, XtselectWord, XtselectLine, XtselectParagraph,
            XtselectAll, XtselectNull}
```

For the default case, two rapid pointer clicks highlight the current word, three clicks highlight the current line, four clicks highlight the current paragraph, and five clicks highlight the entire text If the timeout value is exceeded, the next pointer click returns to the first entry in the selection array The selection array is not copied by the Text widget. The client must allocate space for the array and cannot deallocate or change it until the Text widget is destroyed or until a new selection array is set

Translations and Actions
Many standard keyboard editing facilities are supported by the event bindings The following actions are supported.

Cursor Movement	Delete
forward-character	delete-next-character
backward-character	delete-previous-character
forward-word	delete-next-word
backward-word	delete-previous-word
forward-paragraph	delete-selection
backward-paragraph	
beginning-of-line	
end-of-line	Selection
next-line	select-word
previous-line	select-all
next-page	select-start
previous-page	select-adjust
beginning-of-file	select-end
end-of-file	extend-start
scroll-one-line-up	extend-adjust
scroll-one-line-down	extend-end
New Line	Miscellaneous
newline-and-indent	redraw-display
newline-and-backup	insert-file
newline	do-nothing
Kill	Unkill
kill-word	unkill
backward-kill-word	stuff
kill-selection	insert-selection

Cursor Movement	Delete
kill-to-end-of-line	
kill-to-end-of-paragraph	

- A page corresponds to the size of the Text window. For example, if the Text window is 50 lines in length, scrolling forward one page is the same as scrolling forward 50 lines.

- The **delete** action deletes a text item. The **kill** action deletes a text item and puts the item in the kill buffer (X cut buffer 1).

- The **unkill** action inserts the contents of the kill buffer into the text at the current position. The **stuff** action inserts the contents of the paste buffer (X cut buffer 0) into the text at the current position. The **insert-selection** action retrieves the value of a specified X selection or cut buffer, with fall-back to alternative selections or cut buffers.

The default event bindings for the Text widget are:

```
char defaultTextTranslations[] = ''\
    Ctrl<Key>F:          forward-character() \n\
    Ctrl<Key>B:          backward-character() \n\
    Ctrl<Key>D:          delete-next-character() \n\
    Ctrl<Key>A:          beginning-of-line() \n\
    Ctrl<Key>E:          end-of-line() \n\
    Ctrl<Key>H:          delete-previous-character() \n\
    Ctrl<Key>J:          newline-and-indent() \n\
    Ctrl<Key>K:          kill-to-end-of-line() \n\
    Ctrl<Key>L:          redraw-display() \n\
    Ctrl<Key>M:          newline() \n\
    Ctrl<Key>N:          next-line() \n\
    Ctrl<Key>O:          newline-and-backup() \n\
    Ctrl<Key>P:          previous-line() \n\
    Ctrl<Key>V:          next-page() \n\
    Ctrl<Key>W:          kill-selection() \n\
    Ctrl<Key>Y:          unkill() \n\
    Ctrl<Key>Z:          scroll-one-line-up() \n\
    Meta<Key>F:          forward-word() \n\
    Meta<Key>B:          backward-word() \n\
    Meta<Key>I:          Insert-file() \n\
    Meta<Key>K:          kill-to-end-of-paragraph() \n\
    Meta<Key>V:          previous-page() \n\
    Meta<Key>Y:          stuff() \n\
    Meta<Key>Z:          scroll-one-line-down() \n\
    :Meta<Key>d:         delete-next-word() \n\
    :Meta<Key>D:         kill-word() \n\
    :Meta<Key>h:         delete-previous-word() \n\
    :Meta<Key>H:         backward-kill-word() \n\
    :Meta<Key>\<:        beginning-of-file() \n\
    :Meta<Key>\>:        end-of-file() \n\
    :Meta<Key>]:         forward-paragraph() \n\
```

Athena
Widgets

```
 Meta<Key>[:               backward-paragraph() \n\
~Shift Meta<Key>Delete     delete-previous-word() \n\
 Shift Meta<Key>Delete     backward-kill-word() \n\
~Shift Meta<Key>Backspace  delete-previous-word() \n\
 Shift Meta<Key>Backspace  backward-kill-word() \n\
<Key>Right                 forward-character() \n\
<Key>Left·                 backward-character() \n\
<Key>Down                  next-line() \n\
<Key>Up:                   previous-line() \n\
<Key>Delete                delete-previous-character() \n\
<Key>BackSpace.            delete-previous-character() \n\
<Key>Linefeed.             newline-and-indent() \n\
<Key>Return                newline() \n\
<Key>                      insert-char() \n\
<FocusIn>.                 focus-in() \n\
<FocusOut>                 focus-out() \n\
<Btn1Down>                 select-start() \n\
<Btn1Motion>               extend-adjust() \n\
<Btn1Up>.                  extend-end(PRIMARY, CUT_BUFFER0) \n\
<Btn2Down>                 insert-selection(PRIMARY, CUT_BUFFER0) \n\
<Btn3Down>.                extend-start() \n\
<Btn3Motion>.              extend-adjust() \n\
<Btn3Up>:                  extend-end(PRIMARY, CUT_BUFFER0) \
```

A user-supplied resource entry can use application-specific bindings, a subset of the supplied default bindings, or both The following is an example of a user-supplied resource entry that uses a subset of the default bindings·

```
Xmh*Text.Translations    \\e
     <Key>Right:         forward-character() \\en\\e
     <Key>Left           backward-character() \\en\\e
     Meta<Key>F·         forward-word() \\en\\e
     Meta<Key>B          backward-word() \\en\\e
    .Meta<Key>]·         forward-paragraph() \\en\\e
    .Meta<Key>[:         backward-paragraph() \\en\\e
     <Key>               insert-char()
```

An augmented binding that is useful with the *xclipboard* utility is.

```
*Text Translations  #override \\e
     Button1 <Btn2Down> extend-end(CLIPBOARD)
```

The Text widget fully supports the X selection and cut buffer mechanisms The following actions can be used to specify button bindings that will cause Text to assert ownership of one or more selections, to store the selected text into a cut buffer, and to retrieve the value of a selection or cut buffer and insert it into the text value

insert-selection(*name*[,*name*,...])
> Retrieves the value of the first (left-most) named selection that exists or the cut buffer that is not empty and inserts it into the input stream The specified name can

be that of any selection (for example, PRIMARY or SECONDARY) or a cut buffer (i.e., CUT_BUFFER0 through CUT_BUFFER7). Note that case matters.

select-start()

> Unselects any previously selected text and begins selecting new text.

select-adjust()
extend-adjust()

> Continues selecting text from the previous start position.

start-extend()

> Begins extending the selection from the farthest (left or right) edge.

select-end(name[,name, ...])
extend-end(name[,name, ...])

> Ends the text selection, asserts ownership of the specified selection(s) and stores the text in the specified cut buffer(s). The specified name can be that of a selection (for example, PRIMARY or SECONDARY) or a cut buffer (i.e., CUT_BUFFER0 through CUT_BUFFER7). Note that case is significant. If CUT_BUFFER0 is listed, the cut buffers are rotated before storing into buffer 0.

Programmatic Interface

A Text widget lets both the user and the application take control of the text being displayed. The user takes control with the scroll bar or with key strokes defined by the event bindings. The scroll bar option places the scroll bar on the left side of the window and can be used with any editing mode. The application takes control with procedure calls to the Text widget to:

- Display text at a specified position.
- Highlight specified text areas.
- Replace specified text areas.

The text that is selected within a Text window may be assigned to an X selection or copied into a cut buffer and can be retrieved by the application with the Intrinsics XtGetSelection-Value or the Xlib XFetchBytes functions respectively. Several standard selection schemes (e.g., character/word/paragraph with multiclick) are supported through the event bindings.

- To create a Text string widget, use XtCreateWidget and specify the class variable asciiStringWidgetClass.
- To create a Text file widget, use XtCreateWidget and specify the class variable asciiDiskWidgetClass.

  If you want to create an instance of the class textWidgetClass, you must provide a source and a sink when the widget is created. The Text widget cannot be instantiated without both.

- To enable an application to select a piece of text, use XtTextSetSelection.

```
typedef long XtTextPosition,

void XtTextSetSelection(w, left, right)
    Widget w,
    XtTextPosition left, right,
```

where:

w	Specifies the window ID
left	Specifies the character position at which the selection begins
right	Specifies the character position at which the selection ends

If redisplay is not disabled, this function highlights the text and makes it the PRIMARY selection.

• To unhighlight previously highlighted text in a window, use XtTextUnsetSelection.

```
void XtTextUnsetSelection(w)
    Widget w,
```

• To enable the application to get the character positions of the selected text, use XtText-GetSelectionPos

```
void XtTextGetSelectionPos(w, pos1, pos2)
    Widget w,
    XtTextPosition *pos1, *pos2;
```

where

w	Specifies the window ID
pos1	Specifies a pointer to the location to which the beginning character position of the selection is returned.
pos2	Specifies a pointer to the location to which the ending character position of the selection is returned

If the returned values are equal, there is no current selection

• To enable an application to replace text, use XtTextReplace

```
int XtTextReplace(w, start_pos, end_pos, text)
    Widget w,
    XtTextPosition start_pos, end_pos,
    XtTextBlock *text;
```

where.

w	Specifies the window ID
start_pos	Specifies the starting character position of the text replacement
end_pos	Specifies the ending character position of the text replacement
text	Specifies the text to be inserted into the file

The `XtTextReplace` function deletes text in the specified range (*startPos, end-Pos*) and inserts the new text at *start_pos*. The return value is `XawEditDone` if the replacement is successful, `XawPositionError` if the edit mode is `XttextAppend` and *start_pos* is not the last character of the source, or `XawEditError` if either the source was read-only or the range to be deleted is larger than the length of the source.

The `XtTextBlock` structure (defined in *<X11/Text.h>* contains:

```
typedef struct {
    int firstPos;
    int length;
    char *ptr;
    Atom format;
} XtTextBlock, *TextBlockPtr;
```

The *firstPos* field is the starting point to use within the *ptr* field. The value is usually zero. The *length* field is the number of characters that are transferred from the *ptr* field. The number of characters transferred is usually the number of characters in *ptr*. The *format* field is not currently used, but should be specified as `FMT8BIT`. The `XtTextReplace` arguments *start_pos* and *end_pos* represent the text source character positions for the existing text that is to be replaced by the text in the `XtTextBlock` structure. The characters from *start_pos* up to but not including *end_pos* are deleted, and the characters that are specified by the text block are inserted in their place. If *start_pos* and *end_pos* are equal, no text is deleted and the new text is inserted after *start_pos*.

Only ASCII text is currently supported, and only one font can be used for each Text widget.

•   To redisplay a range of characters, use `XtTextInvalidate`.

```
void XtTextInvalidate(w, from, to)
    Widget w;
    XtTextPosition from, to;
```

The `XtTextInvalidate` function causes the specified range of characters to be redisplayed immediately if redisplay is enabled or the next time that redisplay is enabled.

•   To enable redisplay, use `XtTextEnableRedisplay`.

```
void XtTextEnableRedisplay(w)
    Widget w;
```

The `XtTextEnableRedisplay` function flushes any changes due to batched updates when `XtTextDisableRedisplay` was called and allows future changes to be reflected immediately.

•   To disable redisplay while making several changes, use `XtTextDisableRedisplay`.

```
void XtTextDisableRedisplay(w)
    Widget w;
```

The `XtTextDisableRedisplay` function causes all changes to be batched until `XtTextDisplay` or `XtTextEnableRedisplay` is called

- To display batched updates, use `XtTextDisplay`

```
void XtTextDisplay(w)
    Widget w,
```

The `XtTextDisplay` function forces any accumulated updates to be displayed

- To notify the source that the length has been changed, use `XtTextSetLastPos`.

```
void XtTextSetLastPos(w, last),
    Widget w,
    XtTextPosition last,
```

The `XtTextSetLastPos` function notifies the text source that data has been added to or removed from the end of the source

The following procedures are convenience procedures that replace calls to `XtSetValues` or `XtGetValues` when only a single resource is to be modified or retrieved

- To assign a new value to `XtNtextOptions` resource, use `XtTextChangeOptions`.

```
void XtTextChangeOptions(w, options)
    Widget w,
    int options,
```

- To obtain the current value of `XtNtextOptions` for the specified widget, use `XtTextGetOptions`

```
int XtTextGetOptions(w)
    Widget w,
```

- To obtain the character position of the left-most character on the first line displayed in the widget (that is, the value of `XtNdisplayPosition`), use `XtTextTopPosition`

```
XtTextPosition XtTextTopPosition(w)
    Widget w,
```

- To move the insertion caret to the specified source position, use `XtTextSetInsertionPoint`

```
void XtTextSetInsertionPoint(w, position)
    Widget w,
    XtTextPosition position,
```

The text will be scrolled vertically if necessary to make the line containing the insertion point visible The result is equivalent to setting the `XtNinsertPosition` resource

- To obtain the current position of the insertion caret, use `XtTextGetInsertionPoint`

```
XtTextPosition XtTextGetInsertionPoint(w)
    Widget w,
```

The result is equivalent to retrieving the value of the `XtNinsertPosition` resource

- To replace the text source in the specified widget, use `XtTextSetSource`.

```
void XtTextSetSource(w, source, position)
      Widget w;
      XtTextSource source;
      XtTextPosition position;
```

A display update will be performed if redisplay has not been disabled.

- To obtain the current text source for the specified widget, use `XtTextGetSource`.

```
XtTextSource XtTextGetSource(w)
      Widget w;
```

Creating Sources and Sinks

The following functions for creating and destroying text sources and sinks are called automatically by `asciiStringWidget` and `asciiDiskWidget` and it is therefore only necessary for the client to use them when creating an instance of `textWidgetClass`.

- To create a new ASCII text sink, use `XtAsciiSinkCreate`.

```
XtTextSink XtAsciiSinkCreate(w, args, num_args)
      Widget w;
      ArgList args;
      Cardinal num_args;
```

The resources required by the sink are qualified by the name and class of the parent and the sub-part name `XtNtextSink` and class `XtCTextSink`.

- To deallocate an ASCII text sink, use `XtAsciiSinkDestroy`.

```
void XtAsciiSinkDestroy(sink)
      XtTextSink sink;
```

The sink must not be in use by any widget or an error will result.

- To create a new text disk source, use `XtDiskSourceCreate`.

```
XtTextSource XtDiskSourceCreate(w, args, num_args)
      Widget w;
      ArgList args;
      Cardinal num_args;
```

The resources required by the source are qualified by the name and class of the parent and the sub-part name `XtNtextSource` and class `XtCTextSource`.

- To deallocate a text disk source, use `XtDiskSourceDestroy`.

```
void XtDiskSourceDestroy(source)
      XtTextSource source;
```

The source must not be in use by any widget or an error will result.

- To create a new text string source, use `XtStringSourceCreate`.

```
XtTextSource XtStringSourceCreate(w, args, num_args)
      Widget w;
```

```
ArgList args,
Cardinal num_args,
```

The resources required by the source are qualified by the name and class of the parent and the sub-part name XtNtextSource and class XtCTextSource.

To deallocate a text string source, use XtStringSourceDestroy

```
void XtStringSourceDestroy(source)
    XtTextSource source;
```

The source must not be in use by any widget or an error will result.

Viewport

Name

viewportWidgetClass — scrollable widget for geometry management.

Synopsis

```
#include <X11/StringDefs.h>
#include <X11/Intrinsic.h>
#include <X11/XawMisc.h>            /* <X11/Misc.h> in R2 */
#include <X11/Viewport.h>
widget = XtCreateWidget(widget, viewportWidgetClass,...);
```

Class Hierarchy

Core → Composite → Viewport

Description

The Viewport widget consists of a frame window, one or two Scrollbars, and an inner window (usually containing a child widget). The frame window is determined by the viewing size of the data that is to be displayed and the dimensions to which the Viewport is created. The inner window is the full size of the data that is to be displayed and is clipped by the frame window. The Viewport widget controls the scrolling of the data directly. No application callbacks are required for scrolling.

When the geometry of the frame window is equal in size to the inner window, or when the data does not require scrolling, the Viewport widget automatically removes any scroll bars. The forceBars option causes the Viewport widget to display any scroll bar permanently.

Resources

When creating a Viewport widget instance, the following resources are retrieved from the argument list or from the resource database:

Name	Type	Default	Description
XtNallowHoriz	Boolean	FALSE	Flag to allow horizontal scroll bars
XtNallowVert	Boolean	FALSE	Flag to allow vertical scroll bars
XtNbackground	Pixel	XtDefault-Background	Window background color
XtNbackground-Pixmap	Pixmap	None	Window background pixmap
XtNborderColor	Pixel	XtDefault-Foreground	Window border color
XtNborderPixmap	Pixmap	None	Window border pixmap
XtNborderWidth	Dimension	1	Width of the border in pixels
XtNdestroy-Callback	XtCallbackList	NULL	Callback for XtDestroyWidget
XtNforceBars	Boolean	FALSE	Flag to force display of scroll bars
XtNheight	Dimension	height of child	Height of the widget

Name	Type	Default	Description
XtNmappedWhen- Managed	Boolean	TRUE	Whether XtMapWidget is automatic
XtNsensitive	Boolean	TRUE	Whether widget should receive input
XtNtranslations	TranslationTable	None	Event-to-action translations
XtNuseBottom	Boolean	FALSE	Flag to indicate bottom/top bars
XtNuseRight	Boolean	FALSE	Flag to indicate right/left bars
XtNwidth	Dimension	width of child	Width of the widget
XtNx	Position	0	x coordinate within parent
XtNy	Position	0	y coordinate within parent

The Viewport widget manages a single child widget. When the size of the child is larger than the size of the Viewport, the user can interactively move the child within the Viewport by repositioning the Scrollbars.

The default size of the Viewport before it is realized is the width and/or height of the child. After it is realized, the Viewport will allow its child to grow vertically or horizontally if Xt- NallowVert or XtNallowHoriz were set, respectively. If the corresponding vertical or horizontal scrolling were not enabled, the Viewport will propagate the geometry request to its own parent and the child will be allowed to change size only if the (grand) parent allows it. Regardless of whether or not scrolling was enabled in the corresponding direction, if the child requests a new size smaller than the Viewport size, the change will be allowed only if the parent of the Viewport allows the Viewport to shrink to the appropriate dimension.

Programmatic Interface

- To create a Viewport widget instance, use XtCreateWidget and specify the class variable viewportWidgetClass.

- To insert a child into a Viewport widget, use XtCreateWidget and specify the widget ID of the previously created Viewport as the parent.

- To remove a child from a Viewport widget, use XtUnmanageChild or XtDestroy- Widget and specify the widget ID of the child.

- To delete the inner window, any children, and the frame window, use XtDestroy- Widget and specify the widget ID of the Viewport widget.

See Also

Scrollbar

VPaned

Name

vPanedWidgetClass — geometry-managing widget for vertical tiles.

Synopsis

```
#include <X11/StringDefs.h>
#include <X11/Intrinsic.h>
#include <X11/XawMisc.h>          /* <X11/Misc.h> in R2 */
#include <X11/VPaned.h>
widget = XtCreateWidget(widget, vPanedWidgetClass,...);
```

Class Hierarchy

Core → Composite → Constraint → VPaned

Description

The VPaned widget manages children in a vertically tiled fashion. A region, called a grip, appears on the border between each child. When the pointer is positioned on a grip and pressed, an arrow is displayed that indicates the significant pane that is being resized. While keeping the pointer button down, the user can move the pointer up or down. This, in turn, changes the window borders, causing one pane to shrink and some other pane to grow. The cursor indicates the pane that is of interest to the user; some other pane in the opposite direction will be chosen to grow or shrink an equal amount. The choice of alternate pane is a function of the XtNmin, XtNmax and XtNskipAdjust constraints on the other panes. With the default bindings, button 1 resizes the pane above the selected grip, button 3 resizes the pane below the selected grip and button 2 repositions the border between two panes only.

Resources

When creating a VPaned widget instance, the following resources are retrieved from the argument list or from the resource database:

Name	Type	Default	Description
XtNbackground	Pixel	XtDefault-Background	Window background color
XtNbackground-Pixmap	Pixmap	None	Window background pixmap
XtNbetweenCursor	Cursor	XC_sb_left_arrow	Cursor for changing the boundary between two panes
XtNborderColor	Pixel	XtDefault-Foreground	Window border color
XtNborderPixmap	Pixmap	None	Window border pixmap
XtNborderWidth	Dimension	1	Border width (pixels)
XtNdestroy-Callback	XtCallbackList	NULL	Callbacks for XtDestroy-Widget
XtNforeground	Pixel	Black	Pixel value for the foreground color

Name	Type	Default	Description
XtNgripCursor	Cursor	XC_sb_v_double_arrow	Cursor for grip when not active
XtNgripIndent	Position	10	Offset of grip from margin (pixels)
XtNgrip-Translations	TranslationTable	Internal	Button bindings for grip
XtNheight	Dimension	sum of child heights	Height of vPane
XtNlowerCursor	Cursor	XC_sb_down_arrow	Cursor for resizing pane below grip
XtNmappedWhen-Managed	Boolean	TRUE	Whether XtMapWidget is automatic
XtNrefigureMode	Boolean	On	Whether vPane should adjust children
XtNsensitive	Boolean	TRUE	Whether widget receives input
XtNtranslations	TranslationTable	None	Event-to-action translations
XtNupperCursor	Cursor	XC_sb_up_arrow	Cursor for resizing pane above grip
XtNwidth	Dimension	width of widest child	Width of vPane
XtNx	Position	0	x position of vPane
XtNy	Position	0	y position of vPane

Constraints

During the creation of a child pane, the following resources, by which the VPaned widget controls the placement of the child, can be specified in the argument list or retrieved from the resource database:

Name	Type	Default	Description
XtNallowResize	Boolean	FALSE	If FALSE, ignore child resize requests
XtNmax	Dimension	Unlimited	Maximum height for pane
XtNmin	Dimension	1	Minimum height for pane
XtNskipAdjust	Boolean	FALSE	TRUE if the VPaned widget should not automatically resize pane

Programmatic Interface

- To create a VPaned widget instance, use XtCreateWidget and specify the class variable vPanedWidgetClass.

  Once the parent frame is created, you then add panes to it. Any type of widget can be paned.

- To add a child pane to a VPaned frame, use XtCreateWidget and specify the widget ID of the VPaned widget as the parent of each new child pane.

- To delete a pane from a vertically paned window frame, use XtUnmanageWidget or XtDestroyWidget and specify the widget ID of the child pane.

- To enable or disable a child's request for pane resizing, use XtPanedAllowResize.

```
void XtPanedAllowResize(w, allow_resize)
    Widget w;
    Boolean allow_resize;
```

where:

    w   Specifies the widget ID of the child widget pane.

    allow_resize   Enables or disables a pane window for resizing requests.

If *allow_resize* is TRUE, the VPaned widget allows geometry requests from the child to change the pane's height. If *allow_resize* is FALSE, the VPaned widget ignores geometry requests from the child to change the pane's height. The default state is TRUE before the VPaned widget is realized and FALSE after it is realized. This procedure is equivalent to changing the XtNallowResize resource for the child.

- To change the minimum and maximum height settings for a pane, use XtPanedSetMinMax.

```
void XtPanedSetMinMax(w, min, max)
    Widget w;
    int min, max;
```

where:

    w   Specifies the widget ID of the child widget pane.

    min   is the minimum height of the child, expressed in pixels.

    max   is the maximum height of the child, expressed in pixels.

This procedure is equivalent to setting the XtNmin and XtNmax resources for the child.

- To enable or disable automatic recalculation of pane sizes and positions, use XtPanedSetRefigureMode.

```
void XtPanedSetRefigureMode(w, mode)
    Widget w;
    Boolean mode;
```

where:

    w   Specifies the widget ID of the VPaned widget.

    mode   Enables or disables refiguration.

You should set the mode to FALSE if you add multiple panes to or remove multiple panes from the parent frame after it has been realized, unless you can arrange to manage all the panes at once using XtManageChildren. After all the panes are added, set the mode to TRUE. This avoids unnecessary geometry calculations and "window dancing."

- To delete an entire VPaned widget and all associated data structures, use XtDestroy-Widget and specify the widget ID of the VPaned widget. All the children of the VPaned widget are automatically destroyed at the same time

X Toolkit Intrinsics
Appendices

This section of the book contains release notes, handy lists of functions, macros, and procedures, as well useful reference information on data types, translation table syntax, resource file format, standard errors, and the like.

Alphabetical and Group Summaries

This quick reference is intended to help you find and use the right function for a particular task. It organizes the Section 1 and Section 2 reference pages into two lists:

- Alphabetical listing of functions, macros, and prototype procedures.
- Listing of functions, macros, and prototype procedures by groups.

Alphabetical Listing

In Table A-1 below, all entries begin with *Xt*. Some entries are indented under a heading to improve readability; the heading should be prefixed to the entry names.

Table A-1. Alphabetical Listing of Functions

Function	Description
XtAcceptFocusProc	Prototype procedure to accept or reject keyboard focus.
XtActionProc	Prototype procedure for registering action tables.
XtAdd ...	
Actions	Register an action table with the Resource Manager.
Callback	Add a callback procedure to a widget's callback resource.
Callbacks	Add a list of callback procedures to a given widget's callback list.
Converter	Register a new resource converter.
EventHandler	Register a procedure to handle events.
ExposureToRegion	Merge Expose and GraphicsExpose events into a region.
Grab	Redirect user input to a modal widget.
Input	Register a new file as an input source for an application.
RawEventHandler	Register an event handler without selecting for the event.
TimeOut	Create a timeout value.
WorkProc	Register a work procedure for an application.
XtAlmostProc	Prototype set_values_almost method.

Function	Description
XtApp ...	
AddActions	Declare an action table and register it with the Resource Manager.
AddConverter	Register a new resource converter for an application.
AddInput	Register a new file as an input source for a given application.
AddTimeOut	Invoke a procedure after a specified timeout.
AddWorkProc	Register a work procedure for a given application.
CreateShell	Create additional top-level widget.
Error	Call the installed fatal error procedure.
ErrorMsg	Call the high-level fatal error handler.
GetErrorDatabase	Obtain the error database.
GetErrorDatabaseText	Obtain the error database text for an error or a warning.
GetSelectionTimeout	Get the current selection timeout value.
MainLoop	Process input from a given application.
NextEvent	Return next event from an application's input queue.
PeekEvent	Nondestructively examine the head of an application's input queue.
Pending	Determine if there are any events in an application's input queue.
ProcessEvent	Process one input event.
SetErrorHandler	Register a procedure to be called on fatal error conditions.
SetErrorMsgHandler	Register a procedure to be called on fatal error conditions.
SetSelectionTimeout	Set the Intrinsics selection timeout.
SetWarningHandler	Register a procedure to be called on nonfatal error conditions.
SetWarningMsgHandler	Register a procedure to be called on nonfatal error conditions.
Warning	Call the installed nonfatal error procedure.
WarningMsg	Call the installed high-level warning handler.
XtArgsFunc	Prototype set_values_hook method.
XtArgsProc	Prototype procedure for get_values_hook method.
XtAugmentTranslations	Nondestructively merge new translations with widget's existing ones.
XtBuildEventMask	Retrieve a widget's event mask.
XtCallAcceptFocus	Call a widget's accept_focus procedure.
XtCallbackExclusive	Callback function to pop up a widget.
XtCallbackNone	Callback function to pop up a widget.
XtCallbackNonexclusive	Callback function to pop up a widget.
XtCallbackPopdown	Pop down a widget from a callback routine.
XtCallbackProc	Prototype callback procedure.
XtCallCallbacks	Execute the procedures in a widget's callback list.
XtCalloc	Allocate an array and initialize elements to zero.
XtCaseProc	Prototype procedure called to convert the case of keysyms.
XtCheckSubclass	In DEBUG mode, verify a widget's class.
XtClass	Obtain a widget's class.
XtCloseDisplay	Close a display and remove it from an application context.
XtConfigureWidget	Move and/or resize widget.
XtConvert	Convert resource type.
XtConvertCase	Determine upper-case and lower-case versions of a keysym.
XtConverter	Prototype of a resource converter procedure.

Function	Description
XtConvertSelectionProc	Prototype procedure to return selection data.
XtCreate ...	
ApplicationContext	Create an application context.
ApplicationShell	Create an additional top-level widget.
ManagedWidget	Create and manage a child widget.
PopupShell	Create a pop-up shell.
Widget	Create an instance of a widget.
Window	Create widget's working window.
XtDatabase	Obtain the resource database for a particular display.
XtDestroy ...	
ApplicationContext	Destroy an application context and close its displays.
GC	Release 2 compatible function to free up read-only GCs.
Widget	Destroy a widget instance.
XtDirectConvert	Perform resource conversion and cache result.
XtDisownSelection	Indicate that selection data is no longer available.
XtDispatchEvent	Dispatch registered handlers for an event.
XtDisplay	Return the display pointer for the specified widget.
XtDisplayInitialize	Initialize a display and add it to an application context.
XtError	Call the low-level fatal error handler.
XtErrorHandler	Prototype for low-level error and warning handlers.
XtErrorMsg	Call the high-level fatal error handler.
XtErrorMsgHandler	Prototype for high-level error and warning handlers.
XtEventHandler	Prototype procedure to handle input events.
XtExposeProc	Prototype expose method used in Core widget class.
XtFree	Free an allocated block of storage.
XtGeometryHandler	Prototype procedure to handle geometry requests.
XtGet ...	
ApplicationResources	Update base-offset resource list (by application).
ErrorDatabase	Obtain the error database.
ErrorDatabaseText	Obtain the error database text for an error or a warning.
GC	Obtain a read-only, sharable GC.
ResourceList	Retrieve default values for a resource list.
SelectionTimeout	Get the current selection timeout value.
SelectionValue	Obtain the complete selection data.
SelectionValues	Obtain selection data in multiple formats.
Subresources	Update base-offset resource list (by name or class).
Subvalues	Copy from base-offset resource list to the argument list.
Values	Copy resources from a widget to the argument list.
XtHasCallbacks	Determine the status of a widget's callback list.
XtInitialize	Initialize toolkit and display.
XtInitProc	Prototype initialize procedure for a widget class.
XtInputCallbackProc	Prototype procedure called to handle file events.

Function	Description
XtInstall ...	
Accelerators	Install a widget's accelerators on another widget.
AllAccelerators	Install all accelerators from a widget and its descendants onto a destination.
XtIsComposite	Test whether a widget is a subclass of the Composite widget class.
XtIsConstraint	Test whether a widget is a subclass of the Constraint widget class.
XtIsManaged	Determine whether a widget is managed by its parent.
XtIsRealized	Determine whether a widget has been realized.
XtIsSensitive	Check the current sensitivity state of a widget.
XtIsShell	Test whether a widget is a subclass of the Shell widget class.
XtIsSubclass	Determine whether a widget is a subclass of a class.
XtKeyProc	Prototype procedure to translate a key.
XtLoseSelectionProc	Prototype procedure called by the Intrinsics when another client claims the selection.
XtMainLoop	Continuously process events.
XtMakeGeometryRequest	Request parent to change child's geometry.
XtMakeResizeRequest	Request parent to change child's size.
XtMalloc	Allocate storage.
XtManageChild	Add a widget to its parent's list of managed children.
XtManageChildren	Add widgets to their parent's list of managed children.
XtMapWidget	Map a widget to its display.
XtMergeArgLists	Merge two ArgList structures.
XtMoveWidget	Move a widget on the display.
XtNameToWidget	Translate a widget name to a widget instance.
XtNew	Allocate storage for one instance of a data type.
XtNewString	Copy an instance of a string.
XtNextEvent	Return next event from input queue.
XtNumber	Determine the number of elements in a fixed-size array.
XtOffset	Determine the byte offset of a field within a structure.
XtOpenDisplay	Open, initialize, and add a display to an application context.
XtOrderProc	Prototype procedure for ordering the children of composite widget instances.
XtOverrideTranslations	Merge new translations, overwriting widget's existing ones.
XtOwnSelection	Indicate that selection data is available.
XtParent	Return the parent widget for the specified widget.
XtParse ...	
AcceleratorTable	Compile an accelerator table into its internal representation.
TranslationTable	Compile a translation table into its internal representation.
XtPeekEvent	Nondestructively examine the head of an application's input queue.
XtPending	Determine if there are any events in an application's input queue.
XtPopdown	Unmap a pop-up shell.
XtPopup	Map a pop-up shell.
XtProc	Prototype procedure to initialize data for a widget class.
XtProcessEvent	Process one input event.

Table A-1. Alphabetical Listing of Functions (continued)

Function	Description
XtQueryGeometry	Query a child widget's preferred geometry.
XtRealizeProc	Prototype procedure called when widget is realized.
XtRealizeWidget	Realize a widget instance.
XtRealloc	Change the size of an allocated block of storage.
XtRegisterCaseConverter	Register a case converter.
XtReleaseGC	Deallocate a shared GC when it is no longer needed.
XtRemove ...	
AllCallbacks	Delete all procedures from a callback list.
Callback	Delete a procedure from a callback list.
Callbacks	Delete a list of procedures from a callback list.
EventHandler	Remove a previously registered event handler.
Grab	Redirect user input from modal widget back to normal destination.
Input	Cancel source of alternate input events.
RawEventHandler	Remove a raw event handler.
TimeOut	Clear a timeout value.
WorkProc	Remove a work procedure.
XtResizeWidget	Resize a child or sibling widget.
XtResizeWindow	Resize a widget according to the values of its core dimensions.
XtResourceDefaultProc	Prototype procedure passed as a resource converter of type XtRCallProc.
XtScreen	Return the screen pointer for the specified widget.
XtSelectionCallbackProc	Prototype procedure called when requested selection data arrives.
XtSelectionDoneProc	Prototype procedure called after a data transfer completes.
XtSet ...	
Arg	Construct or modify an argument list dynamically.
ErrorHandler	Register a procedure to be called on fatal error conditions.
ErrorMsgHandler	Register a procedure to be called on nonfatal error conditions.
KeyboardFocus	Redirect keyboard input to a child widget.
KeyTranslator	Register a key translator.
MappedWhenManaged	Change the value of a widget's map_when_managed field.
SelectionTimeout	Set value of selection timeout.
Sensitive	Set the sensitivity state of a widget.
Subvalues	Copy from ArgList to base-offset resource list.
Values	Copy resources from ArgList to widget.
ValuesFunc	Prototype procedure for various set_values methods.
WarningHandler	Register a procedure to be called on nonfatal error conditions.
WarningMsgHandler	Register a high-level procedure to be called on nonfatal error conditions.
XtStringConversion-Warning	Emit boilerplate string conversion error message.
XtStringProc	Prototype procedure for display_accelerator method.
XtSuperclass	Obtain a widget's superclass.
XtTimerCallbackProc	Prototype callback procedure invoked when timeouts expire.
XtToolkitInitialize	Initialize the X Toolkit internals.

Function	Description
XtTranslateCoords	Translate an x-y coordinate pair from widget coordinates to root coordinates.
XtTranslateKey	Invoke the currently registered keycode-to-keysym translator.
XtTranslateKeycode	Invoke the currently registered keycode-to-keysym translator.
XtUninstallTranslations	Remove existing translations.
XtUnmanageChild	Remove a widget from its parent's managed list.
XtUnmanageChildren	Remove a list of children from a parent widget's managed list.
XtUnmapWidget	Unmap a widget explicitly.
XtUnrealizeWidget	Destroy the windows associated with a widget and its descendants.
XtWarning	Call the installed low-level warning handler.
XtWarningMsg	Call the installed high-level warning handler.
XtWidgetProc	Common prototype procedure for widget methods.
XtWidgetToApplication-Context	Get the application context for a given widget.
XtWindow	Return the window of the specified widget.
XtWindowToWidget	Translate a window and display pointer into a widget instance.
XtWorkProc	Perform background processing.

Group Listing with Brief Descriptions

The Section 1 and Section 2 reference pages are listed under the following groups:

Application Contexts	Graphics Context	Resource Management
Argument Lists	Initialization	Selections
Callbacks	Keyboard Handling	Translations and Actions
Error Handling	Memory Allocation	Widget Information
Event Handling	Methods	Widget Lifecycle
Geometry Management	Pop Ups	Window Manipulation

Application Contexts

XtApp*	Application-context versions of other Xt functions.
XtCreateApplicationContext	Create an application context.
XtDestroyApplicationContext	Destroy an application context and close its displays.
XtDisplayInitialize	Initialize a display and add it to an application context.
XtOpenDisplay	Open, initialize, and add a display to an application context.
XtToolkitInitialize	Initialize the X Toolkit internals.

Argument Lists

XtNumber	Determine the number of elements in a fixed-size array.
XtOffset	Determine the byte offset of a field within a structure.
XtSetArg	Construct or modify an argument list dynamically.

Callbacks

XtAddCallback	Add a callback procedure to a widget's callback resource.
XtAddCallbacks	Add a list of callback procedures to a given widget's callback list.
XtCallbackProc	Prototype callback procedure.
XtCallCallbacks	Execute the procedures in a widget's callback list.
XtHasCallbacks	Determine the status of a widget's callback list.
XtRemoveAllCallbacks	Delete all procedures from a callback list.
XtRemoveCallback	Delete a procedure from a callback list.
XtRemoveCallbacks	Delete a list of procedures from a callback list.

Error Handling

XtAppError	Call the installed fatal error procedure.
XtAppErrorMsg	Call the high-level fatal error handler.
XtAppGetErrorDatabase	Obtain the error database.
XtAppGetErrorDatabaseText	Obtain the error database text for an error or a warning.
XtAppSetErrorHandler	Register a procedure to be called on fatal error conditions.
XtAppSetErrorMsgHandler	Register a procedure to be called on fatal error conditions.
XtAppSetWarningHandler	Register a procedure to be called on nonfatal error conditions.
XtAppSetWarningMsgHandler	Register a procedure to be called on nonfatal error conditions.
XtAppWarning	Call the installed nonfatal error procedure.
XtAppWarningMsg	Call the installed high-level warning handler.
XtError	Call the low-level fatal error handler.
XtErrorHandler	Prototype for low-level error and warning handlers.
XtErrorMsg	Call the high-level fatal error handler.
XtErrorMsgHandler	Prototype for high-level error and warning handlers.
XtGetErrorDatabase	Obtain the error database.
XtGetErrorDatabaseText	Obtain the error database text for an error or a warning.
XtSetErrorHandler	Register a procedure to be called on fatal error conditions.
XtSetErrorMsgHandler	Register a procedure to be called on nonfatal error conditions.
XtSetWarningHandler	Register a procedure to be called on nonfatal error conditions.
XtSetWarningMsgHandler	Register a high-level procedure to be called on nonfatal error conditions.
XtStringConversionWarning	Emit boilerplate string conversion error message.
XtWarning	Call the installed low-level warning handler.
XtWarningMsg	Call the installed high-level warning handler.

Event Handling

XtAddEventHandler	Register a procedure to handle events.
XtAddExposureToRegion	Merge Expose and GraphicsExpose events into a region.
XtAddInput	Register a new file as an input source for an application.
XtAddRawEventHandler	Register an event handler without selecting for the event.
XtAddTimeOut	Create a timeout value.
XtAddWorkProc	Register a work procedure for an application.
XtAppAddInput	Register a new file as an input source for a given application.
XtAppAddTimeOut	Invoke a procedure after a specified timeout.
XtAppAddWorkProc	Register a work procedure for a given application.
XtAppMainLoop	Process input from a given application.
XtAppNextEvent	Return next event from an application's input queue.
XtAppPeekEvent	Nondestructively examine the head of an application's input queue.
XtAppPending	Determine if there are any events in an application's input queue.
XtAppProcessEvent	Process one input event.
XtBuildEventMask	Retrieve a widget's event mask.
XtDispatchEvent	Dispatch registered handlers for an event.
XtEventHandler	Prototype procedure to handle input events.
XtInputCallbackProc	Prototype procedure called to handle file events.
XtMainLoop	Continuously process events.
XtNextEvent	Return next event from input queue.
XtPeekEvent	Nondestructively examine the head of an application's input queue.
XtPending	Determine if there are any events in an application's input queue.
XtProcessEvent	Process one input event.
XtRemoveEventHandler	Remove a previously registered event handler.
XtRemoveInput	Cancel source of alternate input events.
XtRemoveRawEventHandler	Remove a raw event handler.
XtRemoveTimeOut	Clear a timeout value.
XtRemoveWorkProc	Remove a work procedure.
XtTimerCallbackProc	Prototype callback procedure invoked when timeouts expire.
XtWorkProc	Perform background processing.

Geometry Management

XtAlmostProc	Prototype set_values_almost method.
XtConfigureWidget	Move and/or resize widget.
XtGeometryHandler	Prototype procedure to handle geometry requests.
XtMakeGeometryRequest	Request parent to change child's geometry.
XtMakeResizeRequest	Request parent to change child's size.
XtMoveWidget	Move a widget on the display.
XtOrderProc	Prototype procedure for ordering the children of composite widget instances.
XtQueryGeometry	Query a child widget's preferred geometry.
XtResizeWidget	Resize a child or sibling widget.
XtUnmanageChild	Remove a widget from its parent's managed list.
XtUnmanageChildren	Remove a list of children from a parent widget's managed list.

Graphics Context

DestroyGC	Release 2 compatible function to free up read-only GCs.
XtGetGC	Obtain a read-only, sharable GC.
XtReleaseGC	Deallocate a shared GC when it is no longer needed.

Initialization

XtAppCreateShell	Create additional top-level widget.
XtCloseDisplay	Close a display and remove it from an application context.
XtCreateApplicationShell	Create an additional top-level widget.
XtInitialize	Initialize toolkit and display.

Keyboard Handling

XtAcceptFocusProc	Prototype procedure to accept or reject keyboard focus.
XtCallAcceptFocus	Call a widget's accept_focus procedure.
XtCaseProc	Prototype procedure called to convert the case of keysyms.
XtConvertCase	Determine upper-case and lower-case versions of a keysym.
XtKeyProc	Prototype procedure to translate a key.
XtRegisterCaseConverter	Register a case converter.
XtSetKeyTranslator	Register a key translator.
XtSetKeyboardFocus	Redirect keyboard input to a child widget.
XtTranslateKey	Invoke the currently registered keycode-to-keysym translator.
XtTranslateKeycode	Invoke the currently registered keycode-to-keysym translator.

Memory Allocation

XtCalloc	Allocate an array and initialize elements to zero.
XtDestroyGC	Release 2 compatible function to free up read-only GCs.
XtFree	Free an allocated block of storage.
XtGetGC	Obtain a read-only, sharable GC.
XtMalloc	Allocate storage.
XtMergeArgLists	Merge two ArgList structures.
XtNew	Allocate storage for one instance of a data type.
XtNewString	Copy an instance of a string.
XtRealloc	Change the size of an allocated block of storage.
XtReleaseGC	Deallocate a shared GC when it is no longer needed.

Methods

XtAlmostProc	Prototype set_values_almost method.
XtArgsFunc	Prototype set_values_hook method.
XtArgsProc	Prototype procedure for get_values_hook method.
XtExposeProc	Prototype expose method used in Core widget class.
XtGeometryHandler	Prototype procedure to handle geometry requests.
XtInitProc	Prototype initialize procedure for a widget class.
XtOrderProc	Procedure for ordering the children of composite widget instances.
XtProc	Prototype procedure to initialize data for a widget class.
XtRealizeProc	Prototype procedure called when widget is realized.
XtSetValuesFunc	Prototype procedure for various set_values methods.
XtStringProc	Prototype procedure for display_accelerator method.
XtWidgetProc	Common prototype procedure for widget methods.

Pop Ups

MenuPopdown	Built-in action for popping down a widget.
MenuPopup	Built-in action for popping up a widget.
XtAddGrab	Redirect user input to a modal widget.
XtCallbackExclusive	Callback function to pop up a widget.
XtCallbackNone	Callback function to pop up a widget.
XtCallbackNonexclusive	Callback function to pop up a widget.
XtCallbackPopdown	Pop down a widget from a callback routine.
XtCreatePopupShell	Create a pop-up shell.
XtRemoveGrab	Redirect user input from modal widget back to normal destination. MenuPopdown MenuPopup
XtPopdown	Unmap a pop-up shell.
XtPopup	Map a pop-up shell.

Resource Management

XtAddConverter	Register a new resource converter.
XtAppAddConverter	Register a new resource converter for an application.
XtArgsFunc	Prototype set_values_hook method.
XtArgsProc	Prototype procedure for get_values_hook method.
XtConvert	Convert resource type.
XtConverter	Prototype of a resource converter procedure.
XtDatabase	Obtain the resource database for a particular display.
XtDirectConvert	Perform resource conversion and cache result.
XtGetApplicationResources	Update base-offset resource list (by application).
XtGetResourceList	Retrieve default values for a resource list.
XtGetSubresources	Update base-offset resource list (by name or class).
XtGetSubvalues	Copy from base-offset resource list to the argument list.
XtGetValues	Copy resources from a widget to the argument list.
XtResourceDefaultProc	Prototype procedure passed as a resource converter of type Xt-RCallProc.
XtSetMappedWhenManaged	Change the value of a widget's map_when_managed field.
XtSetSensitive	Set the sensitivity state of a widget.
XtSetSubvalues	Copy from ArgList to base-offset resource list.
XtSetValues	Copy resources from ArgList to widget.

Selections

XtAppGetSelectionTimeout	Get the current selection timeout value.
XtAppSetSelectionTimeout	Set the Intrinsics selection timeout.
XtConvertSelectionProc	Prototype procedure to return selection data.
XtDisownSelection	Indicate that selection data is no longer available.
XtGetSelectionTimeout	Get the current selection timeout value.
XtGetSelectionValue	Obtain the complete selection data.
XtGetSelectionValues	Obtain selection data in multiple formats.
XtLoseSelectionProc	Prototype procedure called by the Intrinsics when another client claims the selection.
XtOwnSelection	Indicate that selection data is available.
XtSetSelectionTimeout	Set value of selection timeout.
XtSelectionCallbackProc	Prototype procedure called when requested selection data arrives.
XtSelectionDoneProc	Prototype procedure called after a data transfer completes.

Translations and Actions

XtActionProc	Prototype procedure for registering action tables.
XtAddActions	Register an action table with the Resource Manager.
XtAppAddActions	Declare an action table and register it with the Resource Manager.
XtAugmentTranslations	Nondestructively merge new translations with widget's existing ones.
XtInstallAccelerators	Install a widget's accelerators on another widget.
XtInstallAllAccelerators	Install all accelerators from a widget and its descendants onto a destination.
XtOverrideTranslations	Merge new translations, overwriting widget's existing ones.
XtParseAcceleratorTable	Compile an accelerator table into its internal representation.
XtParseTranslationTable	Compile a translation table into its internal representation.
XtUninstallTranslations	Remove existing translations.

Widget Information

XtCheckSubclass	In DEBUG mode, verify a widget's class.
XtClass	Obtain a widget's class.
XtDisplay	Return the display pointer for the specified widget.
XtIsComposite	Test whether a widget is a subclass of the Composite widget class.
XtIsConstraint	Test whether a widget is a subclass of the Constraint widget class.
XtIsManaged	Determine whether a widget is managed by its parent.
XtIsRealized	Determine whether a widget has been realized.
XtIsSensitive	Check the current sensitivity state of a widget.
XtIsShell	Test whether a widget is a subclass of the Shell widget class.
XtIsSubclass	Determine whether a widget is a subclass of a class.
XtNameToWidget	Translate a widget name to a widget instance.
XtParent	Return the parent widget for the specified widget.
XtScreen	Return the screen pointer for the specified widget.
XtSuperclass	Obtain a widget's superclass.
XtWidgetToApplicationContext	Get the application context for a given widget.
XtWindow	Return the window of the specified widget.
XtWindowToWidget	Translate a window and display pointer into a widget instance.

Widget Lifecycle

XtCreateManagedWidget	Create and manage a child widget.
XtCreateWidget	Create an instance of a widget.
XtDestroyWidget	Destroy a widget instance.
XtManageChild	Add a widget to its parent's list of managed children.
XtManageChildren	Add widgets to their parent's list of managed children.
XtMapWidget	Map a widget to its display.
XtRealizeWidget	Realize a widget instance.
XtUnmapWidget	Unmap a widget explicitly.
XtUnrealizeWidget	Destroy the windows associated with a widget and its descendants.

Window Manipulation

XtCreateWindow	Create widget's working window
XtResizeWindow	Resize a widget according to the values of its core dimensions
XtTranslateCoords	Translate an x-y coordinate pair from widget coordinates to root coordinates

B

X Toolkit Data Types

This appendix summarizes the data types used as arguments or return values in Xt Intrinsics functions. Unless otherwise noted, these types are defined in the header file *X11/Intrinsic.h*. Data types (which include simple typedefs as well as structures and enums) are listed alphabetically. Defined symbols (for example, constants used to specify the value of a mask or a field in a structure) or other data types used only to set structure members are listed with the data type in which they are used.

ArgList

An `ArgList` is used for setting resources in calls to create a widget (`XtCreate-Widget`, `XtCreateManagedWidget`, `XtCreatePopupShell`) as well as in calls to set or get resources (`XtSetValues`, `XtGetValues`, `XtSetSubvalues`, `XtGetSubvalues`, `XtSetSubresources`, `XtGetSubresources`). It is defined as follows in *<X11/Intrinsic.h>*:

```
typedef struct {
    String     name;
    XtArgVal   value;
} Arg, *ArgList;
```

The `name` field is typically a defined constant of the form `XtNresourcename` from either *<X11/StringDefs.h>* or a widget public header file. It identifies the name of the argument to be set. The `value` field is an `XtArgVal`, a system-dependent typedef chosen to be large enough to hold a pointer to a function or a long. In the MIT R3 release, it is a long.

Atom

To optimize communication with the server, a property is never referenced by name, but by a unique integer ID called an Atom. Standard atoms are defined in *<X11/Xatom.h>* using defined symbols beginning with `XA_`; nonstandard atoms can be obtained from the server by calling the Xlib function `XInternAtom`. The Xmu library supports an atom-caching mechanism to reduce the number of `XInternAtom` calls that may be required. For more information, see Chapter 10, *Interclient Communication*, in Volume Four, *X Toolkit Intrinsics Programming Manual*.

Boolean

A typedef from *<X11/Intrinsic h>* used to indicate TRUE (1) or FALSE (0) Use either the symbols TRUE or FALSE, defined in *<X11/Xlib h>* or TRUE or FALSE, defined in *<X11/Intrinsic h>*.

Cardinal

A typedef from *<X11/Intrinsic h>* used to specify any unsigned numeric value

Dimension

A typedef from *<X11/Intrinsic h>* used to specify window sizes. The Dimension data type was introduced in R3 to increase portability. R2 applications that specified dimensions as int should use Dimension instead

Display

A structure defined in *<X11/Xlib.h>* that contains information about the display the program is running on Display structure fields should not be accessed directly, Xlib provides a number of macros to return essential values. In Xt, a pointer to the current Display is returned by a call to XtDisplay. XtOpenDisplay can be used to explicitly open more than one Display.

EventMask

A typedef from *<X11/Intrinsic h>* used to specify which events are selected by an event handler. Specify the value as the bitwise OR of any of the following symbols defined in *<X11/X h>*:

Event Mask Symbol	Circumstances
NoEventMask	No events
KeyPressMask	Keyboard down events
KeyReleaseMask	Keyboard up events
ButtonPressMask	Pointer button down events
ButtonReleaseMask	Pointer button up events
EnterWindowMask	Pointer window entry events
LeaveWindowMask	Pointer window leave events
PointerMotionMask	All pointer motion events
PointerMotionHintMask	Fewer pointer motion events
Button1MotionMask	Pointer motion while button 1 down
Button2MotionMask	Pointer motion while button 2 down
Button3MotionMask	Pointer motion while button 3 down
Button4MotionMask	Pointer motion while button 4 down
Button5MotionMask	Pointer motion while button 5 down
ButtonMotionMask	Pointer motion while any button down
KeymapStateMask	Any keyboard state change on EnterNotify, LeaveNotify, FocusIn, or FocusOut
ExposureMask	Any exposure (except GraphicsExpose and NoExpose)
VisibilityChangeMask	Any change in visibility
StructureNotifyMask	Any change in window configuration
ResizeRedirectMask	Redirect resize of this window
SubstructureNotifyMask	Notify about reconfiguration of children

Event Mask Symbol	Circumstances
SubstructureRedirectMask	Redirect reconfiguration of children
FocusChangeMask	Any change in keyboard focus
PropertyChangeMask	Any change in property
ColormapChangeMask	Any change in colormap
OwnerGrabButtonMask	Modifies handling of pointer events

plus the following symbol defined in <X11/Intrinsic.h>:

XtAllEvents   All of the above masks: ((EventMask) -1L)

See Appendix C, *Event Reference*, for more information on each of the events selected by these mask values. The XtBuildEventMask function returns the event mask representing the logical OR of all event masks registered on the widget with XtAddEvent-Handler, as well as event masks registered as a result of translations and accelerators installed on the widget.

GC

A Graphics Context. A pointer to a structure of this type is returned by the Xlib call XCreateGC or the Xt call XtGetGC. (The latter call does client-side caching of GCs to reduce the number of identical GCs that are created.) GCs are used by all Xlib drawing calls. The members of this structure should not be accessed directly. Values can be changed by passing an XGCValues structure to XtGetGC or the Xlib XCreateGC or XChangeGC. Values can be read with XGetGCValues.

Opaque

As its name implies, a typedef designed for portability, whose contents are not to be used.

Position

A typedef from <X11/Intrinsic.h> used to specify x and y coordinates. The Position data type was introduced in R3 to increase portability. R2 applications that specified coordinates as int should use Position instead.

Region

An arbitrary set of pixels on the screen. Usually, a region is either a rectangular area, several overlapping or adjacent rectangular areas, or a general polygon. A Region is actually a typedef from <X11/Xutil.h> pointing to an internal data structure called an _XRegion. There are a number of Xlib functions for creating and manipulating regions; the members of the structure should not be accessed directly. For more information, see Volume Two, *Xlib Reference Manual*. In Xt, the only use is in the call XtAdd-ExposureToRegion.

Screen

A structure that describes the characteristics of a screen (one or more of which make up a display). A pointer to a list of these structures is a member of the Display structure. A pointer to a structure of this type is returned by XGetWindowAttributes. Xlib Macros are provided to access most members of this structure.

```
typedef struct {
    XExtData *ext_data;        /* hook for extension to hang data */
```

```
    struct _XDisplay *display;/* back pointer to display structure */
    Window root;              /* root window ID */
    int width, height;        /* width and height of screen */
    int mwidth, mheight;      /* width and height of in millimeters */
    int ndepths;              /* number of depths possible */
    Depth *depths;            /* list of allowable depths on the screen */
    int root_depth;           /* bits per pixel */
    Visual *root_visual;      /* root visual */
    GC default_gc;            /* GC for the root root visual */
    Colormap cmap;            /* default colormap */
    unsigned long white_pixel;
    unsigned long black_pixel;/* white and black pixel values */
    int max_maps, min_maps;   /* max and min colormaps */
    int backing_store;        /* Never, WhenMapped, Always */
    Bool save_unders;
    long root_input_mask;     /* initial root input mask */
Screen;
```

The XtScreen macro can be used in Xt to return the current screen

String
>   A typedef for char *.

Time
>   An unsigned long value containing a time value in milliseconds The constant CurrentTime is interpreted as the time in milliseconds since the server was started. The Time data type is used in event structures and as an argument to XtAddTimeOut.

Widget
>   A structure returned by calls to create a widget, such as XtInitialize, XtCreate-Widget, XtCreateManagedWidget, and XtCreatePopupShell. The members of this structure should not be accessed directly from applications; they should regard it as an opaque pointer. Type Widget is actually a pointer to a widget instance structure. Widget code accesses instance variables from this structure.

Window
>   A structure maintained by the server, and known on the client side only by an integer ID In Xt, a widget's window can be returned by the XtWindow macro. Given the window, the corresponding widget can be returned by XtWindowToWidget

XEvent
>   A union of all thirty event structures. The first member is always the type, so it is possible to branch on the type, and do event-specific processing in each branch For more information on the individual event structures, see Appendix C, *Event Reference*.

XGCValues
>   A structure defined in *<X11/Xlib h>* that is used to set the values in a Graphics Context using the XtGetGC function, or the Xlib functions XCreateGC, XChangeGC, or XGetGCValues.

```
typedef struct {
    int function;             /* logical operation */
    unsigned long plane_mask; /* plane mask */
    unsigned long foreground; /* foreground pixel */
    unsigned long background; /* background pixel */
```

```
    int line_width;               /* line width */
    int line_style;         /* LineSolid, LineOnOffDash,
                               LineDoubleDash */
    int cap_style;          /* CapNotLast, CapButt,
                               CapRound, CapProjecting */
    int join_style;         /* JoinMiter, JoinRound, JoinBevel */
    int fill_style;         /* FillSolid, FillTiled,
                               FillStippled, FillOpaqueStippled */
    int fill_rule;          /* EvenOddRule, WindingRule */
    int arc_mode;           /* ArcChord, ArcPieSlice */
    Pixmap tile;            /* pixmap for tiling operations */
    Pixmap stipple;         /* 1 plane pixmap for stippling */
    int ts_x_origin;        /* offset for tile or stipple operations */
    int ts_y_origin;
    Font font;              /* default text font for text operations */
    int subwindow_mode;/* ClipByChildren, IncludeInferiors */
    Bool graphics_exposures;  /* should exposures be generated? */
    int clip_x_origin; /* origin for clipping */
    int clip_y_origin;
    Pixmap clip_mask;  /* bitmap clipping; other calls for rects */
    int dash_offset;   /* patterned/dashed line information */
    char dashes;
} XGCValues;
```

For more information on the meaning and use of each of the members, see Chapter 5, *The Graphics Context*, in Volume One, *Xlib Programming Manual*. The second argument of XtGetGC is a mask that specifies which members of the structure are being set. See XtGCMask below for details.

XrmDatabase

A pointer to an internal resource manager datatype. Members of this structure should not be accessed directly. An XrmDatabase can be returned by the Xt calls XtDatabase (a resource database) or XtGetErrorDatabase (an error message database).

XrmOptionDescRec

A structure used to define command line options, passed to XtInitialize, Xt-DisplayInitialize, or XtOpenDisplay. The structure is defined as follows in <*X11/Xresource.h*>:

```
typedef struct {
    char           *option;   /* Option abbreviation in argv */
    char           *specifier;/* Resource specifier */
    XrmOptionKind argKind;    /* Which style of option it is */
    caddr_t        value;     /* Val to provide if XrmoptionNoArg */
} XrmOptionDescRec, *XrmOptionDescList;
```

The value for the argKind element is specified by one of the following enum values, defined in the same file:

```
typedef enum {
    XrmoptionNoArg,      /* Value specified in OptionDescRec.value */
    XrmoptionIsArg,      /* Value is the option string itself */
    XrmoptionStickyArg,/* Value immediately follows option */
    XrmoptionSepArg,     /* Value is next argument in argv */
    XrmoptionResArg,     /* Resource and value in next arg in argv */
    XrmoptionSkipArg,    /* Ignore this opt and next arg in argv */
```

```
    XrmoptionSkipLine   /* Ignore this opt and rest of argv */
} XrmOptionKind;
```

XrmOptionKind

    See XrmOptionDescRec.

XrmValue

    A structure defined in *<X11/Xresource.h>*, used in XtConvert and other resource conversion routines.

```
typedef struct {
    unsigned int    size;
    caddr_t         addr;
} XrmValue, *XrmValuePtr;
```

XrmValuePtr

    See XrmValue

XtAccelerators

    A pointer to an opaque internal type, a compiled accelerator table. A pointer to an Xt-Accelerators structure is returned by a call to XtParseAcceleratorTable. Usually, the compiled accelerator table is produced automatically by resource conversion of a string accelerator table stored in a resource file.

XtActionList

    A typedef for _XtActionsRec, defined as follows in *<X11/Intrinsic h>*.

```
typedef struct _XtActionsRec *XtActionList;

typedef struct _XtActionsRec{
    char        *string;
    XtActionProc proc;
} XtActionsRec;
```

Actions are added by calls to XtAddActions or XtAppAddActions. By convention, the string and the function name are identical, except that the function name begins with an upper-case letter, as in the example:

```
static XtActionsRec two_quits[] = {
    {"confirm", Confirm},
    {"quit", Quit},
};
```

This mapping from strings to function pointers is necessary to allow translation tables to be specified in resource files, which are made up entirely of strings.

XtActionProc

    The typedef for an action procedure. See XtActionProc(2) for details

XtAddressMode

    An enumerated type that specifies the possible values for the *address_mode* field of an XtConvertArgRec. See XtConvertArgRec below for details

XtAppContext

    A pointer to an internal structure used to hold data specific to a particular application context. An XtAppContext can be returned by a call to

XtCreateApplicationContext. The application context being used by a widget can be returned by XtWidgetToApplicationContext. All standard Xt routines use a default application context; routines for handling explicit application contexts almost all have names containing the string App.

XtCallbackList

A structure defined as follows in *<X11/Intrinsic.h>*:

```
typedef struct _XtCallbackRec*    XtCallbackList;

typedef struct _XtCallbackRec {
    XtCallbackProc  callback;
    caddr_t         closure;
} XtCallbackRec;
```

An XtCallbackList is statically defined just after the callback function itself is declared or defined. Then the callback list is used to set a callback resource with any of the calls that set resources, including XtCreateWidget. In most documentation, the closure member is referred to as *client_data*. In application code, when Xt-AddCallback and XtRemoveCallback are used, an XtCallbackList is not required.

XtCallbackProc

The typedef for callback functions. See XtCallbackProc(2) for details.

XtCallbackStatus

An enumerated type that defines the return values from XtHasCallbacks:

```
typedef enum {
    XtCallbackNoList,  /* Callback resource doesn't exist */
    XtCallbackHasNone, /* Resource exists, but no callbacks on it */
    XtCallbackHasSome  /* Resource exists, and callbacks
                          are registered for it */
} XtCallbackStatus;
```

XtConvertArgList

A structure used in calls to XtAddConverter to specify how the converter will access the values to be converted. The structure is defined as follows in *<X11/Intrinsic.h>*:

```
typedef struct {
    XtAddressMode   address_mode;
    caddr_t         address_id;
    Cardinal        size;
} XtConvertArgRec, *XtConvertArgList;
```

The enumerated type XtAddressMode specifies the possible values for the address_mode field, which controls how the *address_id* field should be interpreted.

```
typedef enum {
    XtAddress,          /* address */
    XtBaseOffset,       /* offset */
    XtImmediate,        /* constant */
    XtResourceString,   /* resource name string */
    XtResourceQuark     /* resource name quark */
} XtAddressMode;
```

By specifying the address mode as XtBaseOffset, you can use XtOffset to find the appropriate widget resource, much as you do in a resource list.

XtConvertArgRec

See XtConvertArgList.

XtConverter

The typedef for resource converters. See XtConverter(2) for details.

XtConvertSelectionProc

The typedef for the selection conversion procedure registered by a call to XtOwn-Selection. See XtConvertSelectionProc(2) for details.

XtErrorHandler

The typedef for low-level error or warning handlers. See XtErrorHandler(2) for details.

XtErrorMsgHandler

The typedef for high-level error or warning message handlers. See XtErrorMsg-Handler(2) for details.

XtEventHandler

The typedef for event handlers. See XtEventHandler(2) for details.

XtGCMask

A mask used in calls to XtGetGC that indicates which fields in the XGCValues structure are to be used. The mask consists of a bitwise OR of the following symbols:

Member	Mask	Default
function	GCFunction	GXcopy
plane_mask	GCPlaneMask	all 1's
foreground	GCForeground	0
background	GCBackground	1
line_width	GCLineWidth	0
line_style	GCLineStyle	LineSolid
cap_style	GCCapStyle	CapButt
join_style	GCJoinStyle	JoinMiter
fill_style	GCFillStyle	FillSolid
fill_rule	GCFillRule	EvenOddRule
tile	GCTile	pixmap filled with foreground pixel
stipple	GCStipple	pixmap filled with 1's
ts_x_origin	GCTileStipXOrigin	0
ts_y_origin	GCTileStipYOrigin	0
font	GCFont	(implementation dependent)
subwindow_mode	GCSubwindowMode	ClipByChildren
graphics_exposures	GCGraphicsExposures	TRUE
clip_x_origin	GCClipXOrigin	0
clip_y_origin	GCClipYOrigin	0
clip_mask	GCClipMask	None

Member	Mask	Default
dash_offset	GCDashOffset	0
dashes	GCDashList	4 (i.e., the list [4, 4])
arc_mode	GCArcMode	ArcPieSlice

XtGeometryMask

See XtWidgetGeometry.

XtGeometryResult

An enumerated type used as the return value of the XtQueryGeometry, XtMake-GeometryRequest, and XtMakeResizeRequest functions. It is defined as follows in <*X11/Intrinsic.h*>:

```
typedef enum {
    XtGeometryYes,     /* Request accepted */
    XtGeometryNo,      /* Request denied */
    XtGeometryAlmost,  /* Request denied but willing to take reply */
    XtGeometryDone     /* Request accepted and done */
} XtGeometryResult;
```

XtGrabKind

An enumerated type used in calls to XtPopup to specify the nature of the grab to be asserted by the pop-up widget.

```
typedef enum {
    XtGrabNone,
    XtGrabNonexclusive,
    XtGrabExclusive
} XtGrabKind;
```

An exclusive grab constrains input to the widget actually making the grab (the latest widget in a pop-up cascade), while a non-exclusive grab allows input to any widget in the cascade.

XtInputCallbackProc

The typedef for the procedure registered by a call to XtAddInput. See XtInput-CallbackProc(2) for details.

XtInputId

A unique ID returned by a call to XtAddInput; used to remove an input source with XtRemoveInput.

XtInputMask

A mask used in calls to XtProcessEvent to indicate which types of events should be processed. This mask is made up of a bitwise OR of the following symbols defined in <*X11/Intrinsic.h*>:

XtIMXEvent	Process X Events.
XtIMTimer	Process timeouts registered with XtAddTimeout.
XtIMAlternateInput	Process alternate input sources registered with XtAddInput.
XtIMAll	Process all three types of events.

An `XtInputMask` is returned by `XtPending` to indicate what type of events are in the event queue Don't confuse these values with `XtInputNoneMask`, `XtInput-WriteMask`, `XtInputReadMask`, and `XtInputExceptMask`, which are used in calls to `XtAddInput` to indicate whether the file should be monitored for reads, writes, or exception conditions

XtIntervalId

A unique ID returned by a call to `XtAddTimeout`, used to remove a timeout with `Xt-RemoveTimeout`. Remember that timeouts are automatically removed when the time expires.

XtLoseSelectionProc

The typedef for the lose selection procedure registered by a call to `XtOwnSelection` See `XtLoseSelectionProc`(2) for details.

XtResourceList

A structure used to declare widget or application resources, and to retrieve the current value of resources using `XtGetSubresources`, `XtGetSubvalues`, or `XtGet-ResourceList` It is defined as follows in *<X11/Intrinsic h>*:

```
typedef struct _XtResource {
    String resource_name;       /* specify using XtN symbol */
    String resource_class;      /* specify using XtC symbol */
    String resource_type;       /* actual data type of variable */
    Cardinal resource_size;     /* specify using sizeof() */
    Cardinal resource_offset;   /* specify using XtOffset() */
    String default_type;        /* will be conv'ted to resource_type */
    caddr_t default_address;    /* address of default value */
} XtResource,

typedef struct _XtResource  *XtResourceList,
```

See Chapter 9, *Resource Management and Type Conversion*, in Volume Four, *X Toolkit Intrinsics Programming Manual*, for a detailed description of the `XtResource` structure.

XtSelectionCallbackProc

The typedef for the selection callback procedure registered by a call to `XtGet-SelectionValue` or `XtGetSelectionValues`. See `XtSelection-CallbackProc`(2) for details.

XtSelectionDoneProc

The typedef for the selection completion procedure registered by a call to `XtOwn-Selection` See `XtSelectionDoneProc`(2) for details

XtTimerCallbackProc

The typedef for the procedure to be invoked after a timeout registered by a call to `Xt-AddTimeout` See `XtTimerCallbackProc`(2) for details.

XtTranslations

A pointer to an opaque internal type, a compiled translation table. A pointer to an `Xt-Translations` structure is returned by a call to `XtParseTranslationTable`.

Usually, the compiled translation table is produced automatically by resource conversion of a string translation table stored in a resource file.

XtWidgetGeometry

A structure used to pass in and return data about widget geometry in calls to `XtQuery-Geometry` and `XtMakeGeometryRequest`. It is defined as follows in *<X11/Intrinsic.h>*:

```
typedef struct {
    XtGeometryMask request_mode;
    Position x, y;
    Dimension width, height, border_width;
    Widget sibling;
    int stack_mode;
} XtWidgetGeometry;
```

The *request_mode* field specifies which of the other fields are to be used, or (for returned structures) contain valid values. It is made up of a bitwise OR of the following symbols defined in *<X11/X.h>*:

```
#define CWX              (1<<0)
#define CWY              (1<<1)
#define CWWidth          (1<<2)
#define CWHeight         (1<<3)
#define CWBorderWidth    (1<<4)
#define CWSibling        (1<<5)
#define CWStackMode      (1<<6)
```

plus the following symbol from *<X11/Intrinsic.h>*:

```
#define XtCWQueryOnly    (1 << 7)
```

which means that this call is a query only, and none of the values should be used; the return value should show what would happen if the geometry request were made. (In case you're wondering, the CW prefix stands for "ConfigureWindow"— these symbols are also used by the Xlib `XConfigureWindow` call.)

The *stack_mode* field specifies the relationship between the current widget and a *sibling* widget specified in the same call. It is specified using one of the following symbols defined in *<X11/X.h>*:

Below	Place widget below sibling or on bottom of stack if no sibling.
TopIf	Place widget on top of stack if obscured.
BottomIf	Place widget on bottom if it obscures sibling.
Opposite	If sibling occludes the widget, put widget on top of stack, but if widget occludes sibling, put widget on the bottom.

plus the following symbol from *<X11/Intrinsic.h>*:

XtSMDontChange	Don't change the stacking order.

If no sibling widget is specified in the call, the stacking order is relative to any sibling.

XtWorkProc

The typedef for the work procedure registered by a call to XtAddWorkProc. See Xt-WorkProc(2) for details.

XtWorkProcId

The unique identifier returned by a call to XtAddWorkProc and used as an argument in XtRemoveWorkProc.

C
Event Reference

This appendix describes each event in detail. It covers how the event is selected, what translation table symbols are valid for each event type, when each event occurs, the information contained in each event structure, and the side effects of the event, if any. Each event is described on a separate reference page.

Table C-1 lists each event mask, its associated event types, and the associated structure definition. See Chapter 7, *Events*, in Volume One, *Xlib Programming Manual*, for more information on events. See also Chapter 7, *Events, Translations, and Accelerators*, in Volume Four, *X Toolkit Intrinsics Programming Manual*.

Table C-1. Event masks, event types, and event structures

Event Mask	Event Type	Structure
KeyPressMask	KeyPress	XKeyPressedEvent
KeyReleaseMask	KeyRelease	XKeyReleasedEvent
ButtonPressMask	ButtonPress	XButtonPressedEvent
ButtonReleaseMask	ButtonRelease	XButtonReleasedEvent
OwnerGrabButtonMask	n/a	n/a
KeymapStateMask	KeymapNotify	XKeymapEvent
PointerMotionMask PointerMotionHintMask ButtonMotionMask Button1MotionMask Button2MotionMask Button3MotionMask Button4MotionMask Button5MotionMask	MotionNotify	XPointerMovedEvent
EnterWindowMask	EnterNotify	XEnterWindowEvent
LeaveWindowMask	LeaveNotify	XLeaveWindowEvent
FocusChangeMask	FocusIn	XFocusInEvent

Table C-1. Event Masks, Event Types, and Event Structures (continued)

Event Mask	Event Type	Structure
	FocusOut	XFocusOutEvent
ExposureMask	Expose	XExposeEvent
(selected in GC by graphics_expose member)	GraphicsExpose NoExpose	XGraphicsExposeEvent XNoExposeEvent
ColormapChangeMask	ColormapNotify	XColormapEvent
PropertyChangeMask	PropertyNotify	XPropertyEvent
VisibilityChangeMask	VisibilityNotify	XVisibilityEvent
ResizeRedirectMask	ResizeRequest	XResizeRequestEvent
StructureNotifyMask	CirculateNotify ConfigureNotify DestroyNotify GravityNotify MapNotify ReparentNotify UnmapNotify	XCirculateEvent XConfigureEvent XDestroyWindowEvent XGravityEvent XMapEvent XReparentEvent XUnmapEvent
SubstructureNotifyMask	CirculateNotify ConfigureNotify CreateNotify DestroyNotify GravityNotify MapNotify ReparentNotify UnmapNotify	XCirculateEvent XConfigureEvent XCreateWindowEvent XDestroyWindowEvent XGravityEvent XMapEvent XReparentEvent XUnmapEvent
SubstructureRedirectMask	CirculateRequest ConfigureRequest MapRequest	XCirculateRequestEvent XConfigureRequestEvent XMapRequestEvent
(always selected)	MappingNotify	XMappingEvent
(always selected)	ClientMessage	XClientMessageEvent
(always selected)	SelectionClear	XSetSelectClearEvent
(always selected)	SelectionNotify	XSelectionEvent
(always selected)	SelectionRequest	XSelectionRequestEvent

Meaning of Common Structure Elements

Example C-1 shows the XEvent union and a simple event structure that is one member of the union. Several of the members of this structure are present in nearly every event structure. They are described here before we go into the event-specific members (see also Section 8.2.2 in Volume One, *Xlib Programming Manual*).

Example C-1. XEvent union and XAnyEvent structure

```
typedef union _XEvent {
    int type;              /* must not be changed; first member */
    XAnyEvent xany;
    XButtonEvent xbutton;
    XCirculateEvent xcirculate;
    XCirculateRequestEvent xcirculaterequest;
    XClientMessageEvent xclient;
    XColormapEvent xcolormap;
    XConfigureEvent xconfigure;
    XConfigureRequestEvent xconfigurerequest;
    XCreateWindowEvent xcreatewindow;
    XDestroyWindowEvent xdestroywindow;
    XCrossingEvent xcrossing;
    XExposeEvent xexpose;
    XFocusChangeEvent xfocus;
    XNoExposeEvent xnoexpose;
    XGraphicsExposeEvent xgraphicsexpose;
    XGravityEvent xgravity;
    XKeymapEvent xkeymap;
    XKeyEvent xkey;
    XMapEvent xmap;
    XUnmapEvent xunmap;
    XMappingEvent xmapping;
    XMapRequestEvent xmaprequest;
    XMotionEvent xmotion;
    XPropertyEvent xproperty;
    XReparentEvent xreparent;
    XResizeRequestEvent xresizerequest;
    XSelectionClearEvent xselectionclear;
    XSelectionEvent xselection;
    XSelectionRequestEvent xselectionrequest;
    XVisibilityEvent xvisibility;
} XEvent;

typedef struct {
    int type;
    unsigned long serial;/* # of last request processed by server */
    Bool send_event;     /* TRUE if this came from SendEvent request */
    Display *display;     /* display the event was read from */
    Window window;        /* window on which event was requested in
                           * event mask */
} XAnyEvent;
```

The first member of the XEvent union is the type of event. When an event is received (with XNextEvent, for example), the application checks the type member in the XEvent union. Then the specific event type is known and the specific event structure (such as xbutton) is used to access information specific to that event type.

Before the branching depending on the event type, only the XEvent union is used. After the branching, only the event structure which contains the specific information for each event type should be used in each branch. For example, if the XEvent union were called report, the report.xexpose structure should be used within the branch for Expose events.

You'll notice that each event structure also begins with a type member. This member is rarely used, since it is an identical copy of the type member in the XEvent union.

Most event structures also have a window member. The only ones that don't are selection events (SelectionNotify, SelectionRequest, and SelectionClear) and events selected by the graphics_exposures member of the GC (GraphicsExpose and NoExpose). The window member indicates the event window that selected and received the event. This is the window where the event arrives if it has propagated through the hierarchy as described in Section 7.2.1., in Volume Four, *X Toolkit Intrinsics Programming Manual*. One event type may have two different meanings to an application, depending on which window it appears in.

Many of the event structures also have a display and/or root member. The display member identifies the connection to the server that is active. The root member indicates which screen the window that received the event is linked to in the hierarchy. Most programs only use a single screen and therefore don't need to worry about the root member. The display member can be useful since you can pass the display variable into routines by simply passing a pointer to the event structure, eliminating the need for a separate display argument.

All event structures include a serial member, that gives the number of the last protocol request processed by the server. This is useful in debugging, since an error can be detected by the server but not reported to the user (or programmer) until the next routine that gets an event. That means several routines may execute successfully after the error occurs. The last request processed will often indicate the request that contained the error.

All event structures also include a send_event flag, which if True indicates that the event was sent by XSendEvent (i.e., by another client rather than by the server).

The following pages describe each event type in detail. The events are presented in alphabetical order, each on a separate page. Each page describes the circumstances under which the event is generated, the mask used to select it, the structure itself, its members, and useful programming notes. Note that the description of the structure members does not include those members common to many structures. If you need more information on these members, please refer to this introductory section.

ButtonPress, ButtonRelease

When Generated

There are two types of pointer button events: `ButtonPress` and `ButtonRelease`. Both contain the same information.

Translation Abbreviations

In translation tables, the event type `ButtonPress` or `ButtonRelease` may be used, or use one of the abbreviations shown in the following table.

Abbreviation	Description
BtnDown	Any pointer button pressed
Btn1Down	Pointer button 1 pressed
Btn2Down	Pointer button 2 pressed
Btn3Down	Pointer button 3 pressed
Btn4Down	Pointer button 4 pressed
Btn5Down	Pointer button 5 pressed
BtnUp	Any pointer button released
Btn1Up	Pointer button 1 released
Btn2Up	Pointer button 2 released
Btn3Up	Pointer button 3 released
Btn4Up	Pointer button 4 released
Btn5Up	Pointer button 5 released

Select With

May be selected separately, using `ButtonPressMask` and `ButtonReleaseMask`.

XEvent Structure Name

```
typedef union _XEvent {
. . .
XButtonEvent xbutton;
. . .
} XEvent;
```

Event Structure

```
typedef struct {
int type;                /* of event */
unsigned long serial;    /* # of last request processed by server */
Bool send_event;         /* TRUE if this came from SendEvent request */
Display *display;        /* display the event was read from */
Window window;           /* event window it is reported relative to */
Window root;             /* root window that the event occurred under */
Window subwindow;        /* child window */
Time time;               /* when event occurred, in milliseconds */
int x, y;                /* pointer coords relative to receiving window */
int x_root, y_root;      /* coordinates relative to root */
unsigned int state;      /* mask of all buttons and modifier keys */
unsigned int button;     /* button that triggered event */
```

```
Bool same_screen,          /* same screen flag */
} XButtonEvent;
typedef XButtonEvent XButtonPressedEvent;
typedef XButtonEvent XButtonReleasedEvent;
```

Event Structure Members

subwindow If the source window is the child of the receiving window, then the subwindow member is set to the ID of that child.

time   The server time when the button event occurred, in milliseconds. Time is declared as unsigned long, so it wraps around when it reaches the maximum value of a 32 bit number (every 49.7 days).

x, y   If the receiving window is on the same screen as the root window specified by root, then x and y are the pointer coordinates relative to the receiving window's origin. Otherwise, x and y are zero.

When active button grabs and pointer grabs are in effect (see Volume One, *Xlib Programming Manual*, Section 9.4 and Volume Four, *X Toolkit Intrinsics Programming Manual*, Section 12.2.2) the coordinates relative to the receiving window may not be within the window (they may be negative or greater than window height or width).

x_root, y_root

           The pointer coordinates relative to the root window which is an ancestor of the event window. If the pointer was on a different screen, these are zero

state   The state of all the buttons and modifier keys just before the event, represented by a mask of the button and modifier key symbols: Button1Mask, Button2Mask, Button3Mask, Button4Mask, Button5Mask, ShiftMask, ControlMask, LockMask, Mod1Mask, Mod2Mask, Mod3Mask, Mod4Mask, and Mod5Mask. If a modifier key is pressed and released when no other modifier keys are held, the ButtonPress will have a state member of 0 and the ButtonRelease will have a nonzero state member indicating that itself was held just before the event.

button   A value indicating which button changed state to trigger this event. One of the constants: Button1, Button2, Button3, Button4, or Button5.

same_screen

           Indicates whether the pointer is currently on the same screen as this window This is always TRUE unless the pointer was actively grabbed before the automatic grab could take place.

Notes

Unless an active grab already exists, or a passive grab on the button combination that was pressed already exists at a higher level in the hierarchy than where the ButtonPress occurred, an automatic active grab of the pointer takes place when a ButtonPress occurs. Because of the automatic grab, the matching ButtonRelease is sent to the same application that received the ButtonPress event. If OwnerGrabButtonMask has been selected, the ButtonRelease event is delivered to the window which contained the pointer when the button was released, as long as that window belongs to the same client as the window in which the ButtonPress event occurred. If the ButtonRelease occurs outside of the client's windows, or OwnerGrabButtonMask was not selected, the ButtonRelease is delivered to the window in which the ButtonPress occurred. The grab is terminated when all buttons are released. During the grab, the cursor associated with the grabbing window will track the pointer anywhere on the screen.

If the application has invoked a passive button grab on an ancestor of the window in which the ButtonPress event occurs, then that grab takes precedence over the automatic grab, and the ButtonRelease will go to that window, or it will be handled normally by that client depending on the owner_events flag in the XGrabButton call.

CirculateNotify

When Generated

A `CirculateNotify` event reports a call to change the stacking order, and it includes whether the final position is on the top or on the bottom. This event is generated by `XCirculateSubwindows`, `XCirculateSubwindowsDown`, or `XCirculate-SubwindowsUp`. See also the `CirculateRequest` and `ConfigureNotify` events

Translation Abbreviations

In translation tables, the event type `CirculateNotify` may be used, or use the abbreviation `Circ`.

Select With

This event is selected with `StructureNotifyMask` in the `XSelectInput` call, for the window to be moved, or with `SubstructureNotifyMask`, for the parent of the window to be moved.

XEvent Structure Name

```
typedef union _XEvent {
    . . .
    XCirculateEvent xcirculate;
    . . .
} XEvent;
```

Event Structure

```
typedef struct {
    int type;
    unsigned long serial; /* # of last request processed by server */
    Bool send_event;      /* TRUE if this came from SendEvent request */
    Display *display;     /* display the event was read from */
    Window event;
    Window window;
    int place;            /* PlaceOnTop, PlaceOnBottom */
} XCirculateEvent;
```

Event Structure Members

`event`   The window receiving the event. If the event was selected by `Structure-NotifyMask`, event will be the same as window. If the event was selected by `SubstructureNotifyMask`, event will be the parent of window.

`window`   The window that was restacked

`place`   Either `PlaceOnTop` or `PlaceOnBottom`. Indicates whether the window was raised to the top or bottom of the stack

CirculateRequest

When Generated

A `CirculateRequest` event reports when `XCirculateSubwindows`, `XCirculate-SubwindowsDown`, `XCirculateSubwindowsUp`, or `XRestackWindows` is called to change the stacking order of a group of children.

This event differs from `CirculateNotify` in that it delivers the parameters of the request before it is carried out. This gives the client that selects this event (usually the window manager) the opportunity to review the request in the light of its window management policy before executing the circulate request itself or to deny the request. (`CirculateNotify` indicates the final outcome of the request.)

Translation Abbreviations

In translation tables, the event type `CirculateNotify` may be used, or use the abbreviation `CircRec`.

Select With

This event is selected for the parent window with `SubstructureRedirectMask`.

XEvent Structure Name

```
typedef union _XEvent {
    . . .
    XCirculateRequestEvent xcirculaterequest;
    . . .
} XEvent;
```

Event Structure

```
typedef struct {
    int type;
    unsigned long serial; /* # of last request processed by server */
    Bool send_event;      /* TRUE if this came from SendEvent request */
    Display *display;     /* display the event was read from */
    Window parent;
    Window window;
    int place;            /* PlaceOnTop, PlaceOnBottom */
} XCirculateRequestEvent;
```

Event Structure Members

parent   The parent of the window that was restacked. This is the window that selected the event.

window   The window being restacked.

place   `PlaceOnTop` or `PlaceOnBottom`. Indicates whether the window was to be placed on top or on the bottom of the stacking order.

ClientMessage

When Generated

A ClientMessage event is sent as a result of a call to XSendEvent by a client to a particular window. Any type of event can be sent with XSendEvent, but it will be distinguished from normal events by the send_event member being set to TRUE. If your program wants to be able to treat events sent with XSendEvent as different from normal events, you can check the send_event member, or you can provide a translation for ClientMessage events

Translation Abbreviations

In translation tables, the event type ClientMessage may be used, or use the abbreviation Message.

Select With

There is no event mask for ClientMessage events, and they are not selected with XSelectInput. Instead XSendEvent directs them to a specific window, which is given as a window ID the PointerWindow or the InputFocus.

XEvent Structure Name

```
typedef union _XEvent {
    ...
    XClientMessageEvent xclient;
    ..
} XEvent;
```

Event Structure

```
typedef struct {
    int type;
    unsigned long serial; /* # of last request processed by server */
    Bool send_event,      /* TRUE if this came from SendEvent request */
    Display *display;     /* display the event was read from */
    Window window;
    Atom message_type;
    int format;
    union {
        char b[20];
        short s[10];
        long l[5];
    } data;
} XClientMessageEvent;
```

Event Structure Members

message_type

An atom that specifies how the data is to be interpreted by the receiving client. The X server places no interpretation on the type or the data, but it must be a list of 8-bit, 16-bit, or 32-bit quantities, so that the X server can correctly swap bytes as necessary. The data always consists of twenty 8-bit values, ten 16-bit values, or five 32-bit values, although each particular message might not make use of all of these values.

444   X Toolkit Intrinsics Reference Manual

format   Specifies the format of the property specified by `message_type`. This will be on of the values 8, 16, or 32.

ColormapNotify

When Generated

A `ColormapNotify` event reports when the colormap attribute of a window changes or when the colormap specified by the attribute is installed, uninstalled, or freed. This event is generated by `XChangeWindowAttributes`, `XFreeColormap`, `XInstallColormap`, and `XUninstallColormap`.

Translation Abbreviations

In translation tables, the event type `ColormapNotify` may be used, or use the abbreviation `Clrmap`.

Select With

This event is selected with `ColormapChangeMask`.

XEvent Structure Name

```
typedef union _XEvent {
    . . .
    XColormapEvent xcolormap;
    . . .
} XEvent;
```

Event Structure

```
typedef struct {
    int type;
    unsigned long serial; /* # of last request processed by server */
    Bool send_event;      /* TRUE if this came from SendEvent request */
    Display *display;     /* display the event was read from */
    Window window;
    Colormap colormap;    /* A colormap or None */
    Bool new;
    int state;            /* ColormapInstalled, ColormapUninstalled */
} XColormapEvent;
```

Event Structure Members

window   The window whose associated colormap or attribute changes.

colormap The colormap associated with the window, either a colormap ID or the constant None. It will be None only if this event was generated due to an XFree-Colormap call.

new   TRUE when the colormap attribute has been changed, or FALSE when the colormap is installed or uninstalled.

state   Either `ColormapInstalled` or `ColormapUninstalled`; it indicates whether the colormap is installed or uninstalled.

ConfigureNotify

When Generated

A ConfigureNotify event announces actual changes to a window's configuration (size, position, border, and stacking order). See also the CirculateRequest event.

Translation Abbreviations

In translation tables, the event type ConfigureNotify may be used, or use the abbreviation Configure.

Select With

This event is selected for a single window by specifying the window ID of that window with StructureNotifyMask. To receive this event for all children of a window, specify the parent window ID with SubstructureNotifyMask.

XEvent Structure Name

```
typedef union _XEvent {
    . . .
    XConfigureEvent xconfigure;
    . . .
} XEvent;
```

Event Structure

```
typedef struct {
    int type;
    unsigned long serial; /* # of last request processed by server */
    Bool send_event;      /* TRUE if this came from SendEvent request */
    Display *display;      /* display the event was read from */
    Window event;
    Window window;
    int x, y;
    int width, height;
    int border_width;
    Window above;
    Bool override_redirect;
} XConfigureEvent;
```

Event Structure Members

event   The window that selected the event. The event and window members are identical if the event was selected with StructureNotifyMask.

window   The window whose configuration was changed.

x, y   The final coordinates of the reconfigured window relative to its parent.

width, height
        The width and height in pixels of the window after reconfiguration.

border_width
        The width in pixels of the border after reconfiguration.

above   If this member is None, then the window is on the bottom of the stack with respect
to its siblings. Otherwise, the window is immediately on top of the specified sibling window

override_redirect
The override_redirect attribute of the reconfigured window. If TRUE, it
indicates that the client wants this window to be immune to interception by the
window manager of configuration requests Window managers normally should
ignore this event if override_redirect is TRUE.

ConfigureRequest

When Generated

A `ConfigureRequest` event reports when another client attempts to change a window's size, position, border, and/or stacking order.

This event differs from `ConfigureNotify` in that it delivers the parameters of the request before it is carried out. This gives the client that selects this event (usually the window manager) the opportunity to revise the requested configuration before executing the `XConfigureWindow` request itself or to deny the request. (`ConfigureNotify` indicates the final outcome of the request.)

Translation Abbreviations

In translation tables, the event type `ConfigureRequest` may be used, or use the abbreviation `ConfigureReq`.

Select With

This event is selected for any window in a group of children by specifying the parent window with `SubstructureRedirectMask`.

XEvent Structure Name

```
typedef union _XEvent {
    ...
    XConfigureRequestEvent xconfigurerequest;
    ...
} XEvent;
```

Event Structure

```
typedef struct {
    int type;
    unsigned long serial; /* # of last request processed by server */
    Bool send_event;      /* TRUE if this came from SendEvent request */
    Display *display;      /* display the event was read from */
    Window parent;
    Window window;
    int x, y;
    int width, height;
    int border_width;
    Window above;
    int detail;           /* Above, Below, TopIf, BottomIf, Opposite */
    unsigned long value_mask;
} XConfigureRequestEvent;
```

Event Structure Members

parent   The window that selected the event. This is the parent of the window being configured.

window   The window that is being configured.

x, y   The requested position for the upper-left pixel of the window's border relative to the origin of the parent window.

`width, height`
> The requested width and height in pixels for the window

`border_width`
> The requested border width for the window

`above` None, Above, Below, TopIf, BottomIf, or Opposite. Specifies the sibling window on top of which the specified window should be placed If this member has the constant None, then the specified window should be placed on the bottom

Notes

The geometry is derived from the XConfigureWindow request that triggered the event.

CreateNotify

When Generated

A CreateNotify event reports when a window is created.

Translation Abbreviations

In translation tables, the event type CreateNotify may be used, or use the abbreviation Create.

Select With

This event is selected on children of a window by specifying the parent window ID with SubstructureNotifyMask. (Note that this event type cannot be selected by StructureNotifyMask).

XEvent Structure Name

```
typedef union _XEvent {
    . . .
    XCreateWindowEvent xcreatewindow;
    . . .
} XEvent;
```

Event Structure

```
typedef struct {
    int type;
    unsigned long serial;    /* # of last request processed by server */
    Bool send_event;          * TRUE if this came from SendEvent request */
    Display *display;        /* display the event was read from */
    Window parent;           /* parent of the window */
    Window window;           /* window ID of window created */
    int x, y;                /* window location */
    int width, height;       /* size of window */
    int border_width;        /* border width */
    Bool override_redirect;/* creation should be overridden */
} XCreateWindowEvent;
```

Event Structure Members

parent   The ID of the created window's parent.

window   The ID of the created window.

x, y   The coordinates of the created window relative to its parent.

width, height   The width and height in pixels of the created window.

border_width   The width in pixels of the border of the created window.

override_redirect

The override_redirect attribute of the created window. If TRUE, it indicates that the client wants this window to be immune to interception by the window manager of configuration requests. Window managers normally should ignore this event if override_redirect is TRUE.

Notes

For descriptions of these members, see the XCreateWindow function and the XSet-
WindowAttributes structure

DestroyNotify

When Generated

A `DestroyNotify` event reports that a window has been destroyed.

Translation Abbreviations

In translation tables, the event type `DestroyNotify` may be used, or use the abbreviation `Destroy`.

Select With

To receive this event type on children of a window, specify the parent window ID and pass `SubstructureNotifyMask` as part of the `event_mask` argument to `XSelectInput`. This event type cannot be selected with `StructureNotifyMask`.

XEvent Structure Name

```
typedef union _XEvent {
    . . .
    XDestroyWindowEvent xdestroywindow;
    . . .
} XEvent;
```

Event Structure

```
typedef struct {
    int type;
    unsigned long serial; /* # of last request processed by server */
    Bool send_event;      /* TRUE if this came from SendEvent request */
    Display *display;     /* display the event was read from */
    Window event;
    Window window;
} XDestroyWindowEvent;
```

Event Structure Members

event   The window that selected the event.

window   The window that was destroyed.

EnterNotify, LeaveNotify

When Generated

`EnterNotify` and `LeaveNotify` events occur when the pointer enters or leaves a window.

When the pointer crosses a window border, a `LeaveNotify` event occurs in the window being left and an `EnterNotify` event occurs in the window being entered. Whether or not each event is queued for any application depends on whether any application selected the right event on the window in which it occurred.

In addition, `EnterNotify` and `LeaveNotify` events are delivered to windows that are *virtually crossed*. These are windows that are between the origin and destination windows in the hierarchy but not necessarily on the screen. Further explanation of virtual crossing is provided two pages following.

Translation Abbreviations

In translation tables, the event types `EnterNotify` and `LeaveNotify` may be used, or use one of the abbreviations shown in the following table.

Abbreviation	Description
`Enter`	Pointer entered window
`EnterWindow`	Pointer entered window
`Leave`	Pointer left window
`LeaveWindow`	Pointer left window

The Core widget field `compress_enterleave` controls whether pairs of `EnterNotify` and `LeaveNotify` events with no intervening events are ignored. For more information, see Chapter 8, *More Input Techniques*, in Volume Four, *X Toolkit Intrinsics Programming Manual*.

Select With

Each of these events can be selected separately with `XEnterWindowMask` and `XLeave-WindowMask`.

XEvent Structure Name

```
typedef union _XEvent {
    ...
    XCrossingEvent xcrossing;
    ...
} XEvent;
```

Event Structure

```
typedef struct {
    int type;              /* of event */
    unsigned long serial;  /* # of last request processed by server */
    Bool send_event;       /* TRUE if this came from SendEvent request */
    Display *display;      /* display the event was read from */
    Window window;         /* event window it is reported relative to */
    Window root;           /* root window that the event occurred on */
    Window subwindow;      /* child window */
```

```
    Time time;              /* milliseconds */
    int x, y;               /* pointer x, y coordinates in receiving window */
    int x_root, y_root;     /* coordinates relative to root */
    int mode;               /* NotifyNormal, NotifyGrab, NotifyUngrab */
    int detail;             /* NotifyAncestor, NotifyVirtual, NotifyInferior,
                             * NotifyNonLinear, NotifyNonLinearVirtual */
    Bool same_screen;       /* same screen flag */
    Bool focus;             /* Boolean focus */
    unsigned int state;     /* key or button mask */
} XCrossingEvent;
typedef XCrossingEvent XEnterWindowEvent;
typedef XCrossingEvent XLeaveWindowEvent;
```

Event Structure Members

subwindow In a LeaveNotify event, if the pointer began in a child of the receiving window then the child member is set to the window ID of the child. Otherwise, it is set to None. For an EnterNotify event, if the pointer ends up in a child of the receiving window then the child member is set to the window ID of the child. Otherwise, it is set to None.

time The server time when the crossing event occurred, in milliseconds. Time is declared as unsigned long, so it wraps around when it reaches the maximum value of a 32 bit number (every 49.7 days).

x, y The point of entry or exit of the pointer relative to the event window.

x_root, y_root
 The point of entry or exit of the pointer relative to the root window.

mode Normal crossing events or those caused by pointer warps have mode NotifyNormal; events caused by a grab have mode NotifyGrab; and events caused by a released grab have mode NotifyUngrab.

detail The value of the detail member depends on the hierarchical relationship between the origin and destination windows and the direction of pointer transfer. Determining which windows receive events and with which detail members is quite complicated. This topic is described in the next section.

same_screen
 Indicates whether the pointer is currently on the same screen as this window. This is always TRUE unless the pointer was actively grabbed before the automatic grab could take place.

focus If the receiving window is the focus window or a descendant of the focus window, the focus member is TRUE; otherwise it is FALSE.

state The state of all the buttons and modifier keys just before the event, represented by a mask of the button and modifier key symbols: Button1Mask,

Button2Mask, Button3Mask, Button4Mask, Button5Mask, Shift-
Mask, ControlMask, LockMask, Mod1Mask, Mod2Mask, Mod3Mask,
Mod4Mask, and Mod5Mask.

Virtual Crossing and the detail Member

Virtual crossing occurs when the pointer moves between two windows that do not have a
parent-child relationship. Windows between the origin and destination windows in the hierarchy receive EnterNotify and LeaveNotify events. The detail member of each of
these events depends on the hierarchical relationship of the origin and destination windows and
the direction of pointer transfer.

Virtual crossing is an advanced topic that you shouldn't spend time figuring out unless you
have an important reason to use it. I have never seen an application that uses this feature, and I
know of no reason for its extreme complexity. With that word of warning, proceed

Let's say the pointer has moved from one window, the origin, to another, the destination. First
we'll specify what types of events each window gets, and then the detail member of each of
those events

The window of origin receives a LeaveNotify event and the destination window receives an
EnterNotify event, if they have requested this type of event. If one is an inferior of the
other, the detail member of the event received by the inferior is NotifyAncestor and the
detail of the event received by the superior is NotifyInferior. If the crossing is between
parent and child, these are the only events generated.

However, if the origin and destination windows are not parent and child, other windows are *virtually crossed* and also receive events. If neither window is an ancestor of the other, ancestors
of each window up to but not including the least common ancestor receive LeaveNotify
events if they are in the same branch of the hierarchy as the origin and EnterNotify events
if they are in the same branch as the destination. These events can be used to track the motion
of the pointer through the hierarchy.

- In the case of a crossing between a parent and a child of a child, the middle child receives a
  LeaveNotify with detail NotifyVirtual.

- In the case of a crossing between a child and the parent of its parent, the middle child
  receives an EnterNotify with detail NotifyVirtual.

- In a crossing between windows whose least common ancestor is two or more windows
  away, both the origin and destination windows receive events with detail Notify-
  Nonlinear. The windows between the origin and the destination in the hierarchy, up to
  but not including their least common ancestor, receive events with detail Notify-
  NonlinearVirtual. The least common ancestor is the lowest window from which both
  are descendants.

- If the origin and destination windows are on separate screens, the events and details generated are the same as for two windows not parent and child, except that the root windows
  of the two screens are considered the least common ancestor. Both root windows also
  receive events.

Table C-2 shows the event types generated by a pointer crossing from window *A* to window *B* when window *C* is the least common ancestor of *A* and *B*.

Table C-2. Border Crossing Events and Window Relationship

LeaveNotify	EnterNotify
Origin window (*A*)	Destination window (*B*)
Windows between *A* and *B* exclusive if *A* is inferior	Windows between *A* and *B* exclusive if *B* is inferior
Windows between *A* and *C* exclusive	Windows between *B* and *C* exclusive
Root window on screen of origin if different from screen of destination	Root window on screen of destination if different from screen of origin

Table C-3 lists the detail members in events generated by a pointer crossing from window *A* to window *B*.

Table C-3. Event detail Member and Window Relationship

detail Flag	Window Delivered To
NotifyAncestor	Origin or destination when either is descendant.
NotifyInferior	Origin or destination when either is ancestor.
NotifyVirtual	Windows between *A* and *B* exclusive if either is descendant.
NotifyNonlinear	Origin and destination when *A* and *B* are two or more windows distant from least common ancestor *C*.
NotifyNonlinearVirtual	Windows between *A* and *C* exclusive and between *B* and *C* exclusive when *A* and *B* have least common ancestor *C*. Also on both root windows if *A* and *B* are on different screens.

For example, Figure C-1 shows the events that are generated by a movement from a window (window *A*) to a child (window *B1*) of a sibling (window *B*). This would generate three events: a LeaveNotify with detail NotifyNonlinear for the window *A*, an EnterNotify with detail NotifyNonlinearVirtual for its sibling window *B*, and an EnterNotify with detail NotifyNonlinear for the child (window *B1*).

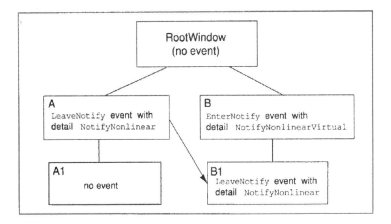

Figure C-1. Events generated by a move between windows

EnterNotify and LeaveNotify events are also generated when the pointer is grabbed, if the pointer was not already inside the grabbing window. In this case, the grabbing window receives an EnterNotify and the window containing the pointer receives a LeaveNotify event, both with mode NotifyUngrab. The pointer position in both events is the position before the grab. The result when the grab is released is exactly the same except that the two windows receive EnterNotify instead of LeaveNotify and vice versa.

Figure C-2 demonstrates the events and details caused by various pointer transitions, indicated by heavy arrows.

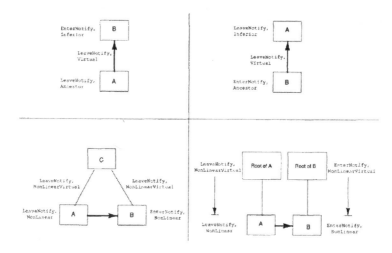

Figure C-2. Border crossing events and detail member for pointer movement from window A to window B, for various window relationships

Expose

————————————————————— — xexpose —

When Generated

An Expose event is generated when a window becomes visible or a previously invisible part of a window becomes visible. Only InputOutput windows generate or need to respond to Expose events; InputOnly windows never generate or need to respond to them The Expose event provides the position and size of the exposed area within the window and a rough count of the number of remaining exposure events for the current window.

Only when an application adds drawing capability to a widget from the application will a translation or event handler for Expose events be necessarily. Xt automatically calls the expose method of each widget in response to these events.

Translation Abbreviations

In translation tables, the event type Expose is the only valid string; there are no abbreviations.

The Core widget field compress_exposures controls whether contiguous Expose events are coalesced before calling a widget's expose method. For more information, see , in .

Select With

This event is selected with ExposureMask.

XEvent Structure Name

```
typedef union _XEvent {
    . . .
    XExposeEvent xexpose;
    .
} XEvent;
```

Event Structure

```
typedef struct {
    int type;
    unsigned long serial; /* # of last request processed by server */
    Bool send_event;      /* TRUE if this came from SendEvent request */
    Display *display;     /* display the event was read from */
    Window window;
    int x, y;
    int width, height,
    int count;            /* if nonzero, at least this many more */
} XExposeEvent;
```

Event Structure Members

x, y — The coordinates of the upper-left corner of the exposed region relative to the origin of the window.

width, height — The width and height in pixels of the exposed region.

count — The approximate number of remaining contiguous Expose events that were generated as a result of a single function call.

Notes

Notes

A single action such as a window movement or a function call can generate several exposure events on one window or on several windows. The server guarantees that all exposure events generated from a single action will be sent contiguously, so that they can all be handled before moving on to other event types. This allows an application to keep track of the rectangles specified in contiguous Expose events, set the clip_mask in a GC to the areas specified in the rectangle using XSetRegion or XSetClipRectangles, and then finally redraw the window clipped with the GC in a single operation after all the Expose events have arrived. The last event to arrive is indicated by a count of 0. In Release 2, XUnionRectWith- Region can be used to add the rectangle in Expose events to a region before calling XSet- Region.

If your application is able to redraw partial windows, you can also read each exposure event in turn and redraw each area.

FocusIn, FocusOut

When Generated

FocusIn and FocusOut events occur when the keyboard focus window changes, as a result of an XSetInputFocus call. They are much like EnterNotify and LeaveNotify events except that they track the focus rather than the pointer.

When a focus change occurs, a FocusOut event is delivered to the old focus window and a FocusIn event to the window which receives the focus. In addition, windows in between these two windows in the window hierarchy are virtually crossed and receive focus change events, as described below. Some or all of the windows between the window containing the pointer at the time of the focus change and the root window also receive focus change events, as described below.

Translation Abbreviations

In translation tables, the event types FocusIn and FocusOut may be used; there are no abbreviations.

Select With

FocusIn and FocusOut events are selected with FocusChangeMask. They cannot be selected separately.

XEvent Structure Name

```
typedef union _XEvent {
    ...
    XFocusChangeEvent xfocus;
    ...
} XEvent;
```

Event Structure

```
typedef struct {
    int type;               /* FocusIn or FocusOut */
    unsigned long serial;   /* # of last request processed by server */
    Bool send_event;        /* TRUE if this came from SendEvent request */
    Display *display;        /* display the event was read from */
    Window window;          /* window of event */
    int mode;               /* NotifyNormal, NotifyGrab, NotifyUngrab */
    int detail;             /* NotifyAncestor, NotifyVirtual, Notify-
                             * Inferior, NotifyNonLinear, NotifyNonLinear-
                             * Virtual, NotifyPointer, NotifyPointerRoot,
                             * NotifyDetailNone */
} XFocusChangeEvent;
typedef XFocusChangeEvent XFocusInEvent;
typedef XFocusChangeEvent XFocusOutEvent;
```

Event Structure Members

mode   For events generated when the keyboard is not grabbed, mode is Notify-
        Normal; when the keyboard is grabbed, mode is NotifyGrab; and when a key-
        board is ungrabbed, mode is NotifyUngrab.

detail   The detail member identifies the relationship between the window that receives
          the event and the origin and destination windows. It will be described in detail
          after the description of which windows get what types of events.

Notes

The *keyboard focus* is a window that has been designated as the one to receive all keyboard
input irrespective of the pointer position. Only the keyboard focus window and its descendants
receive keyboard events. By default, the focus window is the root window. Since all windows
are descendants of the root, the pointer controls the window that receives input.

Most window managers allow the user to set a focus window, to avoid the problem where the
pointer sometimes gets bumped into the wrong window and your typing doesn't go to the
intended window. If the pointer is pointing at the root window, all typing is usually lost since
there is no application for this input to propagate to. Some applications may set the keyboard
focus so that they can get all keyboard input for a given period of time, but this practice is not
encouraged.

Focus events are used when an application wants to act differently when the keyboard focus is
set to another window or to itself. FocusChangeMask is used to select FocusIn and
FocusOut events.

When a focus change occurs, A FocusOut event is delivered to the old focus window and a
FocusIn event is delivered to the window which receives the focus. Windows in between in
the hierarchy are virtually crossed and receive one focus change event each depending on the
relationship and direction of transfer between the origin and destination windows. Some or all
of the windows between the window containing the pointer at the time of the focus change and
that window's root window can also receive focus change events. By checking the detail
member of FocusIn and FocusOut events, an application can tell which of its windows can
receive input.

The detail member gives clues about the relationship of the event receiving window to the
origin and destination of the focus. The detail member of FocusOut and FocusIn events
is analogous to the detail member of LeaveNotify and EnterNotify events, but with
even more permutations to make life complicated.

Virtual Focus Crossing and the detail Member

We will now embark on specifying the types of events sent to each window and the detail
member in each event, depending on the relative position in the hierarchy of the origin window
(old focus), destination window (new focus), and the pointer window (window containing
pointer at time of focus change). Don't even try to figure this out unless you have to.

Table C-4 shows the event types generated by a focus transition from window *A* to window *B* when window *C* is the least common ancestor of *A* and *B*, and *P* is the window containing the pointer. This table includes most of the events generated, but not all of them. It is quite possible for a single window to receive more than one focus change event from a single focus change.

Table C-4. FocusIn and FocusOut Events and Window Relationship

FocusOut	FocusIn
Origin window (*A*)	Destination window (*B*)
Windows between *A* and *B* exclusive if *A* is inferior	Windows between *A* and *B* exclusive if *B* is inferior
Windows between *A* and *C* exclusive	Windows between *B* and *C* exclusive
Root window on screen of origin if different from screen of destination	Root window on screen of destination if different from screen of origin
Pointer window up to but not including origin window if pointer window is descendant of origin	Pointer window up to but not including destination window if pointer window is descendant of destination
Pointer window up to and including pointer window's root if transfer was from PointerRoot	Pointer window up to and including pointer window's root if transfer was to PointerRoot

Table C-5 lists the detail members in events generated by a focus transition from window *A* to window *B*, with *P* being the window containing the pointer.

Table C-5. Event detail Member and Window Relationship

detail Flag	Window Delivered To
NotifyAncestor	Origin or destination when either is descendant.
NotifyInferior	Origin or destination when either is ancestor.
NotifyVirtual	Windows between *A* and *B* exclusive if either is descendant.
NotifyNonlinear	Origin and destination when *A* and *B* are two or more windows distant from least common ancestor *C*.
NotifyNonlinearVirtual	Windows between *A* and *C* exclusive and between *B* and *C* exclusive when *A* and *B* have least common ancestor *C*. Also on both root windows if *A* and *B* are on different screens.

detail Flag	Window Delivered To
NotifyPointer	Window *P* and windows up to but not including the origin or destination windows.
NotifyPointerRoot	Window *P* and all windows up to its root, and all other roots, when focus is set to or from Pointer-Root.
NotifyDetailNone	All roots, when focus is set to or from None.

The following two pages show all the possible combinations of focus transitions and of origin, destination, and pointer windows and shows the types of events that are generated and their detail member. Solid lines indicate branches of the hierarchy. Dotted arrows indicate the direction of transition of the focus. At each end of this arrow are the origin and destination windows, windows *A* to *B*. Arrows ending in a bar indicate that the event type and detail described are delivered to all windows up to the bar.

In any branch, there may be windows that are not shown. Windows in a single branch between two boxes shown will get the event types and details shown beside the branch.

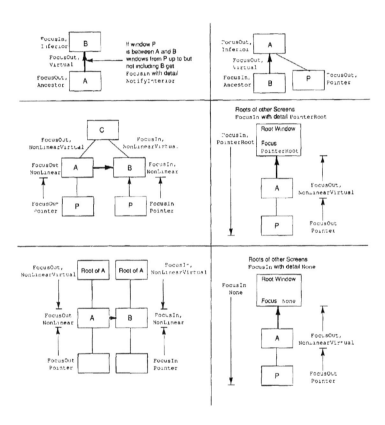

Figure C-3. FocusIn and FocusOut event schematics

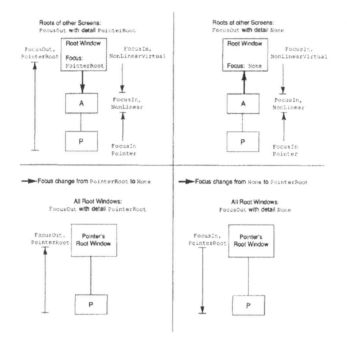

Figure C-3. FocusIn and FocusOut event schematics (continued)

FocusIn and FocusOut events are also generated when the keyboard is grabbed, if the focus was not already assigned to the grabbing window. In this case, all windows receive events as if the focus was set from the current focus to the grab window. When the grab is released, the events generated are just as if the focus was set back.

GraphicsExpose, NoExpose

When Generated

GraphicsExpose events indicate that the source area for a XCopyArea or XCopyPlane request was not available because it was outside the source window or obscured by a window. NoExpose events indicate that the source region was completely available

Neither of these events are used in Xt's automatic processing of Expose events. If a widget needs to use them, it must provide a translation or event handler for them and then call its expose method directly.

Translation Abbreviations

In translation tables, the event types GraphicsExpose and NoExpose may be used, or use the abbreviations GrExp or NoExp.

Select With

These events are not selected with XSelectInput but are sent if the GC in the XCopyArea or XCopyPlane request had its graphics_exposures flag set to TRUE. If graphics_exposures is TRUE in the GC used for the copy, either one NoExpose event or one or more GraphicsExpose events will be generated for every XCopyArea or XCopyPlane call made.

XEvent Structure Name

```
typedef union _XEvent {
    .   .
    XNoExposeEvent xnoexpose;
    XGraphicsExposeEvent xgraphicsexpose;
    .
} XEvent;
```

Event Structure

```
typedef struct {
    int type;
    unsigned long serial; /* # of last request processed by server */
    Bool send_event;      /* TRUE if this came from SendEvent request */
    Display *display;      /* display the event was read from */
    Drawable drawable,
    int x, y;
    int width, height;
    int count;            /* if nonzero, at least this many more */
    int major_code;       /* core is CopyArea or CopyPlane */
    int minor_code;       /* not defined in the core */
} XGraphicsExposeEvent;

typedef struct {
    int type;
    unsigned long serial; /* # of last request processed by server */
    Bool send_event,      /* TRUE if this came from SendEvent request */
    Display *display;      /* display the event was read from */
    Drawable drawable;
```

```
    int major_code;     /* core is CopyArea or CopyPlane */
    int minor_code;     /* not defined in the core */
} XNoExposeEvent;
```

Event Structure Members

drawable   A window or an off-screen pixmap. This specifies the destination of the graphics request that generated the event.

x, y   The coordinates of the upper-left corner of the exposed region relative to the origin of the window.

width, height   The width and height in pixels of the exposed region.

count   The approximate number of remaining contiguous GraphicsExpose events that were generated as a result of the XCopyArea or XCopy-Plane call.

major_code   The graphics request used. This may be one of the symbols CopyArea or CopyPlane, or a symbol defined by a loaded extension.

minor_code   Zero unless the request is part of an extension.

Notes

Expose events and GraphicsExpose events both indicate the region of a window that was actually exposed (x, y, width, and height). Therefore they can often be handled similarly.

GravityNotify

xgravity—

When Generated

A GravityNotify event reports when a window is moved because of a change in the size of its parent. This happens when the win_gravity attribute of the child window is something other than StaticGravity or UnmapGravity.

Translation Abbreviations

In translation tables, the event type GravityNotify may be used, or use the abbreviation Grav.

Select With

This event is selected for a single window by specifying the window ID of that window with StructureNotifyMask. To receive notification of movement due to gravity for a group of siblings, specify the parent window ID with SubstructureNotifyMask.

XEvent Structure Name

```
typedef union _XEvent {
    ...
    XGravityEvent xgravity;
    ...
} XEvent;
```

Event Structure

```
typedef struct {
    int type;
    unsigned long serial; /* # of last request processed by server */
    Bool send_event;      /* TRUE if this came from SendEvent request */
    Display *display;     /* display the event was read from */
    Window event;
    Window window;
    int x, y;
} XGravityEvent;
```

Event Structure Members

event   The window that selected the event.

window The window that was moved.

x, y   The new coordinates of the window relative to its parent.

KeymapNotify

When Generated

A KeymapNotify event reports the state of the keyboard and occurs when the pointer or keyboard focus enters a window. KeymapNotify events are reported immediately after EnterNotify or FocusIn events. This is a way for the application to read the keyboard state as the application is "woken up," since the two triggering events usually indicate that the application is about to receive user input.

Translation Abbreviations

In translation tables, the event type KeymapNotify may be used, or use the abbreviation Keymap.

Select With

This event is selected with KeymapStateMask.

XEvent Structure Name

```
typedef union _XEvent {
    . . .
    XKeymapEvent xkeymap;
    . . .
} XEvent;
```

Event Structure

```
typedef struct {
    int type;
    unsigned long serial; /* # of last request processed by server */
    Bool send_event;      /* TRUE if this came from SendEvent request */
    Display *display;      /* display the event was read from */
    Window window;
    char key_vector[32];
} XKeymapEvent;
```

Event Structure Members

window   Reports the window which was reported in the window member of the preceeding EnterNotify or FocusIn event.

key_vector   A bit vector or mask, each bit representing one physical key, with a total of 256 bits. For a given key, its keycode is its position in the keyboard vector. You can also get this bit vector by calling XQueryKeymap.

Notes

The serial member of KeymapNotify does not contain the serial number of the most recent Protocol Request processed, because this event always follows immediately after FocusIn or EnterNotify events in which the serial member is valid.

KeyPress, KeyRelease

When Generated

KeyPress and KeyRelease events are generated for all keys, even those mapped to modifier keys such as Shift or Control.

Translation Abbreviations

In translation tables, the event types KeyPress and KeyRelease may be used, or use one of the abbreviations shown in the following table.

Abbreviation	Description
Key	Key pressed
KeyDown	Key pressed
Ctrl	KeyPress with Ctrl modifier
Meta	KeyPress with Meta modifier
Shift	KeyPress with Shift modifier
KeyUp	Key released

To execute an action in response to the press or release of an individual key, you can use any of the above abbreviations in combination with a detail. For example, in the translation:

```
<Key>a:    append()
```

the append action is invoked when the key "a" is pressed, regardless of which modifiers are being held. For more information on how to use translations to manage key events, see Chapter 7, *Events, Translations, and Accelerators*, in Volume Four, *X Toolkit Intrinsics Programming Manual*.

Select With

Each type of keyboard event may be selected separately with KeyPressMask and KeyReleaseMask.

XEvent Structure Name

```
typedef union _XEvent {
    . . .
    XKeyEvent xkey;
    . . .
} XEvent;
```

Event Structure

```
typedef struct {
    int type;               /* of event */
    unsigned long serial;   /* # of last request processed by server */
    Bool send_event;        /* TRUE if this came from SendEvent request */
    Display *display;        /* display the event was read from */
    Window window;          /* event window it is reported relative to */
    Window root;            /* root window that the event occurred on */
    Window subwindow;       /* child window */
    Time time;              /* milliseconds */
```

```
    int x, y;              /* pointer coords relative to receiving window */
    int x_root, y_root;    /* coordinates relative to root */
    unsigned int state;    /* modifier key and button mask */
    unsigned int keycode;  /* server-dependent code for key */
    Bool same_screen;      /* same screen flag */
} XKeyEvent;
typedef XKeyEvent XKeyPressedEvent;
typedef XKeyEvent XKeyReleasedEvent;
```

Event Structure Members

subwindow   If the source window is the child of the receiving window, then the `subwindow` member is set to the ID of that child.

time   The server time when the button event occurred, in milliseconds. `Time` is declared as `unsigned long`, so it wraps around when it reaches the maximum value of a 32-bit number (every 49.7 days).

x, y   If the receiving window is on the same screen as the root window specified by `root`, then `x` and `y` are the pointer coordinates relative to the receiving window's origin. Otherwise, x and y are zero.

When active button grabs and pointer grabs are in effect (see Volume One, *Xlib Programming Manual*, Section 9.4 and Volume Four, *X Toolkit Intrinsics Programming Manual*, Chapter 12, *Menus, Gadgets, and Cascaded Pop Ups*, Section 12.2.1), the coordinates relative to the receiving window may not be within the window (they may be negative or greater than window height or width).

x_root, y_root
            The pointer coordinates relative to the root window which is an ancestor of the event window. If the pointer was on a different screen, these are zero.

state   The state of all the buttons and modifier keys just before the event, represented by a mask of the button and modifier key symbols: `Button1Mask`, `Button2Mask`, `Button3Mask`, `Button4Mask`, `Button5Mask`, `ShiftMask`, `ControlMask`, `LockMask`, `Mod1Mask`, `Mod2Mask`, `Mod3Mask`, `Mod4-Mask`, and `Mod5Mask`.

keycode   The `keycode` member contains a server-dependent code for the key that changed state. As such it should be translated into the portable symbol called a keysym before being used. It can also be converted directly into ASCII with `XLookupString`. For a description and examples of how to translate keycodes, see Volume One, Section 9.1.1, and Volume Four, Section 13.4.

Notes

Remember that not all hardware is capable of generating release events, and that only the main keyboard (a-z, A-Z, 0-9), Shift, and Control keys are always found.

Keyboard events are analogous to button events, though of course there are many more keys than buttons, and the keyboard is not automatically grabbed between press and release

All the structure members have the same meaning as described for `ButtonPress` and `ButtonRelease` events except that `button` is replaced by `keycode`.

MapNotify, UnmapNotify

When Generated

The X server generates MapNotify and UnmapNotify events when a window changes state from unmapped to mapped or vice versa. In most cases, Xt widgets are mapped in the final step of the process of realizing the application, initiated with XtRealizeWidget.

Translation Abbreviations

In translation tables, the event types MapNotify and UnmapNotify may be used, or use the abbreviations Map or Unmap.

Select With

To receive these events on a single window, use StructureNotifyMask in the call to XSelectInput for the window. To receive these events for all children of a particular parent, specify the parent window ID and use SubstructureNotifyMask.

XEvent Structure Name

```
typedef union _XEvent {
    . . .
    XMapEvent xmap;
    XUnmapEvent xunmap;
    . . .
} XEvent;
```

Event Structure

```
typedef struct {
    int type;
    unsigned long serial; /* # of last request processed by server */
    Bool send_event;      /* TRUE if this came from SendEvent request */
    Display *display;      /* display the event was read from */
    Window event;
    Window window;
    Bool override_redirect;  /* Boolean, is override set */
} XMapEvent;

typedef struct {
    int type;
    unsigned long serial; /* # of last request processed by server */
    Bool send_event;      /* TRUE if this came from SendEvent request */
    Display *display;      /* display the event was read from */
    Window event;
    Window window;
    Bool from_configure;
} XUnmapEvent;
```

Event Structure Members

event   The window that selected this event.

window   The window that was just mapped or unmapped.

override_redirect (XMapEvent only)
> TRUE or FALSE. The value of the override_redirect attribute of the window
> that was just mapped.

from_configure (XUnmapEvent only)
> TRUE if the event was generated as a result of a resizing of the window's parent
> when the window itself had a win_gravity of UnmapGravity. See the
> description of the win_gravity attribute in Volume One, Section 4.3.4. FALSE
> otherwise.

MappingNotify

When Generated

A `MappingNotify` event is sent when any of the following is changed by another client: the mapping between physical keyboard keys (keycodes) and keysyms, the mapping between modifier keys and logical modifiers, or the mapping between physical and logical pointer buttons. These events are triggered by a call to `XSetModifierMapping` or `XSetPointer-Mapping`, if the return status is `MappingSuccess`, or by any call to `XChangeKeyboard-Mapping`.

This event type should not be confused with the event that occurs when a window is mapped; that is a `MapNotify` event. Nor should it be confused with the `KeymapNotify` event, which reports the state of the keyboard as a mask instead of as a keycode.

Translation Abbreviations

In translation tables, the event type `MappingNotify` may be used, or use the abbreviation `Mapping`.

Select With

The X server sends `MappingNotify` events to all clients. It is never selected and cannot be masked with the window attributes.

XEvent Structure Name

```
typedef union _XEvent {
    . . .
    XMappingEvent xmapping;
    . . .
} XEvent;
```

Event Structure

```
typedef struct {
    int type;
    unsigned long serial; /* # of last request processed by server */
    Bool send_event;      /* TRUE if this came from SendEvent request */
    Display *display;      /* display the event was read from */
    Window window;         /* unused */
    int request;           /* one of MappingModifier, MappingKeyboard,
                            * MappingPointer */
    int first_keycode;     /* first keycode */
    int count;             /* range of change with first_keycode*/
} XMappingEvent;
```

Event Structure Members

request   The kind of mapping change that occurred: `MappingModifier` for a successful `XSetModifierMapping` (keyboard Shift, Lock, Control, Meta keys), `MappingKeyboard` for a successful `XChangeKeyboardMapping` (other keys), and `MappingPointer` for a successful `XSetPointerMapping` (pointer button numbers).

first_keycode
> If the request member is MappingKeyboard or MappingModifier, then first_keycode indicates the first in a range of keycodes with altered mappings Otherwise it is not set.

count   If the request member is MappingKeyboard or MappingModifier, then count indicates the number of keycodes with altered mappings. Otherwise it is not set.

Notes

If the request member is MappingKeyboard, clients should call XRefreshKeyboard-Mapping.

The normal response to a request member of MappingPointer or MappingModifier is no action. This is because the clients should use the logical mapping of the buttons and modifiers to allow the user to customize the keyboard if desired. If the application requires a particular mapping regardless of the user's preferences, it should call XGetModifierMapping or XGetPointerMapping to find out about the new mapping.

MapRequest

When Generated

A MapRequest event occurs when the functions XMapRaised and XMapWindow are called.

This event differs from MapNotify in that it delivers the parameters of the request before it is carried out. This gives the client that selects this event (usually the window manager) the opportunity to revise the size or position of the window before executing the map request itself or to deny the request. (MapNotify indicates the final outcome of the request.)

Translation Abbreviations

In translation tables, the event type MapRequest may be used, or use the abbreviation Map-Req.

Select With

This event is selected by specifying the window ID of the parent of the receiving window with SubstructureRedirectMask. (In addition, the override_redirect member of the XSetWindowAttributes structure for the specified window must be FALSE.)

XEvent Structure Name

```
typedef union _XEvent {
    . . .
    XMapRequestEvent xmaprequest;
    . . .
} XEvent;
```

Event Structure

```
typedef struct {
    int type;
    unsigned long serial; /* # of last request processed by server */
    Bool send_event;      /* TRUE if this came from SendEvent request */
    Display *display;      /* display the event was read from */
    Window parent;
    Window window;
} XMapRequestEvent;
```

Event Structure Members

parent   The ID of the parent of the window being mapped.

window   The ID of the window being mapped.

MotionNotify

When Generated

A MotionNotify event reports that the user moved the pointer or that a program warped the pointer to a new position within a single window.

Translation Abbreviations

In translation tables, the event type MotionNotify may be used, or use one of the abbreviations shown in the following table.

Abbreviation	Description
Motion	Pointer moved
PtrMoved	Pointer moved
MouseMoved	Pointer moved
BtnMotion	Pointer moved with any button held down
Btn1Motion	Pointer moved with button 1 held down
Btn2Motion	Pointer moved with button 2 held down
Btn3Motion	Pointer moved with button 3 held down
Btn4Motion	Pointer moved with button 4 held down
Btn5Motion	Pointer moved with button 5 held down

The Core widget field compress_motion determines whether the widget gets all motion events or only periodic position updates. For more information, see Chapter 8, *More Input Techniques*, in Volume Four, *X Toolkit Intrinsics Programming Manual*.

Select With

This event is selected with PointerMotionMask, PointerMotionHintMask, ButtonMotionMask, Button1MotionMask, Button2MotionMask, Button3-MotionMask, Button4MotionMask, and Button5MotionMask. These masks determine the specific conditions under which the event is generated.

XEvent Structure Name

```
typedef union _XEvent {
    ...
    XMotionEvent xmotion;
    ...
} XEvent;
```

Event Structure

```
typedef struct {
    int type;               /* of event */
    unsigned long serial;   /* # of last request processed by server */
    Bool send_event;        /* TRUE if this came from SendEvent request */
    Display *display;       /* display the event was read from */
    Window window;          /* event window it is reported relative to */
    Window root;            /* root window that the event occurred on */
    Window subwindow;       /* child window */
    Time time;              /* milliseconds */
```

```
    int x, y;              /* pointer coords relative to receiving window */
    int x_root, y_root;    /* coordinates relative to root */
    unsigned int state;    /* button and modifier key mask */
    char is_hint;          /* is this a motion hint */
    Bool same_screen;      /* same screen flag */
} XMotionEvent;
typedef XMotionEvent XPointerMovedEvent;
```

Event Structure Members

subwindow   If the source window is the child of the receiving window, then the subwindow member is set to the ID of that child.

time   The server time when the button event occurred, in milliseconds. Time is declared as unsigned long, so it wraps around when it reaches the maximum value of a 32 bit number (every 49.7 days).

x, y   If the receiving window is on the same screen as the root window specified by root, then x and y are the pointer coordinates relative to the receiving window's origin. Otherwise, x and y are zero.

            When active button grabs and pointer grabs are in effect (see Section 9.4 in Volume One, *Xlib Programming Manual*, and Section 12.2.1 in Volume Four, *X Toolkit Intrinsics Programming Manual*) the coordinates relative to the receiving window may not be within the window (they may be negative or greater than window height or width).

x_root, y_root

            The pointer coordinates relative to the root window which is an ancestor of the event window. If the pointer was on a different screen, these are zero.

state   The state of all the buttons and modifier keys just before the event, represented by a mask of the button and modifier key symbols: Button1Mask, Button2Mask, Button3Mask, Button4Mask, Button5Mask, ShiftMask, ControlMask, LockMask, Mod1Mask, Mod2Mask, Mod3Mask, Mod4Mask, and Mod5Mask.

is_hint   Either the constant NotifyNormal or NotifyHint. NotifyHint indicates that the PointerMotionHintMask was selected. In this case, just one event is sent when the mouse moves, and the current position can be found by calling XQueryPointer, or by examining the motion history buffer with XGetMotionEvents, if a motion history buffer is available on the server. NotifyNormal indicates that the event is real, but it may not be up to date since there may be many more later motion events on the queue.

same_screen

            Indicates whether the pointer is currently on the same screen as this window. This is always TRUE unless the pointer was actively grabbed before the automatic grab could take place.

Notes

If the processing you have to do for every motion event is fast, you can probably handle all of them without requiring motion hints. However, if you have extensive processing to do for each one, you might be better off using the hints and calling XQueryPointer or using the history buffer if it exists. XQueryPointer is a round-trip request, so it can be slow

EnterNotify and LeaveNotify events are generated instead of MotionEvents if the pointer starts and stops in different windows.

PropertyNotify

When Generated

A PropertyNotify event indicates that a property of a window has changed or been deleted. This event can also be used to get the current server time (by appending zero-length data to a property). PropertyNotify events are generated by XChangeProperty, XDeleteProperty, XGetWindowProperty, or XRotateWindowProperties.

Translation Abbreviations

In translation tables, the event type PropertyNotify may be used, or use the abbreviation Prop.

Select With

This event is selected with PropertyChangeMask.

XEvent Structure Name

```
typedef union _XEvent {
    . . .
    XPropertyEvent xproperty;
    . . .
} XEvent;
```

Event Structure

```
typedef struct {
    int type;
    unsigned long serial; /* # of last request processed by server */
    Bool send_event;      /* TRUE if this came from SendEvent request */
    Display *display;     /* display the event was read from */
    Window window;
    Atom atom;
    Time time;
    int state;            /* NewValue, Deleted */
} XPropertyEvent;
```

Event Structure Members

window   The window whose property was changed, not the window that selected the event.

atom   The property that was changed.

state   Either PropertyNewValue or PropertyDelete. Whether the property was changed to a new value or deleted.

time   The time member specifies the server time when the property was changed.

ReparentNotify

When Generated

A ReparentNotify event reports when a client successfully reparents a window.

Translation Abbreviations

In translation tables, the event type ReparentNotify may be used, or use the abbreviation Reparent.

Select With

This event is selected with SubstructureNotifyMask by specifying the window ID of the old or the new parent window or with StructureNotifyMask by specifying the window ID.

XEvent Structure Name

```
typedef union _XEvent {
    ...
    XReparentEvent xreparent;
    ...
} XEvent;
```

Event Structure

```
typedef struct {
    int type;
    unsigned long serial; /* # of last request processed by server */
    Bool send_event;      /* TRUE if this came from SendEvent request */
    Display *display;      /* display the event was read from */
    Window event;
    Window window;
    Window parent;
    int x, y;
    Bool override_redirect;
} XReparentEvent;
```

Event Structure Members

window   The window whose parent window was changed.

parent   The new parent of the window.

x, y   The coordinates of the upper-left pixel of the window's border relative to the new parent window's origin.

override_redirect

The override_redirect attribute of the reparented window. If TRUE, it indicates that the client wants this window to be immune to meddling by the window manager. Window managers normally should not have reparented this window to begin with.

ResizeRequest

When Generated

A `ResizeRequest` event reports another client's attempt to change the size of a window. The X server generates this event type when another client calls `XConfigureWindow`, `XResizeWindow`, or `XMoveResizeWindow`. If this event type is selected, the window is not resized. This gives the client that selects this event (usually the window manager) the opportunity to revise the new size of the window before executing the resize request or to deny the request itself.

Translation Abbreviations

In translation tables, the event type `ResizeRequest` may be used, or use the abbreviation `ResReq`.

Select With

To receive this event type, specify a window ID and pass `ResizeRedirectMask` as part of the `event_mask` argument to `XSelectInput`. Only one client can select this event on a particular window. When selected, this event is triggered instead of resizing the window.

XEvent Structure Name

```
typedef union _XEvent {
    . . .
    XResizeRequestEvent xresizerequest;
    . . .
} XEvent;
```

Event Structure

```
typedef struct {
    int type;
    unsigned long serial; /* # of last request processed by server */
    Bool send_event;      /* TRUE if this came from SendEvent request */
    Display *display;     /* display the event was read from */
    Window window;
    int width, height;
} XResizeRequestEvent;
```

Event Structure Members

window   The window whose size another client attempted to change.

width, height The requested size of the window, not including its border.

SelectionClear

When Generated

A SelectionClear event reports to the current owner of a selection that a new owner is being defined.

Translation Abbreviations

In translation tables, the event type SelectionClear may be used, or use the abbreviation SelClr.

However, all selection events are normally handled automatically by Xt's selection mechanism, and therefore no translations are needed

Select With

This event is not selected. It is sent to the previous selection owner when another client calls XSetSelectionOwner for the same selection

XEvent Structure Name

```
typedef union _XEvent {
    ...
    XSelectionClearEvent xselectionclear,
    ...
} XEvent;
```

Event Structure

```
typedef struct {
    int type;
    unsigned long serial; /* # of last request processed by server */
    Bool send_event;      /* TRUE if this came from SendEvent request */
    Display *display;     /* display the event was read from */
    Window window;
    Atom selection,
    Time time;
} XSelectionClearEvent;
```

Event Structure Members

window   The window that is receiving the event and losing the selection.

selection   The selection atom specifying the selection that is changing ownership

time   The last-change time recorded for the selection.

486   X Toolkit Intrinsics Reference Manual

SelectionNotify

When Generated

A `SelectionNotify` event is sent only by clients, not by the server, by calling `XSend-Event`. The owner of a selection sends this event to a requestor (a client that calls `XConvertSelection` for a given property) when a selection has been converted and stored as a property or when a selection conversion could not be performed (indicated with property `None`).

Translation Abbreviations

In translation tables, the event type `SelectionNotify` may be used, or use the abbreviation `Select`.

However, all selection events are normally handled automatically by Xt's selection mechanism, and therefore no translations are needed.

Select With

There is no event mask for `SelectionNotify` events, and they are not selected with `XSelectInput`. Instead `XSendEvent` directs the event to a specific window, which is given as a window ID: `PointerWindow`, which identifies the window the pointer is in, or `InputFocus`, which identifies the focus window.

XEvent Structure Name

```
typedef union _XEvent {
    . . .
    XSelectionEvent xselection;
    . . .
} XEvent;
```

Event Structure

```
typedef struct {
    int type;
    unsigned long serial; /* # of last request processed by server */
    Bool send_event;      /* TRUE if this came from SendEvent request */
    Display *display;     /* display the event was read from */
    Window requestor;     /* must be next after type */
    Atom selection;
    Atom target;
    Atom property;        /* Atom or None */
    Time time;
} XSelectionEvent;
```

Event Structure Members

The members of this structure have the values specified in the `XConvertSelection` call that triggers the selection owner to send this event, except that the `property` member will return either the atom specifying a property on the requestor window with the data type specified in `target`, or it will be `None`, which indicates that the data could not be converted into the `target` type.

SelectionRequest

xselectionrequest—

When Generated

A SelectionRequest event is sent to the owner of a selection when another client requests the selection by calling XConvertSelection.

Translation Abbreviations

In translation tables, the event type SelectionRequest may be used, or use the abbreviation SelReq.

However, all selection events are normally handled automatically by Xt's selection mechanism, and therefore no translations are needed.

Select With

There is no event mask for SelectionRequest events, and they are not selected with XSelectInput.

XEvent Structure Name

```
typedef union _XEvent {
    ...
    XSelectionRequestEvent xselectionrequest;
    ...
} XEvent;
```

Event Structure

```
typedef struct {
    int type,
    unsigned long serial; /* # of last request processed by server */
    Bool send_event,      /* TRUE if this came from SendEvent request */
    Display *display;     /* display the event was read from */
    Window owner;         /* must be next after type */
    Window requestor;
    Atom selection;
    Atom target;
    Atom property;
    Time time;
} XSelectionRequestEvent;
```

Event Structure Members

The members of this structure have the values specified in the XConvertSelection call that triggers this event.

The owner should convert the selection based on the specified target type, if possible. If a property is specified, the owner should store the result as that property on the requestor window, and then send a SelectionNotify event to the requestor by calling XSendEvent. If the selection cannot be converted as requested, the owner should send a SelectionNotify event with property set to the constant None.

When Generated

A `VisibilityNotify` event reports any change in the visibility of the specified window. This event type is never generated on windows whose class is `InputOnly`. All of the window's subwindows are ignored when calculating the visibility of the window.

Translation Abbreviations

In translation tables, the event type `VisibilityNotify` may be used, or use the abbreviation `Visible`.

Most widgets do not need to provide a translation for this event, because the Core widget field `visible_interest` provides a simplified form of the same information. For more information, see Chapter 8, *More Input Techniques*, in Volume Four, *X Toolkit Intrinsics Programming Manual*.

Select With

This event is selected with `VisibilityChangeMask`.

XEvent Structure Name

```
typedef union _XEvent {
    ...
    XVisibilityEvent xvisibility;
    ...
} XEvent;
```

Event Structure

```
typedef struct {
    int type;
    unsigned long serial; /* # of last request processed by server */
    Bool send_event;      /* TRUE if this came from SendEvent request */
    Display *display;     /* display the event was read from */
    Window window;
    int state;            /* VisibilityUnobscured,*/
                          /* VisibilityPartiallyObscured, or */
                          /* VisibilityObscured */
} XVisibilityEvent;
```

Event Structure Members

state   A symbol indicating the final visibility status of the window: `Visibility-Unobscured`, `VisibilityPartiallyObscured`, or `Visibility-Obscured`.

Notes

Table C-6 lists the transitions that generate `VisibilityNotify` events and the corresponding `state` member of the `XVisibilityEvent` structure.

Table C-6. The State Element of the XVisibilityEvent Structure

Visibility Status Before	Visibility Status After	State Member
Partially obscured, fully obscured, or not viewable	Viewable and completely unobscured	`VisibilityUnobscured`
Viewable and completely unobscured, or not viewable	Viewable and partially obscured	`VisibilityPartially-` `Obscured`
Viewable and completely unobscured, or viewable and partially obscured, or not viewable	Viewable and partially obscured	`VisibilityPartially-` `Obscured`

D
Standard Errors and Warnings

The two sections below summarize all errors and warnings that the Toolkit can generate. The information has this form:

Message Name
    `Message Type`   Default message

Note that many messages have more than one type; however, all Toolkit errors and warnings have class `XtToolkitError`.

Error Messages

allocError
`calloc`	Cannot perform calloc
`malloc`	Cannot perform malloc
`realloc`	Cannot perform realloc

communicationError
`select`	Select failed

internalError
`shell`	Shell's window manager interaction is broken

invalidArgCount
`xtGetValues`	Argument count > 0 on NULL argument list in XtGetValues
`xtSetValues`	Argument count > 0 on NULL argument list in XtSetValues

invalidClass
`constraintSetValue`	Subclass of Constraint required in CallConstraintSetValues
`xtAppCreateShell`	XtAppCreateShell requires non-NULL widget class
`xtCreatePopupShell`	XtCreatePopupShell requires non-NULL widget class
`xtCreateWidget`	XtCreateWidget requires non-NULL widget class
`xtPopdown`	XtPopdown requires a subclass of shellWidgetClass
`xtPopup`	XtPopup requires a subclass of shellWidgetClass

invalidDimension
`xtCreateWindow`	Widget %s has zero width and/or height
`shellRealize`	Shell widget %s has zero width and/or height

invalidDisplay
    xtInitialize   Cannot open display

invalidGeometryManager
    xtMakeGeometryRequest XtMakeGeometryRequest -- parent has no geometry manger

invalidParameter
    removePopupFromParent RemovePopupFromParent requires non-NULL popuplist
    xtAddInput   Invalid condition passed to XtAddInput

invalidParameters
    xtMenuPopupAction   MenuPopup wants exactly one argument
    xtmenuPopdown   XtMenuPopdown called with num_params != 0 or 1

invalidParent
    realize   Application shell is not a windowed widget?
    xtCreatePopupShell   XtCreatePopupShell requires non-NULL parent
    xtCreateWidget   XtCreateWidget requires non-NULL parent
    xtMakeGeometryRequest XtMakeGeometryRequest – NULL parent. Use SetValues instead
    xtMakeGeometryRequest XtMakeGeometryRequest – parent not composite
    xtManageChildren   Attempt to manage a child when parent is not Composite
    xtUnmanageChildren   Attempt to unmanage a child when parent is not Composite

invalidPopup
    xtMenuPopup   Cannot find pop up in _XtMenuPopup
    xtMenuPopup   Cannot find pop up in _XtMenuPopup

invalidProcedure
    inheritanceProc   Unresolved inheritance operation
    realizeProc   No realize class procedure defined

invalidWindow
    eventHandler   Event with wrong window

missingEvent
    shell   Events are disappearing from under Shell

noAppContext
    widgetToApplication-   Couldn't find ancestor with display information
    Context

noPerDisplay
    closeDisplay   Couldn't find per display information
    getPerDisplay   Couldn't find per display information

noSelectionProperties
    freeSelectionProperty Internal error no selection property context for display

nullProc
    insertChild   NULL insert_child procedure

subclassMismatch
    xtCheckSubclass   Widget class %s found when subclass of %s expected: %s

translationError

mergingTablesWithCycles Trying to merge translation tables with cycles, and cannot resolve this cycle

wrongParameters

cvtIntOrPixelToXColor	Pixel-to-color conversion needs screen and colormap arguments
cvtStringToCursor	String-to-cursor conversion needs screen argument
cvtStringToFont	String-to-font conversion needs screen argument
cvtStringToFontStruct	String-to-cursor conversion needs screen argument
cvtStringToPixel	String-to-pixel conversion needs screen and colormap arguments

Warning Messages

ambigiousParent

xtManageChildren	Not all children have same parent in XtManageChildren
xtUnmanageChildren	Not all children have same parent in XtUnmanageChildren

communicationError

windowManager	Window Manager is confused

conversionError

string	Cannot convert string "%s" to type "%s"

displayError

invalidDisplay	Cannot find display structure

grabError

grabDestroyCallback	XtAddGrab requires exclusive grab if spring_loaded is TRUE
grabDestroyCallback	XtAddGrab requires exclusive grab if spring_loaded is TRUE
xtRemoveGrab	XtRemoveGrab asked to remove a widget not on the grab list

initializationError

xtInitialize	Initializing Resource Lists twice

invalidArgCount

getResources	Argument count > 0 on NULL argument list

invalidCallbackList

xtAddCallbacks	Cannot find callback list in XtAddCallbacks
xtCallCallback	Cannot find callback list in XtCallCallbacks
xtOverrideCallback	Cannot find callback list in XtOverrideCallbacks
xtRemoveAllCallback	Cannot find callback list in XtRemoveAllCallbacks
xtRemoveCallbacks	Cannot find callback list in XtRemoveCallbacks

invalidChild

xtManageChildren	NULL child passed to XtManageChildren
xtUnmanageChildren	NULL child passed to XtUnmanageChildren

invalidDepth

setValues	Cannot change widget depth

invalidGeometry
    xtMakeGeometryRequest   Shell subclass did not take care of geometry in XtSetValues

invalidParameters
    compileAccelerators   String to AcceleratorTable needs no extra arguments
    compileTranslations   String to TranslationTable needs no extra arguments
    mergeTranslations   MergeTM to TranslationTable needs no extra arguments

invalidParent
    xtCopyFromParent   CopyFromParent must have non-NULL parent

invalidPopup
    unsupportedOperation   Pop-up menu creation is only supported on ButtonPress or Enter-Notify events

invalidProcedure
    deleteChild   NULL delete_child procedure in XtDestroy
    inputHandler   XtRemoveInput Input handler not found
    set_values_almost   set_values_almost procedure shouldn't be NULL

invalidResourceCount
    getResources   Resource count > 0 on NULL resource list

invalidResourceName
    computeArgs   Cannot find resource name %s as argument to conversion

invalidShell
    xtTranslateCoords   Widget has no shell ancestor

invalidSizeOverride
    xtDependencies   Representation size %d must match superclass's to override %s

invalidTypeOverride
    xtDependencies   Representation type %s must match superclass's to override %s

invalidWidget
    removePopupFromParent   RemovePopupFromParent,widget not on parent list

noColormap
    cvtStringToPixel   Cannot allocate colormap entry for "%s"

registerWindowError
    xtRegisterWindow   Attempt to change already registered window
    xtUnregisterWindow   Attempt to unregister invalid window

translation error
    nullTable   Cannot remove accelerators from NULL table
    nullTable   Tried to remove non-existant accelerators

translationError
    ambiguousActions   Overriding earlier translation manager actions
    mergingNullTable   Old translation table was null, cannot modify
    nullTable   Cannot translate event through NULL table
    unboundActions   Actions not found %s
    xtTranslateInitialize   Initializing Translation manager twice

translationParseError

showLine	... found while parsing "%s"
parseError	Translation table syntax error: %s
parseString	Missing ".LP

typeConversionError

noConverter   No type converter registered for "%s" to "%s" conversion

versionMismatch

widget   Widget class %s version mismatch: widget %d vs. intrinsics %d

wrongParameters

cvtIntToBool	Integer-to-Bool conversion needs no extra arguments
cvtIntToBoolean	Integer-to-Boolean conversion needs no extra arguments
cvtIntToFont	Integer-to-Font conversion needs no extra arguments
cvtIntToPixel	Integer-to-Pixel conversion needs no extra arguments
cvtIntToPixmap	Integer-to-Pixmap conversion needs no extra arguments
cvtIntToShort	Integer-to-Short conversion needs no extra arguments
cvtStringToBool	String-to-Bool conversion needs no extra arguments
cvtStringToBoolean	String-to-Boolean conversion needs no extra arguments
cvtStringToDisplay	String-to-Display conversion needs no extra arguments
cvtStringToFile	String-to-File conversion needs no extra arguments
cvtStringToInt	String-to-Integer conversion needs no extra arguments
cvtStringToShort	String-to-Integer conversion needs no extra arguments
cvtStringToUnsignedChar	String-to-Integer conversion needs no extra arguments
cvtXColorToPixel	Color-to-Pixel conversion needs no extra arguments

E
Resource File Format

A resource file contains text representing the default resource values for an application or set of applications. The resource file is an ASCII text file that consists of a number of lines with the following EBNF syntax:

```
resourcefile  = {line "\n"}
line          = (comment | production)
comment       = "!" string
production     = resourcename ":" string
resourcename  = ["*"] name {("." | "*") name}
string        = {<any character not including eol>}
name          = {"A"-"Z" | "a"-"z" | "0"-"9"}
```

If the last character on a line is a backslash (\), that line is assumed to continue onto the next line.

To include a newline character in a string, use \n

Translation Table Syntax

Notation

Syntax is specified in EBNF notation with the following conventions:

- [a]   Means either nothing or "a"
- { a }   Means zero or more occurrences of "a"

All terminals are enclosed in double quotation masks (" "). Informal descriptions are enclosed in angle brackets (< >).

Syntax

The translation table file has the following syntax:

```
translationTable   = [ directive ] { production }
directive          = { "#replace" | "#override" | "#augment" } "\n"
production         = lhs ":" rhs "\n"
lhs                = ( event | keyseq ) { "," (event | keyseq) }
keyseq             = """ keychar {keychar} """
keychar            = [ "^" | "$" | "\" ] <ISO Latin 1 character>
event              = [modifier_list] "<"event_type">" [ "(" count["+"] ")" ] {detail}
modifier_list      = ( ["!" | ":"] {modifier} ) | "None"
modifier           = ["~"] modifier_name
count              = ("1" | "2" | "3" | "4" | ...)
modifier_name      = "@" <keysym> | <see ModifierNames table below>
event_type         = <see Event Types table below>
detail             = <event specific details>
rhs                = { name "(" [params] ")" }
name               = namechar { namechar }
namechar           = { "a"-"z" | "A"-"Z" | "0"-"9" | "$" | "_" }
params             = string {"," string}.
string             = quoted_string | unquoted_string
```

```
quoted_string   = """ {<Latin 1 character>} """
unquoted_string = {<Latin 1 character except space, tab, ",", newline, ")">}
```

It is often convenient to include newlines in a translation table to make it more readable. In C, indicate a newline with a "\n".

```
"<Btn1Down>:        DoSomething()\\en\\c
<Btn2Down>:         DoSomethingElse()"
```

Modifier Names

The modifier field is used to specify normal X keyboard and button modifier mask bits. Modifiers are legal on event types `KeyPress`, `KeyRelease`, `ButtonPress`, `Button-Release`, `MotionNotify`, `EnterNotify`, `LeaveNotify`, and their abbreviations; however, parsing a translation table that contains modifiers for any other events generates an error.

- If the `modifier_list` has no entries and is not `None`, it means "don't care" on all modifiers.

- If an exclamation point (!) is specified at the beginning of the modifier list, it means that the listed modifiers must be in the correct state and no other modifiers can be asserted.

- If any modifiers are specified and an exclamation point (!) is not specified, it means that the listed modifiers must be in the correct state and "don't care" about any other modifiers.

- If a modifier is preceded by a tilde (~), it means that that modifier must not be asserted

- If `None` is specified, it means no modifiers can be asserted.

- If a colon (:) is specified at the beginning of the modifier list, it directs the Intrinsics to apply any standard modifiers in the event to map the event keycode into a keysym. The default standard modifiers are Shift and Lock, with the interpretation as defined in Volume Zero, *X Protocol Reference Manual*. The resulting keysym must exactly match the specified keysym, and the nonstandard modifiers in the event must match the modifier_list. For example, `:<Key>a` is distinct from `:<Key>A`, and `:Shift<Key>A` is distinct from `:<Key>A`.

- If a colon (:) is not specified, no standard modifiers are applied. Then, for example, "<Key>A" and "<Key>a" are equivalent

In key sequences, a circumflex (^) is an abbreviation for the Control modifier, a dollar sign ($) is an abbreviation for Meta, and a backslash (\) can be used to quote any character, in particular a double quote ("), a circumflex (^), a dollar sign ($), and another backslash (\). Briefly:

No modifiers:	None <event> detail
Any modifiers:	<event> detail
Only these modifiers:	! mod1 mod2 <event> detail
These modifiers and any others:	mod1 mod2 <event> detail

The use of None for a modifier_list is identical to the use of and exclamation point with no modifers.

Table F-1. Modifier Keys

Modifier	Abbreviation	Meaning
Ctrl	c	Control modifier bit
Shift	s	Shift modifier bit
Lock	l	Lock modifier bit
Meta	m	Meta key modifier (see below)
Hyper	h	Hyper key modifier (see below)
Super	su	Super key modifier (see below)
Alt	a	Alt key modifier (see below)
Mod1		Mod1 modifier bit
Mod2		Mod2 modifier bit
Mod3		Mod3 modifier bit
Mod4		Mod4 modifier bit
Mod5		Mod5 modifier bit
Button1		Button1 modifier bit
Button2		Button2 modifier bit
Button3		Button3 modifier bit
Button4		Button4 modifier bit
Button5		Button5 modifier bit
ANY		Any combination

A key modifier is any modifier bit whose corresponding keycode contains the corresponding left or right keysym. For example, *m* or *Meta* means any modifier bit mapping to a keycode whose keysym list contains XK_Meta_L or XK_Meta_R. Note that this interpretation is for each display, not global or even for each application context. The Control, Shift, and Lock modifier names refer explicitly to the corresponding modifier bits; there is no additional interpretation of keysyms for these modifiers.

Because it is possible to associate arbitrary keysyms with modifiers, the set of modifier key modifiers is extensible. The "@" <keysym> syntax means any modifier bit whose corresponding keycode contains the specified keysym.

A modifier_list/keysym combination in a translation matches a modifiers/keycode combination in an event in the following cases:

- If a colon (:) is used, the Intrinsics call the display's XtKeyProc with the keycode and modifiers. To match:

  ```
  (modifiers & ~modifiers_return)
  ```

  must equal modifier_list, and keysym_return must equal the given keysym.

- If (:) is not used, the Intrinsics mask off all "don't care" bits from the modifiers. This value must be equal to modifier_list. Then, for each possible combination of "don't care" modifiers in the modifier_list, the Intrinsics call the display's

`XtKeyProc` with the keycode and that combination ORed with the cared-about modifier bits from the event. `keysym_return` must match the keysym in the translation.

Event Types

The `EventType` field describes `XEvent` types. Currently defined `EventType` values are listed in Table F-2 below.

Table F-2. EventType Values

Type	Meaning
`Key` or `KeyDown`	`KeyPress`
`KeyUp`	`KeyRelease`
`BtnDown`	`ButtonPress`
`BtnUp`	`ButtonRelease`
`Motion, PtrMoved,` `or MouseMoved`	`MotionNotify`
`Enter` or `EnterWindow`	`EnterNotify`
`Leave` or `LeaveWindow`	`LeaveNotify`
`FocusIn`	`FocusIn`
`FocusOut`	`FocusOut`
`Keymap`	`KeymapNotify`
`Expose`	`Expose`
`GrExp`	`GraphicsExpose`
`NoExp`	`NoExpose`
`Visible`	`VisibilityNotify`
`Create`	`CreateNotify`
`Destroy`	`DestroyNotify`
`Unmap`	`UnmapNotify`
`Map`	`MapNotify`
`MapReq`	`MapRequest`
`Reparent`	`ReparentNotify`
`Configure`	`ConfigureNotify`
`ConfigureReq`	`ConfigureRequest`
`Grav`	`GravityNotify`
`ResReq`	`ResizeRequest`
`Circ`	`CirculateNotify`
`CircReq`	`CirculateRequest`
`Prop`	`PropertyNotify`
`SelClr`	`SelectionClear`
`SelReq`	`SelectionRequest`
`Select`	`SelectionNotify`
`Clrmap`	`ColormapNotify`
`Message`	`ClientMessage`
`Mapping`	`MappingNotify`

The supported abbreviations are listed in Table F-3.

Table F-3. Modifier Key Abbreviations

Abbreviation	Meaning
Ctrl	KeyPress with control modifier
Meta	KeyPress with meta modifier
Shift	KeyPress with shift modifier
Btn1Down	ButtonPress with Btn1 detail
Btn1Up	ButtonRelease with Btn1 detail
Btn2Down	ButtonPress with Btn2 detail
Btn2Up	ButtonRelease with Btn2 detail
Btn3Down	ButtonPress with Btn3 detail
Btn3Up	ButtonRelease with Btn3 detail
Btn4Down	ButtonPress with Btn4 detail
Btn4Up	ButtonRelease with Btn4 detail
Btn5Down	ButtonPress with Btn5 detail
Btn5Up	ButtonRelease with Btn5 detail
BtnMotion	MotionNotify with any button modifier
Btn1Motion	MotionNotify with Button1 modifier
Btn2Motion	MotionNotify with Button2 modifier
Btn3Motion	MotionNotify with Button3 modifier
Btn4Motion	MotionNotify with Button4 modifier
Btn5Motion	MotionNotify with Button5 modifier

The detail field is event-specific and normally corresponds to the detail field of an XEvent, for example, <Key>A. If no detail field is specified, then ANY is assumed.

A keysym can be specified as any of the standard keysym names, a hexadecimal number prefixed with *0x* or *0X*, an octal number prefixed with *0*, or a decimal number. A keysym expressed as a single digit is interpreted as the corresponding Latin 1 keysym. For example, *0* is the keysym XK_0. Other single character keysyms are treated as literal constants from Latin 1, for example, *!* is treated as 0x21. Standard keysym names are as defined in <X11/keysymdef.h> with the XK_ prefix removed. (See Appendix H, *Keysyms*, in Volume Two, *Xlib Reference Manual*.)

Canonical Representation

Every translation table has a unique, canonical text representation This representation is passed to a widget's `display_accelerator` method to describe the accelerators installed on that widget. The table below shows the canonical representation of a translation table file. (See also the section on "Syntax" earlier in this appendix.)

```
translationTable   = { production }
production         = lhs ":" rhs "\n"
lhs                = event { "," event }
event              = [modifier_list] "<"event_type">" [ "(" count["+"] ")" ] {detail}
modifier_list      = ["!" | ":"] {modifier}
modifier           = ["~"] modifier_name
count              = ("1" | "2" | "3" | "4" | ...)
modifier_name      = "@" <keysym> | <see canonical modifier names below>
event_type         = <see canonical event types below>
detail             = <event specific details>
rhs                = { name "(" [params] ")" }
name               = namechar { namechar }
namechar           = { "a"-"z" | "A"-"Z" | "0"-"9" | "$" | "_" }
params             = string ["," string].
string             = quoted_string
quoted_string      = """ {<Latin 1 character>} """
```

The canonical modifier names are.

```
Button1    Mod1    Ctrl
Button2    Mod2    Shift
Button3    Mod3    Lock
Button4    Mod4
Button5    Mod5
```

The canonical event types are.

```
ButtonPress       DestroyNotify    KeyPress         PropertyNotify
ButtonRelease     EnterNotify      KeyRelease       ReparentNotify
CirculateNotify   Expose           LeaveNotify      ResizeRequest
CirculateRequest  FocusIn          MapNotify        SelectionClear
ClientMessage     FocusOut         MappingNotify    SelectionNotify
ColormapNotify    GraphicsExpose   MapRequest       SelectionRequest
ConfigureNotify   GravityNotify    MotionNotify     UnmapNotify
ConfigureRequest  KeymapNotify     NoExpose         VisibilityNotify
CreateNotify
```

Examples

- Always put more specific events in the table before more general ones:

```
Shift <Btn1Down> : twas()\n\
<Btn1Down> : brillig()
```

- For double-click on Button 1 Up with Shift, use this specification:

```
Shift<Btn1Up>(2) : and()
```

This is equivalent to the following line with appropriate timers set between events:

```
Shift<Btn1Down>,Shift<Btn1Up>,Shift<Btn1Down>,Shift<Btn1Up> : and()
```

- For double-click on Button 1 Down with Shift, use this specification:

```
Shift<Btn1Down>(2) : the()
```

This is equivalent to the following line with appropriate timers set between events:

```
Shift<Btn1Down>,Shift<Btn1Up>,Shift<Btn1Down> : the()
```

- Mouse motion is always discarded when it occurs between events in a table where no motion event is specified:

```
<Btn1Down>,<Btn1Up> : slithy()
```

This is taken, even if the pointer moves a bit between the down and up events. Similarly, any motion event specified in a translation matches any number of motion events. If the motion event causes an action procedure to be invoked, the procedure is invoked after each motion event.

- If an event sequence consists of a sequence of events that is also a non-initial subsequence of another translation, it is not taken if it occurs in the context of the longer sequence. This occurs mostly in sequences like the following:

```
<Btn1Down>,<Btn1Up> : toves()\n\
<Btn1Up> : did()
```

The second translation is taken only if the button release is not preceded by a button press or if there are intervening events between the press and the release. Be particularly aware of this when using the repeat notation, above, with buttons and keys because their expansion includes additional events, and when specifying motion events because they are implicitly included between any two other events. In particular, pointer motion and double-click translations cannot coexist in the same translation table.

- For single click on Button 1 Up with Shift and Meta, use this specification:

```
Shift Meta <Btn1Down>, Shift Meta<Btn1Up>: gyre()
```

- You can use a plus sign (+) to indicate "for any number of clicks greater than or equal to count"; for example:

```
Shift <Btn1Up>(2+) : and()
```

- To indicate `EnterNotify` with any modifiers, use this specification:

      <Enter> : gimble()

- To indicate `EnterNotify` with no modifiers, use this specification:

      None <Enter> : in()

- To indicate `EnterNotify` with Button 1 Down and Button 2 Up and "don't care" about the other modifiers, use this specification:

      Button1 ~Button2 <Enter> : the()

- To indicate `EnterNotify` with Button1 Down and Button2 Down exclusively, use this specification:

      ! Button1 Button2 <Enter> : wabe()

  You do not need to use a tilde (~) with an exclamation point (!)

G
StringDefs.h Header File

StringsDefs.h
Header File

This appendix lists the contents of the *StringDefs.h* header file. The contents are classified by resource names, class types, representation types, and constants.

Table G-1. Resource Names

Resource Name	Value
XtNaccelerators	"accelerators"
vXtNallowHoriz	"allowHoriz"
XtNallowVert	"allowVert"
XtNancestorSensitive	"ancestorSensitive"
XtNbackground	"background"
XtNbackgroundPixmap	"backgroundPixmap"
XtNborderColor	"borderColor"
XtNborder	"borderColor"
XtNborderPixmap	"borderPixmap"
XtNborderWidth	"borderWidth"
XtNcallback	"callback"
XtNcolormap	"colormap"
XtNdepth	"depth"
XtNdestroyCallback	"destroyCallback"
XtNeditType	"editType"
XtNfont	"font"
XtNforceBars	"forceBars"
XtNforeground	"foreground"
XtNfunction	"function"
XtNheight	"height"
XtNhSpace	"hSpace"
XtNindex	"index"
XtNinnerHeight	"innerHeight"
XtNinnerWidth	"innerWidth"
XtNinnerWindow	"innerWindow"
XtNinsertPosition	"insertPosition"
XtNinternalHeight	"internalHeight"

Table G-1. Resource Names (continued)

Resource Name	Value
XtNinternalWidth	"internalWidth"
XtNjustify	"justify"
XtNknobHeight	"knobHeight"
XtNknobIndent	"knobIndent"
XtNknobPixel	"knobPixel"
XtNknobWidth	"knobWidth"
XtNlabel	"label"
XtNlength	"length"
XtNlowerRight	"lowerRight"
XtNmappedWhenManaged	"mappedWhenManaged"
XtNmenuEntry	"menuEntry"
XtNname	"name"
XtNnotify	"notify"
XtNorientation	"orientation"
XtNparameter	"parameter"
XtNpopupCallback	"popupCallback"
XtNpopdownCallback	"popdownCallback"
XtNreverseVideo	"reverseVideo"
XtNscreen	"screen"
XtNscrollProc	"scrollProc"
XtNscrollDCursor	"scrollDownCursor"
XtNscrollHCursor	"scrollHorizontalCursor"
XtNscrollLCursor	"scrollLeftCursor"
XtNscrollRCursor	"scrollRightCursor"
XtNscrollUCursor	"scrollUpCursor"
XtNscrollVCursor	"scrollVerticalCursor"
XtNselection	"selection"
XtNselectionArray	"selectionArray"
XtNsensitive	"sensitive"
XtNshown	"shown"
XtNspace	"space"
XtNstring	"string"
XtNtextOptions	"textOptions"
XtNtextSink	"textSink"
XtNtextSource	"textSource"
XtNthickness	"thickness"
XtNthumb	"thumb"
XtNthumbProc	"thumbProc"
XtNtop	"top"
XtNtranslations	"translations"
XtNuseBottom	"useBottom"
XtNuseRight	"useRight"
XtNvalue	"value"
XtNvSpace	"vSpace"

Resource Name	Value
XtNwidth	"width"
XtNwindow	"window"
XtNx	"x"
XtNy	"y"

Table G-2. Class Types

Class Type	Value
XtCAccelerators	"Accelerators"
XtCBackground	"Background"
XtCBoolean	"Boolean"
XtCBorderColor	"BorderColor"
XtCBorderWidth	"BorderWidth"
XtCCallback	"Callback"
XtCColormap	"Colormap"
XtCColor	"Color"
XtCCursor	"Cursor"
XtCDepth	"Depth"
XtCEditType	"EditType"
XtCEventBindings	"EventBindings"
XtCFile	"File"
XtCFont	"Font"
XtCForeground	"Foreground"
XtCFraction	"Fraction"
XtCFunction	"Function"
XtCHeight	"Height"
XtCHSpace	"HSpace"
XtCIndex	"Index"
XtCInterval	"Interval"
XtCJustify	"Justify"
XtCKnobIndent	"KnobIndent"
XtCKnobPixel	"KnobPixel"
XtCLabel	"Label"
XtCLength	"Length"
XtCMappedWhenManaged	"MappedWhenManaged"
XtCMargin	"Margin"
XtCMenuEntry	"MenuEntry"
XtCNotify	"Notify"
XtCOrientation	"Orientation"
XtCParameter	"Parameter"
XtCPixmap	"Pixmap"

Table G-2. Class Types (continued)

Class Type	Value
XtCPosition	"Position"
XtCScreen	"Screen"
XtCScrollProc	"ScrollProc"
XtCScrollDCursor	"ScrollDownCursor"
XtCScrollHCursor	"ScrollHorizontalCursor"
XtCScrollLCursor	"ScrollLeftCursor"
XtCScrollRCursor	"ScrollRightCursor"
XtCScrollUCursor	"ScrollUpCursor"
XtCScrollVCursor	"ScrollVerticalCursor"
XtCSelection	"Selection"
XtCSensitive	"Sensitive"
XtCSelectionArray	"SelectionArray"
XtCSpace	"Space"
XtCString	"String"
XtCTextOptions	"TextOptions"
XtCTextPosition	"TextPosition"
XtCTextSink	"TextSink"
XtCTextSource	"TextSource"
XtCThickness	"Thickness"
XtCThumb	"Thumb"
XtCTranslations	"Translations"
XtCValue	"Value"
XtCVSpace	"VSpace"
XtCWidth	"Width"
XtCWindow	"Window"
XtCX	"X"
XtCY	"Y"

Table G-3. Representation Types

Representation Type	Value
XtRAcceleratorTable	"AcceleratorTable"
XtRBoolean	"Boolean"
XtRCallback	"Callback"
XtRCallProc	"CallProc"
XtRColor	"Color"
XtRCursor	"Cursor"
XtRDimension	"Dimension"
XtRDisplay	"Display"
XtREditMode	"EditMode"
XtRFile	"File"

Table G-3. Representation Types (continued)

Representation Type	Value
XtRFont	"Font"
XtRFontStruct	"FontStruct"
XtRFunction	"Function"
XtRGeometry	"Geometry"
XtRImmediate	"Immediate"
XtRInt	"Int"
XtRJustify	"Justify"
XtRLongBoolean	"LongBoolean"
XtROrientation	"Orientation"
XtRPixel	"Pixel"
XtRPixmap	"Pixmap"
XtRPointer	"Pointer"
XtRPosition	"Position"
XtRShort	"Short"
XtRString	"String"
XtRStringTable	"StringTable"
XtRUnsignedChar	"UnsignedChar"
XtRTranslationTable	"TranslationTable"
XtRWindow	"Window"

StringsDefs.h Header File

Table G-4. Constants

Constant	Value
Boolean Enumeration:	
XtEoff	"off"
XtEfalse	"false"
XtEno	"no"
XtEon	"on"
XtEtrue	"true"
XtEyes	"yes"
Orientation Enumeration:	
XtEvertical	"vertical"
XtEhorizontal	"horizontal"
Text Edit Enumeration:	
XtEtextRead	"read"
XtEtextAppend	"append"
XtEtextEdit	"edit"

Table G-4. Constants (continued)

Constant	Value
Color Enumeration:	
XtExtdefaultbackground	"xtdefaultbackground"
XtExtdefaultforeground	"xtdefaultforeground"
Font:	
XtExtdefaultfont	"xtdefaultfont"

H
Release Notes

This appendix summarizes the changes to the Intrinsics between Release 2 and Release 3. Where significant, these differences have also been noted on the appropriate page in this manual.

- Many bugs have been fixed, including the ability to create more than 896 widgets, to destroy the last widget in an application, to call XtDestroyWidget from within a destroy_callback, to call XtNextEvent recursively from input or timer callbacks, and to call XtOverrideTranslations or XtAugmentTranslations after the target widget has been realized.

- An additional source for application resource specifications has been added; see XAPPLRESDIR under XtDisplayInitialize.

- In Release 2, XtGetValues would overwrite an entire longword, regardless of the size of the resource being retrieved. XtGetValues now works correctly on most machine architectures. Applications that relied on the broken behavior will have to be fixed. In particular, only the number of bytes specified by the resource size will be copied; not an entire (long) word.

- The definitions of the types Dimension and Position have changed. Correct code will not be affected by this, but code that assumed that Dimensions and Positions were ints may break. In particular, all cases where pointers to such fields are used will need to be checked. In the standard interfaces, the only such places are calls to Xt-MakeResizeRequest and XtGetValues. Widgets that pass pointers in callbacks or other public interfaces will also need to be checked. This change plus the preceeding bugfix require all application calls to XtGetValues to be checked for correctness, especially those that refer to XtNx, XtNy, XtNwidth, XtNheight and Xt-NborderWidth.

- XtGetValues and XtSetValues on callback lists now work consistently with the public callback list structures. That is, in Release 2, when you used XtGetValues on a callback list, it did not return an XtCallbackList, as would be expected. This has been fixed in Release 3.

- XtSetKeyboardFocus works correctly in Release 3; it was broken in Release 2, especially in handling grabs.

- The link *Atoms.h* has been removed; use *StringDefs.h*.

- Support for selections has been added.

- New syntax in translation tables allows resource specifications to provide translations that are merged with the default widget translations, rather than completely replacing them. See XtAugmentTranslations and XtOverrideTranslations.

- The translation table syntax has been extended to completely support keysym names as modifier and detail fields. Better support for indicating upper/lower case sensitivity in translations has been added, plus hooks for providing non-standard case converters and non-standard keycode to keysym converters.

- Application contexts have been added to several interfaces to allow for re-entrant libraries. The old interfaces remain supported for compatibility and will use a global default context. See XtCreateApplicationContext.

- Multiple display connections are now supported. Displays opened with XOpen-Display can also be registered with the Toolkit by making a call to XtDisplay-Initialize

- A new routine, XtReleaseGC, must be used in place of XtDestroyGC if the application is using XtGetGC on multiple displays

- XtInitialize has been split up into four separate routines: XtToolkit-Initialize, XtCreateApplicationContext, XtOpenDisplay, and Xt-AppCreateShell XtInitialize remains supported as a convenience routine for simple applications.

- Additional standard command line options have been defined: *-selectionTimeout* and *+synchronous*

- The resource database created by the Intrinsics can now be accessed directly, using *Xrm* routines, if desired

- A per-user application class defaults file has been added, which will be loaded into the resource database immediately after the system-wide application class defaults and before the user preference resources.

- Widget subclasses can now provide default values for superclass resources that override the superclass's default before the superclass initialize procedure is called.

- Resource lists can now specify as default values the Black and White pixels and the default font assigned by the server. Reverse video is implemented only for these two pixels. See XtDefaultForeground, XtDefaultBackground and XtDefault-Font

- Support for computing default values for resources at run-time has been added. See Xt-RCallProc.

- Additional error and warning message interfaces have been defined that allow customization of error messages and provide for textual substitution in the message. All internal error messages generated by the Intrinsics use these new interfaces.

- A routine to determine if X input, alternate input, or timer input is available without actually processing any has been added. See XtAppPending

- `XtDispatchEvent` now returns a Boolean indicating whether or not a widget was found to which to dispatch the event.

- A function to return the full event mask for a widget has been added. See `XtBuildEventMask`.

- Limited support for background processing has been added. See `XtAddWorkProc`.

- Support for accelerators has been added to the translation manager. Accelerators are event bindings that trigger actions in a widget other than the one in which the event(s) occurred. See `XtInstallAccelerators`.

- Resource hierarchies are no longer qualified by an additional name and class to the left of the `ApplicationShellWidget` name and class. This may have compatibility implications for existing resource files that contain full resource names, and for applications that used `XtCreateApplicationShell`.

- Colormap and depth fields have been added to the Core widget class so that widgets can specify values different from their parent's values.

- The Core class has two new fields: a `display_accelerator` method for the new accelerators capability and a field to allow future additions to the Core class without requiring a recompile of all widgets. Widget class initializers should be updated to initialize these to `XtInheritDisplayAccelerator` and `NULL`, respectively. Old widgets will continue to work without updating.

- The interface to the `accept_focus` procedure now has a time parameter and a new interface to it, `XtCallAcceptFocus`, has been added. The `accept_focus` procedure must now return a Boolean to indicate whether or not the widget actually wanted the focus. Widgets implementing an `accept_focus` procedure will have to be updated.

- The Composite widget class dropped the `move_focus_to_next` and `move_focus_to_prev` fields. The Composite class also added a field to allow for future expansion. Widget class initializers for all composite widgets must be modified to remove the initializers for the first two and initialize the last to `NULL`.

- The `num_mapped_children` field has been dropped from the `CompositePart`. Most widgets that used this field probably had bugs.

- A new flag, `CWQueryOnly`, has been added to geometry requests. A geometry manager is expected to return the same information whether or not this flag is set, but to not actually make any geometry changes if `CWQueryOnly` is set. Geometry managers will have to be updated.

- Any widget may be specified as the parent in `XtCreateWidget`. Children of non-composite widgets may not be managed (via `XtManageChild`), nor may they make geometry requests.

- The inquiry function `XtIsManaged` has been added.

- A new routine, `XtGetResourceList` has been added to return the complete resource list for a widget class.

- The built-in `MenuPopdown` action procedure now accepts an optional (shell) widget name.

- `XtRealizeWidget` now respects the `map_when_managed` attribute for all widgets, including Shells.

- `XtCreateWindow` and `ShellRealize` will now report more helpful error messages when a widget is to be realized with a width or height of 0.

- Shell will now allow geometry changes via `XtSetValues` when the `XtNallow-ShellResize` resource is FALSE.

- The *new* argument to `set_values` routines now contains the real widget (was formerly the *current* argument). This will affect widgets that make explicit geometry requests within their `set_values` routine. Widgets should never assume the geometry in "new" is what they will actually get; instead, they should rely on a call to their Resize procedure to inform them of changes.

- `XtDestroyWidget` will now automatically call `XtRemoveAllCallbacks` on every callback list for each destroyed widget; widget destroy procedures are no longer required to do so.

Master Index

The Master Index combines Volumes Four and Five index entries, making it easy to look up the appropriate references to a topic in either volume. PM refers to the X Toolkit Intrinsics Programming Manual. RM refers to the X Toolkit Intrinsics Reference Manual.

Index

The Master Index combines Volumes Four and Five index entries, making it easy to look up the appropriate references to a topic in either volume. PM refers to the X Toolkit Intrinsics Programming Manual. RM refers to the X Toolkit Intrinsics Reference Manual.

The alphabetical sequence of the index is highlighted by the bolding of primary entries.

adding display RM 135-136, XtOpenDisplay
    PM 98, 396, RM·195-196
creating RM 115-116
destroying and closing displays RM 127
explicit PM 98
main loop for multiple PM 394
multiple PM.394
    (see also XtCreateApplicationContext)
    (see also XtDestroyApplicationContext)
    (see also XtWidgetToApplicationContext)
application, application resources PM 80, data
    structure PM 81, retrieving values PM 85
application-defaults file, about PM·32, 36,
    245, directory PM 36, naming conven-
    tions PM·32, 36
applicationShellWidgetClass PM 270,
    RM 346-353
Arg structure PM 92
argc PM 33, 91, 272
ArgList (see argument lists)
ArgsProc RM 327
ARGSUSED PM 42
arguments, argument lists, about PM 92, 496,
    constructing/modifying dynamically
    RM 232-233, creating PM 92, creating
    dynamically PM 93, creating with
    XtSetArg PM 93-94, example PM 92-93,
    merging ArgList RM·186, XtMergeAr-
    gLists RM.186
argument styles PM.90
command line RM 13
to actions PM 113, 124
to type converters PM 259-260
argv PM 33, 91, 272
array, (see also XtNumber)
allocating RM 105
elements, determining number RM 192
(see also XtCalloc)
aspect ratio PM 274
Athena widgets, about PM:17, 496
    Box PM 66, RM 357-358
    Command PM 19, 40-43, 47, 65, RM 359-362
    Dialog PM 71, 75, 340-341, RM 363-364
    Form PM 68-69, 325-340, RM 365-367
    Grip PM 66, RM 368-369
    inheritance among PM 18
    Label PM.19, 36, 240, RM 370-372
    List RM 373-377
    MenuButton PM 367
    Scroll PM 15, 39, 42, 66, 109, RM 378-382
    Simple PM 19
    SimpleMenu PM 349, 367-371, 378-381
    Template RM 383-390

Text PM 75, 150, 264, 280, RM 391-402
Viewport PM 107, 310, 314, RM 403-404
Vpaned PM 66
VPaned PM 310
Vpaned RM 405-408
atoms, about PM 288, 496
    obtaining, example PM 291, 292
    predefined PM 291
    standard PM 299
augmenting translations PM 48

B

background PM 53, 496
    background processing PM 231, RM 323-324
    pixmap PM 53
    window attribute PM 156
backing store PM 257, 496
    window attribute PM 156
binding, tight vs. loose (resources) PM 244
bit gravity PM 496
bit plane PM 497
bit_gravity window attribute PM 156
bitmap PM 279, 497
    bitmap files PM 104
    BitmapEdit widget, about PM 66, 104, 177,
        314, 461
    BitmapEditClassRec, example PM 138-139
    BitmapEditRec, example PM 139
bitwise RM 50, 95
Boolean values PM 253
border PM 497
    border crossing events RM 454-459
    border width PM 306
    border window attribute PM 156
bounding box PM 171, RM 295
Box widget PM.21, 61-71, 206-211, 351-358
    examples PM 61-66
    geometry management RM 357-358
    resources RM 357-358
BulletinBoard widget PM 409
ButtonPress events PM:196, 353, RM 439-441
ButtonRelease events PM 196, 353,
    RM 439-441
buttons, (see also command buttons)
    grabbing PM 497
    mapping RM 477
byte order PM 497

C

caching, old size PM:179
 standard atoms PM:299
 type conversions PM:260
 Xmu; initializing PM:300
callbacks, about PM:26, 30, 39, 497; RM:6,
  330, 429
 adding PM:40, 42; more than one at a time
  PM:80; to callback list RM:46-47; to callback resource RM:44-45
 arguments to PM:42
 callback list, about PM:79, RM:6; deleting
  method RM:219; deleting method list
  RM:220; determining status RM:160;
  executive methods RM:104; popping
  down widget RM:102-103; popping up
  widget RM:98-101; XtCallbackExclusive
  RM:98-99; XtCallbackNone RM:100;
  XtCallbackNonexclusive RM:101;
  XtCallbackPopdown RM:102-103; XtCall-
  backs RM:104; XtHasCallbacks
  RM:160; XtRemoveCallback RM:219;
  XtRemoveCallbacks RM:220
 contrasted with actions PM:46
 format PM:42
 naming conventions PM:42
 passing data PM:77-79
 pop-up functions PM:79
 procedure RM:279-280
 (see also XtAddCallback, XtCallbackProc)
 (see also XtTimerCallbackProc)
Caption widget, about PM:409
cascading pop ups, about PM:345-347,
  362-367
 example PM:363-365
case converter PM:200
 registering RM:216
 (see also XtRegisterCaseConverter)
chained methods (see inheritance)
change_managed method PM:306-308, 319,
  497; RM:340
 in constraint widgets PM:338-339
CirculateNotify events RM:442
CirculateRequest events RM:443
class, about PM:18, 498
 class name; defined in Core class part PM:150
 class part PM:137; combining into class
  record PM:138; lack of new fields
  PM:138
 class record PM:136; allocating storage
  PM:140; BitmapEdit widget PM:138-139;
  contents PM:136

class_initialize method PM:153, 258, 381,
  498; RM:331
class_part_init method PM:153, 331; RM:331
 hierarchy (see widget classes); Athena widgets
  PM:153; gadgets PM:375
 structures PM:136-162
 subclass; about RM:14
client, about PM:6, 498
 ClientMessage events RM:444-445
 client-server model PM:6
clipping region PM:498
color PM:53, 56, 120, 156-158, 253-254, 276
 color names PM:433
 colorcell, about PM:436, 498; read-only
  PM:438; read/write PM:438; shared
  PM:437
 colormap, about PM:53, 436, 498; installing
  PM:276; window attribute PM:156
 ColormapNotify events RM:446
 determining available PM:436
 displaying PM:436
 false PM:277
 hexadecimal specification PM:434
 RGB model PM:435
 specifying PM:433
command buttons PM:404, 406, 417;
  RM:359-362
command line options (see options)
 compiling PM:34
Command widget PM:206-210, 353-359, 362,
  366, 404-406, 417; RM:359-362
 creating RM:362
 destroying RM:362
 resources RM:359-361
compiling Xt PM:34
composite widgets,
 as parent and child PM:320
 change_managed method RM:340
 class, about PM:16, 21, 137; XtNinsertPosi-
  tion resource PM:324
 composite widget class; about PM:61
 delete_child method RM:340
 general purpose PM:409, 421
 geometry_manager method RM:340-341
 insert_child method RM:339-340
 insert_position method RM:342
 importance PM:408
 initial size PM:309
 inserting children PM:323
 menus and control areas PM:418
 ordering method; XtOrderProc RM:310
 reasons for writing PM:305
 resources (see resources)

widget_size PM:150; xrm_clas PM:150;
resize method PM:154, 165, 177-180, 306,
309, 316, 336-337, 380, 510; RM:333;
set_values method PM:154, 165-166,
174-176, 311-312, 315, 512; RM:319,
334-335, 343
Core class part initializing; example
PM:148-149
Core class structure; compress_exposures field
PM:172, RM:297; in gadgets PM:375
Core widget class (see also XtExposeProc);
XtN (see resources)
Core widget class PM:17, 19, 52, 137, 499;
RM:327-337; class pointer PM:119;
class_initialize method RM:331;
class_part_initialize method RM:331;
compress_enterleave field PM:234; com-
press_exposure field PM:234; com-
press_motion field PM:234; destroy
method RM:332; display_accelerator
method RM:336; drawing into from application PM:117, 118, 119; expose method
PM:171-172; RM:296, 332-333; get_val-
ues_hood method RM:335; hidden superclasses PM:155; initialize method
RM:328-329, 330-331; initialize_hook
method RM:336; instance default size
PM:119; methods RM:330; query_geome-
try method RM:336-337; realize method
RM:331-332; resize method RM:333;
resources PM:52; set_values method
RM:334-335; set_values_almost method
RM:335; set_values_hood method
RM:335; superclasses PM:374; visi-
ble_interest field PM:230; widgetClass
class pointer PM:119
CoreClassPart structure PM:139
CorePart structure PM:139
instance record; height field PM:308; width
field PM:308
instance; setting size PM:119
counter incrementing inside XtSetArg PM:51
CreateNotify events RM:451-452
Ctrl key (see modifiers)
cursor PM:157, 253, 499
cursor window attribute PM:157
cut and paste (see selections)

D

data types RM:423
database (see also XtDatabase); obtaining for
display RM:126
DECNet PM:280
decoration PM:31, 279
default size PM:180
delete_child method PM:306, 323-324, 500;
RM:340
depth PM:53, 169, 500
dereference PM:500
descendants PM:500
destroy method PM:154, 165, 183, 500;
RM:332
DestroyNotify events RM:453
details in translations (see translations)
device PM:500
dialog boxes PM:371
cascading PM:371
grabs in PM:371
without grabs PM:371
Dialog widget RM:363-364
adding children RM:364
creating RM:364
destroying RM:364
removing children RM:364
resources RM:363-364
DirectColor PM:500
directories, font PM:438
display, (see also XtDisplayInitialize)
about PM:6, 500
adding; XtOpenDisplay RM:195-196
closing RM:108
connecting to multiple PM:396
depth PM:436
DISPLAY environment variable PM:53
lists PM:171; RM:295
pointer; returning for widget RM:134
display_accelerator method, (see also
XtStringProc); PM:211; RM:320, 336
initializing RM:135-136
(see also XtCloseDisplay)
distributed processing, about PM:7
DoesBackingStore Xlib macro PM:156
DoesSaveUnders Xlib macro PM:156
double-clicks PM:43, 201
downward chaining PM:152
drawing, about PM:119-120, 140, 150-152,
165, 170-174
after Expose event PM:153
bitmap cells PM:161
coordinate system PM:3

due to set_values method changes PM 175
in expose method PM 166
into Core widget PM 117-119
window attributes PM 156-157
drop-down menu (see menus)

E

elements (see array)
encapsulation PM 29, 500
enter/leave compression PM·234
EnterNotify events PM 195-196, 234, 353,
    RM 454-459
EnterWindow events PM 216
environment variables, DISPLAY PM 53
    XAPPLRESDIR PM 245
    XENVIRONMENT PM 245
errors, error database, obtaining RM 74, 75-77,
    144, XtAppGetErrorDatabase RM 74,
    145, XtAppGetErrorDatabaseText
    RM 75-77, 144
    error handling PM 91, 93, and application
        contexts PM 387, calling error resource
        database PM 386, calling fatal error han-
        dler RM:71-73, 85-86, 137-139, 234, XF 2
    listing RM 491
    string conversion error message RM 248
events, event loop (see main loop)
events, (see also exposure)
    (see also XtDispatchEvent)
    (see also XtMainLoop, XtNextEvent)
    about PM 10, 191, 501, RM 7
    accessing specific data RM 437
    as argument of action PM 46
    border crossing RM 454-459
    ButtonPress RM·439-441
    ButtonRelease RM 439-441
    cancelling source RM 224
    CirculateNotify RM.442
    CirculateRequest RM 443
    ClientMessage RM 444-445
    ColormapNotify RM 446
    ConfigureNotify RM 447-448
    ConfigureRequest RM 449-450
    CreateNotify RM 451-452
    DestroyNotify RM:453
    dispatching handlers RM 133
    EnterNotify PM 234, RM 454-459
    EnterWindow PM 216
    event compression PM 501
    event data, using in an action PM 222
    event filters PM 150, 234

event handelrs, about PM·28, 30, 215-220,
    501, RM 7, adding PM 216, dispatching
    RM 133, for nonmaskable events
    PM 219-220, procedure RM 293-294,
    304-305, raw PM·220, reasons to use
    PM 216, registering PM 49-50, register-
    ing raw PM 56-57, removing
    RM 221-222, removing raw RM 225-226,
    XtAddEventHandler RM 49-50, XtAd-
    dRawEventHandler RM.56-57,
    XtEventHandler RM 293-294, XtIn-
    putCallbackProc RM 304-305, XtRemo-
    veEventHandler RM·221-222, XtRemo-
    veRawEventHandler RM·225-226
event masks, about PM 216, 501, RM 424,
    retrieving RM 95-96, table PM 216,
    XtBuildEventMask RM 95-96
event members, common RM 438
event processing RM 84, XtAppProcessEvent
    RM 84
event propagation PM 501
event queue PM.234, peeking PM 234
event sequences, sharing initial events
    PM 204, sharing noninitial events PM 204
event source PM 501
event structure PM 221
event-driven programming, about PM 10-11
event_mask window attribute PM 157
expose PM:10
Expose PM 23, 153, 235, RM 460-461
FocusIn PM 216; RM 462-467
FocusOut PM 216; RM.462-467
frozen event PM 502
GraphicsExpose PM 193, 220, RM 468-469
GravityNotify RM 470
in action routines PM 124
in gadgets PM.373
input events, XtRemoveInput RM 224
KeymapNotify RM 471
KeyPress RM 472-474
KeyRelease RM 472-474
LeaveNotify PM 234, RM·454-459
LeaveWindow PM 216
list of types and structure names PM 223
MapNotify RM 475-476
MappingNotify RM 477-478
MapRequest RM 479
mocking up from action PM 171, RM 295
MotionNotify PM 216, 234, RM 480-482
next event; returning RM 191
NoExpose PM 193, RM 468-469
nonmaskable PM·191, 207, 218
processing RM 176

processing one event; XtProcessEvent RM:209
propagation PM:207
PropertyNotify RM:483
ReparentNotify RM:484
ResizeRequest RM:485
returning next event RM:80
selecting PM:207
SelectionClear PM:280, 289; RM:486
SelectionNotify PM:280, 290, 295; RM:487
SelectionRequest PM:280, 282, 290-291; RM:488
structures RM:438
translation table abbreviations PM:192-193
UnmapNotify RM:475-476
using inside actions or event handlers PM:221; RM:271
VisibilityNotify RM:489-490
XEvent; example PM:221; RM:271
(see also XtAppNextEvent, XtAppPending)
examples, actions; actions table PM:45; adding actions PM:43-45; in gadget parent PM:380-381; using event data in PM:222; widget actions PM:184-185
adding; accelerators PM:206; event handler PM:218-219; RM:294; resource list to class structure PM:145; scrollbars to application PM:109, 111; work procedure PM:231-232
application resource data structure PM:81
BitmapEditClassRec PM:138-139, 138
BitmapEditRec PM:139
calculating scrollbar thumb size PM:113-116
cascading pop-up menu PM:363, 365
constraint resources PM:68-69
constraint widget change_managed method PM:338-339
constraint widget; refiguring child locations PM:333-335
converting; default value of resource PM:254-255; selection PM:293-294; standard selections PM:300-301; RM:284-285
creating; argument list PM:92; argument lists with XtSetArg PM:93, 94; GCs from initialize method PM:169-170; icon pixmap PM:278-279
creating pop up; work procedure RM:323
creating; widget hierarchy PM:61-63
declaring; resource list PM:240; widget class record pointer PM:155
destroy method PM:183
drawing into Core widget PM:118-119
explicitly invoking converter PM:261

expose method PM:171-172; RM:296; in gadget parent PM:378-379
gadget class structure PM:376
gadget instance structure PM:377
geometry_manager method in constraint widget PM:332-333
get_values_hook method PM:265; RM:277
hardcoding resources PM:92
highlighting selection PM:284-288
initialize method PM:166-168; in constraint widget PM:330
initializing; Core class part PM:148-149; Xmu atom caching PM:300
installing accelerators in multiple widgets PM:209
interactions between resources PM:55
laying out child widgets PM:317-319
main loop (custom) PM:233
menu using SimpleMenu widget PM:368-370
nonmaskable event handlers PM:219-220
obtaining; atom PM:291-292; source code availability PM:34
options table PM:88-89
passing arguments to converter PM:259
passing data PM:77-79
pasting selection PM:295-296
placing; drop-down menu PM:360, 361; pop-up menu PM:354, 357
pop ups; work procedure to create PM:232
pop-up menu (spring-loaded); using Box widget PM:354-358
public function to get widget data PM:105
query_geometry method PM:182; in composite widget PM:316-317; in constraint widget PM:339
reading; from file PM:224-226; from pipe PM:226-227
registering resource converter PM:258
removing timeouts PM:229-230
resize method PM:177, 179; in composite widget PM:316; in constraint widget PM:336-337; in gadget parent PM:380
resource definition in widget PM:143-145
resource list PM:82-83
resource value; getting PM:51
retrieving; application resources PM:85-86; resource default at run-time PM:256
setting; resources for widget hierarchy PM:64; resources with XtSetValues PM:50; window attributes in realize method PM:157; XtNinput PM:276
set_values method PM:174-175; in composite widget PM:316

Master Index

obtaining RM:146-147
read-only PM·168
reasons for PM 119
setting with resources PM 170
graphics (see also drawing)
GraphicsExpose events PM 193, 220; RM 51,
468-469
graphics primitive PM 503
gravity PM·503
GravityNotify events RM 470
GrayScale PM 503
Grip widget class PM 19, RM 368-369
resources RM 368

H

hardcoding, resources PM·38, 91, 92
translations PM 48
header files, not included twice PM 139
private PM 508
public PM 508
height PM 308
checking in initialize method PM 166
hello world in Xt PM 31
hexadecimal color specification PM 434
hints PM 270-279, 503
icon position PM 273
position PM 55
size PM·273
size increment PM·273
hook RM 158, 244
host access list PM.503
hotspot, in cursor PM 503
Hyper key (see modifiers)

I

ICCCM PM·11, 269, 288, 291, 298-302
icon, pop-ups PM 272
setting, name PM 278; pixmap PM 269,
277-278
starting application as PM 273
identifier PM.503
ifndef statement, to prevent include files from
being read in twice PM.139
implementation file (see widget)
include files PM 30, 50, 53, 136, 139
in widget implementation PM 141
inferiors PM 503
inheritance, about PM·18, 49, 54, 148-158
adding features to superclass PM 157

among Athena Widgets PM 18
among Motif widgets PM 399
among Open Look widgets PM 399
in widget class and instance record
PM 137-138
of AT&T PM 405
of chained methods PM 152
of conflicting methods PM 157
of Core resources PM 52, 54
of self-contained methods PM.151-152
of superclass method PM 155
resources PM 143-145
single vs multiple PM 503
specifying NULL for chained methods
PM 152-153
styles PM 151-152
using XtInherit constants PM:151
widget not using resource value PM 56
initial size PM 308
initialize method PM 153, 165-170, 315, 503,
RM 328-331
(see also XtInitProc)
(see also XtProc)
calling XInternAtom from PM.291
in constraint widget PM 330
initialize_hook method PM 153, 265, 503,
RM 336
input queue, determining events RM 83, 205
(see also XtAppNextEvent)
(see also XtAppPeekEvent)
(see also XtAppPending)
(see also XtPeekEvent)
examining head RM 81-82, 204
input, from file PM·224-226
from pipe PM 226-227
input events method RM 293-294
input focus PM 504
input manager PM 504
input source masks PM 224
InputOnly window PM 504
InputOutput window PM 504
InputOutput window RM 460
insert_child method PM 306, 323-324, 504,
RM 339-340
insert_position method RM 339, 342
instance, about PM 18, 504
instance record PM 136, adding variables to
PM 139, allocating storage PM 140, BitmapEdit widget PM 139, contents
PM 136
instance structure PM·166
part structure, constraints in PM 327
structures PM 135-162

Inter-Client Communication Conventions
Manual (see ICCCM)
Intrinsics, about PM:8, 504; RM:2
    functions and macros; MenuPopdown
        PM:352; MenuPopup PM:352
    Intrinsic.h PM:30, 141
    IntrinsicP.h PM:141
    selection timeout RM:87

J

JumpProc RM:381

K

key events (see events or translations)
key translation, registering RM:238
    (see also XtKeyProc)
    (see also XtSetKeyTranslator)
keyboard focus, about PM:274, 389, 391, 504
    (see also XtAcceptFocusProc)
    (see also XtNinput resource)
    (see also XtSetKeyboardFocus)
    accept/reject method RM:269
    redirecting input RM:236-237
    setting PM:275
    styles PM:275
    window RM:462
keyboard grabbing (see grabs)
keyboard, mapping RM:477
    shortcuts (see accelerators)
keycodes, about PM:194, 391, 505
    translating; keycode-to-keysym RM:252-255;
        XtTranslateKey RM:252-253; XtTransla-
        teKeycode RM:254-255
KeymapNotify events RM:471
KeyPress events PM:194, 196, 391;
    RM:472-474
KeyRelease events PM:194, 196; RM:472-474
keysyms, about PM:194, 391, 505
    (see also XtCaseProc)
    (see also XtConvertCase)
    converting case PM:200; RM:281-282
    determining case RM:114
    key generated PM:198
    keysymdef.h PM:194, 197
    naming conventions PM:195

L

Label widget class, about PM:177;
    RM:370-372
    creating RM:372
    destroying RM:372
    resources RM:370-372
laying out child widgets, example PM:317,
    319
layout Form method PM:329
LeaveNotify events PM:195-196, 234, 353;
    RM:454-459
LeaveWindow events PM:216
lint PM:42
List widget class, about PM:19, RM:373-377
    creating RM:375
    destroying RM:375
    listWidgetClass RM:373-377
    resources RM:373-375
loose bindings PM:244, 505

M

macros PM:388-389
main loop PM:30, 34
    (see also XtAppMainLoop)
    (see also XtMainLoop)
    customizing; example PM:233
    internals PM:233
mapping, about PM:33, 53, 505
    (see also widget, mapping)
    button RM:477
    keyboard RM:477
    MapNotify events RM:475-476
    MappingNotify events PM:193; RM:477-478
    MapRequest events RM:479
    pop-up shell; XtPopup RM:207-208
    unmapping pop-up shell; XtPopdown
        RM:206
    widgets; XtMapWidget RM:185
mechanism without policy PM:10, 269
memory allocation PM:392
    for widget instance record PM:150
MenuPopdown PM:352; RM:39
MenuPopup PM:352, 357; RM:40-41
    argument to PM:358
menus, about PM:345-381, 408
    accelerators in PM:367, 371
    cascading PM:347, 362
    drop-down PM:347, 359
    grabbing pointer PM:353
    panes in PM:349

object-oriented programming, about PM:506
obscure PM:506
occlude PM:506
OOP (see object-oriented programming)
optimization PM:124, 179, 394
options -xrm PM:86, 88
options, abbreviating PM:87
    argument styles PM:90
    command line PM:86; styles PM:90
    custom PM:246
    defining your own PM:88
    handling errors in PM:91
    options table; example PM:88-89; xbitmap
        PM:106
    standard PM:86, 87; RM:13-14
OR operator RM:50, 95, 221, 225
overriding, override redirect PM:272
    override_redirect window attribute PM:157
    OverrideShell widget class PM:272;
        RM:346-353
    standard options PM:91
    translations PM:48-49

P

padding PM:506
parent PM:506
    parent window PM:507
parsing, command-line arguments PM:88-91
    translations PM:48
part (vs. record) PM:137
pipe input PM:226-227
pixel values PM:120, 507
pixmap, about PM:53, 171, 257, 507; RM:295
    freeing PM:183
    icon PM:277
    updating in widget PM:116
placing, drop-down menu; example
        PM:360-361
    pop-up menu; example PM:354, 357
plane PM:507
    (see also bit plane)
    plane mask PM:507
pointer PM:507
    events (see events or translations)
    grabbing (see also grabs), PM:507
    pointing device PM:507
pop ups, about PM:17, 70, 507; RM:8
    cascading pop ups; about PM:345
    creating in work procedure PM:232; RM:323
    creating just before popping up PM:76
    from callback function PM:75

linking group PM:272
modal PM:348, 505
modeless PM:348, 506
moving to desired position PM:75
OverrideShell PM:272
sensitivity PM:372
spring-loaded PM:348, 513; RM:8
using PM:71-74
when application is iconified PM:272
pop-up menus PM:345
    (spring-loaded) using Box widget PM:354-358
pop-up shell, (see also XtCreatePopupShell)
    creating RM:119-121
    mapping RM:207-208
    unmapping RM:206
portability PM:92, 224, 376, 391-394
position, about PM:55, 253
    hints PM:273
    relative to root window PM:279
    setting with resources PM:55
PRIMARY selection PM:281
printer fonts, see (fonts)
private header file (see widget)
private instance variables PM:140
process input RM:79
    (see also XtAppMainLoop)
program structure PM:30
properties, about PM:280, 508
    and atoms PM:288
PropertyNotify events RM:483
protocol, about PM:5
PseudoColor PM:508
public, functions, about PM:104, 158; naming
        conventions PM:114; reasons to use
        PM:106
    header file (see widget)
    instance variables (see resources)
    routines PM:340
pull down menu (see menus)

Q

quarks PM:262, 508
query_geometry method, about PM:154, 165,
        180-182, 306, 321, 508; RM:336-337
    in composite widget PM:316-317
    in constraint widget PM:339
    in gadgets PM:378
querying preferred geometry PM:320

R

R4 PM 96
  initialize_hook and set_values_hook obsoles-
    cence RM 277
raise PM·509
raw event handlers PM 220, RM 56-57
real estate PM 509
realization, about PM 33, 172, 176; RM 296
realize method PM 153, 274, 310, 315, 509,
  RM 331-332
RealizeProc RM 327
rectangle PM 509
RectObj class PM:155, 374, 377
redirect PM 509
redrawing PM 23
reference pages, list RM·411, 416
regions PM·172, 379, RM·51, 297
registering/declaring actions (see actions)
registering, callbacks RM 44-45, list
  RM 46-47
  converters PM 257-260, RM:48, 62-64, 216
  event handlers PM 218-220, RM 49-50
  fatal error condition procedure PM 385-388,
    RM 85-86, 234
  file RM.54-55, 65-66
  nonfatal error condition procedure
    PM 385-388, RM 88-89, 235, 246-247
  raw event handlers RM 56-57
  work procedures PM.231-233, RM·59, 68
Release 4, (R4) PM 36, 345-346, 372
removing, callbacks RM 218-220
  grabs RM 223
  input RM 224
  raw event handlers RM 225-226
  timeouts RM 227, example PM 229-230
  work procedures PM 232
reparenting, about PM 279, 361, 509
ReparentNotify events RM 484
reply PM 509, RM 341
representation type PM 81-83, 239, 241, 509
request PM 510
resize method PM 154, 165, 177-180, 306, 309,
  316, 336-337, 380, 510; RM 333
ResizeRequest events RM 485
resizing, about PM 65, 305, 311
  caching old size PM 179
  parent widget RM 333
  reasons PM 322
resource conversion RM 131
resource list, copying (see also XtGetSubvalues, XtSetSubvalues)
  copying from ArgList RM 242-243

copying to argument list RM 156-157
resource list, retrieving, (see also
  XtGetResourceList)
  (see also XtGetApplicationResources)
resource list, updating, (see also
  XtGetSubResources)
  default values, retrieving RM 148-149
  updating RM 141-143; by name or class
    RM 154-155
resources RM 338-339
resources, (see also resource list)
  about PM 22-23, 32, 36, 49, 52-54, 239-242,
    510, RM 6-8
  advantages of hardcoding PM 38
  and set_values method PM 174-176
  application PM 80
  changing value PM:174
  checking validity PM 166
  class PM.83
  classes and instances PM 37
  comment character in files PM 244
  constraint PM 68
  constraint widget RM 343-345
  copying, from ArgList to widget
    RM 244-245, from widget to argument list
    RM 158-159, XtGetValues RM 158-159,
    XtSetValues RM 244-245
  declaring resource list, example PM 240
  default address, interpreting PM 242
  default value; converting PM 254-255; set-
    ting PM 83, 255
  defined by Core PM 52
  defined in widget implementation file
    PM 143-145
  defining characteristics PM 83-84
  defining in widget PM 143-145
  Form widget PM 68, 326
  format, of definitions PM 243-244
  getting from application PM.50
  getting resource value, example PM.51
  in instance record PM 140
  inheritance of PM 49, 143-145
  interactions between PM 54-57, example
    PM 55
  loading, from .Xdefaults PM 55, with xrdb
    PM 55
  looking up values PM 243-251
  loose bindings PM 244
  name PM 83
  naming conventions PM 240
  precedence rules PM 249-251
  registering resource converter; example
    PM 258

S

save-set PM 511
save_under window attribute PM 156
saving under PM 156
scan line PM 511
  order PM 511
screen, screen fonts (see fonts)
  about PM 6, 511
scrollbars, about PM 15, 409, 422, 512
  adding to application PM 109, example
    PM 109
  adding to xbitmap PM 108
  and Expose events PM 114
  calculating thumb size PM 113-116, example
    PM 113-116
  controlling scrolling area RM·378-382
  creating PM 112
  Scroll widget PM·19
  Scrollbar widget PM 108-111, RM 378-382,
    creating RM 380, destroying RM 380,
    resources RM 378-380
  scrollbarWidgetClass RM 378-382
  setting thumb values RM 381
selections PM 269, 280-302, 512
  SelectionClear events RM 486
  SelectionNotify events RM 487
  SelectionRequest events RM 488
  and CurrentTime PM 289
  asserting ownership PM.288-289
  converting, selection PM.293-294, standard
    selections PM 299-301; RM:284-285
  deleting PM.301
  disowning PM 302
  handling large selections PM 301, RM 285
  highlighting selected data PM 284, 287-288
  highlighting selection; example PM 284,
    287-288
  losing selection PM 289-297
  pasting data PM 292
  pasting selection PM 295-297, example
    PM 295-296
  querying for desired target PM 298-302
  requesting selection PM 289-290
selections, selection data RM 132, 198-199
  method RM:316-317, obtaining RM 151,
    obtaining in multiple formats RM 152-153
  (see also XtConvertSelectionProc)
  (see also XtDisownSelection, XtSelection-
    CallbackProc)
  (see also XtGetSelectionValue, XtGetSelec-
    tionValues)
  (see also XtOwnSelection)

selections, selection method
  (see XtLoseSelectionProc, XtSelection-
    DoneProc)
selections, selection timeout (see timeouts)
  SelectionClear events PM.280, 289
  SelectionNotify events PM 280, 290, 295
  SelectionRequest events PM 193, 280, 282,
    290-291
  setting timeout PM 302
  target types PM 290-292
  XA_CLIPBOARD PM 288, 301-302
  XA_MULTIPLE PM 301, RM 285
  XA_PRIMARY PM 281, 288
  XA_SECONDARY PM·288
  XA_TARGETS PM 291, 298
self-contained methods (see inheritance)
sensitivity PM.54, 75, 92
  checking state, XtIsSensitive RM 173
  in pop-up callbacks PM 372
  setting state, XtSetSensitive RM 241
server, about PM 6, 512
  server code, guide to PM 491
  server grabbing PM 512
  server resources, freeing PM 183
set_values method PM 154, 165- 166, 174-176,
    311-312, 315, 512, RM 319, 334-335, 343
  (see also XtSetArgsFunc, XtSetValues, XtSet-
    ValuesFunc)
  change to PM 456
  in composite widget PM 316
  redrawing due to changes in PM 175
set_values_almost method PM 154, 312,
    322-323, 512, RM 273-274, 335
  in gadgets PM 378
set_values_hook method PM 154, 265-266,
    512, RM 275-276, 335
Shell RM 346-353
  environment variables (see environment vari-
    ables)
Shell, default value PM 458, RM.351-352
  Shell types, ApplicationShell RM 346, Over-
    rideShell RM 346, Shell RM 347,
    TopLevelShell RM 346; TransientShell
    RM 346, VendorShell RM 347, WMShell
    RM 347
  Shell widget class, about PM 17, 21, 32, 55,
    61, 66, 269, RM 346-353, reason for invisi-
    bility PM 63, resources PM 271, 272-277,
    279, types RM 346-347, XtIsShell
    RM 174; XtNbasewidth PM.272
sibling PM 512

single-line input field PM:280
sink, in Athena Text widget PM:264
size PM:305
  hints PM:273
  preferences PM:320
  sizeof PM:150
Sme gadgets PM:367-378
SmeBSB gadgets PM:367-378
SmeLine gadget PM:367-378
software architecture, about PM:8
source code, obtaining; example PM:34
source files for widget PM:135
source, in Athena Text widget PM:264
spring-loaded pop up (see pop ups)
stacking order PM:306, 341, 513
StaticColor PM:513
StaticGray PM:513
status PM:513
stdio.h PM:141
stipple PM:513
storage, storage block
  allocating RM:181; for data type RM:189;
    XtNew RM:189
  freeing RM:140; (see also XtFree)
  resizing RM:215
  (see also XtMalloc)
string, copying; XtNewString RM:190
StringDefs.h PM:83
StringDefs.h header file PM:30, 50, 141;
    RM:507
string, error message; XtStringConver-
    sionWarning RM:248
StringToWidget resource converter PM:69
structure, (see also XtOffset)
  determining field's byte offset RM:193-194
  of Xt applications PM:30
subclass, about PM:19, 513
submenus (menus, cascading)
subparts PM:150, 154, 264-266
subresources PM:150, 154, 264-266
Super key (see modifiers)
superclass, about PM:19, 149, 513
syntax functions PM:91

T

TCP/IP PM:280
templateWidgetClass RM:383-390
Text widget, about PM:19, 414, 424;
    RM:391-402
  creating RM:397
  default bindings RM:395-396

edit modes RM:392
  resources RM:392-394
tight bindings PM:244, 513
tiling, about PM:53, 513
time PM:513
timeouts, about PM:227
  adding PM:227
  and visibility interest PM:230
  callback method RM:321
  example PM:228-229
  invoking procedure after timeout RM:67
  removing PM:229-230
  selection timeout; setting RM:240; value
    RM:78, 87, 150
  (see also XtAddTimeout, XtAppAddTimeOut)
  (see also XtAppSetSelectionTimeout, XtGet-
    SelectionTimeout)
  (see also XtRemoveTimeOut, XtSetSelection-
    Timeout)
  (see also XtTimerCallbackProc)
toolkits, initializing internals RM:250
  initializing toolkit and display RM:161-165
  (see also XtInitialize, XtToolkitInitialize)
top-level widget (see Shell widget)
  top-level window PM:514
  topLevelShell widget class PM:270;
    RM:346-353
training in Xlib PM:489
TransientShell widget class PM:70, 74, 270;
    RM:346-353
Translation Manager (see actions)
translations, # augment directive PM:48
  ! modifier symbol PM:200
  # override directive PM:48
  # replace directive PM:48
  (see also accelerators)
  (see also actions)
  (see also XtOverrideTranslations)
  about PM:27, 39, 43, 47, 53, 514; RM:7
  augmenting PM:48
  colon modifier symbol PM:200-201
  compiling; table RM:202-203; when widget
    class initialized PM:147; XtParseTransla-
    tionTable RM:202-203
  defining; default in Core class part PM:150;
    in source PM:49
  details in PM:194-196
  differences between directives PM:191
  directives PM:191
  double-clicks PM:201
  event abbreviations PM:192-193
  event sequences PM:201-203
  hardcoding PM:48

in widget implementation file PM 145-147
inheritance PM 146
interactions between PM 203-207
keyboard events PM 194-195
merging PM·112, 203
merging widget translations RM 93-94
merging/overwriting RM 197
modifiers PM 196-201, 198
modifiers and event sequences PM 202
Motion events PM 202
newlines in PM 190
*Notify details PM 195
order PM 203-204
overriding PM 48-49
parsing PM 48
removing RM 256
replacing PM 48, 49
resource converters PM 253
syntax PM 190
tilde modifier symbol PM 199
translation table PM 514; RM·499, example
    PM 47, syntax PM:457
(see also XtAugmentTranslations)
(see also XtUninstallTranslations)
traversal, post-order PM 508
    pre-order PM 508
TrueColor PM 514
type converters, (see also resources)
    about PM 93
    caching PM 260
    explicitly invoking PM 261, example
        PM 261
    format PM 262-264
    passing arguments to PM 259
    registering PM 257-260
type property PM.514
typedefs PM 140
types converters, passing arguments to;
    example PM 259

U

unmanaging widget PM 319
UnmapNotify events RM 475-476
upward chaining PM 152
uunet PM 34
uwm PM 346

V

varargs PM 95, 427
variables, resource PM 446
VendorShell widget class PM:275
viewable PM 514
Viewport widget, creating RM 404
Viewport, Viewport widget, destroying
    RM 404, inserting child RM 404, remov-
    ing child RM 404, resources RM 403-404
ViewportWidgetClass RM 403-404
virtual colormaps PM·276
virtual crossing RM 456
visibility interest PM 150, 230-231
VisibilityNotify events PM 150, 193,
    RM 489-490
visible PM 514
visual PM 514
    class PM 514
VPaned, VPaned widget; about RM·405-408,
    adding pane RM 406, change height set-
    tings RM 407, child resources RM 406,
    deleting pane RM 406, destroying
    RM 408, disabling auto-reconfiguring
    RM 407, disabling pane resizing RM 407,
    disabling resources RM.405-406, enabling
    auto-reconfiguring RM 407, enabling pane
    resizing RM 407
VPanedWidgetClass RM 405-408

W

warnings (see error handling)
    calling high-level RM 91-92, 261-262
    handler, (see XtAppWarningMsg, XtWarning,
        XtWarningMsg)
    listing RM 491
widget
    about PM 8, 15, 514, RM.2
    actions, example PM 184-185
    adding to parent list PM 17, RM.182-184,
        XtManageChild RM 182, XtManageChil-
        dren RM 183-184
    application context PM.97-98; getting
        RM 263, XtWidgetToApplicationContext
        RM 263
    as data type PM 33
    BitmapEdit PM 66, 103-132, 177, 314, 461
    Box widget PM 21, 351; RM 357-358,
        example PM 61
    call accept_focus method RM 97
    callback list (see callbacks)

Master Index

O'Reilly & Associates, Inc.
Creators and Publishers of Nutshell Handbooks

Nutshell Handbooks

Learning the UNIX Operating System
DOS Meets UNIX
Learning the vi Editor
UNIX in a Nutshell, System V
UNIX in a Nutshell, Berkeley

Handbooks on Communications:

!%@:: A Directory of Electronic
Mail Addressing and Networks
Using UUCP and Usenet
Managing UUCP and Usenet

Handbooks on Programming:

Using C on the UNIX System
Checking C Programs with lint
Understanding and Using COFF
Programming with curses
termcap and terminfo
Managing Projects with make

The X Window System series

Vol. 0 *X Protocol Reference Manual*
Vol. 1 *Xlib Programming Manual*
Vol. 2 *Xlib Reference Manual*
Vol. 3 *X Window System User's Guide*
Vol. 4 *X Toolkit Intrinsics*
Programming Manual
Vol. 5 *X Toolkit Intrinsics Reference*
Manual
Vol. 7 *XView Programming Manual*

For HyperCard on Macintosh:

UNIX in a Nutshell for HyperCard
(includes 1.8MB of HyperCard
stackware, *User's Guide*, and a copy of
Learning the UNIX Operating System)

Other UNIX books:

UNIX Text Processing

Send me more information on:

☐ Retail sales
☐ Licensing
☐ Review copies for instructors
☐ Magazine press kits for new books
☐ Education policy
☐ Bookstore locations
☐ Overseas distributors
☐ Additional copy of Nutshell News
☐ Upcoming books on the subject:

....
....

☐ Writing a Nutshell Handbook

O'Reilly & Associates, Inc.
Creators and Publishers of Nutshell Handbooks

Nutshell Handbooks

Learning the UNIX Operating System
DOS Meets UNIX
Learning the vi Editor
UNIX in a Nutshell, System V
UNIX in a Nutshell, Berkeley

Handbooks on Communications:

!%@:: A Directory of Electronic
Mail Addressing and Networks
Using UUCP and Usenet
Managing UUCP and Usenet

Handbooks on Programming:

Using C on the UNIX System
Checking C Programs with lint
Understanding and Using COFF
Programming with curses
termcap and terminfo
Managing Projects with make

The X Window System series

Vol. 0 *X Protocol Reference Manual*
Vol. 1 *Xlib Programming Manual*
Vol. 2 *Xlib Reference Manual*
Vol. 3 *X Window System User's Guide*
Vol. 4 *X Toolkit Intrinsics*
Programming Manual
Vol. 5 *X Toolkit Intrinsics Reference*
Manual
Vol. 7 *XView Programming Manual*

For HyperCard on Macintosh:

UNIX in a Nutshell for HyperCard
(includes 1.8MB of HyperCard
stackware, *User's Guide*, and a copy of
Learning the UNIX Operating System)

Other UNIX books:

UNIX Text Processing

Send me more information on:

☐ Retail sales
☐ Licensing
☐ Review copies for instructors
☐ Magazine press kits for new books
☐ Education policy
☐ Bookstore locations
☐ Overseas distributors
☐ Additional copy of Nutshell News
☐ Upcoming books on the subject:

....
....

☐ Writing a Nutshell Handbook

www.ingramcontent.com/pod-product-compliance
Lightning Source LLC
LaVergne TN
LVHW012208040326
832903LV00003B/190